NATURE WALKS
IN
SOUTHERN INDIANA

A

and the

Hoosier Chapter / Sierra Club

with

Cartography by: Aileen Buckley

Drawings by: Debbie Wilkerson

Edited by: Alfred Strickholm

Author at Cedar Bluffs

NATURE WALKS IN SOUTHERN INDIANA

" To a people, these sanctuaries

of the spirit are necessary

for sanity and growth and

I use the word "sanctuary"

advisedly, for they are

places not only for recreation

and enjoyment, but inspiration."

- Theodore Clement Steele (1884-1926)

This Book is Dedicated to the Centennial of the Founding of the Sierra Club in 1892 and its Founder, John Muir, who spent part of his youth in Indianapolis where he began his thousand mile journey to Florida.

Books by Alan McPherson

Wild Food Plants of Indiana and Adjacent States
Wild Plants of the Urban West
Nature Walks in Orange County, CA

Published by the Hoosier Chapter of the Sierra Club
6140 North College Ave, Indianapolis, IN 46220   (317) 253-2687

Edited by: Alfred Strickholm
Cartography by: Aileen Buckley
Drawings by: Debbie Wilkerson
Photography by: Alan McPherson.

Cover: Jackson-Washington State Forest

ISBN 0-9628469-0-2

Second printing: Aug 1993

Distribution and Marketing: Hoosier Chapter/Sierra Club
6140 North College Ave, Indianapolis, IN 46220 (317) 253-2687

Printed by: McNaughton and Gunn, Inc., Lithographers.
Manufactured in the United States of America

CONTENTS: NATURE WALKS IN SOUTHERN INDIANA

Quotation by Paul Tillich / New Harmony

5

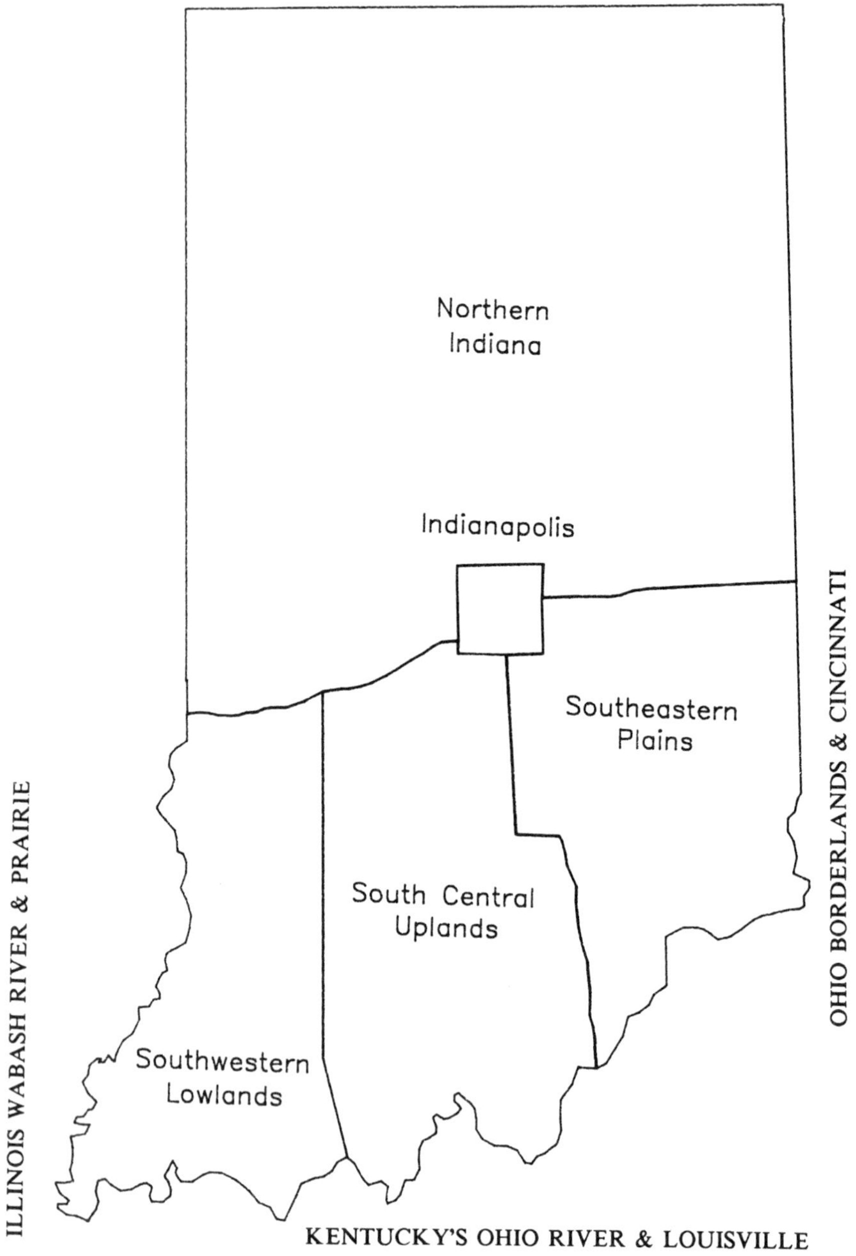

Northern Indiana

Indianapolis

Southeastern Plains

South Central Uplands

Southwestern Lowlands

ILLINOIS WABASH RIVER & PRAIRIE

OHIO BORDERLANDS & CINCINNATI

KENTUCKY'S OHIO RIVER & LOUISVILLE

NATURE WALKS IN SOUTHERN INDIANA: A LISTING

Clear Cut Aftermath / Wyandotte Woods

FOREWORD

"... To explore, enjoy, and preserve the nation's forests, waters, wildlife, and wilderness..."

- Sierra Club

This nature and hiking guide to southern Indiana had a simple beginning when the Uplands Group of the Sierra Club would regularly meet and talk of the poorly known and beautiful places that some of us had visited on our hikes. Eventually, there came the slow realization that if these places were to ever succumb to man's development and commercialization, they would be lost forever. It became important that our joy in these places be preserved for our children and generations to come. Part of our heritage consists of the wild and natural places of Indiana, just as the original pioneers experienced them. True, most of Indiana had been clear cut, but wild natural places still existed and the Charles Deam wilderness had finally become a reality through tremendous efforts of the Sierra Club and others recognizing its worth.

The Sierra Club members realized that only with public awareness, use, and appreciation of the wild and natural areas, could they be preserved. From these thoughts came the incentive to develop this guide book. Alan McPherson provided the major impetus to start by offering to spend a "year in the bush" by exploring and hiking throughout southern Indiana. His dedication to walking and describing the beauty of southern Indiana is unparalleled. At a critical time, Aileen Buckley provided her expertise in cartography. Without her, this guide may never have materialized. During the evolution of this guide, it acquired a broader scope, namely to provide a range of nature outings for all, from parents with children and others not able to endure longer hikes, to outings for the serious backpacker.

The wild and natural regions described here have some areas preserved and others not, but clearly all deserve of preservation for posterity. With population increasing and pressures to exploit the last remaining land, all that will remain of the wild and beautiful places are those what we save today. Once gone, they are gone forever. When on an outing it is hoped that users of this guide will remember and appreciate the following saying attributed to Henry Thoreau, and restated by John Muir, the founder of the Sierra Club:

"...In Wilderness is preservation of the soul..."

Alfred Strickholm
Hoosier Chapter / Sierra Club

Trail Sign at Patoka Lake

PREFACE

Southern Indiana residents and visitors are fortunate in having an abundance of natural beauty to enjoy. The moderate climate permits year around outdoor activities in a diverse and unique landscape. Getting outside and walking whether at a wilderness area or urban park is a memorable experience.

We, the members of the Sierra Club, appreciate the varied public and private lands that are open to visitation. We commend the many individuals and groups who established these life sustaining natural resources. This compilation of nature walks informs the general public where they are located in southern Indiana.

There are trails for all seasons. Trails that lead to deep cool and refreshing forested ravines and coves. Trails along ridgetops with open panoramic year around vistas. Trails that lead through renewing wildflower filled meadows and up hillslopes ablaze in autumn's deciduous colors. There are even "trails" for rainy days which access natural history museums, botanical and zoological gardens and historical monuments, buildings and grounds.

With Nature Walks in Southern Indiana the walking enthusiast will be able to locate over 100 trails ranging from easy to moderate. The majority of the nature experiences in this guide may be walked in one day. The first four sections of the book includes trails located in the 42 southern Indiana counties south of Interstate highway 70, the "New National Road". In addition, Indianapolis and neighboring border areas of Ohio, Kentucky and Illinois are included.

All nature walks were experienced, photographed and written by the author between 1975 and 1987. The author thanks Tom Bertolacini of Photo Solutions for the care in printing the photos. Aileen Buckley designed the highway and trail maps that accompany the text with some assistance from Al Strickholm who also did the arduous task of editing. Debra Wilkerson drew the pen and ink drawings of native wildlife. She also typed the manuscript from my writings into a usable form. The brief write-ups include a capsule heading at the page top that list place, town and county, name of the United State Geological Survey USGS map 1: 24,000 if needed, trail or trails distance, acreage, activities and fees. The main focus of the write-ups is about outstanding site features, trailhead location, trail surface and description and highway travel directions. More than a trail guide, fauna, flora, folklore, history, geology and other recreational sites and activities are mentioned to further enhance and enjoy the many splendors.

Development of this easy-to-use guide was encouraged by the members of the Uplands Group at Bloomington, Indiana especially Kent and Terry Wilson, Al Strickholm, Lois Ormond and Debra Wilkerson. A special thank you with deep gratitude to all individuals who generously contributed to the making of this guide.

Alan McPherson

Muscatatuck National Wildlife Refuge

DISCOVERING SOUTHERN INDIANA: OVERVIEW

Southern Indiana's natural beauty and fairly mild climate makes an ideal setting to explore year around. Spring and fall months are especially ideal to set out on foot. A basic motor skill, walking, especially in natural surroundings, is considered the way to a lifetime of health and happiness. Fortunately nature walks are plentiful throughout the Hoosier state particularly the southern half. Knowing a trail exists, what to expect and how to arrive are the three basic questions this guidebook addresses.

The nature walks are listed by natural geographical sections and administrative division. The main body includes 3 southern Indiana regional trail sections: Southeastern Plains, South Central Uplands, and the Southwestern Lowlands plus a section about trips in the Hoosier National Forest. The nature walks are numbered and correspond to a regional map at the beginning of each of the 4 main sections. Expanded listings of nature walks will be found in four additional sections: Indianapolis Nature Walks, Ohio Borderlands and Cincinnati, Kentucky's Ohio River Valley and Louisville, the Illinois Prairie, Ozarks and Wabash River Valley.

Municipal, township, county, state and federal governmental agencies administer public accessible parklands for recreation and other purposes. So do many private organizations such as The Nature Conservancy, a national conservation organization whose objective is the preservation and protection of environmentally significant land.

No special skills are required to be a walker but to further enhance your enjoyment and safety in the outdoors there are tips that are worthy of mention. Plan and study ahead your special needs for either a short walk, a day hike or several overnites. Consider your physical comfort in our humid continental climate. Soft soled footwear such as quality tennis shoes or lightweight hiking shoes are best for the terrain of southern Indiana. The average walking speed is 3 miles per hour or 20 minutes per mile. Good fitting and roomy clothing are essential. Cotton for summer and wool for winter. Layering, dark clothing, natural wool, some cottons, and high-tech synthetics are best for winter. Be cautious of frostbite, hypothermia and dehydration in winter and heat exhaustion and stroke in summer. Several sporting and outdoor stores have all hiking and backpacking needs in our area.

Suggested day pack essentials or options may include raingear, maps, compass, flashlight, pocket knife, water, butane lighter, first aid kit, whistle, dry food and fresh fruit, toilet paper, bug repellent and a guidebook to your favorite nature study like birds or geology. A hat, sunglasses and binoculars and the gear should fit nicely in one or two day or fanny packs.

Backpacking for overnights will require additional gear of course, especially in winter. An extra change of clothes and evening wear may include a sweater or light coat, wool socks, and a parka. Sleeping gear such as bag, ground pad and cloth, and tent adds to the pounds. Cooking gear and food will also add to your load and may require heavier shoes for support.

Other overnight items that may be included are candles, repair kits, toilet articles, towel, garden trowel. Plastic bags may serve as emergency raincoats for backpacks or for hikers. If matches are preferred you may waterproof the heads with nail polish. Gear should be compact, simple, and light, generally speaking. All in all, you can explore without expensive gear. Before leaving always tell your family or friends your hiking plans and make sure your vehicle is road worthy to take you and others to a destination and back. Arrive alive.

Trail quality and their conditions will vary from experience to experience. Few trails are paved and handicapped accessible. Trail brochures are available at some trailheads such as nature preserves and other trails are unmarked such as the Charles C. Deam Wilderness Area. Be aware that herbicides such as Round-Up are known to be used to control overgrown trails. When planning a hike consider the length of daytime especially during the short days of late fall and winter. Steep hills will cut your hiking time in half. Trail rules may vary but basically all expect fire control, trash and sanitary containment and respect for private property and people. Hikers should be aware of the potential dangers of hunters during the fall hunting season. Accidents do occur.

Offtrail exploration is more secure if a compass and maps are available. Topographic quadrangle maps feature natural detail with symbols. On a map in the scale of 1:24,000, 1 inch on the map equals 2,000 feet in the real setting. Color is used somewhat real to life: Green for woodland, brown lines for contour earth, blue for water and black for human works. Topo and other maps may be purchased from:

Publications Office
Indiana Geological Survey
Geology Building
Indiana University
10th Street and Walnut Grove
Bloomington, IN 47401

Map Sales
612 State Office Building
Indianapolis, IN 46204

Maps may also be checked out at the Geology Library, Indiana University. Several backpacking and outdoor stores carry topographic maps in the larger cities. Prices vary. Expect to pay between $2.25 and $4.00 each.

Hayes Regional Arboretum

Insect pests are also a part of being outside and southern Indiana has its small share of noxious creatures. Chiggers, harvest mites or red bugs are prolific mainly from early June to late September. The near invisible larvae of the mite (Arachnid) feeds on humans and other animals by dropping off brushy or herbaceous vegetation and feeds by piercing the skin. They cause a red welt by injecting a fluid that breaks down the tissue and a tube is formed in which the chigger lives and feeds. The larvae bites ankles, waist and arm pits. Little can be done after bitten except apply itch relief ointments or take a salt water bath. Best prevention entails staying away and applying sulphur-vaseline ointment around the legs and ankles. Kerosene is reputed to be the best. Drugstore insecticides are available.

Adult eastern North American wood ticks or "dog ticks" are a particular problem mainly in early spring to mid-spring but are found during warm weather in grassy open areas and woodlands. Ticks are crab-shaped and the largest of the mites, closely related to chiggers. They transmit disease such as Rocky Mountain spotted fever which is uncommon in Indiana. They are unlikely to transmit Lyme disease. Ticks feed on the blood by injecting their mouth parts into the skin.

The Lone Star (Deer, Turkey) tick of the southcentral US is found in certain national forest lands primarily in Perry County. Introduced from Missouri white-tail deer stock in the 1940's, the extremely difficult to see minute "seed" tick is common in grassy areas from June to frost in Perry County and particularly at Mogan Ridge. This tick can transmit Lyme disease. Prevention with sulphur and kerosene or commercial spray as you would chiggers. If a tick does attach, use alcohol or kerosene to make it "back-out". Do not leave the infectious mouthparts behind.

Beaver Activity

The female mosquito is a problem in a few areas of southern Indiana but nothing in comparison with northern Indiana. The pesky flying insect is usually common in low swamp areas or poorly drained bottomlands particularly at sunset, night and sunrise. 52 species occur in Indiana and one, the Culex species does carry disease. Malaria, a bane of the pioneer, is carried by mosquitoes. There are numerous insect repellents which are effective which include the component DEET, and most hikers have a favorite. Mosquitoes are seldom seen in southern Indiana after mid August but with wet and hot summers they will persist until frost.

The female deer fly, like the female mosquito, needs blood for protein to produce young. Deer flies breed in wet areas and are especially noticeable along reservoirs or wet woodland or swamp. A hat, longsleeve shirt and pants help keep them from biting as do certain insecticides. They are strong fliers and will pursue their victims for miles. Usually they are not seen after mid July but may persist as late as mid August.

The wood eye gnat can be a pest of the eye, ear, nose and mouth in late summer. Repellents work to a degree. Black widows are common in southern Indiana in trash dumps, outhouses, stumps, stone walls and beneath objects. They are shy but quite poisonous especially for small children. Fortunately there is an anti-venom. The brown recluse is rarely found. An annoying but harmless spider of late summer is the spiny woods spider who builds its webs seemingly everywhere along the trail. Yellow jackets, bees, hornets, and wasps may sting sometimes repeatedly. Centipedes rarely bite and are non-poisonous. Baking soda moistened is reputed to relieve the bite and sting of insects.

Copperhead

There are 35 types of snakes found in Indiana. The common harmless snakes in southern Indiana include the garter, water, brown, racers, rat and king and green snakes. Be advised that non-poisonous snakes will bite if disturbed. Snakes are usually active from April to October and most are basically nocturnal but do venture out in the day. Occasionally hikers will come across a garter or black racer basking in a sunny opening along the trail.

The copperhead and the timber rattlesnake are the two poisonous snakes found in southern Indiana primarily in the undisturbed land of the state and national forests. Water moccasin or cottonmouth, often confused with the watersnake, has been recently reported in isolated areas of extreme southwestern Indiana. The cottonmouth is black, thick bodied and aquatic. They are nervous and aggressive and have a more serious bite than the copperhead, the most common poisonous snake in Indiana. The pygmy prairie massasauga rattlesnake is found in low swampy areas of the northern 2 tiers of counties and does not present a concern in southern Indiana.

The copperhead inhabits high, rocky, dry upland ridges in the south half of Indiana however it is also found under rocks near streams and wood piles. Its bite is rarely fatal. It is difficult to see on the forest floor since the snake's chestnut brown body and red-bronze copper head blend well with the leaf litter. Like the rattlesnake, the copperhead is a pit viper with retractable hollow fangs and bears young alive in September. Watch out for this "highland moccasin" when stepping over logs since there is no warning of their presence and they will strike from any position.

The timber rattlesnake inhabits similar rocky hilly terrain as the copperhead. They do not always "rattle" before striking but may lie quiet and hopefully unnoticed. The thick body is yellow with black "V" shaped bands and a dark tail. The rattlesnake's bite may be fatal in a few hours if the poison is not extracted and/or anti-venom taken. Seek help if stricken, and try to remain calm as possible. Brown County State Park nature center has an excellent collection on display of captured snakes including these two poisonous reptiles.

Poison ivy should be identified and learned to be avoided. If you encounter the vine use rubbing alcohol to remove the oils and then bath as soon as possible. Woodland stinging nettle can be painful as can be greenbriar and briars from roses, rasp and blackberry canes. It is remotely possible that an encounter with a skunk may result in being sprayed. Even more remote is a bite from a rabid raccoon or other animal. The safety rule for lightning is seek out dense woods, ravines, ditches and groves of immature trees and not shelter underneath large solitary trees, hilltops, high ground, or rock ledge outcrops. The spring months especially April-May are tornado season.

Some natives believe there are 6 seasons in southern Indiana. January and February are the winter months. March 1 to April 15th brings the cool early spring. April 15 to June 1st is when the late spring occurs. From June to October 1st there are four hot months of summer. Indian Summer is from October 1st to November 15. The cooler mild autumn period is from November 15 to January 1st.

After a long hike, treat your feet to a warm soaking, a cool rinse, easy drying, and maybe some foot powder. Put on a fresh pair of socks if handy. Be flexible and prepared for all your trips in the outdoors. Whether hiking with a friend or alone, always inform others of your route.

Trail routes are always changing. New trails are being added, old trails neglected or re-routed, improved or abandoned. All trails herein have been read and checked for accuracy but errors may exist. Errors and corrections should be brought to the attention of the author through the publishers, the Hoosier Chapter/Sierra Club, 6140 North College Ave. Indianapolis, IN 46220. Be aware the Sierra Club and the author are not responsible for any accidents that may incur while using this guide.

NATURE WALKS IN THE SOUTHEASTERN PLAINS

Anderson Falls
Fall Fork of Clifty Creek

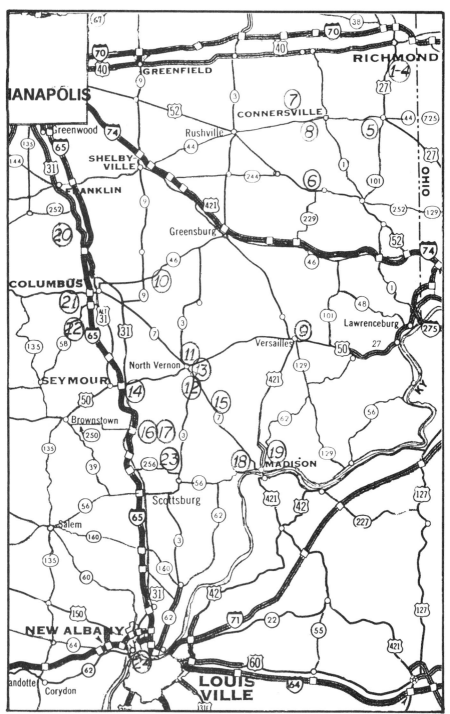

SOUTHEASTERN PLAINS

SOUTHEASTERN PLAINS: OVERVIEW

For the most part, the plains of southeastern Indiana appear as a glaciated flat and level landscape with some rolling relief. However hikers will enjoy the steep canyon like ravines along the Ohio River and Whitewater valleys at Clifty Falls and Whitewater State Park. Basically the area is bordered by I-70 on the north, I-65 on the west, the Ohio River on the south and the Indiana-Ohio state line. Three natural geographic regions subdivide the southeastern plains: Dearborn Upland, Muscatatuck Regional Slope and the Scottsburg Lowland. These 3 subregions within the "plains" do not end at the state lines, but extend naturally into Ohio and Kentucky as well as central Indiana.

Some relief to the flatness is the Whitewater River valley and its numerous short tributaries comprised of the Dearborn Upland, a deeply dissected plain. There are steep slopes, deep draws with cutting streams and uplands. Hikeable properties in this area include Whitewater Canal, Whitewater Gorge Trail, Shrader-Weaver Nature Preserve and Mary Gray Bird Sanctuary. Unfortunately no public accessible trails exist in the beautiful Ohio River counties of Dearborn, Ohio, and Switzerland.

West of the Dearborn Upland is the Muscatatuck Regional Slope, a broad, flat westward-sloping upland. Guthrie Woods and Wells Woods are fine natural representatives of the "flatwoods", a conspicuous feature of the "slope" on the east but contrasts sharply with the high ridge escarpment on the west with the Norman Upland.

The Scottsburg Lowland is a broad flat valley land. The average elevation is around 600 feet. Hardy Lake, Muscatatuck National Wildlife Refuge and Anderson Falls represent this lowland. Excellent views of the low flat valley may be seen from Skyline Drive at Jackson-Washington State Forest and Clark State Forest at the firetower.

Leon Wilkinson

1. RICHMOND IN/NATURE PLACES

ACTIVITIES: park, zoo, E. G. Hill Memorial Rose Garden, picnicking, shelterhouses, amphitheater, playgrounds, tennis, archery lake, fishing, concessions, greenhouse tours, downtown nature walk

The 194 acre century old Glen Miller Park, named after the original owner features several points of interest for the urban nature walker. A small zoo that contains several barnyard and exotic animals is located along Lower Drive across from the park office. Buffalo are fenced in along west North Drive. Near the Lower Drive entrance along National Road East/US 40 is the E.G. Hill Memorial Rose Garden that grows 300 roses representing 73 varieties. This lovely garden park in the "City of Roses" was developed by Hills Roses, where group tours only one month in advance, are guided thru the 40 greenhouse acres at 2117 Peacock Street. (Ph. 317-955-TOUR). Hills' ships over 25 million cut hothouse roses annually. Starting in 1881, they have hybridized and introduced several rose varieties including Golden Fantasie, Colillion, Forever Yours and Promise Me. There are 16 other annual and perennial floral gardens in Glen Miller Park.

Walking west of the rose garden uphill at the 23rd Street Entrance is the Madonna of the Trail statue, one of the many placed along the National Road west by the DAR commemorating the bravery of pioneer women in the new land. Picnic tables and shelters are located in the wooded area along east North Drive. Accessible from North Drive east of the picnic area is Elks Road and Hayes Regional Arboretum.

Handsome formal plantings landscape the Downtown Promenade/Mall year around on Main Street/National Road/US 40 between 5th and 10th Streets. These 5 city blocks of circular fountains and foliage have been awarded landscape architectural recognition.

Glen Miller Park

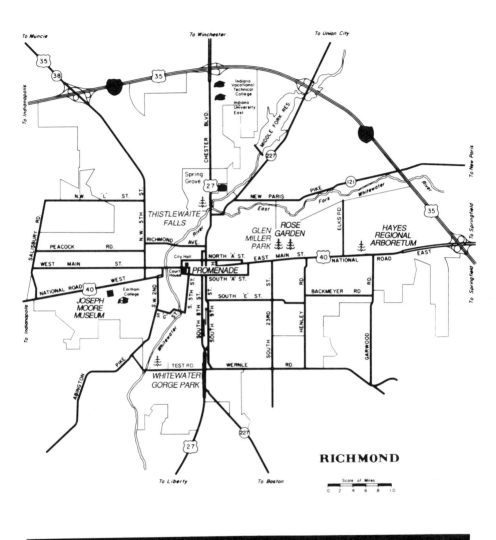

RICHMOND

Scale of Miles
0 2 4 6 8 10

2. HAYES REGIONAL ARBORETUM

Richmond, IN/Wayne County
USGS MAP(S): New Paris 1:24,000
TRAIL(S) DISTANCE: 7 trails total 6.9 miles / 3.5 mile auto tour
  / winter ski route
ACREAGE: 355 acres
ACTIVITIES: hiking, nature study, nature center, naturalists, snow
  ski, auto tour, arboretum, bird sanctuary, rose garden, gift shop,
  guided tours, environmental education (publications, classes,
  workshops, lecture programs, field trips), special events

A private non-profit organization, Hayes Regional Arboretum has been actively engaged in environmental education, scientific research, outdoor recreation and community horticultural services since 1963. The arboretum is privately endowed by the Stanley W. Hayes Research Foundation, Inc. The focus of the regional arboretum is a 10-acre Native Woody Plant Preserve that botanically represents an informal collection of 179 trees, shrubs and vines of the Whitewater Valley and its tributaries of southeastern Indiana and southwestern Ohio. In addition the arboretum includes a converted dairy-barn-nature-center, classrooms, Indiana's first solar greenhouse, a spring house, native fern garden, a reservable Woodland Chapel, an All-America Rose Test Garden, a 3.5 mile auto tour and gift shop. There are 4 easy to moderate trails that wind through the grounds.

At the main entrance parking lot, directly behind the nature center and between the solar greenhouse is the trailhead for two easy marked loop trails: Beech-Maple Trail (7/8 mile) and the Snail Trail (1 1/8 mile). Both well maintained pathways have trail numbered interpretive stations that correspond with trailhead-available brochures. The Beech-Maple Trail is a study in ecological succession, tree identification, natural and social history. The path leads thru a climax forest, crossing and recrossing the gravel auto tour road 3 times, looping around Research Pond and back to end behind the Classroom Annex and Children's Garden at the main entrance parking lot.

The Snail Trail visits a variety of wildlife habitats: old revegetating fields, woodlands, aquatic, field, and forest edge. Access to the Springhouse Trail (1/4 mile) and the Springhouse is located just beyond Trail Marker 8. Turn right at the gravel road and walk across the parking lot. This short walk guides thru the native fern garden along a shady hillside and back to the Springhouse and Snail Trail. The Snail Trail ends at the nature center/solar greenhouse trailhead.

After obtaining a token coin from the naturalist at the nature center, you may enter the 3.5 mile auto tour. A guide book is also available that traces the route and its interesting points. Trees, shrubs and vines have been identified in the guide as well as being uniquely marked along the route.

The next walking section begins south of the Hayes House at the Native Woody Plant Preserve, the All America Rose Test Garden and the Brice Hayes Memorial Fountain. The Native Woody Plant Preserve Trail (1/2 mile) wanders throughout the arboretum parkland preserve. The auto tour route ends at Hayes Arboretum Road.

The summer hours (March 1 - December 24)) are Tuesday thru Saturday 9:00 am to 5:00 pm, Sunday 1:00 pm to 5:00 pm and closed Mondays. The winter hours (December 26 to February 28) Tuesday thru Saturday are 9:00 am to 5:00 pm.

The Hayes Regional Arboretum is located at 801 Elks Road in east Richmond. From I-70 take the US 40 west exit and drive 2.5 miles west and turn north onto Elks Road and proceed 1/2 mile to the main entrance gate.

Hayes Regional Arboretum
801 Elks Road
Richmond, IN 47374
317-962-3745

School Group, Hayes Regional Arboretum

3. WHITEWATER GORGE PARK TRAIL

Richmond, IN/Wayne County
USGS MAP(S): Richmond 1:24,000
TRAIL(S) DISTANCE: 3.5 miles one way/7 miles round trip
ACREAGE: 100 acres of river corridor
ACTIVITIES: hiking, natural and social history

The Whitewater Gorge Park Trail is the result of governmental agencies and private organizations working in cooperation towards a common goal. This urban nature hike extends over 3.5 linear miles one-way thru mostly a steep walled, semi-natural canyon however there are sections of the trail that are definitely 'city'. The path is marked, easy to moderately rugged in difficulty and mainly follows the west side of the canyon wall with the exception of the Bridge Avenue area. There is a section north of West Main Street and south of Richmond Avenue where the hike is on the road edge of Sim Hodgin Parkway (about 250 paces). Negative points include missing trail markers, missing steps on staircases, trash and vandalism. There are 9 bridges and 8 sets of staircases. The trail requires about 3 1/2 hours to hike round-trip from Thistlethwaite Falls near Spring Grove Park south to Test Road.
There are 5 access trail points:

Spring Grove Park: Park north along Waterfall Road preferably in Spring Grove Park. Trailhead is at Thistlethwaite Falls along West Fork Branch.
Bridge Avenue: Park along Bridge Avenue and enter southeast side of Bridge and follow the level parkland along stream.
Sim Hodgin Parkway: Park alongside the parkway near Weir Dam and south of dam.
High School Parking Lot: North of South G Street at Whitewater Boulevard.
Test Road: Park at the park gate and hike 100 yards north to trailhead.

Starting north and going south, Thistlethwaite Falls will be the first outstanding natural feature. Just downstream is a 20 acre bird sanctuary for at least 50 species. The trail goes up the bank at Bridge Avenue and heads across the bridge and follows a section of level floodplain on the east band of West Branch. A information sign describes the abundance of fossils discovered in the exposed bedrock: bryozoans or moss animals, brachiopods or lamp shells and marine animals, stromatoporoid. Geologists refer to these 450 million years old fossils as the Richmond Group of the Whitewater Formation.

The confluence of West Fork with the East Fork of the Whitewater River occurs near the junction of the Norfolk & Western RR and Sam Hodgin Parkway. From the confluence south past the Richmond Avenue Bridge, Weir Dam, to nearly the Main Street Bridge is 'urban'. There are several historic points in this area: the city's first public utility, a former water-powered flour mill, the dam and views of the Wayne County courthouse.

South of the Main Street Bridge the atmosphere becomes more natural as you move away from the downtown above. Ruins of the old National Road Bridge, the Starr Piano Company building, Gennett Recording Studio, the old river ford, and old quarries are pointed out in the trail guide. South of G Street the trail reaches its most natural development. The flood plain is wide and well forested with riparian flora. The trail forms a loop to Test Park; one trail follows the canyon wall to the decaying foundations of the Test Woolen Mill and the other trail follows alongside the river. Test Road is the end of the trail. This unique hike was made possible from the glacial meltwaters of the Wisconsin Ice Age (22,000 years before) carving its way thru the bedrock.

Trail guides may be obtained from the Wayne County Convention & Tourism Bureau at 600 Promenade, Richmond, IN 47374. The city park office headquartered at Glen Miller Park, 2400 National Road will also have information.

Thistlethwaite Falls

4. JOSEPH MOORE MUSEUM OF NATURAL HISTORY and TEETOR PLANETARIUM

Richmond, IN/Wayne County
Earlham College/National Road West/US 40
(317) 983-1303 or 1210
ACTIVITIES: natural history museum, group tours, planetarium shows, gift shop

Joseph Moore, teacher, college president, geologist was the founder and early curator of this excellent natural history museum that was later named in his honor. The talented Professor Moore established the "working" museum in 1847 as a teaching collection and research center. The facility is staffed by students who design exhibits, maintain the collection, lead tours, and teach classes. The museum is open to the general public for informal visitation 1 pm to 4 pm Monday, Wednesday and Friday, September thru November (fall semester) and January to May (spring semester). The December and summer hours are 1 pm to 5 pm on Sundays. The Ralph Teetor Planetorium is also housed here, presenting visual programs and lectures about the stars and astronomy. The planetarium is open 1 pm to 5 pm on Sundays.

The collection of natural specimens are displayed on two levels: main floor and lower level. An Indiana excavated mastodon skeleton is displayed near the picture window along with the complete skeleton of a giant beaver and a fullsize cast of a giant ground sloth.

In addition, the Paleontology area includes a 100 million year old Antrodemusital or carnivorous dinosaur. Indiana mammals and birds, insects, arachnids, crustaceans, reptiles, amphibians, fish, shells, plants, minerals and the famous Whitewater Gorge Ordovician fossils are exhibited on the main floor. The lower level is the Children's Discovery Room that includes a live snake collection. Ta-ah, an Egyptian mummy, is also placed here.

The Joseph Moore Museum of Natual History is located west of downtown Richmond just south of the National Road/US 40 on the Earlham College campus. Visitor parking is available on the campus.

John Iverson, Director
Joseph Moore Museum of Natural History
Earlham College
Richmond, IN 47374

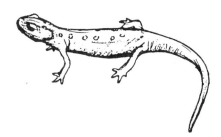

30

5. WHITEWATER MEMORIAL STATE PARK

Liberty, IN/Union County
USGS MAP(S): New Fairfield, Liberty 1:24,000
TRAIL(S) DISTANCE: 6 trails total 11 miles
ACREAGE: 1,710 acres/ Whitewater Lake 200 acres
ACTIVITIES: hiking, nature preserve, naturalist service, solar
heated visitors center, picnicking, picnic shelters, playground,
playfields, bicycling, lake fishing, Whitewater Valley Bicycle Route,
non-motorized boating, launch ramps, beach swimming, lifeguards,
bathhouse, concessions, saddle barn, bridle trails, horsemen camp,
Class A & B camping, rally, youth tent, family cabins, dumping
station, grocery store, cultural arts programs
FEE(S): entrance, camping, cabins, horse rental, canoe, paddleboat and
rowboat rentals, bicycle rental, shelterhouse reservations

Whitewater Memorial State Park was established in 1949 as a living parkland memorial to the men and women who served in World War II. Union, Fayette, Wayne and Franklin County residents worked together successfully to acquire the property. The park occupies the lower valley and adjacent hills of Silver Creek, a tributary of the nearby Brookville Reservoir and East Fork of the Whitewater River. Six easy-to-rugged, well-marked trails encircle Whitewater Lake.

Trail 2 and 3 are very popular, well maintained linear trails that follow the east shoreline of Whitewater Lake. Trail 3 is a one mile one-way trip from the beach area north to the Silver Creek bridge crossing and the beginning of Trail 4. Several campground spurs lead up and downhill connecting the lakeshore trail. Deer, raccoon and songbirds frequent the trailsides, especially at twilight. Trail 2 is actually a southern extension of Trail 3. It follows the Whitewater lakeside from the south side of the beach area south along lake bluffs, across a picnic shelter area, beside a cove ravine and uphill to end at the boat dock area.

Trail 1 is a moderate 1 3/4 mile winding linear trail that begins at the main park road southeast of the saddle barn entrance. Due to the trail's close proximity to the horse trail, it is utilized by riders and a section has been designated for both hikers and riders. Closer to the lake, the hills and ravines are more heavily wooded. Trail 1 ends at the boat dock parking area and connects Trail 2.4, and 5.

Trail 4 begins along the west bank of Silver Creek in the north area of the park. The area is scenic and wildlife rich as it crosses a wooded marsh south 3/4 mile to North Point Vista. Trail 4 continues as it follows the west lakeshore bluffs and draws around to the south lakeside and the spillway parking area. The Hornbeam Nature Preserve is where the trail forms a reconnecting loop thru the 37 acre preserve. The dedicated forest has a sizeable hornbeam tree population of water or blue beech as well as hophornbeam or ironwood. These shade tolerant trees are members of the Birch family and are regarded as weed trees by foresters but ornamentals by gardeners. The "hornbeam" means "tough wood" in reference to the hard, "iron-like" wood. Trail 4 connects trails 5 and 3.

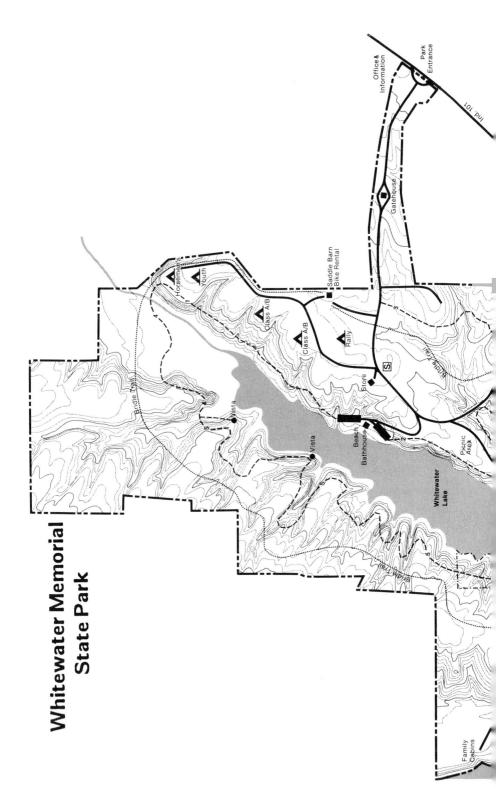

Whitewater Memorial State Park

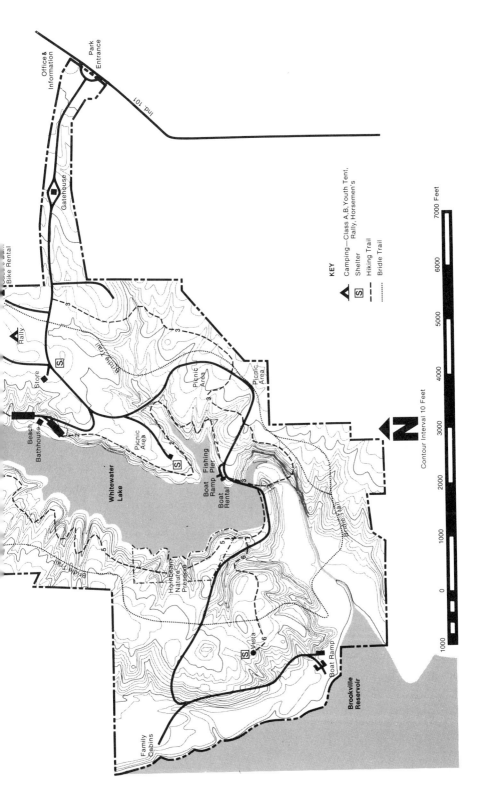

Trail 5 is 1 1/2 mile loop trail that crosses the main park road and heads southwest thru a climax beech-maple forest ravine to cross a horse trail then on to follow the hill top to a sheltered vista where the young trees are reclaiming the view of Brookville Reservoir. The trail continues south winding back around to the east following along Silver Creek, past seep springs and returns to the spillway parking area. A parking lot adjacent west of Hornbeam Nature Preserve has ample parking for access to Trails 4 and 5.

Trail 6 is a moderate 2 1/4 mile loop trail that has an assortment of scenic areas. The trail heads north through a hardwood forest, crossing the main park road, continuing north through another hardwood forest before turning south at the cabin area. The trail continues south following along the edge of Brookville Reservoir where aquatic wildlife may be found. The trail then returns to the Silver Creek Ramp picnic area. A parking lot here has ample parking for access to trail 6.

Be advised that horsemen ride the footpaths quite often so expect to walk alongside muddy eroded trails even at the Hornbeam Nature Preserve. Whitewater Memorial State Park entrance is located 1 mile south of Liberty on SR 101.

Immediately south and west of the state park is the 5,260 acre, 16 mile long Brookville Reservoir. Mounds State Recreation Area, Scenic Drive and Bon Hill Recreation Site are part of the 12,000 land acres where some established hiking is available. In addition to Mounds SRA's 1.5 mile peninsular beach trail, near the Mound Hills, there are several short spur trails that lead from the campground down to the boat ramp and wooded shores. A scenic roadway follows the 1,000 foot lake bluff from Garr Hill Ramp south to Bon Well Hill. There is a short nature trail between the boat ramp, dam and Lookout Point. Other recreational activities at Brookville Reservoir include, picnicking, playground, playfields, shelters, swimming beaches, boating, boat rentals, marinas, bathhouses, water skiing, cross country winter skiing, concessions, Class AA, A, and B camping, dumping station, gate fee.

The Brookville Reservoir main office is located at SR 101 and Mounds Road at the entrance of Mounds State Recreation Area.

6. WHITEWATER CANAL TRAIL & STATE HISTORIC SITE

Metamora, IN/Franklin County
USGS MAP(S): Metamora, Brookville 1:24,000
TRAIL(S) DISTANCE: appx. 6 miles
ACTIVITIES: hiking natural and social history, picnicking, canoeing, tent camping, canal boat ride, gristmill, Whitewater Valley steam RR tour, special annual events, canoe rental, canal boat ride

The Whitewater Canal State Historic Site was established in 1946 under the administration of the DNR's Division of State Museum and Historic Sites to preserve a 14 mile section of the canal and some of its unique features. Historically, the commercial waterway which was constructed between 1836-1847, flowed 76 miles alongside the Whitewater River from Hagerstown to Lawrenceburg with a branch along the Miami River at Cincinnati, Ohio. Fifty-six locks and 7 feeder dams were constructed along the scenic valley route with a elevation fall of 490 feet.

Destructive floods caused considerable damage to the canal thus maintaining the numerous locks, dams and embankments was financially ruinous and led to its subsequent bankruptcy in 1862. At this point in history, railroads were replacing the canals. In a short time the old towpath became a railway bed.

Today the canal flows 14 miles from the Laurel Feeder Dam to Yellow Bank Creek, 3 miles west of Brookville on US 52. Restoration included the Laurel Feeder Dam, Metamora Gristmill, Duck Creek Aqueduct and Millville Lock. The steam powered Whitewater Valley Railroad was also restored by a non-profit organization, making round trip runs from Connersville to Metamora during May to November and special holidays.

The Whitewater Canal Trail begins at the Laurel Feeder Dam (restored 1960) approximately 1.5 miles south of Laurel on the right/east bank of the Whitewater River. Follow the Main Street road 1/4 mile southeast from the crossroads in Laurel and turn south/right onto a gravel road just beyond the West Fork of the Whitewater River bridge. Parking, picnicking, fishing and tent camping are permitted at the dam site and feeder channel. Canoeists or "tubers" may put in at the feeder dam and float the restored 14 mile canal to Yellow Bank Creek, or canoe the adjacent swift West Fork of the Whitewater River downstream to the confluence with the Miami River.

Follow the white metal, one-way blazes on the utility line poles southeast along the gravel road and canal 2.2 miles to where the canal and trail curve northeast and gradually southeast. This is the best natural section of the trail as it follows the south bank of the former towpath. Old tree covered locks and nearby hills convey the feeling of remoteness on this 1 mile section before the trail joins the Whitewater Valley Railroad (old New York Central RR).

Upon reaching the railroad, the trail follows the railroad for approximately 3/4 miles while the canal flows alongside and under low trestle bridges twice. The white blazes are nailed down to the railroad ties. The trail leaves the tracks and follows the canal via a farm lane for approximately 200 yards to US 52 highway where it crosses over to

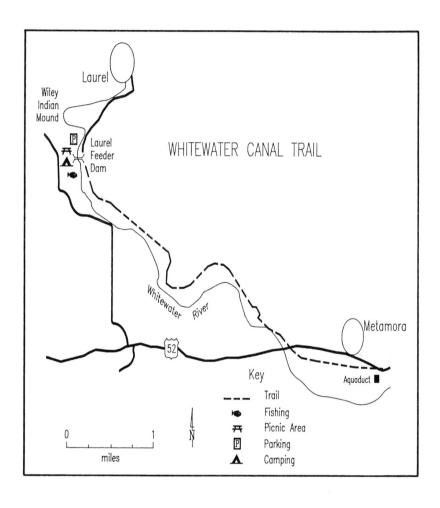

Laurel

Wiley
Indian
Mound

Laurel
Feeder
Dam

WHITEWATER CANAL TRAIL

Whitewater River

Metamora

52

Aquaduct

Key

- - - Trail

Fishing

Picnic Area

P Parking

▲ Camping

0   1

miles

N

the Metamora Main Street road right and then left beyond the railroad crossing.

Follow the Metamora Main Street road east alongside the canal and railroad tracks about 1/2 mile to the town of Metamora and the restored brick gristmill and lock. French buhrstones grind corn and wheat and the meal and flour is available for public sale. A historical museum is located on the second floor. Picnicking may be enjoyed at the easily accessed park on the opposite bank where there are fine views of the working water wheel. The gristmill and museum is closed Mondays but open weekdays noon to 3:30 pm. Weekend hours are Saturday 11 am to 6 pm and Sunday noon to 6:00 pm.

Proceed east along the historic Main street buildings to the replica canal boat Ben Franklin III docked at the corner of Main and Colombia. Tickets may be purchased next to the boat dock May 1st to October 31st every day but Monday. Mules were originally used to pull the boats but now Tony and Rex, 2 American-Belgium horses tow the several ton boat one mile every trip several times a day.

Continue east along the tow path to Duck Creek Aqueduct originally built in 1843. One of a kind, the 80 foot long covered aqueduct bridge literally floats thru the air 16 feet above Duck Creek. The tow path trail continues eastward a short distance to the Millville Lock, dated 1842 and the only operational lock along the entire 14 mile section. From here the trail continues past the Metamora Rest Park and ends at the 50 mile marker east of Metamora about 1 mile. Poison hemlock with its mousey smell is abundant along this section. Brambles and other thick vegetation begins where the rails end but formerly the Whitewater Canal Trail continued on eastwards to Boundary Hill just west of Brookville. If you do not have a car shuttle, you must retrace steps back to Laurel Feeder Dam.

Metamora is located 8 miles west of Brookville on US 52. From I-74 exit north at Batesville onto SR 229.

In addition the nearby 200 acre Franklin County Park offers seasonal Class A and C camping, picnicking, shelterhouses (rentals available), playground and playfields. There are no established nature trails but the hilltop shelter area has a beech-maple forest around its slopes to explore.

Franklin County Park is located southeast of Brookville approximately 1 mile turning right/west on Blue Creek Road driving south another mile to the park entrance on the right. Follow the directional signs.

Historic Site Curator
Whitewater Canal Memorial
Metamora, IN 47030
(317) 647-6512

Whitewater Valley Railroad Co.
300 S. Eastern Ave.
Connersville, IN 47331
(317) 825-2054

Debra Wilkerson

37

7. SHRADER-WEAVER WOODS NATURE PRESERVE

Bentonville, IN/ Fayette County
USGS MAP(S): Connersville 1:24,000
TRAIL(S) DISTANCE: 2 self-guiding trails total 1 1/4 miles
ACREAGE: 108 acres
ACTIVITIES: hiking, nature study, photography, environmental study
  area

Dedicated as a National Natural Landmark, Shrader-Weaver Woods has old growth beech-maple forest as well as abandoned open fields, and a historic 1830 pioneer homestead. This 28 acre stand of climax-aged trees is a rarity and a quality outdoor experience in the logged-out farmland of the eastern Tipton Till Plain. Thanks to the foresight and generosity of the Weaver family and The Nature Conservancy, the impressive forest is now a state nature preserve. Two brief, self-guided, loop trails with 25 marked stations each traverse the preserve. Trail brochures are available at the trailhead registration boxes. Marked trail spurs lead from the parking lot and the pioneer homestead to the nearby trailheads. Mosquitos can be pesky in the wet woodland especially in spring and early summer. Stinging wood nettles can be troublesome along the overgrown trail areas during the warm season.

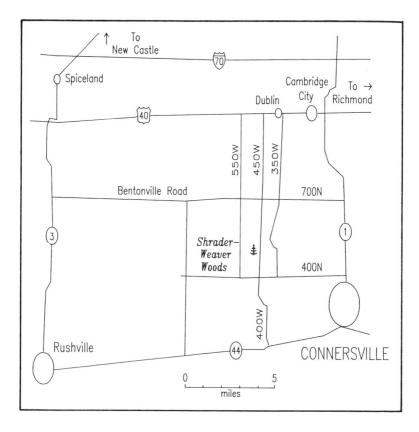

Old Growth Wood Trail is an easy 1/2 mile loop around and about a moist and cool climax forest where sugar maple is common and beech is dominant. Surprisingly, bur oak is the largest tree since few oaks and hickories are present. The open low understory is filled with ironwood, pawpaw, spring wildflowers of violets, trilliums, and spring beauties, ferns, young trees of red elm, beech, maple, tulip poplar, wild cherry, white ash, black walnut and (unfortunately) stinging wood nettle. Once completing the loop continue right/south to the second trail.

The Succession Nature Trail is a moderate 3/4 mile loop thru a revegetating farm field and alluvial woodland along Williams Branch. The 25 stations correspond with the trail brochure to identify flora and examples of forest ecology. Grasses to forbs to brambles to saplings to young trees are the primary stages of secondary succession the abandoned field has taken. The lowland has several different species of oak and hickory, black and white walnuts, hackberry, honey locust, boxelder maple, cork elm, sycamore, blue beech, ash, skunk cabbage, and marsh marigold. This trail has the tendency to be overgrown and muddy in places.

To reach Shrader-Weaver Woods from I-70, exit south on SR 1 and drive 5 1/2 miles thru Milton to the Bentonville Road/CR 700N and proceed west to 450 about 1 mile east of Bentonville. Turn south on 450W and drive 1 3/4 miles to the preserve's parking lot entrance. The preserve is open sunrise to sunset. A resident caretaker lives on the property.

Spore Mushrooms

8. MARY GRAY BIRD SANCTUARY

Columbia, IN/ Fayette County
USGS MAP(S): Alpine, New Salem 1:24,000
TRAIL(S) DISTANCE: 12 trails total 6 miles
ACREAGE: 656 acres
ACTIVITIES: hiking, nature study, picnicking, shelterhouses, Audubon
  Society meetings and programs, Brooks Hall (meeting rooms, museum,
  library), Markle Barn Kitchen, fishing and camping for Audubon
  members public group tours
FEE(S): donations welcome, shelterhouses, Brooks Hall and Markle Barn
  Kitchen are public reservable

Mary Gray Bird Sanctuary, since 1940, has been owned and managed
by the Indiana Audubon Society. The sanctuary was a generous gift from
the late state congressman Finley Gray and spouse Alice Gray in memory
of their daughter. Old abandoned fields, pastures and immature forest
cover the gentle rolling hills and ravines. The main east entrance to the
property follows a 100 yard-long wooded lane to Brooks Hall (usually
closed), the picnic/pond area, resident manager's home and visitors
parking lot. The easy to moderate short trails with plant and animal
names weave and intersect within a short distance from the parking area.
60 bird species have been identified at the property.

Mary Gray Bird Sanctuary

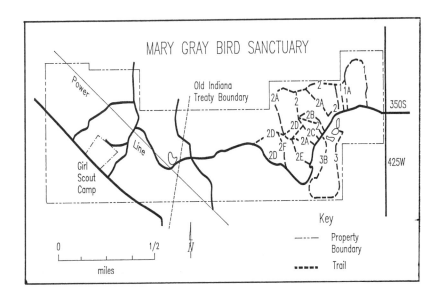

MARY GRAY BIRD SANCTUARY

Wildflower/Trail 1 is a 0.55 mile wooded ravine, ridge and old abandoned pasture loop walk that begins on the east side of the sanctuary resident's home. Nut Grove/Trail 1A is a 0.15 mile bottomland spur to Wildflower Trail. Bluebird, Malus, Craetegus/Trail 2 is a 0.7 mile walk that follows a ravine uphill to a open wildlife food plot. The trail proceeds along the field border to descend thru an allee of crabapple and hawthorn trees, several bluebird boxes, a vista point, back to the service road and left to the visitors parking lot. Trail 2 is intersected with several woodland and meadow spur trails: Beech/2A (0.2 m.), Lonicera/2B (0.2 m.), Viburnum/2C (0.2 m.), Cornus/2D (0.5 m.), Prunus/2E (0.3 m.) and Woods/2F (0.2 m.). Beech/2A has the most mature beech-maple forest area on the grounds. Tulip Poplar/Trail 3, one of the longest trails, begins east of the picnic/pond area and winds thru the natural area to connect Lower Creek/3B (0.4 m.) and returns via ravine to the picnic/pond and parking area. West Pond (1.3 m.) follows the service road west from the parking area to a small wildlife pond and back. The sanctuary is open daily from sunrise to sunset.

Mary Gray Bird Sanctuary is located southwest of Connersville. From SR 44 approximately 3 miles west of Connersville, turn south onto 525W and turn left/east at 150S and drive about one mile to 425W. Turn south/right and drive to the entrance at the junction of 350S. The entrance is 4 miles south of SR 44.

Another route may be taken by driving south on SR 121 from Connersville turning west onto CR 350 and proceeding 3.5 miles to the entrance and junction with CR 425W. The sanctuary entrance is 1.6 miles northwest of Columbia.

Supervisor, RFD #6 Box 165
Connersville, IN 47331 , (317) 825-9788

9. VERSAILLES STATE PARK

Versailles, IN/Ripley County
USGS MAP(S): Milan 1:24,000
TRAIL(S) DISTANCE: 3 trails total 6 miles; no est. trails at 2 nature preserves
ACREAGE: 5,905 acres, 230 acre Versailles Lake
ACTIVITIES: hiking, nature study, nature preserves, nature center, naturalist, bicycling, Hoosier Hills Bike Route, picnicking, shelterhouses, playground, swimming pool, waterslide, lifeguards, bathhouse, concessions, non-motorized boating, boat rental, boat ramp, fishing, saddle barn, bridle trails, horse rental, cultural arts program, Class A camping, youth group camping and building, dumping station
FEE(S): entrance, boat rental, boat launch fee, horse rental, shelter reservations, camping, group camp, swimming pool fee

After Brown County State Park, Versailles State Park is Indiana's second largest outdoor parkland. The National Park Service acquired the property during the depression years and it was developed shortly thereafter by the Civilian Conservation Corps. After 1943, the land was administered by the Indiana Department of Conservation, now known as the Department of Natural Resources.

Three well maintained trails have been designated in the developed north section of the park and two begin and end at the Oak Grove Picnic Shelter area. Two nature preserves are located in the more remote undeveloped south portion of the park.

Trail 1 or Firetower Trail is a moderate 2 1/4 mile loop that begins about 100 feet west of the Oak Grove Picnic Shelter. Proceed south, following the wooden steps, stairs and bridge down the hillside and across the paved park road. Go right uphill and continue along the ridgetop to the fire tower road. There are two vista points in the heavy forest growth. This trail leads through fine specimens of oak, hickory, maple, beech, tulip poplar, black walnut and other native tree specimens. Look for limestone sinkholes along the way. The forest path loops past the fire tower road and alongside sections of the gravel park road to the saddle barn to eventually descend a scenic ravine. The trail junctions with the original park road crossing then climbs uphill along a gravel path to the shelterhouse.

Trail 2 or the Fallen Timber Trail is a moderate 2 3/4 mile trail that begins about 100 feet northeast of the Oak Grove Picnic Shelter area. The trail skirts past the southeast edge of Campground A and across the campground road. The trail descends a firelane and then turns sharply west to follow the south bluffside of Fallen Timber Creek and the north edge of Campground A. A spur trail leads down to Versailles Lake Picnic area, however, to return to Oak Grove Picnic area follow the upland path.

Trail 3 begins north of Fallen Timbers Bridge and proceeds eastward along Fallen Timbers Creek crossing the rockbottom creek three times before joining Trail 2. Visitors may observe the numerous invertebrates that inhabit the creek bottom.

Laughrey Bluff Nature Preserve encompasses 81 scenic acres downstream of Laughrey Creek about 200 yards past Busching Covered Bridge near the park entrance at US 50. A north-facing bluff overlooks Laughrey Creek 200 feet below. The steep slopes and ridgetops support a healthy stand of mixed woods that have been undisturbed since 1940. A waterfall and rock outcrops add to the diversity of the trailless preserve. The best access to this special area is to follow the Laughery Creek streambed or bankside downstream a short way from the covered bridge. Laughrey Creek is named in honor of Col. Archibald Lockry who was killed in a Indian skirmish at the confluence with the Ohio River in 1781.

Dogwood Nature Preserve is 20 acres in size but has several old age hardwoods on a north facing slope and plenty of flowering dogwood understory trees. Along with the high incidence of flowering dogwood, it also includes dense beds of may-apple, sweet cicely and bedstraw. The northeastern corner of the preserve contains an old field in an advanced stage of succession. American beech trees are particularly large and impressive. There are no trails.

To reach Dogwood Nature Preserve follow Cave Road south just beyond the Versailles Park entrance and Laughrey Creek Bridge on US 50. Continue south on Cave Hill Road and turn east on 200S and drive to where the road turns north on 300E. South of this point is Wilson Cemetery. Follow the road lane south to the cemetery and continue on along the west side of fenceline and park property to the preserve.

Versailles State Park is open all year and the entrance is located 1 mile east of Versailles on US 50.

Maidenhair Fern   Wilson

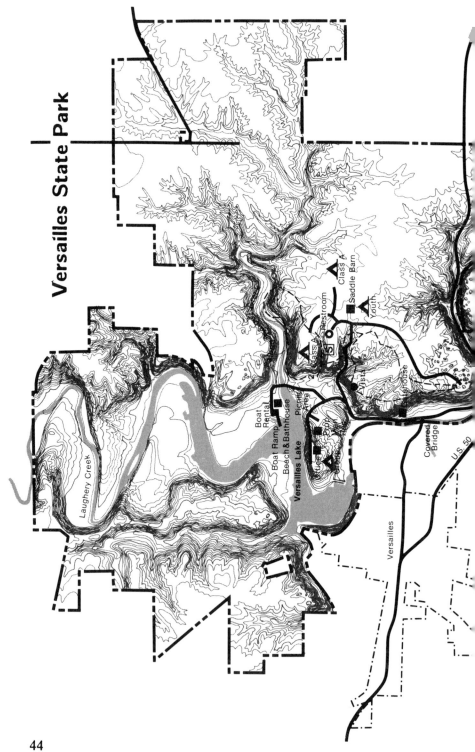

Versailles State Park

Laughery Creek

Versailles Lake

Boat Rental

Boat Ramp

Beach & Bathhouse

Picnic Area

Class A

Restroom

Class A

Vista

Class A

Saddle Barn

Youth

Lighthouse

Covered Bridge

U.S. 50

Versailles

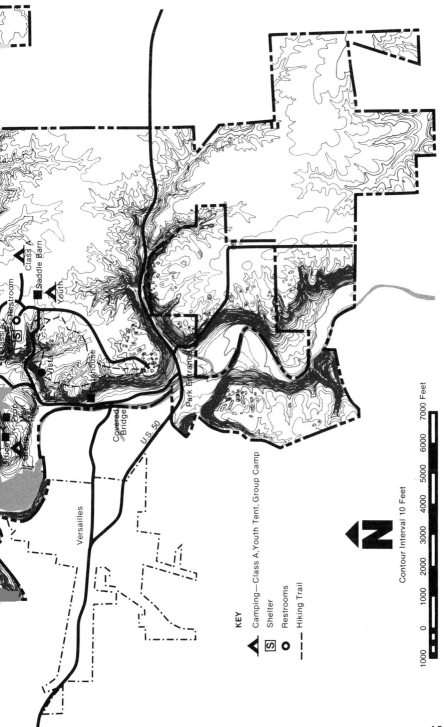

Saddle Barn

Class A

Restroom

Youth

CLASS A

S

Vista

Nature House

Park Entrance

Covered Bridge

U.S. 50

Versailles

KEY

Camping—Class A, Youth Tent, Group Camp

S Shelter

Restrooms

Hiking Trail

N

Contour Interval 10 Feet

1000   0   1000   2000   3000   4000   5000   6000   7000 Feet

10. ANDERSON FALLS

Hartsville, IN/Bartholomew County
USGS MAP(S): Grammer 1:24,000
TRAIL(S) DISTANCE: path 1 moderate 3/4 mile loop/path 2 easy 1/4
  mile loop
ACREAGE: 44 acres
ACTIVITIES: hiking, nature study, picnicking, photography

Positioned on Fall Fork of Clifty Creek, Anderson Falls is almost a scale model of the renowned Niagara Falls especially regarding its geological processes and formation. Historically, the Falls are named after a former landowner, David Anderson, who established a grist mill upstream near the cascade in the late 1830's. Prior to American settlement and the New Purchase Treaty of 1818, the area supported a sizable Miami and Delaware Indian encampment. Around 1900, with more leisure time and improved transportation, the Falls, the local mineral spring, and the immediate wooded surroundings were a favorite place for visitors on weekend outings. In recent years, The Nature Conservancy with combined financial funding purchased the land in 1977, and in 1981 the property was transferred to the Bartholomew County Parks and Recreation Board.

Anderson Falls

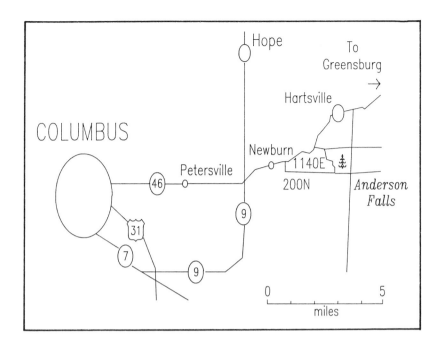

This pleasant nature walk crosses over and meanders alongside the stream and thru the adjoining dense forest. The trail begins across the road from the parking area. A brief all-weather paved path overlooks the 15 foot high waterfall, and several interpretive signs have been posted. Do read them before taking your hike to appreciate the Falls' geologic, natural and social history. Begin your hike a few yards upstream from the Falls stepping over to the other bank on the large evenly placed stones. Although the flow of water is normally low during the summer and fall months, the stream can be occasionally impassable during high water. Proceed on the well defined trail downstream. After a short walk, the 1/4 mile loop trail will be on the right leading up thru the woods and around to the stream again, and back to the stream crossing. Continue on if you want to follow the 3/4 mile path thru the ravines and uphill towards the back of the preserve property to eventually arrive again at the stream bluffs. Once at the streamside continue downstream to the crossing. Marked signs are posted that identify various plants such as white ash, poison ivy and chestnut oak. During the summer, fossils species of brachiopods, crinoids, bryozoans, trilobites, mollusks, and corals may be seen in the soft Waldron shale and limestone outcrops of Fall Fork. The park preserve hours are from sunrise to sunset.

Anderson Falls may be reached by driving east of Columbus on SR 46 to Newbern. Continue driving east thru Newbern on SR 46 to CR 925E and turn south a short distance to the curve east and CR 200N. Proceed about 2 miles on CR 200N and turn north onto CR 1140E and drive about 1/2 mile to the parking area on the west side of the road. Directional signs begin along SR 46 east of Newbern.

11. SELMIER STATE FOREST

North Vernon, IN/Jennings County
USGS MAP(S): Butlerville 1:24,000
TRAIL(S) DISTANCE: no est. trails, only firelanes
ACREAGE: 352 acres
ACTIVITIES: hiking, nature study, picnicking, fishing, hunting

Since 1951 Selmier State Forest has been Indiana's smallest state forest. The farmfields, pine and hardwood stands, and river frontage along the scenic Vernon Fork of the Muscatatuck River, were formerly the estate of Indianapolis entrepreneur Frank Selmier. These lands were willed to the state of Indiana upon his death for usage as a natural resource and public benefit.

There are no hiking trails but there are plenty of firelanes to wander. The Vawter Road follows along the forested bluffs of the same river that flows downstream past Muscatatuck County Park and Crosley State Fish & Wildlife Area. Sizeable native hemlock trees are found on the river bluff between the Summerfield Cemetery and the power line cut/swath. The riverside is by far the most picturesque part of the forest with stream rapids and boulders, rock outcrops, and overhangs. A property map is available at the forest office. Because there are so few places to park on the narrow forest roads it may be best to leave your vehicle at the forest office. Several unnumbered firelanes weave and interlace throughout the manage level woodlots northwest of the river. Some of the firelanes are graveled like White Pine Road but most are vegetated and overgrown during the warm months. There is largemouth bass fishing at Gill Pond near the property entrance and the forest office.

Selmeir State Forest is located 3 miles northeast of North Vernon. Turn north on Main Street from SR 7 & 3 at the railroad tracks and follow Base Road/20W about 2 miles north to 350N (1st crossroads) and turn right. Continue east approximately 1 mile to the forest office on the right side of the road. The day-use property and firelane access road to the river is about 100 yards west before the park office.

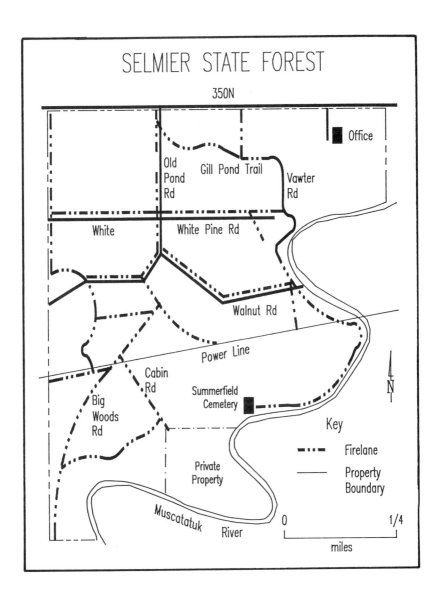

SELMIER STATE FOREST

350N

Office

Old Pond Rd

Gill Pond Trail

Vawter Rd

White

White Pine Rd

Walnut Rd

Power Line

Cabin Rd

Big Woods Rd

Summerfield Cemetery

Private Property

Muscatatuk River

Key

- - ·· - Firelane

——— Property Boundary

0   1/4

miles

N

49

12. CROSLEY STATE FISH & WILDLIFE AREA

Vernon & Butlerville, IN/Jennings County
USGS MAP(S): Vernon, Hayden, Butlerville & Holton 1:24,000
TRAIL(S) DISTANCE: no est. trails/several miles of firelanes
ACTIVITIES: hiking, spelunking, nature study, social history,
picnicking, canoeing, river boat ramp, non-motorized boating,
lake boat ramp, lake, pond & river fishing, wild food foraging,
hunting, archery & rifle range, skeet shoot

Cincinnati businessman, Powell Crosley, famous for the Crosley automobile and refrigerator and former owner of both the Cincinnati Reds baseball team and WLW radio station began land acquisition in 1927 of what is now Crosley State Fish and Wildlife Area. The abandoned farm fields and the logged and abused woodlands were in poor condition and were highly eroded. The new owner set about to develop and restore the land as a personal game preserve and lodge retreat. Mr. Crosley entertained friends, business acquaintances and occasionally members of his Cincinnati Reds baseball team. The 3,100 acre estate was sold to the DNR/Division of Fish & Wildlife in 1958. Since that time an additional 1,000 acres was purchased, making Crosley approximately 4,100 acres in size. Today second growth deciduous hardwoods and pine plantations cover most of the property.

Ponds, marshes, lakes, upland forest and meadows occupy the area located between state Highways 7 and 3. Crosley lake, 14 acres in size, is the largest and most scenic lake with the twelve remaining lakes and ponds averaging 2.5 acres in size. The four marshes range from 2 to 9 acres of water. Parking lots are situated near all lakes, and fisherman's paths encircle the bodies of water. The property's main office is located in the area near Aspen Lake and picnic grounds alongside SR 3, two miles south of Vernon.

West of SR 3 are forested ravines and seven miles of the Muscatatuck River. Several small, seldom explored limestone caves are found along the river and its tributaries. Three caves that range from easy to difficult to discover are Tunnel Mill, Circle Cave and Biehle Cave. Tunnel Mill ruins are located at the north end of the G Area near the Baldwin Cemetery on the south side of the Muscatatuck River across from the town of Vernon. The man made tunnel was created in 1825 to divert water to power the mill. Circle Cave is located near the Shooting Range on the west bank of the river. Biehle Cave is located near the Biehle Branch on CR 300S and 50W just east of the Baltimore & Ohio railroad.

There are no established hiking trails on the property but there are at least 4 miles of firelanes that follow Love Branch and Green Branch and connect Old SR 3. Densely wooded, it is hard to imagine that this was once a state highway going to Vernon.

Twelve miles northeast of North Vernon is Brush Creek Fish and Wildlife Area and Public Fishing Area which is also administered by Crosley Fish & Wildlife Area. Like Crosley SFWA there are no designated trails but a few unique features are found throughout the abandoned farmlands and warrant exploration. Portions of the reservoir lake border the Muscatatuck State School and private property.

Property Manager
Crosley State Fish & Wildlife Area
R.R. #2, Box 87, North Vernon, IN 47265
812-346-5596

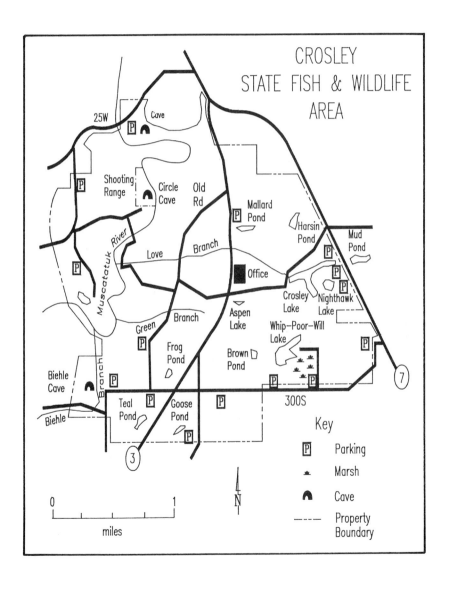

13. MUSCATATUCK COUNTY PARK

North Vernon, IN/Jennings County
USGS MAP(S): Hayden, Jennings 1:24,000
TRAIL(S) DISTANCE: appx. 3 mile total trail network
ACREAGE: 206 acres
ACTIVITIES: hiking, nature study, picnicking, shelterhouses, kitchen
   rental, river fishing, canoeing, recreational fields, bicycle BMX
   track, archery club & range, Senior Citizens Center, Class A camping
FEE(S): shelterhouse rental, kitchen rental, camping

Muscatatuck County Park has a unique social history. Jennings County bought and donated the scenic river bluff land as a state park in the early 1920's and was first known as Vinegar Mills State Park. Vinegar mills was a water powered mill on the Muscatatuck River in the 1830's. Morgan's Confederate Raiders camped here during their brief northern raid during the summer of 1863. A state park inn and cottages were constructed (now the Senior Citizens Center) and the park's name changed to Muscatatuck State Park. From 1953 to 1961 the Division of Fish and Game operated the property as a game farm for bobwhite quail. In 1967 the Indiana DNR returned the parkland to Jennings County and a county park was established.

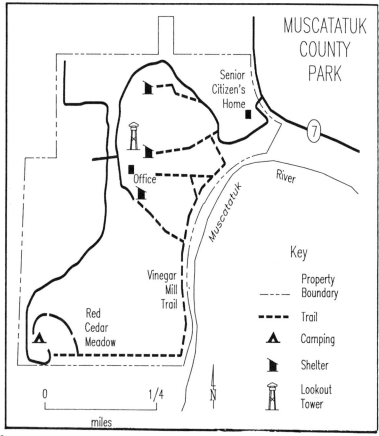

Unmarked yet obvious old state park trails follow ravines, hilltops, hillsides, and river shore. Woodsy paths lead down the steeps river bluffs to the Vernon Fork of the Muscatatuck River from the picnic shelter houses and from behind the park office along the main park blufftop road. The trail (formerly the Vinegar Falls Trail) is very narrow in places along the river where scenic waterfalls and rock outcroppings are found. Chinquapin oak and coralberry thrive on the bluff slopes as well as other oaks, hickories, ash, maples, blue and American beech, ironwood, wild cherry, sycamore, elm, red cedar, redbud and dogwood. Several old spurs lead from the campground. There is a 1/2 mile ravine trail that leads to a old crumbling dam on the northwest portion of the park. Park at the first picnic shelter encountered on the bluff and walk downhill on the road about 100 yards to a conspicuous streamside trail on the north side of the park road. The trail continues upstream to the old concrete dam and beyond to Park Avenue and Elm Street in North Vernon. The name Muscatatuck is derived from a Delaware Indian word, "Mosch-ach-hit-tuk", meaning "clear river" or "land of the winding waters".

Muscatatuck County Park is located between North Vernon and Vernon on SR 7 on the south side of the highway.

White Tail Deer

14. MUSCATATUCK NATIONAL WILDLIFE REFUGE

Seymour, IN/Jackson & Jennings Counties
USGS MAP(S): Chestnut Ridge 1:24,000
TRAIL(S) DISTANCE: 5 foot trails total appx. 3 miles
ACREAGE: 7,724 acres
ACTIVITIES: hiking, visitor center, bird watching, photography,
  bicycling, fishing, non-motorized boating, self-guided interpretive
  trail, self-guided auto tour, waterfowl outlook overlook, wild
  food foraging, hunting
FEE(S): entrance

The sale of federal Duck Stamps provided the needed monies to
establish Muscatatuck National Wildlife Refuge in 1966. Both resident and
migratory waterfowl are seasonally abundant in the lakes, ponds, marshes
and creeks that flow to the winding Muscatatuck River, and the south
boundary of the refuge. The uplands include abandoned fields, grassy
meadows, croplands, young forests, woodlots; ideal habitats for wildlife.
The over 7,000 acre refuge is one of 430 national wildlife refuges in the
United States and is the only one in Indiana. It is administered by the
U.S. Fish and Wildlife Service of the Department of the Interior.

Early spring and mid fall during early morning or late afternoon are
the best times to observe the migratory waterfowl on the refuge although
ducks and geese can be observed year-round. During the migratory
periods birds like mallards, blue-winged teal, shovelers, ring-necked ducks,
lesser scaup, and redheads can be often seen. Colorful wood ducks and
Canada geese are abundant nesting residents. Arriving by late April and
early May are songbirds like the eastern phoebe, gray catbird, Carolina
wren, indigo bunting, and many warblers. Sandhill cranes are commonly
seen flying over in early spring and late fall and osprey can sometimes be
found on the refuge throughout the summer months.

Common and abundant year-round residents include mourning dove,
blue jay, Carolina chickadee, eastern bluebirds, tufted titmouse, white-
breasted nuthatch, robins, northern mockingbird, rufous-sided towhee,
eastern meadowlark, and American goldfinch, along with many species of
woodpeckers and two species of owls. Over 228 bird species have been
observed on the refuge and a bird list is available at the visitors center
as are other brochures, maps, and related information.

The five short foot trails are described as easy to moderate.
Beginning at the visitor center parking lot is the trailhead for a 0.3 mile
long self-guided Chestnut Ridge Interpretive Trail. This trail winds
through a woods across a wetland spring (on a wooden boardwalk) and
travels through a pine forest and grassy, shrub-covered meadow before
looping back to the visitor center.

Endicott Trail is a 0.3 mile long loop trail that is located at the south
end of Endicott Marsh along the auto-tour route. The trail follows a
grassy lane through a young forest and passes a wildlife pond.

The Wood Duck Trail begins at the east end of the parking lot north
of Stanfield Lake. The 0.5 mile path loops thru a wet woods of large
beech, maple, tulip and white oak trees. Wooden bridges have been
provided over wet ravines and wildflowers are especially abundant in this
area in the spring.

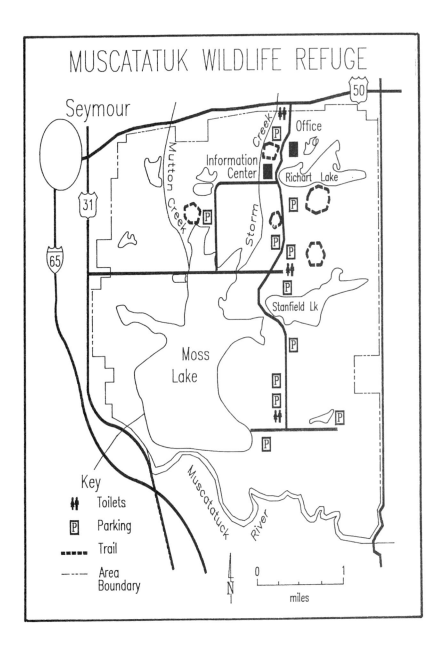

MUSCATATUK WILDLIFE REFUGE

Seymour

Creek

Mutton Creek

Storm Creek

Office

Information Center

Richart Lake

Stanfield Lk

Moss Lake

Muscatatuck River

Key

Toilets

Parking

Trail

Area Boundary

N

0   1

miles

The Richart Trail begins just south of Richart Lake (on the road traveling south from the refuge office). The .8 mile trail travels through a large woods and through shrub-covered meadows before winding down to a waterfowl observation overlook on Richart Lake (and back to the parking lot).

Bird Trail is located on the other side of the road due south of Richart Trail. This 0.5 mile trail follows a grassy fire through old pasture land that has reverted to brush and enters a woods adjacent to a refuge wetland unit.

All five refuge loop trails are marked by a hiking symbol sign. Hikers should also consider off-trail hiking on some of the many abandoned county roads and farm lanes existing on the refuge. One of the best walks for birders to take is to park at the Endicott Marsh corner (along the auto tour road) and walk back (past the "No Vehicle" signs) to Mutton Creek and Mini Marsh. The very scenic walk is easy and is about one half mile (one-way), and during the first week of May is one of the best places in the Midwest to see warblers. Off trail hiking is permitted everywhere on the refuge except in the closed waterfowl sanctuary area in the southwester corner of the refuge.

The Muscatatuck NWR is located 3 miles east of Seymour and I-65 on the south side of US 50. The refuge office (first building on the left or east side of the park road) is open Monday through Friday 8:00 am to 4:30 pm. The refuge is open sunrise to sunset.

Refuge Manager, Muscatatuck National Wildlife Refuge
R.R. 7, Box 189A, Seymour, IN 47274, 812/522-4352

Muscatatuck National Wildlife Area

15. GUTHRIE WOODS
Vernon, IN/Jennings County
USGS MAP(S): Vernon 1:24,000
TRAIL(S) DISTANCE: no est. trails
ACREAGE: 61 acres
ACTIVITIES: explore hiking, nature study, photography

Botanically, Guthrie Woods is known as a "high flatwoods" or "high flats". The level, poorly drained acid soil supports beech, sweet gum, tulip poplar and black gum and some "low flat" tree species such as swamp white oak, red oak and red maple. There are no established trails thru this unique nature preserve, however if one is willing to explore the dense understory the property is open.

Fall or winter are ideal seasons to visit when the forest floor is apt to be dry, and the mosquito/insect populations subside and the thick woods sheds its leaf cover. There is plenty of poison ivy as well as ferns, spicebush, paw paw, maple leaf viburnum, elderberry, and wildflowers including the more northern species and overlooked dwarf ginseng and threatened sweet white violet. The northern portion of the rectangular property is the least disturbed and most natural.

Guthrie Woods was a gift to The Nature Conservancy in 1982 from the Guthrie Trust and the former Nature Study Club of Indiana. Future plans for the woods will be dedication and inclusion as a state of Indiana nature preserve. Guthrie Woods has been dedicated before. A weathering plaque fixed at the corner of the southeastern boundary reads:

> *"Guthrie Woods is forest land*
> *dedicated to Sarah Ann Guthrie for*
> *a perpetual sanctuary as a living*
> *memorial to one who loved trees,*
> *flowers and birds."*

To reach Guthrie Woods drive south on SR 7 from Vernon 6 miles and turn east/left onto County Line Road and continue 1.1 miles to the southwest corner of the property.

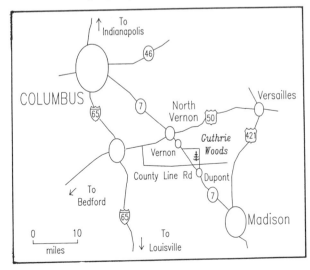

Guthrie Woods Memorial

16. TRIBBETT WOODS
Uniontown, IN/Jennings County
USGS MAP(S): Deputy 1:24,000
TRAIL(S) DISTANCE: no est. trails, old lanes
ACREAGE: 33 acres
ACTIVITIES: hiking, nature study

Open to hiking, this Nature Conservancy property offers visitors a rare wet flatwoods of majestic beech and oak. Exploring the 33 acre, nearly square tract on foot requires weaving trailess through the dense understory of pawpaw and spicebush. The deep woods is excellent for birding. Songbirds such as wood thrush, woodpeckers and warblers frequent the forest canopy. Deerfly and mosquitoes are particularly annoysome during the warmer months. Late fall to early spring are virtually bug-free. Wear tennis shoes that you don't mind getting soaked and muddy since the woods is seasonally wet. The Nature Conservancy's plans are to donate the preserve to the Indiana Division of Nature Preserves.

From I-64 at the Uniontown exit east onto SR 250. Go east on SR 250 about 4 miles and take the first road CR 200W to your left/north past the jog. Go north 2 miles to a gravel road CR 750S and turn right. The large woods is next to the road on the left side of the road 0.5 miles from CR 700W.

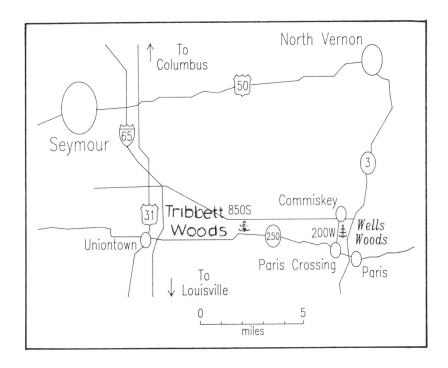

17. WELLS WOODS
Commiskey, IN/Jennings County
USGS MAP(S): Deputy 1:24,000
TRAIL(S) DISTANCE: no est. trails
ACREAGE: 20 acres
ACTIVITIES: hiking, nature study

This rectangular block of southeastern flatwoods is noted for its giant trees and plant diversity. The higher "flats" support beech, sweet gum, tulip poplar and black gum. The woodland depressions or "low flats" grow red or swamp maple and various water-tolerant oaks. Greenbriar and poison ivy are common. The underlying soils are acid, poorly drained and claypan. Biting insects are a problem during summer. Currently there are no trails but they are planned. The flatwoods of southeastern Indiana are basically found in south Decatur, Jennings, Ripley, north Jefferson and parts of Clark Counties.

Wells Woods lies southwest of Guthrie Woods and east of Tribbett Woods in southeastern Jennings County. All three preserves are prime examples of level, seasonally wet forest. From I-65, 8.5 miles south of Seymour, exit SR 250 east at Uniontown. Drive about 10 miles to Paris Crossing and turn north on CR 200W. Proceed north about 2 miles and the woods will be in front of you at the first curve east where there is a parking pullout. Residential homes border the east boundary. The preserve is owned by The Nature Conservancy.

18. CLIFTY FALLS STATE PARK

Madison, IN/Jefferson County
USGS MAP(S): Clifty Falls, Madison West 1:24,000
TRAIL(S) DISTANCE: 9 foot trails total appx. 13 miles
ACREAGE: 1,360 acres
ACTIVITIES: hiking, nature study, nature preserve, nature center, naturalist service, Hoosier Hills Bicycle Route, picnicking, shelterhouses, playgrounds, playfields, swimming pool, water slide, bathhouse, tennis courts, concessions, campground store, Clifty Inn, Class A & C camping, youth tent area, rally camping, dumping station, cultural arts program
FEE(S): entrance, shelter reservations, bicycle rental, camping, inn, swimming pool fee

Clifty Falls and Canyon is one of southern Indiana's most beautiful natural areas. The falls plummet over 60 feet into the steep walled gorge. The falls are most spectacular during the wetter months of the year, November through July. August through October the falls are at low flow. Plant covered boulders are everywhere. Smaller impressive waterfalls cascade over rock ledges along the tributaries. There are scenic bluff top views of the Ohio River and Madison 400 feet above the valley floor near the mouth of the canyon. Fortunately the mid-19th century Madison & Indianapolis railroad scheme failed to materialize since it would have traversed Clifty Canyon's east wall and Dean's Branch. However before the "folly" ran aground, railroad construction was carried out and is evident in the form of piers, trestles, stonework and Tunnel Cave.

The state park was established in 1920 and included most of the canyon and falls area. In 1965 nearly 700 acres of abandoned fields and woods were added and developed into recreational areas. All trails except #9 and #10 explore the falls and canyon area, a dedicated nature preserve. Most of these trails are heavily used and suffering from erosion but efforts are being made to curtail the problem with water bars, bridges, stairs, and re-directing foot traffic.

Trail 1 (also 2 and 3) is a moderate 5/8 mile path that begins at the nature center parking area and leads out on a south facing promontory to the flat platformed observation tower that overlooks the Ohio River Valley. Clifty Creek Power Plant smoke stack towers mar the sweeping panoramic view. From the observation tower the trail passes along the canyon wall northwest to connect Trails 2 and 3. If you continue onto Trail 2 it leads down to Clifty Canyon and up-canyon to the falls. Trail 3 leads to Beech Grove Picnic Shelter and Hoffman Falls. Trail 1 follows Trail 1-2-3 uphill to the main park road. To return to the nature center parking area follow the park road right or south.

Trail 2 is an upward rugged 3 mile streambed hike to Big Clifty Falls and the North Gate Shelter and Picnic Area. Expect to have wet feet since there is plenty of rock hopping and criss crossing Clifty Creek before you reach the falls but its worth it. There are several waterfalls and fossil rich boulders encountered along the scenic way. The trail ascends a wooden staircase at Big Clifty Falls to North Shelter Overlook and Picnic Area.

Trail 3 is a rugged one mile forest path that begins from the intersection with Trail 1 to continue north along the canyon wall between the rim and the creek. The trail switchbacks uphill alongside the main park road west of Poplar Grove Shelter and Picnic Area. The trail continues ridgeside past the Hoffman Branch Ravine and arrives at Beech Grove Shelter and Picnic Area and Hoffman Falls.

Trail 4 is a moderate 3/4 mile walk that starts from Hoffman Falls where there is a observation platform overlooking the 77 foot falls. The trail descends a root exposed rugged path along the canyon rim to a unmarked branching trail fork. One spur heads down the canyon to Trail 2 and the other continues to follow the rim to Lilly Memorial and Trail 5.

Trail 5 is a moderate one mile trail that begins at the Lilly Memorial, descends and heads back along the canyon wall past both ends of Tunnel Cave. A man made 200 yard long tunnel carved through the limestone bedrock to accommodate trains (never used). The trail continues above Dean's Branch to end at Tunnel Falls. To access Trail 6 and to continue hiking up the canyon's northeast side, follow the main park road around Dean's Branch, north or left, to Hickory Grover Shelter and Picnic Area.

Trail 6 is a 1/2 mile rugged trail that begins at Hickory Grove Shelter and Picnic Area and proceeds to hike the canyon wall to Lookout Point where the trail is re-numbered Trail 7.

Trail 7 is a moderate and scenic 1 1/4 mile walk that starts at Lookout Point and continues to follow the canyon rim. After a 1/4 mile the trail forks. The left fork leads to Little Clifty Falls and up wooden stairsteps to the Big Clifty Falls Overlook and North Shelter and Picnic Area. The right fork continues above Little Clifty Creek and crosses over a creek waterfall and overhang to head uphill to the North Shelter and Picnic Area.

Trail 8 is a rugged 4 1/2 mile trek, the longest and most remote hike of the canyon. The trailhead starts west of the North Shelter and Picnic Area and follows a firelane along the west bluff of Clifty Canyon. There are several overlooking canyon vistas. The trail is poorly drained in sections and can be muddy and slick days after a rain. Wallace Falls (79 feet high) is an outstanding natural feature. Trail 8 does access Trail 2 by descending into the gorge near the confluence of Clifty Creek and Dean's Branch. Further downstream the trail accesses Trail 2 again to cross and head uphill to intersect Trail 3 (Poplar Grove/Hoffman Falls) and Trail 1 (Observation Tower/Nature Center).

Trail 9 is a moderate 6/10 mile trail that begins at campsite 49-50 in the Class A campground. The trail passes through mature open woodland and alongside a small tributary creek (that drains to Hoffman Falls) enroute to the swimming pool parking area.

Trail 10 is a 3/4 mile nature trail through old fields. Brochures for this self guiding trail are available at the nature center.

There are two entrances to Clifty Falls State Park. The south gate entrance is located one mile west of Madison on SR 56. The north gate entrance is located on SR 62 northwest of Madison.

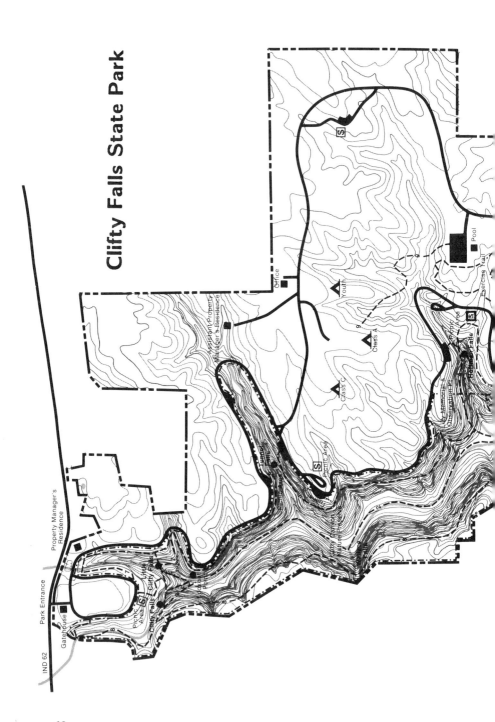

Clifty Falls State Park

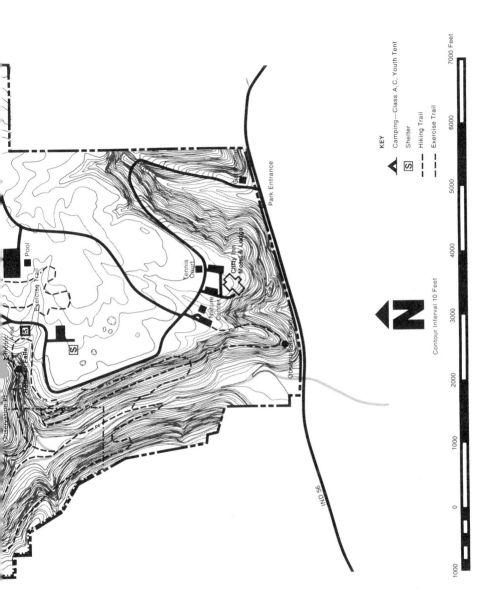

KEY

▲ Camping—Class A, C, Youth Tent

Ⓢ Shelter

--- Hiking Trail

-·- Exercise Trail

N

Contour Interval 10 Feet

1000   0   1000   2000   3000   4000   5000   6000   7000 Feet

Pool

Exercise Trail

Tennis Court

Nature Center

Clifty Inn Motel & Lodge

Park Entrance

IND 56

Observation Tower

Picnic Area

Clifty Falls

19. MADISON IN/NATURE PLACES

ACTIVITIES: visiting landscaped historic gardens/architecture, riverside
   pocket parks, picnicking, camping
FEE(S): entrance fee to historic buildings, camping

First settled in 1809 Madison is one of the oldest, most picturesque, and historically rich communities in southern Indiana. It is known for its architecture and charming Americana atmosphere. Most of the historic mansions between First and Second Streets were constructed from 1830-1860 and reflect the Federal, Classical Revival and Italianate styles. Many of these historical structures are open to public visitation including the beautiful landscaped gardens and grounds that surround them. Many of these reproduced period gardens grow plants that were cultivated by the early to mid-19th century residents. Practical gardeners on the western frontier grew plants not only for their beauty but for food, medicine, fragrance or for other purposes. This nature walk through horticultural history may yield ideas for your own present day garden. In addition, walkabout the downtown area where 133 blocks are listed on the National Register of Historic Places.

A premier example of one well researched period garden is the Talbot-Hyatt Pioneer Garden and House at 301 West 2nd Street between 1st and 2nd Streets at Poplar Street, just west of downtown. Restored by Historic Madison, Inc., the original garden was created in 1820 and the present reproduced garden dates from 1963. Richard C. Talbot arrived in Madison from Pennsylvania in 1814 and purchased the half square block which at that time was a stones throw from the town's limits. Research reveals Mr. Talbot was impressed with the landscaping practices of 18th century England especially curving paths or lines, compact enclosed areas and limited vistas. He made great use of native flowers, shrubs, and trees but also had room for fruits, vegetables, herbs, exotic flowers and shrubs. Raised beds for drainage were constructed and enclosed by rocks. The grounds also include a restored carriage house, an early community well, walkways and enough grass to play croquet as was done on Sunday afternoons of the 19th century. Mr. Talbot may be considered a prosperous, "beforetime suburbanite" that enjoyed gardening. The garden walk is free. Below is a partial list of plants that grow in the Talbot-Hyatt Pioneer Garden:

Bloodroot	Sweet Strawberry Shrub
Bluebells, Virgina	Pinks
Marsh Mallow	Petunias
Wild & Old Fashioned Roses	Squash
Osage Orange	Gooseberries
Wild Cherry	Grapes
Ash, White	Lavender
Maples	Thyme
Mulberry, Red & White	Yucca
Redbud	Native Clematis
Red Cedar	

The nearby J.F.D. Lanier Memorial Home at 511 West 1st Street between Elm and Vine Streets has lovely landscaped grounds that enhance the stately Classic Greek Revival-styled mansion. There are several old sycamores, crabapples, and other flower trees, evergreen shrubs and flower plots. Culinary and medicinal herbs and old fashioned flowers line the walls of the basin or sunken garden east of the mansion. The state of Indiana acquired the property in 1925 and presently the memorial is under the management of the Division of Indiana State Museum and Historic Sites/DNR.

The grounds are in the process of being historically restored to its mid-19th century design thanks to original correspondence and drawings. One picture illustrates that the current front lawn was formerly a garden with diverse plantings. There were two greenhouses; one for citrus fruits and one for flowers. This commendable horticultural historic undertaking will only improve with age and will assist the visitor to have a more complete picture of how residents lived a century or so ago. Tour of the home and grounds are free.

The mansion is open year round. Standard state hours of operation are Wednesday through Saturday 9 am to 5 pm; Tuesday and Sunday 1 to 5 pm. All times are Eastern standard. Additional hours by special arrangement. Telephone (812) 265-3526 for further information.

Preserved by Historic Madison, Inc., the Dr. William Hutchings Office and Hospital at 120 West 3rd Street has authentic furnishings but it is questionable if the backyard herb wall garden was ever cultivated for medicinal herbs. The cultivation of herbs for medicinal purposes was a standard practice in the previous early to mid 19th century (may be more so in the next century). Nonetheless the medicinal herbs growing were utilized in the pioneer doctor pharmacopoeia. The Office, Hospital and Garden are open for a small fee from May 1st to November 1st Monday to Saturday 10 am to 4:30 pm and Saturday 1 pm to 4:30 pm.

Stretch your legs and enjoy the walk around historic Madison. Several other historical sites have gardens such as the side garden at the Jeremiah Sullivan House on 304 West 2nd Street. There are colorful flower container gardening at the Broadway Fountain at Broadway between 3rd and Main Streets. John Paul Park, named in honor of Madison's founder, is at 3rd and Vine. Picnicking is fine at Jaycess, Fireman's, Kiwanis and Cherokee Parks, the Madison's riverside "pocket" parks with riverviews along Vaughn Drive. Tent and trailer camping is available at Vaughn Drive Campsites east of the Ohio River Bridge and at nearby state operated Clifty Falls State Park just west of the Madison city limits.

Historic Madison, Inc.
500 West Street
Madison, IN 47250, (812) 265-2967

Curator, Lanier State Historical Site
511 West First Street
Madison, IN 47250, (812) 265-3526

20 ATTERBURY STATE FISH and WILDLIFE AREA/ JOHNSON COUNTY PARK/ DRIFTWOOD STATE FISHING AREA

Edinburgh, IN/Johnson and Bartholomew Counties
USGS MAP(S): Nineveh, Franklin, Edinburgh 1:24,000
TRAIL(S) DISTANCE: limited designated trails/primarily large areas to walkabout
ACREAGE: Atterbury SFWA 5500 acres/Johnson Co. Pk. 611 acres/ Driftwood SFA 280 acres
ACTIVITIES: picnicking, nature study, non-motorized boating and boat ramps at Atterbury and Driftwood plus year around fishing, hunting, ice skating, Class C primitive camping, wild food foraging, Atterbury pistol, rifle and Archery Range. Johnson County Park: bicycling, volleyball, tennis courts, indoor and outdoor horseshoe pits, picnic shelters, amphitheater, wildlife observation decks, ballfields, historical trails, Class A-C, Group and RV camping
FEES: camping

These three recreational properties were created from deactivated military lands that formerly belonged to the original 43,968 acre Camp Atterbury, a United State government army training center established in the early 1940's. Today Camp Atterbury is known as Atterbury Reserves Forces Training Area and the remaining lands are primarily utilized by the Indiana National Guard and the US Army Reserve. The removal of the old army buildings, the natural and man assisted revegetation, and the establishment of recreation facilities is changing a previous "war prep zone" into a leisure landscape.

While there are not designated hiking trails found on the Atterbury State FWA property there are numerous, seldom used old roads, hunting, fishing and wildlife paths. There are also two wildlife observation decks that overlook the waterfowl nesting wetlands of Coyote Marsh and Honker Haven. The abandoned railroad track is not open to the public from the park area to Schoolhouse road as it is within the the waterfowl resting area. East of Schoolhouse road is open and may be traversed. Be advised that the area is popular among hunters in the fall months when deer, rabbit, quail, grouse, squirrel, woodcock and duck waterfowl may be taken. Some of the best spots to roam about to see the abundant native and migratory water fowl are near the marshes lakes and steams that are located on the west (Nineveh Creek, Stone Arch Lake, Teal Marsh), north (Pisgah Lake, Beaver Bottom, Mallard Marsh, Mink Meadow Marsh), and east (Sugar Creek) perimeters of the property area. Parking is available at or nearby all of these water bodies. A 20 acre primitive campsite is situated along the east bank of Sugar Creek on River Road just off the Main Hospital Road. Stop first at the Manager's Office and Check-In Station to pick up a property map and be informed on the wildlife and hunting scene. In addition, information is available concerning Camp Atterbury's unrestricted areas to hike during dayhours of weekdays. Old roads weave through the eastern portions of the army property including Atterbury Fish and Wildlife property along the Driftwood River. Be certain to check on what areas are available since sections are restricted for explosives and bombing training.

Surrounded on three sides by Atterbury State FWA is the 611 acre Johnson County Park. Primarily an active park with various recreational facilities, there are natural sections in the scouting area, and south picnic area woods. Short interconnecting historical paths wind through the park that identify pioneer contributions to the area. Interestingly, immediately south of the park, near the middle of the property, is a decaying former World War II prisoner of war compound that held German and Italian captured soldiers. To reach Johnson County Park turn north onto Schoolhouse Road from Hospital Road. The park office is located on North Street. From Schoolhouse Road turn west onto North Street and follow the signs to the park office for additional information.

Driftwood State Fishing Area is located just south of Hospital Road near US 31 and access CR 965 N. Just northwest of the property's boundary the confluence of the Big Blue River and Sugar Creek form the Driftwood River. Historically, the Miami Indians called the Driftwood River, "On-gwah-sah-kah", supposedly a literal translation. Formerly sand and gravel pits, Plover, Sandpiper and Meadowlark Lakes account for 100 acres of the property and are well stocked with gamefish. The hiker will enjoy exploring the shoreline on an encircling gravel road of these closely situated lakes as well as the banks of the nearby Big Blue River. Birding's excellent here.

While you are in the general area a visit to Heflen Memorial Park is enjoyable. Basically an active recreational park, the setting is natural along the shores of the Driftwood River. The Bartholomew County park (35.5 acres) has limited hiking but nice views of the river and wooded surroundings. The park is located south of Driftwood State Fishing Area near the Taylorsville I-65 exit. Turn west on the service road at the Standard/Amoco service station and proceed west to the park entrance that dead ends at the Driftwood River. The road to the park is the first road north of I-65 and US 31.

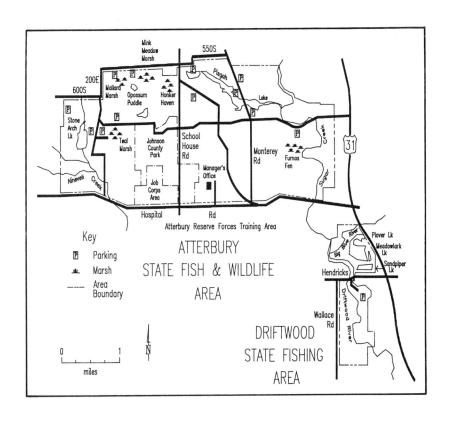

Mink
Meadow
Marsh

550S

200E
600S

Pisgah

Mallard
Marsh

Opossum
Puddle

Honker
Haven

Lake

Stone
Arch
Lk

Teal
Marsh

Johnson
County
Park

School
House
Rd

Monterey
Rd

Furnas
Fen

Creek

Sugar

31

Nineveh   Creek

Job
Corps
Area

Manager's
Office

Hospital   Rd

Atterbury Reserve Forces Training Area

Big Blue River

Plover Lk

Meadowlark
Lk

Hendricks

Sandpiper
Lk

Key

🅿 Parking

🜨 Marsh

- - - - Area
        Boundary

ATTERBURY
STATE FISH & WILDLIFE
AREA

Wallace
Rd

Driftwood River

DRIFTWOOD
STATE FISHING
AREA

0   1

miles

N

D. Atherton

69

21. COLUMBUS, IN/NATURE PLACES

ACTIVITIES: garden walks, walking tour of the downtown architecture and landscape architecture, picnicking, fishing, boating, boat ramp, soccer, horseshoes, ball diamonds, playgrounds, bird watching at city river parks

FEE(S): tours

Situated 40 miles south of Indianapolis and just east of Interstate 65, Columbus is a special city that is known world wide for its architecture. In addition the community's landscape architecture, gardens and parks are equally endowed with design and beauty.

One block east of the City Visitors Center past the Henry Moore sculpture "Large Arch" and adjacent to the Irwin-Sweeney-Miller home is the lovely Irwin Gardens located at 5th Street between Lafayette and Pearl Avenues. This formal nature walk within the heart of the city has several brick and flagstone pathways that lead thru the Pompeiian Italian Garden, the 16th Century Renaissance Garden, and the Herb Garden. Designed by Henry Phillips in 1910, the gardens are chock-full of statuary, gates, vases, terraces, bird baths, a reflecting pool, fountains, a garden house, pergolas, inscriptions and other symbolism. The gardens were as important to Mr. W. Irwin as his home. The gardens are beautiful in all four seasons and especially spring when blossoms are everywhere. Along the walk you will see such ornamental plants as hawthornes, Bradford pear, lindens, junipers, yews, boxwood, wisteria, pyrancantha, Oregon grape, Baltic ivy and numerous seasonal flowers. The separate Herb Garden is planted in a knot fashion with various culinary, medicinal, dye and ornamental herbs. The entrance is on 5th Street and the gardens are open to the public Saturday and Sunday 8 to 4 year around.

A 1 1/2 hour walking tour of the downtown Columbus architectural and landscape architectural marvels designed by noted architects begins one block west of the Irwin Gardens at the Visitors Center (a renovated home) at 5th and Franklin Streets. A 20 minute slide presentation may be viewed and a walking tour map is available for a small fee. There is a charge for a tour guide and arrangements must be made in advance. A taped walking sequence and cassette player may be rented that explains the story behind the 18 buildings in the 13 block area. Public facilities along the tour are usually open 9 to 5 except weekends. Allow extra time for interior visitation.

To fulfill the day, drive to the two riverfront natural parks just west of the downtown area. Millrace Park at 5th Street and Lindsey is bounded by the East Fork of the White River and the confluence of Flatrock Creek. Various park activities include picnicking, two shelterhouses, playground, soccer field, fishing, a boat ramp, horseshoe pits and restrooms. A historical plaque honors an early resident named Patterson who established a mill on the site. Additional history is preserved in the covered bridge that spans a brooklet and is used by motorists. Clifty Covered Bridge was moved to the present park location in 1966. Fire destroyed the bridge and in June 1986 it was replaced by Brownsville Covered Bridge. Millrace Park is open sunrise to 11 p.m. Currently, Mill Race Park is undergoing renovation and should be completed in 1991.

North of Millrace Park a mile or so on Washington and 17th Streets is Noblitt Park. Bordered on the west by the Flatrock River, the park is noted for bird watching. Active facilities include ball diamonds, playground and picnic area. The hours are also sunrise to 11 pm.

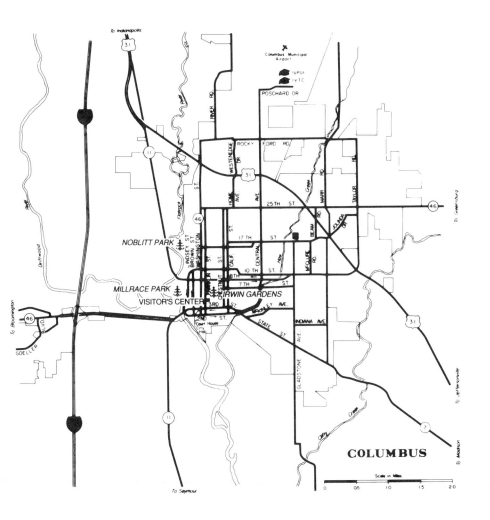

COLUMBUS

22. GROUSE RIDGE PUBLIC FISHING AREA
Ogilville, IN/Bartholowmew County
USGS MAP(S): Waymansville 1:24,000
TRAIL(S) DISTANCE: no established trails
ACREAGE: 160 land acres; 20 water acres
ACTIVITIES: picnicking, hiking, fishing, boat ramp, non- motorized
   boating, limited hunting, primitive Class C camping, wild food
   foraging

There are no formal established trails or outstanding natural features at Grouse Ridge however there is usually plenty of solitude and serenity. As would be expected, an occasional fishermen will be engaged in the pleasure of angling and there are three or four homesites in the surrounding ruralscape but you can usually rest assured that you're on your own.

Revegetating meadow and new forest is found on the north shore and just beyond are the primitive campsites, pit toilets and picnic area. The south side of the lake is a grassy parkland setting where the fishermen frequent and launch their boats. There is an access road on this side of the lake just south of the entrance. The earthwork and concrete dam overflow is situated on the eastern bank. The west shore is the most natural with its dense mixed hardwood forest and where it is possible to hear the drumming or thumping or luckily see the native ruffled grouse (Bonasa umbellus) for whom the fishing area is named.

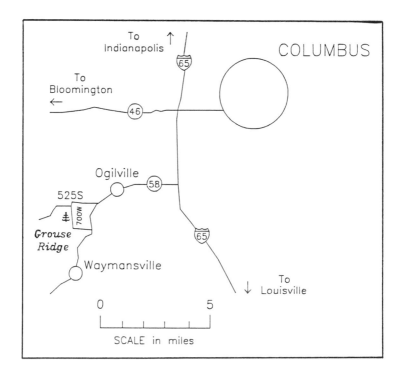

March and April are the mating season months for this medium sized plump gamebird when the male is actively calling his mate. In Indiana, this reddish brown wildfowl is most common in the south central hills especially in neighboring Brown County State Park and Hoosier National Forest and it is possible to find the bird here at Grouse Ridge in the woods and adjacent brushy borders. There is no danger of getting lost when exploring since the park area is small. If you fish, you may catch stocked bluegill, largemouth bass, crappie, and catfish from the lakewaters. Be sure to bring your own drinking water since there are no spigot freshwater outlets. Although not a hiker's paradise, it is a slice of southern Indiana to saunter about and enjoy.

To reach Grouse Ridge PFA drive 10 miles south on I-65 from the Columbus exit 64 to SR 58 and turn west. Proceed west on SR 58 thru Ogilville to CR 525S and turn west and then south on CR 700 W to the entrance. Directional signs are well posted.

Trail Blaze, Hardy Lake

23. HARDY LAKE STATE RECREATION AREA

Austin, IN/Scott & Jefferson Counties
USGS MAP(S) DISTANCE: 5 loop trails/total 6 miles
ACREAGE: 2,062 acres/741 acre lake
ACTIVITIES: hiking, picnicking, shelterhouses, playground, beach
  swimming, bathhouse, concessions, motor and non-motorized boating,
  boat ramp, water skiing, marina, fishing, hunting, environmental
  education programs, class A & C camping, dumping station
FEE(S): entrance, camping, swimming, boat launch service fee,
  row boat rental

Hardy Lake originates from a dam constructed on Quicks Creek in 1970 by the Department of Natural Resources, Division of Reservoir Management.   It is the first state owned Indiana reservoir to have established a nature trail system. Maintained and marked trails rate near the top with Patoka Reservoir for hiking experience. The interconnecting trails and all other recreational facilities are located on the southwest lake shore.   Deerflies can be a nuisance to trail walkers near the reservoir from June to mid-August.

The Lakeshore Nature Trail begins or ends west of the Shale Bluff Campground adjacent to campsite #55. The trail also ends or begins at the Sunnyside Beach parking area. The easy and wide one mile long trail skirts the vegetated lakeshore.   The terrain is wooded and slightly rolling. A .4 mile loop follows the cattail-lined shoreline. Day visitors are advised to begin their hike at the Sunnyside Beach parking lot trailhead since the campground is restricted to registered campers and their guests.

Just south of the Sunnyside Beach area, a spur trail leads west from the Lakeshore Trail through a young woods and open abandoned field, across the main park road to connect with a parking area and the more remote trail loop system.   Four short to long loop trails interconnect in the wooded area. The shortest loop walk is a 1/2 mile path that leads to the pioneer McClain Cemetery, then encircles the old forest grove back to the parking lot. The McClain Cemetery forest loop is well marked and connects the 1.4 mile Peninsula or Island Nature Trail and the 4 mile "B" Loop Trail.

The Peninsula Trail heads north from the forest edge into an open revegetating meadow and along the lakeshore. The trail is ideal for good views of Hardy Lake and its wildlife. Red cedar, sumac, wildflowers and farm grasses are common in the open places. The grassy extra-wide trail loops back to the forest and McClain Cemetery from the land point extending into Hardy Lake. "B" Loop was the most recently constructed trail the summer of 1987. This longest trail, 4 miles long, joins both the Peninsula Nature Trail and the McClain Cemetery Loop. A mile of remote moderately difficult trail follows the points and coves of the extreme north western portion of the lakeshore. The remainder of the trail follows the rolling backcountry of maturing woodlands and abandoned fields, looping back to the other trails. Best trail for natural experiences. Additional loops interconnect "B" loop.

From I-65 exit east on SR 256 and drive through Austin to the junction of SR 256 and SR 203. Turn north and drive 2.5 miles to the Hardy Lake entrance gate. Hardy Lake SRA is located 8 miles northeast of Austin.

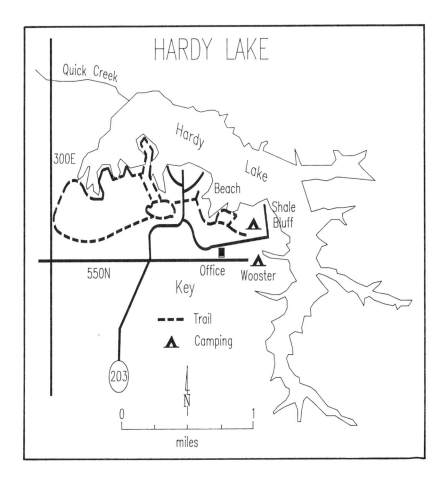

Tulip Tree Flower

24. FALLS OF THE OHIO NATIONAL WILDLIFE CONSERVATION AREA
Clarksville, IN/Clark County
USGS MAP(S): New Albany 1:24,000
TRAIL(S) DISTANCE: no est. trails
ACREAGE: 1,400 ACRES
ACTIVITIES: geology, natural and social history

The Falls of the Ohio National Wildlife Conservation Area includes land in the Ohio River between the Central and K&I railroad bridges and some of the adjacent shorelines of Louisville, Kentucky and Clarksville, Indiana. A 900 acre portion of this conservation area has been designated as an Indiana State Park administered in cooperation with the Army Corps of Engineers. An interpretive center will be constructed to interpret the unique natural and cultural history of the area. Short interpretive trails with outdoor exhibits are also planned.

Before the alteration of the Ohio River for navigational purposes, the "Falls of Ohio River" were a 2 to 3 mile gradual series of descending rapids. The construction of McAlpine Dam and Locks have shifted the main flow of water south exposing the "Falls", a 1.5 mile long ancient coral reef island of Devonian fossils 375 million years old that enabled ancient mastadons to cross the Ohio River. These are the largest such exposed outcroppings in the world. Over 600 hundred species of fossils, various geological strata, limestone outcroppings, niches, reefs, and glacial deposits can be seen. Thea area was declared a National Natural Landmark in 1966.

The wide pothold 22 foot thick limestone shelf requires slow walking and is best explored during the dry early autumn months. Birding is also good in the area during the fall and spring migratory season but nothing like the days when John James Audubon and Alexander Wilson lived and visited here. About a mile west of the fossil beds is the George Rogers Clark home site also to be developed as part of the new state park with interpretive signs and overlooks. It was here that George Rogers Clark lived and started his famous campaign to secure the Northwest Territory. The Falls of the Ohio National Wildlife Conservation Area is administered by the US Army Corps of Engineers, Louisville District and the US Fish and Wildlife Service.

To reach the Falls from I-65, exit at Jeffersonville, the last Indiana exit before crossing the bridge to Louisville, Kentucky. Drive west on South Clark to Mulberry Street 3 blocks, then turn right on Market Street. Market turns into Riverside Drive. Continue west on Riverside Drive. The fossil beds can best be seen west of the 14th Street railroad bridge and McAlpine Dam. A historical marker may be seen at Northwestern Parkway and 26th Streets.

Falls of the Ohio

FALLS CITY AREA

Scale of Miles

79

NATURE WALKS IN THE SOUTH CENTRAL UPLANDS

Trail, McCormick's Creek State Park

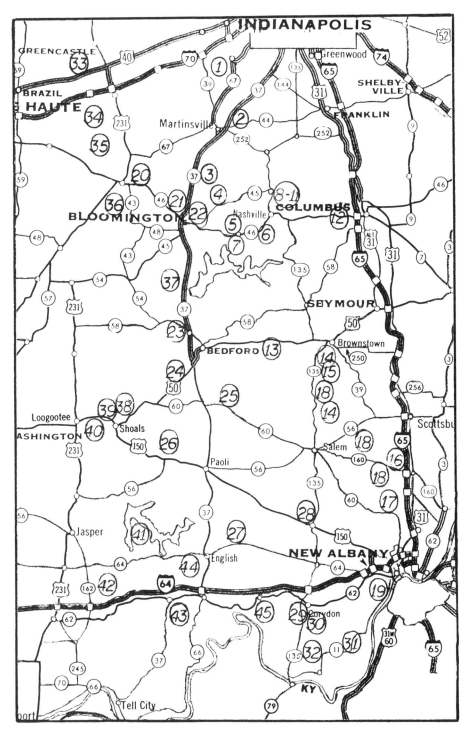

SOUTH CENTRAL UPLANDS

Vic Swain Hill, Knobstone Trail

SOUTH CENTRAL UPLANDS: OVERVIEW

The South Central Uplands are by far the most popular destination of hikers and outdoor recreationists. Three geographic regions are found here in the most rugged and diverse area of Indiana: Norman Upland, Mitchell Plain and Crawford Upland. Roughly the "Uplands" cover the region west of I-65 to the Anderson River, north to Jasper continuing north on SR 56/US 231 to the West Fork of the White River. The northern and southern boundaries of the Uplands are represented by Martinsville and the Ohio River.

The Norman Upland is mostly unglaciated and scenic. The rugged ridges resisted the last ice sheet forcing it to flow down the lowlands to the east. 1,050 foot Weedpatch Hill at Brown County State Park is the highest point in the Norman Upland. Four of our state forests and the Hoosier National Forest/Pleasant Run Area are here and hiking trails abound. The longest foot trail, the Knobstone follows 57 miles of knobs and valleys.

The Mitchell Plain is a west sloping and rolling limestone plain that is situated like a "valley" between two uplands. The karst topography is unique and includes sinkholes, caves and a underground river. McCormicks Creek and Spring Mill State Parks and the Orangeville Rise of the Lost River are places that feature these geological phenomena. The Lost River National Monument proposal would include numerous examples of karst topography accessible via foot trails in Orange County. Communities that have been built on the Mitchell Plain take in Spencer, Bloomington, Mitchell, Bedford, Salem and Corydon.

The third region of the "Uplands" is the Crawford Upland between the Mitchell Plain and the Southwestern Lowlands. It rivals the Norman Upland for ruggedness and beauty. Hikers will enjoy the Hoosier National Forest trails at Hemlock Cliffs, Springs Valley and German Ridge recreational areas. The Patoka Reservoir, Martin State Forest and Cedar Bluffs Nature Preserve are charming places to walk. The Crawford Upland possesses the most diverse types of landforms than found elsewhere in Indiana.

1. GOETHE LINK OBSERVATORY AND MEMORIAL GARDENS
Brooklyn, IN/Morgan County
ACREAGE: 15 acres
ACTIVITIES: observatory programs, landscaped gardens

There are special nights and days of the year when the Goethe Link Observatory is open to the public and the Memorial Gardens are in bloom with visual delights. Located on a high hill of the private Link family estate, the observatory is named in honor of the late Goethe Link, a prominent Indiana University professor and scientist of astronomy who donated the observatory to the university in 1948. Mrs. Helen Link, his wife and a nationally acknowledged expert on daffodils, has planted over 1,100 different varieties which are labelled for public viewing.

During the year the observatory is in use by the staff and students of the astronomy department from Indiana University. There are two public nights a year, weather permitting. Each spring and fall semester the public has the rare opportunity to view the heavens through the 36" inch reflector and 10" refractor telescopes and hear a presentation about the latest happenings in the cosmos.

Admission is by reservation only. Free tickets are available by writing a postcard early each semester to:

> Public Nights
> Swain Hall West
> Room 319
> Indiana University
> Bloomington, IN 47405

Be advised to dress warmly.

The Memorial Gardens are best viewed about the last two weeks in April depending on the weather. The hardy bulbous European herbs of the genus Narcissus are symbolic of spring and the earth's' ability to renew itself from winter sleep. It is spiritually uplifting to see so many flowers in bloom at one time. The English poet, William Wordsworth's poem of 1807 summarizes a spring day at the gardens:

> *"I wandered lonely as a cloud*
> *That floats on high o'er vales and hills,*
> *When all at once I saw a crowd,*
> *A host, of golden daffodils;*
> *Besides the lake, beneath the trees,*
> *Fluttering and dancing in the breeze."*

> - Wm. Wordsworth 1807.

No charge and no reservations are necessary for visiting the gardens.

To reach Goethe Link Observatory and Memorial Gardens drive 5 miles south of Mooresville on SR 67. Turn west onto Observatory Road and follow the signs. The white observatory dome will be noticed on the right hand side as the road curves sharply west about 2 miles from SR 67. Parking is available at the observatory during open house and when the garden is open to the public.

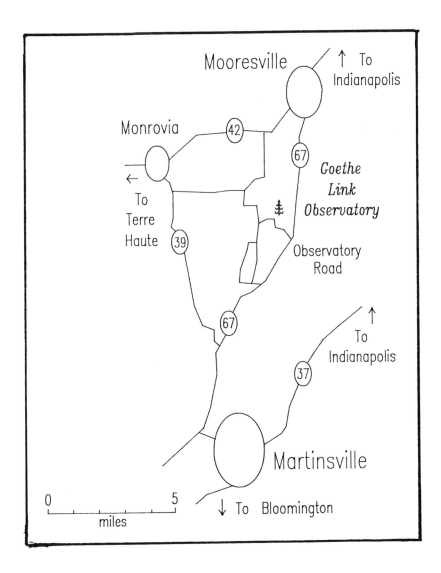

2. CIKANA STATE FISH HATCHERY/GRASSYFORK FISHERIES/ JIMMY NASH CITY PARK

Martinsville, IN/Morgan County
USGS MAP: Martinsville 1:24,000
TRAIL(S) DISTANCE: 1/4 mile one way Cikana SFH. Jimmy Nash
City Park, one mile of parkland meanderings
ACREAGE: Cikana SFH 28 water acres; Grassyfork Fisheries 1500 acres
ACTIVITIES: fish hatchery tours, nature walks, picnicking, swimming,
playground

These three facilities are conveniently located a few driving miles of each other in the Martinsville area and provide a full day educational and recreational outing. Although there is not a great amount of walking involved, there is a good amount of information that can be learned especially about the process of rearing fish and fish hatcheries.

The Cikana State Fish Hatchery is one of seven hatcheries owned and operated by the Indiana Department of Natural Resources, Division of Fish and Wildlife. The basic mission of the state's largest warmwater hatchery is to provide game fish for stocking into the public fishing water of Indiana. The hatchery specializes in bass culture, but other fish are also raised such as hybrid walleye, and catfish. Incidentally, the name Cikana is a Delaware Indian word meaning "bass".

Purchased in 1967 from Grassyfork Fisheries, the Cikana hatchery has two separate units. The north unit, just off SR 37 about 4 miles north of Martinsville, consists of 21 ponds totalling 6 acres of water. The east unit is the more recent acquisition. Located one mile east of SR 37 on SR 44 this facility has 22 acres of rearing ponds. A 1/4 mile nature trail has been recently developed that traverses a small wooded hill overlooking the fish ponds.

30 million fry and 20,000 fingerlings of warmwater fish species reared at Cikana are introduced to these rearing ponds in June. Some spend the entire summer to mid-fall feeding and attaining a size large enough to be stocked into public waters. The fish are difficult to see once introduced to these ponds. Most of the ponds are drained by the end of November. The winter months are used by the team of biologists in preparation for the next producing season.

The spring months especially April and May are the best times to visit the hatchery when the fish are spawning and eggs are being stripped. Individuals and families may stop by to visit. A self-guiding tour brochure is available. Reservations made a week or so in advance may be arranged to have a fisheries biologist lead a tour. A slide show and fish feeding are part of the tour. For further information call (317)-342-5527. The Cikana Fish Hatchery is open 8 am to 5 pm weekdays.

Approximately 1.5 miles west of the Cikana north unit on old SR 37 or East Morgan Street is the private commercially owned and operated Grassyfork Fisheries, one of the worlds largest producers of goldfish (Carassium auratus). Goldfish were first successfully raised in the United States at Martinsville. Grassyfork has been in continuous operation since 1899 and is currently under ownership by Ozark Fisheries of Missouri. Over 50 million goldfish are raised each year and shipped to distributors of wholesale and retail businesses around the world.

The goldfish varieties include Fantail, Redcaps, Calicoes, Moors, Koi, Shebunkins, and Commons. Spawning begins in mid-April and continues until the first of summer. After three to three and one-half months in the growing ponds, the fish will reach marketable size and then be transferred to holding tanks, graded in size and shipped usually by air freight. Grassy fork is also an important grower of water lilies. Their colorful blooms will further enhance your visit. Visitors are welcome to drive through the main office gates to the ponds and the sorting and packing house all year around. The visitation hours are 8 to 11 am and 12 to 4 pm Tuesday through Friday.

After touring the fish hatcheries you may want to picnic at the closeby Martinsville main city park at 360 North Home Street. Jimmy Nash Park has a swimming pool, playground, picnic shelter, duck pond and pathways through wooded hills with open vistas of the city and surrounding valley. To reach the city park from Grassyfork Fisheries continue the drive south into Martinsville on East Morgan Street and follow the directional signs. The park entrance is at the west end of North Home Street.

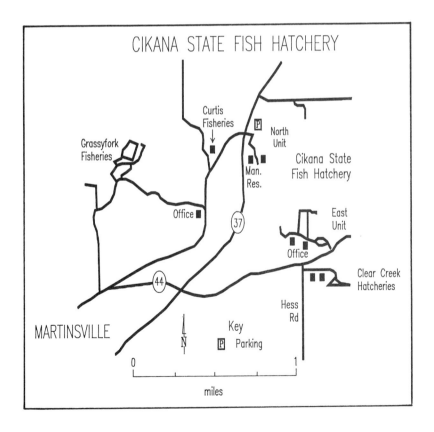

Bryant's Creek Lake, Three Lakes Trail
Morgan-Monroe State Forest

3. MORGAN-MONROE STATE FOREST: AN OVERVIEW

Straddling the county lines of southern Morgan and northeastern Monroe, Morgan-Monroe State Forest originated from small parcels of exhausted and eroded farmlands in the 1930's. Since those times additional tracts were acquired, primarily in Monroe County and thoughtfully managed. Today this healthy and productive green rugged forest of nearly 24,000 acres and 31 separate parcels of land yield thousands of board feet in timber harvests. This state forest is the third largest after Harrison-Crawford and Clark State Forests. Although forestry and related concerns such as wildlife, land, and watershed management are the major concerns at Morgan-Monroe State Forest, recreation plays an important role here as well.

Trail-wise, four well-maintained short and long walking trails have been established: Scout Ridge Nature Preserve, Tree Identification or Dendrology Trail, Three Lakes Trail and the Low Gap Trail. Other recreational fare and facilities include picnicking, five shelterhouses, playground, year around fishing, non-motorized boating (electric, sail, row, canoe) on four small lakes, two boat ramps, ice skating, hunting, wild food foraging, fire tower, two Class C primitive campgrounds for family and a youth group campground, backcountry camping and one primitive cabin rental. Certainly some of the best quality primitive outdoor recreation in southern Indiana is found at this premier state forest.

Morgan-Monroe State Forest is located 6 miles south of Martinsville and 12 miles north of Bloomington on Old SR 37. Well placed directional signs appear along new 37 at the Turkey Track roadside picnic shelter and Old SR 37 road about a mile north of the roadside shelter. Proceed 3 miles east on Old SR 37 to the forest entrance at 6220 Forest Road. Follow Forest Road about 4 miles to the forest office for further information.

TRIP 1: MORGAN-MONROE STATE FOREST

Scout Ridge Nature Preserve/Dendrology Tour
USGS MAP(S): Hindustan 1:24,000
TRAIL(S) DISTANCE: Scout Ridge Trail loop/Dendrology Tour Trail,
   1/2 mile each
ACTIVITIES: hiking, nature study, photography, camping, forestry
FEE(S): camping

Located near the central area of Morgan-Monroe State Forest just north of the administration office are two brief loop trails that introduce the nature walker to the wooded wonderland and its natural arboreal occupants. Situated in close proximity of each other, the Scout Ridge Nature Preserve Trail and the Dendrology Tour Trail may be unhurriedly traversed in two hours or less.

Scout Ridge Nature Preserve is a quiet and serene 15 acre haven that supports a rich variety of flora and fauna. The identified trailhead is found at the end of the forest road north of the forest office and just east of the firetower near the Scout Ridge Campground and Shelter. A self-guiding brochure that identifies 24 corresponding stations along the way is available at the trailhead registration box or at the forest office. The brochure enables the walker to understand the geology and the deciduous forest ecology. The forest path gradually descends alongside the north facing slope into a narrow ravine across and down wooden steps and bridges to Happy Hollow and up to the ridgetop where it began. Besides being exposed to the milieu of vegetation that resides in this predominately beech-maple woodland, one learns about plant succession, recycling, glaciation and other natural phenomena. Parking is available at the firetower, forest office or Scout Ridge picnic shelter area.

The Dendrology Tour or Tree Identification trail begins adjacent north of the forest office parking lot. This trail provides an easy opportunity to view 28 choice select tree specimens that are identified with wooden signs at the base of each. If you are interested to know what woody members comprise the forest communities of south central Indiana's hardwood forest, this is your trail to explore. Follow the trail west as it loops around to the starting point. The latter section of the trail is a fire lane. A trail spur leads off to the north at the junction of the firelane across the paved road through Mason Ridge Campground to the climbable firetower for impressive vistas of the surrounding terrain. Retrace your steps back to the firelane and the parking lot. Anyone would enjoy taking this walk.

TRIP 2: MORGAN-MONROE STATE FOREST

Three Lakes Trail
USGS MAP(S): Hindustan 1:24,000
TRAIL(S) DISTANCE: 10 mile loop
ACTIVITIES: nature study, photograph, hiking

Three Lakes Trail is a sure-favorite for those who are seeking a rousing day-long excursion in attractive natural surroundings. Little used, rough, and guided only by one-way white blazes that appear sporadically on tree trunks, the trail leads over heavily timbered hills and ridges, scenic ravines and creek bottoms to encircle three separate lakes that are popular with fishermen, boaters, picnickers, and hikers.

The trail begins a few yards southwest of Cherry Lake, south of the forest office at the locked gate of a fire lane. Parking is available at the Cherry Lake picnic area for several cars. The trail follows the fire lane briefly before descending into a charming ravine and on through an open meadow, then upwards along a steep ridge to the main forest road. Follow alongside the road for about 100 yards or less and cross over to a fire lane that follows the ridge south and turns southeast to overlook Beanblossom Lake. The trail encircles the lake and continues onward to Bryant Creek Lake, up and down along small hills, across brooklets and alluvial bottoms. Once arriving at Bryant Creek Lake the trail proceeds eastward across the main forest road where the path descends and ascends its way to Cherry Lake. This 5 to 6 hour or more trail is best hiked starting in the early morning while wildlife is still astir and thus allowing yourself ample daylight hours to enjoy nature. Bring the usual food, water, raingear, flashlights and other items in your daypack. Dress for the brushy woods since the trail is overgrown in places.

TRIP 3: MORGAN-MONROE STATE FOREST

Low Gap Trail
USGS MAP(S): Hindustan 1:24,000
TRAIL(S) DISTANCE: 3 mile loop and 9 mile loop
ACTIVITIES: nature study, photography, hiking, overnight backcountry camping
FEE(S): camping permit

Although the Low Gap Trail is a rigorous day's hike with a large section of trail traversing the remote backcountry area, it is somewhat unfulfilling as a walking experience since a large portion of the hike is on fire lanes and old roads. Some of these roads are still public roads which access private landholdings. In addition the last trail segment skirts rather close to the main forest road and its traffic. Despite this, the hike features scenic areas and includes former sections of the Tulip Tree Trace and Yellowwood Trail.

The marked trailhead begins just east of the Beanblossom Road turnoff and Wells Shelterhouse picnic area along the Main Forest Road where parking is available in a small area for 6 to 10 cars. The trail is guided by white blazes infrequently painted on tree trunks as is the Three Lakes Trail. The trail proceeds through the woods a short piece to a fire lane that is followed for some distance south. In time the trail turns east through the woods again and descends steeply into a picturesque ravine with rock overhangs and outcrops. Watch for the blaze that leads to the right uphill out of the ravine to a fire lane. At this point you have the option either to continue on or return via the fire lane back to the parking lot on the three mile loop.

Proceeding on, the trail or actually Landrun Ridge Road continues past an abandoned farm and descends to Low Gap Road and the beginning of the backcountry area. Parking is available here for several vehicles. Overnight backpack camping is permitted without fee but you need to register at the forest office where a backcountry area map is available. It is advised to wear bright colors when hiking during the hunting season for safety reasons.

The trail crosses North Creek and climbs a ridgetop firelane for a distance before sharply descending north into the alluvial bottoms of the East Fork of North Creek. The trail continues through creek bottom and pine plantations gradually climbing upwards to Shipman Ridge where the trail becomes Orcutt Road. Continue westward on Orcutt Road across Low Gap Road onward past private residences and eventually a Tree Demonstration Area. Just before the trail meets the Forest Road, it turns south and follows close to the road all the way back to the parking area. Allow yourself plenty of time for observation and bring the necessary day provisions for a comfortable trip.

Property Manager, Morgan-Monroe State Forest
6220 Forest Road, Martinsville, IN 46151, (317) 342-4026

MORGAN MONROE STATE FOREST

MORGAN MONROE STATE FOREST

1 mile

N

BC

AB

MORGAN-MONROE

Morgan-Monroe State Forest

STATE FOREST

BE

MORGAN MONROE STATE FOREST

BM 612

Cem

26

25

Creek

650

DOWNEY

BC

Robertson

BM 619

Reynolds Ridge

34

35

36

MORGAN CO
MONROE CO

MORGAN
MONROE
STATE FOREST

Taylor Cem

Hollow

Happy

YELLOWWOOD
STATE
FOREST

3

CF

94

MORGAN MONROE STATE FOREST

N

3-Lakes Trail

Main

Forest

Main

DE

Beanblossom
Lake

RGAN-MONROE STATE FOREST

INDIANA HIKING GUIDE

95   96

MORGAN MONROE STATE FOREST

Cherry Lake

3-Lakes Trail

Ma's Road

Blossom Lake

FOREST

BRENTON

STATE FOREST

etween 2 State Properties

MORGAN MONROE STATE FOREST

98

Trails:
3-Lakes Trail
1 Low-Gap Trail

Low Gap Trail, Morgan Monroe Back Country

4. LAKE LEMON RIDDLE POINT
Unionville, IN/Monroe Country
USGS MAP(S): Hindustan 1:24,000
TRAIL(S) DISTANCE: 1/2 mile loop
ACREAGE: 30 acres
ACTIVITIES: picnicking, hiking, shelter, concession/country store, summer beach swimming, water skiing, boat launch ramp, boating, playground, playfield, canoe and rowboat livery, special events, seasonal Class A & C camping
FEE(S): entrance, shelter rental, canoe and rowboat livery, launch permit, camping

The only public park located on the 1,650 acre Lake Lemon, Riddle Point Park and Beach is owned and managed by the City of Bloomington. Jutting out into Lake Lemon, this peninsular park offers visitors a balance of active as well as passive nature oriented recreation. Primarily developed for flood abatement, recreation, and drinking water, the man-made lake contains the contributing waters of Bean Blossom, Bear, Plum and other in-flowing creeks. Completed in 1953, both Monroe and Brown counties share the lake frontage of the reservoir. The lake is named in honor of former Bloomington Mayor, Tom Lemon, who actively pursued its construction.

The self-guiding Tulip Ridge Nature Trail has 12 stations that match with the interpretive trail booklet available at the entrance station. The short easy trail is well suited for families with children as it provides a varied look at the type of plants that inhabit the wooded ridges and ravines in the park. Access to the wood chip footpath is near the entrance gate and adjoining service gravel road. The trail follows the ridge and descends winding gently towards Lake Lemon. Impressive large beech, maple, and tulip trees provide a shady canopy for the numerous ferns and wildflowers inhabiting the coves, slopes and ravines. The trail proceeds past the shoreline and provides fine views through the overhanging branches of the lake. Passing out of the woodland, the trail emerges at the gravel service road. Turn left and continue uphill to rejoin the original trailhead.

To reach Lake Lemon Riddle Point & Beach from Bloomington drive northeast 7 miles on SR 45 and turn left at the park sign onto Tunnel Road bearing right 3 miles to the park entrance.

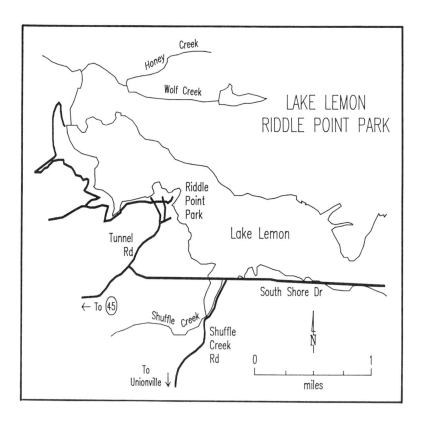

5. YELLOWWOOD STATE FOREST: OVERVIEW

One of the largest of Indiana's state forests, Yellowwood lies entirely within western Brown County and consists of separate parcel holdings totalling 23,250 acres. The most sizeable unbroken tract and the main recreation area is located north of SR 46 and south of SR 45, centering around 133 acre Yellowwood Lake. The place name, "Yellowwood", is derived from the rare Cladrastis lutea, one of the most graceful and lovely flowering American trees largely confined to the mid-southern United States. This native tree, found only in Brown County within Indiana, was originally more common in the state forest before strict logging practices. It is now confined to less than 200 acres on north facing cool slopes and ravines near Crooked Creek Lake, approximately 7 miles south of Yellowwood lake on Crooked Creek Road, south of SR 46. Ogle Hollow State Preserve at Brown County State Park is the ideal place to view the trees in the wild although a single specimen is growing for display at the state forest visitor center. The largest scarlet oak in Indiana (Quercus coccinea), was found here. It measured over 16 feet in circumference and nearly 100 in height and has recently died.

From moderate to rugged and varying greatly in distance, 6 trails are found in Yellowwood State Forest. High King Vista and Jackson Creek Resource Management Trails are situated around Yellowwood Lake. Dubois Family Cemetery Trail and John Floyd Hollow Overlook are 3.5 road miles northeast of the visitor center. The Panther Gap and Brown Co. trails both begin and end at Crooked Creek Lake (s.e. of Belmont, west of Brown County SP). The Ten O'clock Line Trail begins here at Yellowwood Lake and ends 16 miles away at Weed Patch Hill in Brown County SP.

In addition to the hiking trails the state forest includes other outdoor pursuits: picnicking, shelter house, summer-only concessions, playground, boat launch ramp, non-motorized boating (electric trolling, canoeing, sailing, kayaking and row boats that may be rented), ice skating, year around lake fishing on Yellowwood, Crooked Creek and Bear Creek Lakes (Bear Creek is approximately 11 miles north of Yellowwood Lake, north of Trevlac on Bear Creek Road), wild food foraging, hunting (white-tailed deer, ruffed grouse, raccoon, gray and red fox, gray and fox squirrels, eastern cottontail rabbit, wild turkey, and American woodcock), horse bridle trails, Class C primitive camping, a horsemen's camp near the base of the Yellowwood Lake Dam and just south of the primitive campgrounds on Yellowwood Lake Road, group and youth tent camping.

To reach the main recreation area and visitors center of Yellowwood State Forest drive 7 miles west of Nashville on SR 46 to Knights Corner and turn north onto Duncan Road. Go north on Duncan Road one mile following the curve west and turn left once across the North Fork of Salt Creek Bridge. Continue another mile on the paved road and turn north onto Yellowwood Lake Road proceeding 1/2 mile to the visitors center on the west side of the road. Access to Yellowwood may also be found south of Needmore on SR 45. From SR 45 turn onto Lanam Ridge Road and it is 1/2 mile from Highway 45 to the intersection with Yellowwood Lake Road. Turn immediately south on Yellowwood Lake Road and drive 4 miles to the visitors center. State forest directional signs appear at both state road turnoffs.

Jackson Creek Resource Management Trail, Yellowwood State Forest

TRIP 1: YELLOWWOOD STATE FOREST

High King Vista Trail/Jackson Creek Resource Management Trail
USGS MAP(S): Belmont 1:24,000
TRAIL(S) DISTANCE: 0.5 mile High King Vista Trail/ 1.5 miles
    Jackson Creek Resource Management Trail
ACTIVITIES: hiking, nature study, photography, forestry education

The timbered shoreline around Yellowwood Lake offers two frequented foot trails that make a good introductory outing to the state forest. The High King Vista Trail begins southwest of the dam near the entrance fork of the camp road. The plainly marked trailhead identifies access to the

100 foot steep climb up stair steps and switchbacks to the natural "window" view of the lake (nearly overgrown). The shady forested slope supports a variety of ferns including the elegant maidenhair. The trail covers a small segment of the former Scarce-of-Fat trail that looped Caldwell Hollow and Bill Jack Ridge. The return trip to the horse camp retraces the same route.

The Jackson Creek Resource Management Trail is located at the opposite northwest headwaters area of the lake adjacent to the Group camp area along Yellowwood Lake Road, 1 mile from the visitors center. The moderately easy loop trail winds its way through pine and hardwood plantations, across wooden swinging bridges suspended over Jackson Creek, along a marsh and across a steep north facing slope. Available at the visitor center, is a self-guiding trail booklet that basically describes the major role of the State Division of Forestry and the relationship of scientific silviculture and forest ecology. The trail guide also interprets the numbered 24 posted stations that identify trees, birds, ferns, habitats, plant succession, reforestation, timber cultural practices and wildlife management. Of special interest, Jackson Creek is managed as a trout stream. This hike is the right distance to saunter along with no hurry after picnicking or a drive in the car.

TRIP 2: YELLOWWOOD STATE FOREST

Dubois Family Cemetery Trail and John Floyd Hollow Overlook
USGS MAP(S): Belmont 1:24,000
TRAIL(S) DISTANCE: 1/2 mile
ACTIVITIES: hiking, nature study, social history, photography

Removed from the Yellowwood Lake main recreational area, Dubois Family Cemetery and the John Floyd Hollow Overlook is one of the least visited areas of the state forest. Although most people will drive to the site, it is just as conceivable to hike the 4 mile round trip from Yellowwood Lake via the Ten O'clock Line Trail northeast, one mile to the Dubois Ridge Road, and north one mile to the marked trailhead and overlook, returning the same route.

Under a shady canopy of assorted deciduous trees and a northern red pine plantation, the gentle and dry ridge trail emerges after 1/4 mile at the pioneer Dubois Family Cemetery. At the time the Dubois family members were buried in the mid-1840's and 1850's most of the native Indian tribes had gone westward, German and Irish immigrants replaced them, the Democrats controlled the state, New Albany and Madison were the largest towns, the Constitution of 1851 was adopted, the canal age failed, and the Mexican War had been won. The trail loops around to the John Floyd Hollow Overlook where the southwestern vista reveals wooded slopes, ridges and deep ravines, a watershed that contributes to Yellowwood Lake. North up the road 300 yards is Dry Falls Overlook.

If driving, the Dubois Family Cemetery Trail and John Floyd Overlook is 3.5 miles from the visitor center. From the center, drive south on Yellowwood Lake Road to the "T" road, turn left onto the paved road and drive to the stop sign before the North Fork Salt Creek Bridge. Turn onto the Dubois Ridge Road, the road to the extreme left or west, and follow the gravel road about 1.2 miles to the marked trailhead /overlook.

TRIP 3: YELLOWWOOD STATE FOREST

Ten O'Clock Line Trail
USGS MAP(S): Belmont, Nashville 1:24.000
TRAIL(S) DISTANCE: 16 miles
ACTIVITIES: hiking, nature study, photography

One of the longest and rewarding trails in southern Indiana, the Ten O'clock Line Trail begins at Yellowwood Lake at Yellowwood State Forest and stretches 16 miles to the firetower on Weed Patch Hill in Brown County State Park. The easy to downright rough trail requires 6 to 8 hours of somewhat leisurely hiking to complete. A car shuttle between the two points is necessary. Ideally the best time to start is the early morning especially in the spring and fall months.

Opened for year around cross country hiking in 1959, the trail traverses slopes, gravel, paved, logging and fire roads, brooks and streams, shady forests, open fields, ridgetops, a lake and the highest hill in southern Indiana. The trail is guided by eye level white blazes that conspicuously appear at regular intervals on the tree trunks (double blazes means the trail changes direction), and occasional wooden gold lettered and black signs. Beware of farm dogs when walking on the gravel road sections. Unfortunately for hikers, the trail is now shared with horsemen. Be prepared for wet and muddy sections of trail especially in spring when heavy rains can cause the path to turn into a stream. Bring your own water supply (available at Yellowwood lake), food and other comfort items in your day pack.

Historically, the trail's place name commends the Ten O'clock Line Treaty of 1809 or the Treaty of Fort Wayne. The boundary began at the confluence of Raccoon Creek and the Wabash River near Montezuma, Indiana and ran 95 miles southeast to the East Fork of the White River and the Grouseland Treaty Line near Vallonia, Jackson County.

Dubois Cemetery, Yellowwod State Forest

Distrustful of the surveying compass, the Miami Indians agreed that the treaty line follow the direction of the sun's shadow cast by a tree at 10:00 am on September 30, 1809. The Indians sold 2,900,000 acres of land at 1/3 of one cent per acre to Governor William Henry Harrison and the United States government. Although the trail does not intersect with the treaty line, the closest point lies about 1/2 mile south of Yellowwood Lake and Taylor Ridge, along the Brown County Trail.

The trail begins 1/2 mile north of the visitor center on Yellowwood Lake Road near the group campground and south of the inlet bridge where parking is available. The first mile of trail ascends the ridge to a fire lane that soon arrives at Dubois Ridge Road. The trail turns north following the road approximately .4 mile and heads east on a fire lane sidehilling down a steep ridge through a handsome forest 3/4 mile to a unnamed brooklet. Cross over and continue nearly straight 3/4 mile on a old road lane out of the state forest to junction with Duncan Road. Follow the gravel road south just over a mile turning west and then south to a bridge that crosses over the North Fork of Salt Creek. Horsemen may be encountered anywhere after this southern turn. At this intersection, Horsetrail "G" goes west while the Ten O'Clock Line Trail goes east. Continue south .4 mile down the lane past the farmhouse curving east through the wood and by a small stream into Yellowwood State Forest.

Many spring wildflowers grace this area including cardinal flowers, phlox, krigia, trilliums, mayapples, violets and hepaticas. The trail gradually ascends and descends for the next 1 1/4 mile crossing a tributary stream of Somerset Lake and onto Hickory Hill Cemetery. This is a peaceful point to rest and lunch. Proceed south about a 1/2 mile down the gravel cemetery access road to SR 46. Caution cannot be overemphasized at this dangerous crossing. Watch for speeding traffic particularly to the rise in the road to the immediate west.

Proceed around the backside of the abandoned log cabin and cross over Upper Schooner Creek on the suspension bridge. Follow the curving gravel road a half mile or more past a farm house and gravel pit mining area up the slope and the start of Taylor Ridge and Brown County State Park's western boundary. Continue to climb up and down (700-1000 feet) Taylor Ridge for over 2 miles to Taylor Ridge Campground. Aspen, sassafras, chestnut and black oak thrive in the thin rocky soils of the ridge.

Upon reaching Taylor Ridge Campground follow the paved camp road east about a mile or so to the main park road and head right or southeast 1/2 mile to the Civilian Conservation Corps picnic shelter and Hohen Point Vista. From the vista, the trail descends rapidly downhill along the eroded slope to Strahl Lake. Bear right and follow the south lake shoreline around the dam, through the pine plantations to the main park road. Cross over the road and hike up the ridge past more white pine plantations, hardwood forest and open overgrown former fields to descend at Skinner Creek. Follow the creek upstream (also a horse bridle trail and fire lane) for about a mile, watching for a double blaze that turns west into the forest, then proceeds nearly straight uphill to Weed Patch Hill and firetower where the trail ends. Parking is available at the firetower for the car shuttle.

TRIP 4: YELLOWWOOD STATE FOREST

Brown County Trail
USGS MAP(S): Elkinsville, Belmont 1:24,000
TRAIL DISTANCE: approx. 10 mile loop
ACTIVITIES: hiking, bridle trails, nature study, fishing & boating at
   Crooked Creek Lake

Originally the Brown County Trail was a rugged overgrown pathway looping 6 miles through the back country of Yellowwood State Forest, Brown County State Park and the Hoosier National Forest. In recent years, two connecting horse trails "D" and "C" marked and maintained by Brown County State Park have replaced sections of the Brown County Trail along Swain Branch, Miller Ridge and Bales Hollow north to Taylor Ridge. Lettered diamond-shaped markers affixed to trees both ways guide horsemen as well as hikers.

The trailhead of the Brown County Trail loop is at the southeast shore of Crooked Creek Lake, Yellowwood State Forest along Crooked Creek Road southwest of Nashville (Panther Gap Trailhead is also here). On the east shore the trail heads uphill to Miller Ridge and the connecting horse trail "D". Go left/northeast on HT "D" into Brown County State Park to the inverted "Y" trail fork (Ten O'Clock Indian Treaty Line) and turn right onto HT "C" and walk south to Bales Hollow. Going straight would lead to a "T" and the Ten O'Clock Line Trail and Taylor Ridge.

At Bales Hollow bottom the HT "D" and HT "C" becomes HT "B". The Old Brown County Trail headed up Bales Hollow and up ravine and ridge to Miller Ridge and Crooked Creek Lake.

Witch Hazel Flowers

Turn right onto HT "D" and walk south along Little Blue Creek past Petro Hollow and May Branch to the county road. Turn right/west on the county road curving south to Swain Branch. The trail follows Swain Branch upstream and up to Miller Ridge, past old growth Porter Hollow where it eventually connects the Crooked Creek Lake spur. From Hay Branch Ravine north to Crooked Creek Lake spur is also part of the Panther Gap Trail.

To reach Crooked Creek Lake, Brown County Trailhead from SR 46 about 2 miles east of Belmont and 5.1 miles west of Nashville, take Crooked Creek Road south approximately 3.4 miles to the lake parking lot on the east side of the road. Crooked Creek Road leads south to Lake Monroe approximately 3 miles. Map and compass are also suggested especially if you want to explore Porter Hollow of the Hoosier National Forest.

TRIP 5: YELLOWWOOD STATE FOREST

Panther Gap Trail
USGS MAP(S): Elkinsville 1:24,000
TRAIL DISTANCE: 9.4 mile rugged loop
ACTIVITIES: hiking, nature study, backpacking

Both Panther Gap Trail and the Brown County Trail begin and end at the southeast shore of Crooked Creek Lake in Yellowwood State Forest. Basically unmaintained, the trail follows Miller Ridge southwest into the Hoosier National Forest towards the backwaters of Lake Monroe. The trail turns south through Panther Gap down across Panther Creek and Will Hay Branch to loop back north between old growth Panther Hollow and Will Hay Branch to horse trail "D" of Brown County State Park, Miller Ridge, and Crooked Creek Lake trailhead. Other than the maintained horse trail, only occasional visitors and wildlife help to keep the trail somewhat conspicuous. Bring map and compass.

The trail follows across the Crooked Creek Dam uphill to the ridgetop and the old road trail of Miller Ridge. The trail continues south, slowly descending the ridge from 900 feet to 600 feet at Panther Creek valley. The trail proceeds south uphill and through a low saddle in the ridge or gap to Will Hay Branch. Across Hay Branch the trail loops north along an old road with Porter Hollow to the immediate east. The trail connects horse trail "D". Go north/left and follow the ridge back to Miller Ridge and a connecting steep spur to Crooked Creek Lake.

To reach Panther Gap Trailhead at Crooked Creek Lake, Yellowwood State Forest, drive 5.1 miles west of Nashville or 2 miles east of Belmont on S.R. 46 to Crooked Creek Road. Drive south on Crooked Creek Road 3.4 miles to Crooked Creek Lake on the east side of the road. A boat ramp access to Lake Monroe is 3.3 miles further south on Crooked Creek Road.

Property Manager, Yellowwood State Forest
Rt. #5, Box 390, Nashville, IN 47448
(812) 988-7945

N

├── 1 mile ──┤

Resource Management Trail

10 O'clock

Yellowwood
Lake

AB

High King Hill Vista Trail

108

A
D

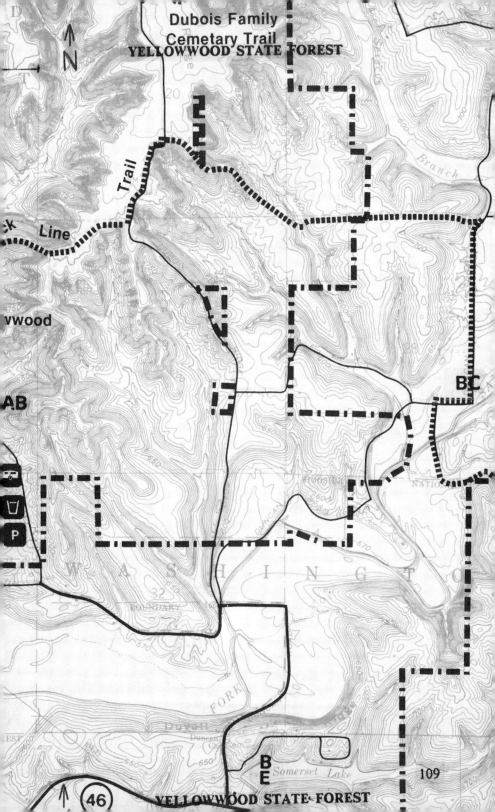

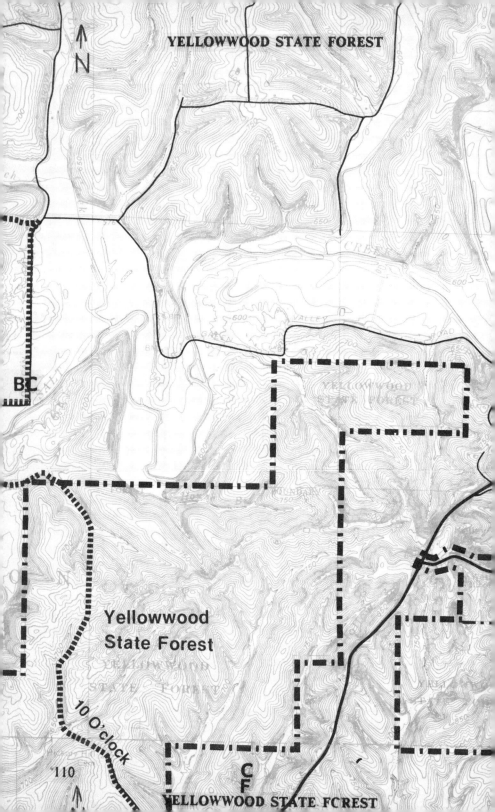

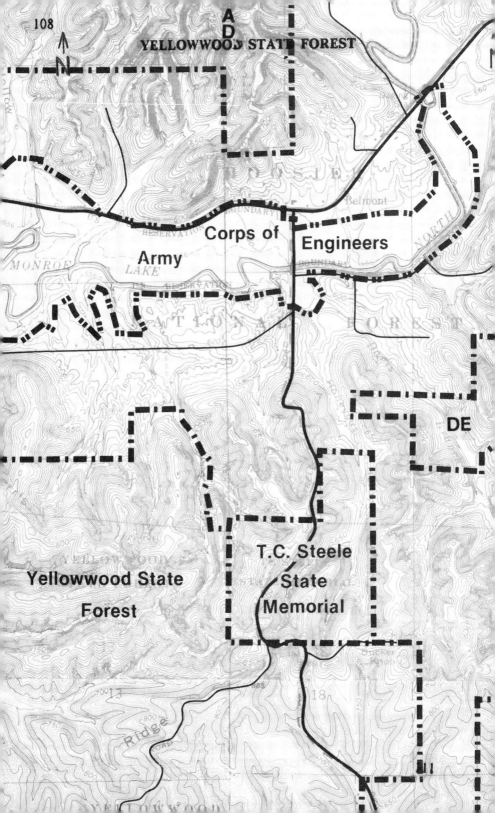

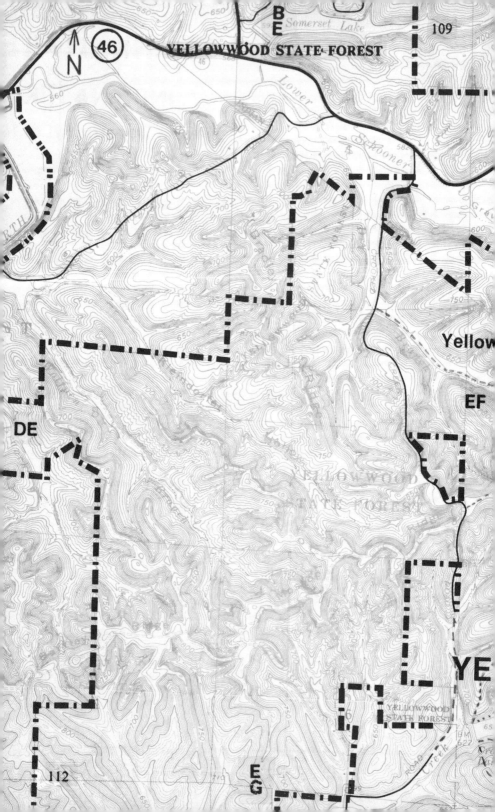

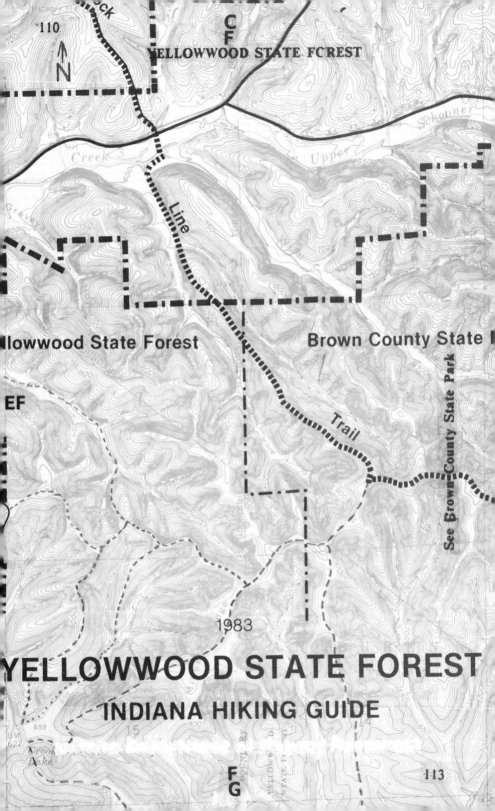

YELLOWWOOD STATE FOREST
INDIANA HIKING GUIDE

YELLOWWOOD STATE FOREST

←N

1 mile

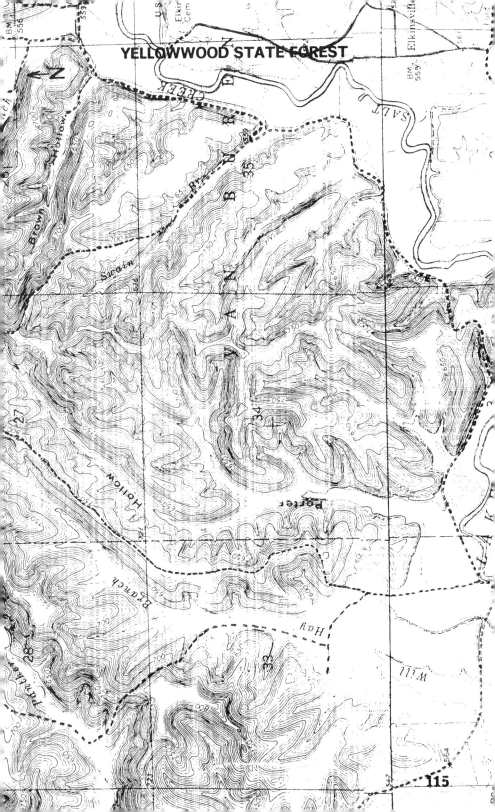

YELLOWWOOD STATE FOREST

6. BROWN COUNTY STATE PARK

Nashville, IN/Brown County
USGS MAP(S): Nashville, Belmont, Story, Elkinsville 1:24,000
TRAIL(S) DISTANCE: 10 trails totalling 15 miles and appx. 7 miles of
    the Ten O'clock Line Trail from Brown County State Park to
    Yellowwood State Forest
ACREAGE: 15,682 acres
ACTIVITIES: nature study, photography, hiking, bridle trails,
    saddle barn, hayrides, pony rides, recreational building,
    picnicking, shelters, fishing lakes, non-motorized boating on
    Ogle Lake, Olympic size pool, self-guiding auto tour and self-
    guiding nature trail, tennis courts, playgrounds, playfields,
    camper supply store, fire tower, cultural arts program (summer),
    park information on radio station 1610 AM, naturalists, year around
    nature center exhibits and programs, Class A and B camping, camper
    store, RV sanitary station, Rally campground, Youth tent camping,
    horsemen's campground, cabins, family housekeeping cabins, Abe
    Martin lodge and restaurant, game room, snack bar, gift shop
FEE(S): entrance, camping, cabins, lodge, saddle horse rental,
    hayrides, pony rides, recreational building rental, shelterhouses

Established in 1929, Brown County State Park has the distinction of possessing the most acreage of any state park in Indiana. Nationally speaking, this Hoosier state park is one of the largest and certainly one of the better known. During the mid 1930's the park was developed by the Civilian Conservation Corps. They planted trees on eroded slopes and ridges and utilized the park's own timber and sandstone to construct buildings. The Corps work is evident today. Some of the more interesting natural resources include the colorful spring and fall foliage, the 1,058 foot Weed Patch Hill (the highest hill in southern Indiana), numerous vistas of the surrounding hillscape and a rare colony of yellowwood trees. Nine well maintained hiking trails and a section of the Ten O'clock Line Trail permit the hiker to explore these natural wonders. The more remote areas of the eastern and southwestern sections of the park are accessible by horse and fire trails.

Trails 1, 2, and 3 are easy to moderate and begin and end at the Abe Martin Lodge where parking is also available. The 1 1/4 mile Trail 1 starts at the northwest front porch of the lodge and descends alongside the slope into a wooded ravine where CCC workers constructed a sandstone fireplace shelter. The trail climbs up out of the ravine where one may cross the lodge road to a playground and family cabins.

The longest and most remote trail in the lodge area, Trail 2 is a 2 mile moderate loop path that encircles the cabin area. Trail 2 also begins at the northwest front porch of the lodge, and at a steady pace may be hiked in a hour. The trail descends down steps to a ravine and then follows the ridge slope to the North Lookout Tower. Continue on across the lodge road and down along the ravine drainage past the base of the family cabins. The trail eventually joins Trail 3 near the amphitheater and ends at the lodge.

Trail 3 begins at the front porch of the lodge. This moderate 3/4 mile loop trail skirts the amphitheater, a picnic area, saddle barn and the main park road until it curves back through a lovely ravine (a continuation of the Trail 2 ravine) that is filled with spicebush, ferns, moss-covered rocks and mixed hardwoods.

Trail 4 is a linear and level 1 1/4 mile trail that connects Trail 5 (Ogle Hollow Nature Preserve) to Trail 7 (Ogle Lake Loop Trail). The path follows the Ogle Hollow ravine bottomland and creek through forest and some open area.

Trail 5 or the 3/4 mile Ogle Hollow Nature Preserve loop trail is the most special and rugged of all the park's hiking trails. The trailhead begins at the parking lot near the entrance to the Ogle Ridge Rally Campground across and north of the park road from the Recreation Building and Conservation Officer's Headquarters. A self-guiding brochure is available at the trailhead registration box. There are 25 interpretative stations in the 41 acre tract that identify the trees, ferns, geology and ecology of the preserve. The rare yellowwood tree (Cladrastis lutea) is the first station on the rugged and steep north facing cove. One of 25 mature trees in the preserve, this leguminous medium-sized tree resembles the American beech in winter but blooms every 2 to 3 years with white fragrant, pea-shaped flowers that clearly identify this handsome species. The yellowwood is rare not only in Indiana but throughout its natural range from southwest Virginia, western North Carolina and northeast Georgia west to Oklahoma.

Lookout Tower, Brown County State Park

Trail 6 or the Strahl Lake Trail is an easy 1 1/4 mile loop around the scenic lake shores. The path is high, wide and dry along the east shore but becomes seasonably wet on the north shore where the ravines drain into the lake. The west shore follows a forested slope and is also part of the Ten O'clock Line Trail. Parking is available below the earth dam and waterfall overflow.

Trail 7 is the Ogle Lake Loop Trail. The moderate to rugged 1 1/2 mile path also encompasses the lakes varied shoreline where you may observe woodland birds. The north shore is the most level and well worn. The west section follows along the tip of the dam. The south shore trail follows the sloping ridge and has scenic views. Follow the shoreline closely along the east shore where the trail appears to climb an upland spur. If you feel energetic, Trails 4, 5 and 7 interconnect providing a total of 6 miles of hiking. Parking is available at the base of the Ogle Lake dam.

Trail 8 is the longest trail (aside from the Ten O'clock Trail) in the park and traverses a variety of habitats. The trail begins either at the West Lookout Tower or Ogle Lake where parking is available at both points. From the West Lookout Tower the path leads alongside the ridge close to the main park road. After walking a short piece, the trail forks south to Ogle Lake or you can continue on the ridge past Tulip Tree Shelter to Hesitation Point Overlook. Avoid the dead end side spurs and be advised the ridge trail can be very muddy during periods of rain making the adjacent park road a viable hiking alternative (to wet muddy feet). From Hesitation Point the trail turns south down the ridge into a ravine along the headwaters of Upper Schooner Creek to Ogle Lake. Before reaching Ogle Lake, the trail forks to the right and leads up over a ridgetop and down a ravine and up a hill to the ridgetop trail that returns to West Lookout Tower. This final section of the trail is a steep but delightful climb if walked cautiously.

Trail 9 is somewhat out of the way to reach especially for the day visitor but worth the extra hike. Since the trailhead is at the end of the Taylor Ridge Campground, the day visitor must park at the nature center and cross over to the campground road and walk about a mile one way to the trailhead. Overall, the 2 mile loop trail in the state park is the most remote. The grade is very gradual as it descends from the ridgetop to the stream bottom and narrow valley. Once reaching the stream, continue upstream where crossing can be wet at times and follow the trail uphill back to the trailhead.

The 10th and most recently developed hike is the Chestnut Oak Trail that begins behind the nature center and descends over 300 feet to Jimmie Strahl Lake. The climb down is somewhat easy as it follows the hillside wooden walkways and stairs but the return rigorous climb follows a separate loop with some switchbacks to the south side of the nature center. The trail is approximately 1 1/2 miles in length and may require a hour or so depending if you want to hike around Strahl Lake. Parking is available at the nature center and do include the center in your visit. The nature center is open daily 9:00 am to 5:00 pm in the summer months, and Wed. - Sat. in the winter.

The choicest section to hike of the Ten O'clock Line Trail starts from the CCC picnic shelter just south of the nature center on the main park road. This 3.5 mile trail segment starts at the vista (note the marked yellow and black trail sign and follow the one-way white blazes) across the park road from the CCC picnic area where it steeply descends along deeply eroded rills to Jimmie Strahl Lake. Upon reaching the lake the trail bear right and follows the shoreline around the dam and through the pine plantation to the park road. Cross the road and continue the walk along a ridge through white pine plantations, oak-hickory woods, and former open fields to descend to Skinner Creek. Follow the creek upstream (also a horse trail and fire lane trail) for about a mile, watching for a double blaze that turns west into the forest and sharply uphill to Weed Patch Hill and the fire tower where the trail ends. Parking is available at the fire tower or the CCC picnic shelter area.

To reach Brown County State Park drive 2 miles east on SR 46 & 135 to the north park entrance or drive 2 miles southwest on SR 46 to the west entrance. A third entrance for horse campers only is off SR 135.

Strahl Lake Spillway, Brown County State Park   119

BROWN COUNTY STATE PARK

N ⊕ ├─── 1 mile ───┤

46

Yellowwood
State Forest

Y.S.F.

AB

Ogle Lak

120

A
D

N ⊕ BROWN COUNTY STATE PARK

BROWN COUNTY STATE PARK

2

1

Abe
Martin Lodge

3

AB

BC

8

7

4

5

gle Lake

121

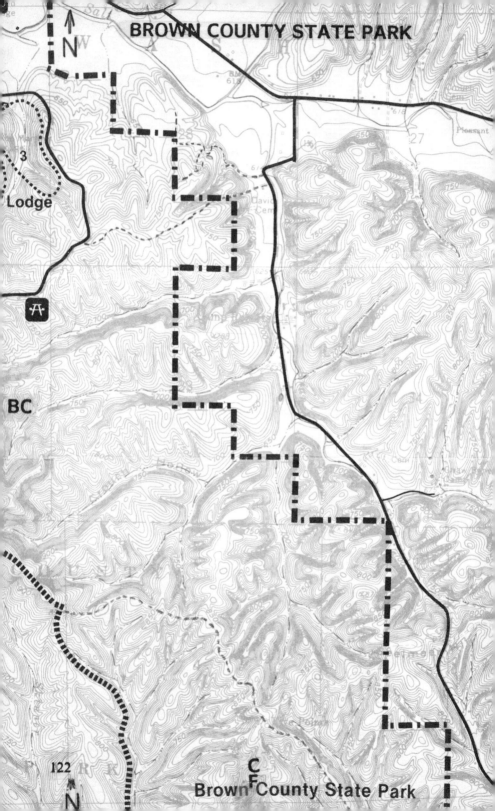

BROWN COUNTY STATE PARK

BC

122

Brown County State Park

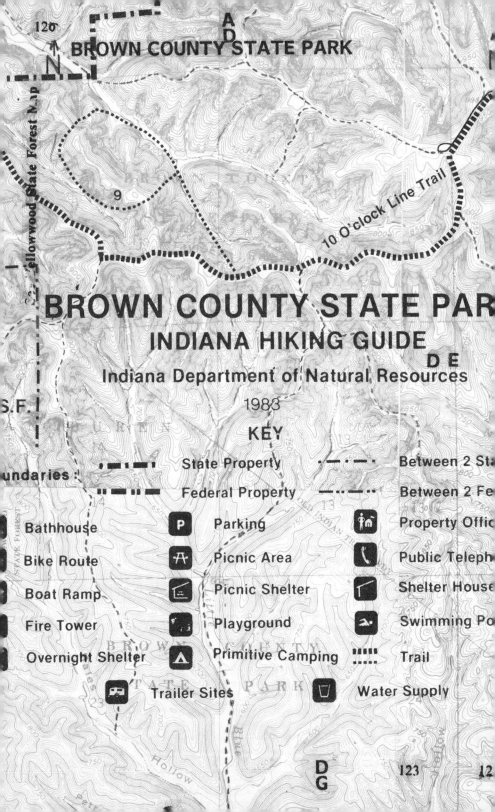

120

N

BROWN COUNTY STATE PARK

A
D

Yellowwood State Forest Map

9

10 O'clock Line Trail

BROWN COUNTY STATE PAR

INDIANA HIKING GUIDE

Indiana Department of Natural Resources

1983

KEY

S.F.

undaries :

State Property		Between 2 Sta
Federal Property		Between 2 Fe
Bathhouse	P Parking	Property Offic
Bike Route	A Picnic Area	Public Teleph
Boat Ramp	Picnic Shelter	Shelter House
Fire Tower	Playground	Swimming Po
Overnight Shelter	Primitive Camping	Trail
Trailer Sites	Water Supply	

BROWN COUNTY STATE PARK

D
G

123

12

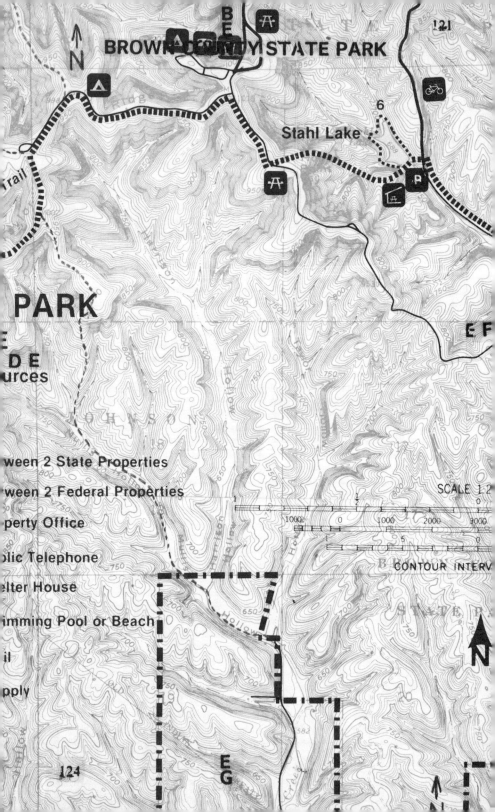

BROWN COUNTY STATE PARK

N

121

6

Stahl Lake

Trail

E F

PARK

D E

urces

ween 2 State Properties

ween 2 Federal Properties

perty Office

lic Telephone

elter House

mming Pool or Beach

il

pply

SCALE 1:2

1000   0   1000   2000   3000

CONTOUR INTERV

STATE P

B

N

124

E G

Brown County State Park

122

N

1:24 000

3000 4000 5000 6000 7000 FEET

1 KILOMETER

1 MILE

INTERVAL 10 FEET

N

Trails:

10 O'clock Line T

Trail #1

Trail #2

Trail #3

125

common summer resident throughout well drained southern Indiana woodlands. Colorful Nature Conservancy signs mark the boundary at the end of the road trail where you may retrace your steps or set off to explore the deep ravines in the general north direction back to your car. Bring your own water and other day use supplies and wear suitable clothing for exposure to greenbrier and other brambles.

To reach Whip-Poor-Will Woods from Brown County State Park north entrance, drive about 1 mile east on SR 46 and turn north at the Shell Station onto Salt Creek Road and drive 7 miles to Gatesville Roadside Park and the general store. Turn east a brief ways and turn off north on Sweetwater Trail and drive 1.2 miles to Mr. Moriah Road. Proceed east on Mt. Moriah Road 1.8 miles to a hairpin curve and farmhouse. Parking is limited alongside the gravel road.

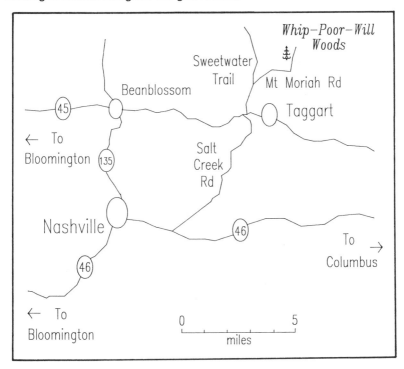

9. LILLY-DICKEY WOODS
Nashville, IN/Brown County
USGS MAP(S): Nashville 1:24,000
TRAIL(S) DISTANCE: appx. 2 mile loop
ACREAGE: 379 acres
ACTIVITIES: hiking, nature study, photography
FEE(S): none but obtain permission from property manager uphill at
    Bear Wallow Trail Headquarters

One of the highest points of elevation in Brown County, the Lilly-Dickey Woods is positioned near the summit of Bear Wallow Hill. Indiana University owns the property and permission to hike the trail should be

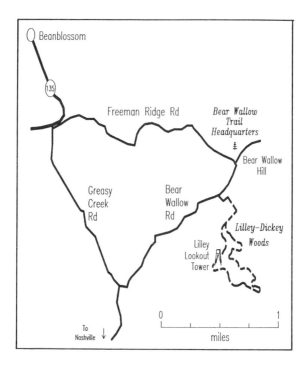

obtained from the preserve manager who resides in the house across Bear Wallow Road from the Flags of the Nations Circle, uphill at the Bear Wallow Hill overlook.

High and dry (800 to 1,000 feet elevation), the easy-to-moderate, loop trail road winds through large growth oak-hickory and mixed deciduous forest that is reputed to have been untouched by agriculture and logging for nearly a century. The recent history reveals the woods formerly belonged to Marcus Dickey, a biographer of Hoosier poet, James Whitcomb Riley. Eli Lilly who founded the Indianapolis based pharmaceutical enterprise and a close friend of Dickey, was instrumental in acquiring the woodland for Indiana University research and teaching.

The first trail mile curves along on grass-covered rocky soil that supports chestnut and black oak trees with an understory of flowering dogwood, greenbriar, viburnum, dryland blueberry and a variety of wildflowers and other herbs. Approximately a third of the way along the trail road is the unclimbable Lilly lookout tower. The trail loops back north and west to a fenced no trespassing area. Follow the fence line downhill a few yards to the return trail road. The north facing slopes, coves and ravines harbor beech-maple forest and other less predominant deciduous trees. Birdlife that may be heard and seen include the pileated woodpecker, blue jay, crow, great horned owl, eastern phoebe, white-breasted nuthatch, a variety of warblers, red-eyed vireo, red-bellied woodpeckers, yellow-bellied sapsucker, red-shouldered and red tailed hawks, turkey vulture, wild turkey and other avifauna. Copperhead snakes are occasionally spotted. The trail may be enjoyed year around.

Pileated Woodpecker Tree, Lilly-Dickey Woods

The old road trail forms a portion of the American Heritage Trail (12.1 mile long) that originates from the Bear Wallow Trail Headquarters, a few hundred yards uphill from the Lilly-Dickey Trailhead.

Lilly-Dickey Woods may be reached by driving from the stop light at Nashville downtown east on Old SR 46 about 1/2 mile to Greasy Creek Road and turning north. Proceed north on Greasy Creek Road to Bear Wallow Road and turn northeast and follow Bear Wallow Road to the summit at Flags of the Nations where parking is available. The trailhead begins 0.4 mile south of the Trail Headquarters at the locked metal gate on the east side of the road.

10. BEAR WALLOW TRAIL HEADQUARTERS
Nashville, IN/Brown County
TRAIL(S) DISTANCE: American Heritage Trail 13 miles/other trails
ACTIVITIES: hiking, camping, indoor overnight sleeping, dining hall, awards and historical program
FEE(S): registration, literature, camping, indoor overnight sleeping, meals, awards

Trail Headquarters is a non-profit organization that maintains and sponsors hiking trails in the Brown County area. The Headquarters is a charming house situated at the top of Bear Wallow Hill on Bear Wallow Hill Road northeast of Nashville where most of the trails begin and end. Individual and group registration is necessary before hiking the trails. Once arriving at the Headquarters, an orientation is given. The most popular hike is the American Heritage Trail, a 13 mile loop that is open year around. Patches and awards are earned upon completion of the hike. Outdoor camping, indoor sleeping, and dining room service are available to participants at moderate expense. If you would like information on the hiking trails sponsored by the Trail Headquarters write:

Ken Tuxhorn, Director, Trail Headquarters, Bear Wallow Hill
Route 4, Box 88, Nashville, IN 47448 (812) 988-2636

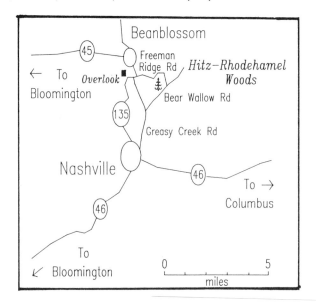

11. HITZ-RHODEHAMEL WOODS
Beanblossom, IN/Brown County
USGS MAP(S): Nashville 1:24,000
TRAIL(S) DISTANCE: part of the Am. Heritage Trail bisects the preserve
ACREAGE: 271 acres
ACTIVITIES: hiking, nature study

This undisturbed woodland occupies a north to south, horseshoe-shaped deep ravine in north central Brown County. Large chestnut oaks thrive along the steep ridgetop rim while a mixture of hardwoods mingle in the stream bottom. The thick tree canopy prohibits all but the shade-loving plants in the sparse understory. Like nearby Whip-Poor-Will Woods, also Nature Conservancy property, the whorled pogonia survives here. The orchid is found on the few open-wooded slopes along with low bush blueberry, huckleberry and partridge-berry. A portion of the American Heritage Trail from the Trail Headquarters at Bear Wallow Hill bisects the property. The linear white metal blazed trail is located near the wooden property sign at the middle of the ridge road and descends into the cove ravine and follows the stream for a short ways before heading southwest to Bear Wallow. The short hike is about a 1/2 mile round trip.

To reach Hitz-Rhodehamel Woods from Nashville drive north on SR 135 approximately 4 miles past the Beanblossom Overlook shelter and turn right/south at Greasy Creek Road, then turn immediately left/east onto Freeman Ridge Road. Continue on Freeman Ridge Road past the row of rustic suburban houses curving north/left. Where the pavement ends and the gravel begins so does the preserve on the south side of the road. The large wooden property sign is obvious. Park alongside the narrow roadway.

12. BARTHOLOMEW COUNTY EDUCATIONAL OUTDOOR LABORATORY
Columbus,IN/ Bartholomew County
USGS MAP(S): Columbus 1:24,000
TRAIL(S) DISTANCE: 1/3 mile and 3/4 mile loops
ACREAGE: 22 acres
ACTIVITIES: plant walk, nature study, nature walk

Nestled between two roadways, a sheltered ravine and hillside harbors the self-guiding nature walk with its 59 posted numbered stations. This "land-between-the-roads", is leased by the Bartholomew County Soil and Water Conservation District from the Irwin Management Company, Inc. as a outdoor learning trail primarily used by school-age children but individuals are welcome to walk the trail as well. Despite its short length, there is worthwhile information to be acquired from the trail brochure that describes the closely situated stations. The loop paths pass under the shady boughs of tall trees, over wooden footbridges, and through an open revegetating, man altered "meadow".

The trail begins behind the Harrison Township Volunteer Fire Department and watertower where parking is available for about 10 cars.

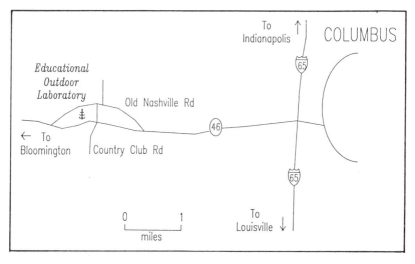

To
Indianapolis ↑

COLUMBUS

65

*Educational
Outdoor
Laboratory*

Old Nashville Rd

← To
Bloomington

Country Club Rd

46

65

0   1
└──────┘
miles

To
Louisville ↓

Basically the trail descends from the hill to the ravine and the return is a gradual climb. The shorter 1/3 mile loop may be preferred by crossing over on a connecting spur at station 16 and go up the hill to station 50 and bear left to the parking lot, otherwise proceed downhill and around to complete the entire loop. The trail brochure is available by writing or visiting the Bartholomew County Soil and Water Conservation District Office at 947 2nd Street in Columbus.   Since brochures are not available at the site, the 59 stations are summarized as follows:

1. Hemlock (Tsuga canadensis) landscaping use, found locally in southern Indiana
2. Flowering Dogwood (Cornus florida) showy understory tree in our region
3. Sugar Maple (Acer saccharum) shade tree, lumber and sap/syrup
4. Crownvetch (Coronilla varia) legume used for erosion control, nat. of Europe
5. Sassafras (Sassafras albidum) landscaping, herbal tea
6. Persimmon (Diospyros virginiana) edible late fall fruits, also landscaping
7. Wild Grape vines (Vitis sp.) wildlife edible
8. Woodpeckers debarking of tree for insects
9. Blue Beech (Carpinus caroliniana) also called American Hornbean or Water-Beech
10. Shagbark Hickory (Carya ovata) lumber tree, edible nuts in fall
11. White Oak (Quercus alba) lumber tree, edible nuts in fall
12. Wild Black Cherry (Prunus serotina) lumber, edible fruit in July
13. Wire fence nailed to tree 40 to 50 years ago but the tree lives on
14. Ferns and their shady, moist habitat
15. Dead Tree and natural decomposition
16. Sumac (Rhus sp.) primary shrub of secondary succession
17. Red Cedar (Juniperus virginiana) lumber, evergreen tree of sunny opens

18. Multi-Flora Rose (Rosa multiflora) planted for wildlife, nat. of Japan
19. Mosses and Lichens
20. Sercia lespedeza and Tall Fescue Grass (Lespedeza "Bushclover" sp.) and (Festuca sp.) erosion control and wildlife habitat
21. Lack of top soil
22. Watershed in miniature
23. Ironwood or Hophornbeam (Ostrya virginiana)
24. Honey Locust (Gleditsia triacanthos) spines found on trunk and limbs
25. Red Oak (Quercus rubra) lumber tree
26. Geology, layers of gray shale and sandstone
27. White Ash (Fraxinus americana) lumber
28. Decomposing log
29. Beech (Fagus grandifolia) smooth bark, favorite tree of wildlife
30. Red Oak (Quercus rubra) dead limbs indication of maturity
31. Red Maple (Acer rubrum) landscaping, tree of wet areas
32. Cottonwood (Populus deltoides) tree of streamsides
33. Black Walnut (Juglans nigra) most valuable tree in Indiana for lumber, edible nut
34. Hackberry (Celtis occidentalis)
35. Paw Paw (Asimina triloba) edible fruits, locally called Indiana Banana
36. Flowering Dogwood (Cornus florida)
37. Dead White Oak serves as a live den tree
38. Black Oak (Quercus velutina) lumber
39. Relationship between soils and what trees and plants thrive
40. Chestnut Oak (Quercus prinus)
41. Pignut Hickory (Carya glabra) lumber, wildlife tree
42. Greenbrier (Smilax sp.) prickly woody vine, wildlife food plant
43. Wild Fern habitat
44. Sugar Maple (Acer saccharum) lumber, landscaping, syrup and sugar
45. Brush and log pile provides wildlife cover
46. Woodland ecology and White Pine (Pinus strobus)
50. Soil erosion near laboratory sign
51. Tulip Tree (Liriodendron tulipifera) Indiana's State Tree
52. White Pine (Pinus strobus) locally native to Indiana at Turkey Run and Dunes
53. Sycamore (Platanus occidentalis) some lumber uses, landscaping esp. in parks
54. Redbud (Cercis canadensis) landscaping, State Tree of Oklahoma
55. Red Pine (Pinus resinosa) native to northern states, State Tree of Minnesota
56. Black Locust (Robinia pseudoacacia) erosion control
57. Black Walnut (Juglans nigra) grows in fertile, deep, well drained soils
58. Slippery Elm or Red Elm (Ulmus rubra) medicine tree for sore throats
59. Hackberry (Celtis occidentalis) warty bark

To reach Bartholomew County Educational Outdoor Laboratory from Interstate 65 at Columbus exit west on SR 46 and drive approximately 3.5 miles to the Country Club Road and turn north or right. Drive to the stop sign a short ways and turn west onto the Old Nashville Road and drive 1/4 mile to the Harrison Township Fire Station and watertower on the left side of the road where parking is available.

13. HEMLOCK BLUFF
Leesville, IN/Lawrence & Jackson Counties
USGS MAP(S): Tunnelton 1:24,000
TRAIL(S) DISTANCE: 1/2 mile loop trail
ACREAGE: 45 acres
ACTIVITIES: hiking, nature study, photography

Appropriately named, Hemlock Bluff supports a fringe of eastern hemlock (Tsuga canadensis) trees intermixed with hardwoods 175 feet above the south bank of Guthrie Creek. The steep sloped sandstone bluff is home to the largest hemlock tree in the state of Indiana (33" diameter and 75' feet tall).

The leaf littered trail heads west along the ridge gradually descending and then switch backing east along the cliff edge where most of the graceful trees cling in the shaded and cool northwest face.   Cedar waxwings, warblers, juncos and other birds are attracted to the evergreens. Trilliums, hepaticas, and rare purple flowering raspberry are also found in the preserve. Open vistas of the valley appear along the well defined trail. The path loops back uphill through beech-maple and red oak forest to return to the parking area.

Another natural area of the preserve is located at the bottom of Hemlock Bluff along Guthrie Creek. By driving east from the parking area and turning the first left onto CR 1200W, you will wind down a steep hillside gravel road to a small parking lot on the left side of the road just before the bridge. There is a short trail to a fine view of the hemlock dotted hillside and the exposed 20 foot high Mississipian shale bank that has been water sculptured by Guthrie Creek.

Hemlock Bluff was acquired jointly by the Garden Club of Indiana and The Nature Conservancy and since 1976 the property has been owned and maintained by the Division of Nature Preserves/DNR.

Hemlock Bluff may be reached by driving east on US 50 from SR 37 at Bedford and turning south near the Lawrence-Jackson County Line on the Leesville Road. Drive 2 miles to Leesville and on the south side of the village, turn left or east on CR 126S and continue 1 1/4 miles into Jackson County to the property's parking area on the left/north side of the road.

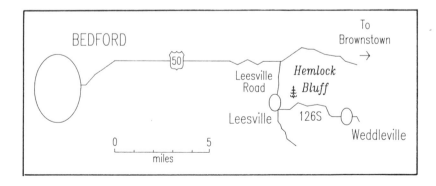

Hemlock Bluff Nature Preserve

14. JACKSON-WASHINGTON STATE FOREST: OVERVIEW

The first land acquisition of the Jackson-Washington State Forest began in the 1930's at south central Jackson County. It was not until the 1950's that property was acquired in northeastern Washington County. Presently over 15,000 acres comprise the state forest which is managed by the multiple-use concept as are all state forest properties.

The Jackson County portion of the forest (6,000 acres) is known for its unglaciated Knobs that rise as much as 300 feet above the Muscatatuck and White River East Fork Valleys. Also called the Brownstown Hills, these prominent rounded Knobs occupy nearly 30 square miles and are in sharp scenic contrast to the surrounding farmscape. This section of the forest provides much of the CCC developed active recreation: picnicking, shelterhouses, fishing and boating (electric) on Knob Lake, a playground, bicycling on the Hoosier Hills Route, horseback riding, primitive camping and other activities. The Hoosier Skyline Drive is approximately a 3 mile motorized (some hiking) drive along the lofty Knobs between the main entrance of the forest southeast of Brownstown and Starve Hollow Road and Lake SRA. (see Starve Hollow SRA)

The Washington County portion of the forest is the Backcountry Area and remains largely undeveloped with the exception of the Knobstone Trail section (15 miles) that heads out of Spurgeon Hollow southeast to Elk Creek State Fish & Wildlife Area (see Knobstone Trail). Delaney Park, a developed Washington County Park is located 1/2 mile north of Spurgeon Hollow (see Delaney Park). Hunting for deer, raccoon, squirrel, grouse and wild turkey is permitted in both Jackson and Washington state forest areas with the exception of the high use areas.

Five easy to very rugged hiking trails totalling nearly 9 miles have been established at the main forest area 2.5 miles southeast of Brownstown on SR 250. Two short trails of moderate-to-rugged difficulty are located on Skyline Drive. Most of these trails lead to the Knob tops, allowing fine vistas of the surrounding countryside.

TRIP 1: JACKSON-WASHINGTON STATE FOREST

Knob Lake Trail Network
USGS MAP(S): Vallonia, Tampico, Brownstown 1:24,000
TRAIL(S) DISTANCE: 5 easy to very rugged trails totalling 8 3/4 miles
ACREAGE: 6,000 acres
ACTIVITIES: hiking, nature study, wild food foraging, picnicking,
   shelterhouses, Hoosier Hills Bicycle Route, boating(electric), boat
   launch ramp, canoeing, sailing, fishing, ice skating, playground,
   horseshoes, horseback riding, primitive camping, youth tent area
FEE(S): camping

Situated in a quiet woodsy hollow, Knob Lake and surroundings offer a day's worth of challenging and beautiful hiking up and down hillsides, along ridgetops, and climbs to the top of Knobs. The five marked trails begin or end at Knob Lake or the nearby campground.

Trail 1 is a 1.5 rugged hike that starts at the extreme north campground loop at the Oven Shelter picnic parking lot. Follow the path 200 feet uphill through the shady cool woods to the ridge top (910 ft. elev.) and the old Lookout Tower site. Continue left along the ridge past the two Trail 10 access points. The trail heads uphill along a highly eroded rocky path to climb another 50 feet to Mt. Baldy/Pinnacle Peak (966 ft. elev.). The vista to the west and south provide a "upclose" look of a Knob "range" making the rigorous climb worth the effort. Retrace your steps back to the trailhead.

Trail 2 is a 1 3/4 mile moderate loop trail that traverses the rugged hills of the southeast property. Although it is a hikers only trail, horsemen will occasionally use the path. Follow Trail 1 uphill and turn right at the old Lookout Tower site and follow the narrow "backbone" ridge down and up to High Point Vista (985 ft. elev.). Continue downridge due south to a second vista point at 900 feet and a third knob overlook point at 850 feet. The trail descends west along the ridge and follows a ravine to the junction with Trail 3 a firelane that will lead to the main park road. Turn right and follow the main park road to Knob Lake and the campground trailhead.

Trail 3 is a 1 mile moderate loop trail around Knob Lake and the backsides of the forest office and maintenance area. The trail heads up at the north tip of Knob Lake and follows the immediate surrounding hillside to the administrative office and a firelane to the main park road. Turn right at the main park road and walk through the pine plantation picnic area to Knob Lake.

Trail 4 is a 1/2 mile easy woodsy walk that begins/ends across from the forest office on the main road. The trail has several up and down hill moments but nothing too invigorating. The trail ends at the firelane gate at the Knob Lake Dam and picnic shelter (former museum). If you follow the firelane north it leads to Trail 10, also a firelane.

Mt. Baldy / Pinnacle Peak, Jackson-Washington State Forest

Trail 10 is a four mile moderate loop hike that basically follows a fire lane up and down the steep hillside, a 200 foot elevation climb and descent. The trail may be accessed from Trail 1, or Trail 4, and a firelane just south of the forest office on the right side of the main road. The trail skirts the northeast shore of Lake Pyoca and there are clearcut areas passed. The firelane trail may be overgrown in summer.

The main entrance of Jackson-Washington State Forest is located 2.5 miles southeast of Brownstown on SR 250.

TRIP 2: JACKSON-WASHINGTON STATE FOREST

Skyline Drive/Tower Trail/Vista Trail
USGS MAP(S): Vallonia 1:24,000
TRAIL(S) DISTANCE: Tower Trail 1 mile/Vista Trail 1/2 mile
ACREAGE: 6,000 acres
ACTIVITIES: hiking, nature study, photography, picnicking,
          shelterhouse, lookout tower, scenic drive

Skyline Drive is a 3 mile paved roadway that follows the ridgeline of the Brownstown Hills or Knobs just south of Brownstown and northeast of Starved Hollow Lake SRA. Skyline Drive may be accessed from three separate ways. About 1/2 north of the main forest entrance on SR 250, turn left or south onto a paved road (Hoosier Hills Bike Route), and then turn right or west onto Skyline Drive. Starve Hollow Road turns left onto Skyline Drive just north of Starve Hollow Lake SRA. Both of these turnoffs are marked by wooden directional signs. A third approach is south from Brownstown on CR 50W.

There are two short hiking trails along Skyline Drive. The 1 mile rugged Tower Trail begins or ends at the backside of the #2 shelterhouse, a fine vista point. The trail descends and follows the ridgeside through a ravine and across a stream up the steep hillside to the ridgetop (switchbacks). The trail levels out the last 1/4 mile to the Lookout Tower. You must either retrace your steps or follow the Skyline Drive road back to the shelterhouse. This trail was overgrown last time hiked.

The second trail is a linear 1/2 mile trail that begins and ends at the picnic area south of the Lookout Tower. From the picnic area the trail goes "out" 1/4 mile onto the long southwestern-oriented ridgetop to descend to a point overlook of Starve Hollow Lake. Retrace your steps back to the picnic area.

TRIP 3: JACKSON-WASHINGTON STATE FOREST

Indian Bitter Nature Preserve
USGS MAP(S): Kossuth, Little York 1:24,000
TRAIL(S) DISTANCE: no est. trails
ACREAGE: 35 acres
ACTIVITIES: nature study

Located a few miles south and west of the northern terminus of Knobstone Trail east of Spurgeon Hollow, this nature preserve is noted for its botanical significance. A rare stand of cucumber magnolia (Magnolia acuminata) are thriving in a cluster grove along a moist sheltered ravine near Delaney Creek. It is a handsome tree more adapted to the middle and southern Appalachian Mountains in moist soils of mountain slopes and valleys. The cucumber magnolia, referring to its dark red vegetable-like fruit, is a member of the Magnoliaceae Family, now known in Indiana from only a few southern counties. In spring solitary bell-shaped flowers appear at the end of the branches. Yellow tulip poplar, our State Tree, is the only other native Magnolia family member found in Indiana. The fruit of cucumber magnolia was used to make "bitters", an alcoholic flavored liquor.

There are no trails as yet in this state nature preserve and no permission is required for entry to the property. The steep slopes and ravines are easily accessible from the adjacent county gravel road that runs alongside the preserves boundaries.

To reach Indian-Bitter Nature Preserve in Jackson-Washington State Forest from Salem go north on SR 135 about 4 miles and turn right and continue 1 3/4 miles and turn north on the paved county road. Continue to Crossroads Church about 2 miles and turn right/east. Continue driving east (instead of turning north at the jog to Delaney Park and Spurgeon-Hollow, Knobstone Trail/north terminus) approximately 3 miles along the ridge base of Delaney Creek curving north another 3/4 mile to the roadside pulloff on the west side of the road and the east boundary of the nature preserve. Additonal access points are on information signs along SR 135.

Property Manager, Jackson-Washington State Forest
R.R. #2, Brownstown, IN 47220, (812) 358-2160

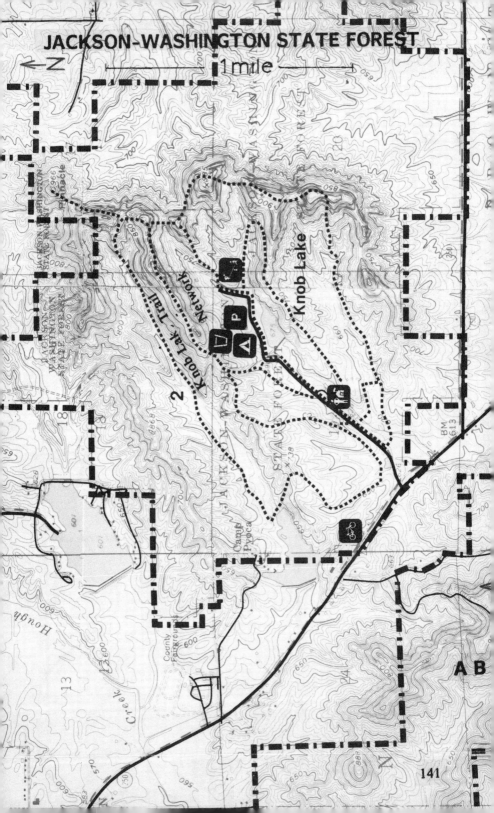

JACKSON-WASHINGTON STATE FOREST

←N ⊢———— 1 mile ————⊣

Knob Lake

Knob Lak. Trail Network

141

JACKSON-WASHINGTON STATE FOREST

A B

P

Skyline Drive

Tower Trail

1

JACKSON-WASHINGTON STATE FOREST

Vista Trail

3

St. Pauls Cem

BM 578 Hollow

BO

Starve

Jackson-Washington
State Forest

STATE FOREST

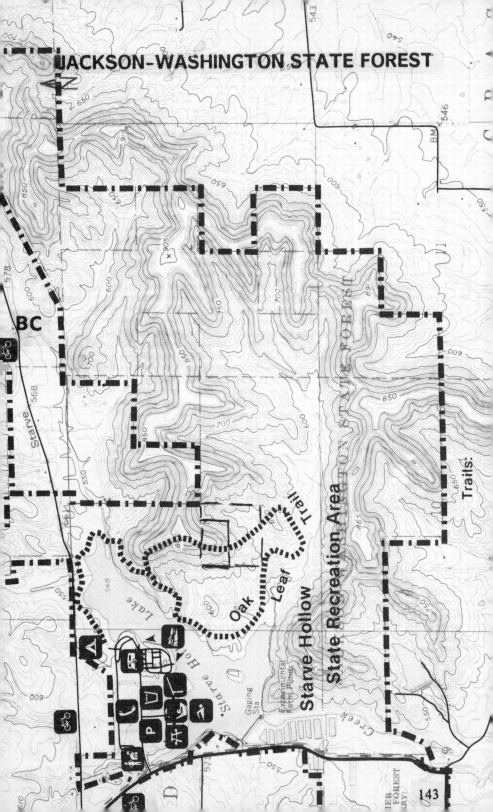

JACKSON-WASHINGTON STATE FOREST

BC

Oak Leaf Trail

Starve Hollow State Recreation Area

Trails:

143

15. STARVE HOLLOW STATE RECREATION AREA

Vallonia, IN/Jackson County
USGS MAP(S): Vallonia 1:24,000
TRAIL(S) DISTANCE: 5 miles
ACREAGE: 300 acres. 145 acre lake
ACTIVITIES: hiking, nature study, nature preserve, nature interpretive
   center, picnicking, shelterhouses, beach swimming, lifeguards,
   bathhouse, sailing, ice skating, canoe and row boat rental,
   boathouse, boat ramp, boating (electric), fishing, concessions,
   bicycling, playground, recreational fields, Class A and B camping
   (electric/non-electric), comfort stations, dumping station, fish
   cleaning station, shelterhouses
FEE(S): entrance, camping, row boat & canoe rental

Starve Hollow Lake was established in 1938 at Jackson-Washington
State Forest near Vallonia. Since that time its popularity over the years
has grown and in recent years the lake and surrounding forest was
designated a state recreational area. Despite the desperate sounding
place name for the hollow, this scenic knob forestland is not "starved"
for outdoor activity.

The 5 mile loop Oak Leaf Nature Trail varies in difficulty from easy
to very rugged however most of the trail is moderately easy. The
trailhead begins near a pier at the last campground loop near campsite
#42. If a day visitor instead of a camper, you will need to park your car
at the visitors lot next to the entry gate. There is a information bulletin
case and posted sign at the trail head. The trail is blazed by a gold oak
leaf carved on a black post at regular intervals.

The first 0.7 mile of trail is close to the shoreline and may be wet at
times despite the gravel path. This trail section has 20 numbered
stations that correspond to a guidebook available from the gate attendant
or property office (YACC developed, 1979). The following stations are:

1. Plant succession	12. Sycamore
2. Sumac	13. Marsh Sedimentation/Plantlife
3. Big Tooth Aspen	14. Marsh and Wildlife
4. Club Moss	15. Marsh and Northern Pike
5. Red Pine	Fingerlings
6. Persimmon	16. Dead Tree/Home to Wildlife
7. Bald Cypress	17. Tulip Poplar
8. Woodpecker Chippings	18. Recycling Stump
9. Horsetail	19. American Beech
10.Sassafras	20. Forestry Management
11. Red Cedar	

The numbered trail section ends at the firelane just beyond the
footbridge over the creek inlet on the northeast side of Starve Hollow
Lake. You may return to the trailhead or continue to the right or
southwest on the firelane uphill to the trail loop intersection
approximately one third of a mile. At the trail intersection go left nearly
straight uphill to the knob ridgetop and pause for the western vista on
the provided rest bench. Continue southward along the chestnut and

scarlet oak narrow ridgetop to a second "natural" vista of the Muscatatuck River Valley. This vista and the immediate surroundings are the designated Knobstone Barrens Nature Preserve. The thin fragile and erosive soils does not permit any large vegetation to take root, therefore the unobstructed view. The nearly 300 feet descent to the ravine below is rugged. Please stay on the provided switchback. At the ravine bottom the trail continues across a stream to the firelane (right). Follow the firelane trail past a log shelterhouse to the loop junction and continue to retrace your steps back to the trailhead. Plans are being made to extend the next section of the Knobstone Trail north, from Spurgeon Hollow to Starve Hollow.

In addition to the Oak Leaf Nature Trail you may want to visit the Driftwood Interpretive Nature Center, Driftwood Fish Hatchery, and the Vallonia Tree Nursery. The nature center is located at the far end of the first campground section. It is open during the summer season only (Memorial to Labor Day). The fish hatchery just beyond the dam is one of the smallest and oldest in the state. The ten holding ponds produce largemouth bass, saugeye (sauger X walleye hybrid), and goldfish to be used as food for the brooding stock. About 3/4 miles south of the Starve Hollow entrance drive is the Vallonia Nursery where over 30 hardwood and softwood tree species are raised for reforestation on wildlife habitat plantings. The nursery is open Monday through Friday from 8 am to 4:30 pm. Ask for a property map at the administration property office.

Another point of interest to visit while in the vicinity of Starve Hollow SRA are the Knobs Overlook Rest Park on US 50 just west of Vallonia.

Marsh and Knob, Starved Hollow Lake   145

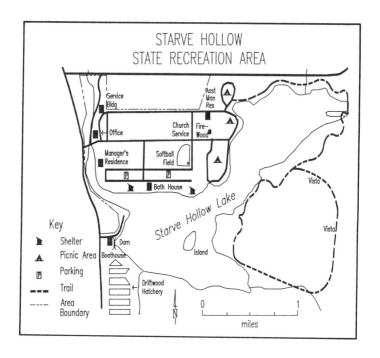

STARVE HOLLOW
STATE RECREATION AREA

Key
- Shelter
- Picnic Area
- Parking
- Trail
- Area Boundary

Service Bldg
Asst Man Res
Office
Church Service
Fire—Wood
Manager's Residence
Softball Field
Bath House
Vista
Vista
Starve Hollow Lake
Dam
Boathouse
Island
Driftwood Hatchery
N
0   1
miles

16. CLARK STATE FOREST: OVERVIEW

Clark State Forest is where Indiana state forestry first began when 2,000 acres of deep valleys and knobs were purchased in 1903. Now twelve times the original purchase, the state forest consists of forested knobs in Washington, Scott and Clark Counties. A large portion of the land was once part of General George Roger Clark's 1783 Grant. Clark was a hero of the American Revolution at Vincennes and the Old Northwest Territory.

Clark State Forest offers rewarding short and long hiking opportunities. Outside of the Knobstone Trail, all trailheads are located near the developed area at Henryville. Deam Lake State Recreation Area, also administered by the State Division of Forestry, was created from 1300 acres of Clark State Forest land and named in honor of Indiana's first state forester Charles C. Deam.

Henryville, the administrative center for Clark State Forest is a developed recreation area with 3 separate trails that begin and end here: 1 mile Resource Management Trail, 0.9 mile White Oak State Nature Preserve and 20 mile Clark State Forest Boy Scout Trail. In addition to trails, the Henryville site offers lake fishing, non-motorized boating, picnicking, shelterhouse, playgrounds, ice skating, bridle trails, horsemen campground, Class C primitive camping and dumping station.

Henryville and Clark State Forest is located adjacent to US 31 on the north edge of town, one mile east from the I-65 exit SR 160, ten miles south of Scottsburg.

TRIP 1: CLARK STATE FOREST
Resource Management Trail
USGS MAP(S): Henryville 1:24,000
TRAIL(S) DISTANCE: 1 mile interpretive loop

It is fitting that one of the first state forests in the United States maintain a walking trail dedicated to forestry practices and wildlife. Labelled interpretive signs have been placed along the service road trail loop. The footpath begins southwest of the picnic area at Oak Lake alongside the main forest road. The hike is level and easy as the route makes its way through oak and hickory woodland, open grassy areas and tulip tree plantations. There are 150 experimental tree plantations here, first planted at the turn of the 20th century. A trail brochure is available.

TRIP 2: CLARK STATE FOREST

White Oak Nature Preserve
USGS MAP(S): Henryville 1:24,000
TRAIL DISTANCE: 0.9 mile self-guiding loop

The 143 acre White Oak Nature Preserve is a fine stand of oak-hickory forest which has been set aside within the state forest at an easily-accessed location north of adjoining Franke Lake. The maintained self-guiding forest trail has 25 numbered stations that correspond to the trail brochure available at the trailhead registration box. White, black, red, scarlet, post and chestnut oak dominate the dry ridges of the woodland. The trailhead for the Clark State Forest Boy Scout Trail has its beginnings in the White Oak Nature Preserve.

The preserve may be reached by taking the main forest road west across the overpass of I-65 and park to the immediate right in the roomy shaded parking area. The trailhead is well marked across the main forest road south.

TRIP 3: CLARK STATE FOREST
Clark State Forest Boy Scout Trail
USGS MAP(S): Henryville 1:24,000
TRAIL(S) DISTANCE: 20 mile rugged loop

In cooperation with the Indiana Division of Forestry, the Boy Scout Troop 31 of New Albany, Indiana developed the 20 mile rugged Clark State Forest Trail. Nearly half of the day hike follows gravel county roads. The other half is located along logging lanes, a section of the Knobstone Trail, and a blazed trail maintained by the Boy Scout troop. The 20 mile hike requires at least 7 to 10 hours and may be shortcutted for a less arduous hike. The trail is marked with wooden signs lettered in yellow. White blazes mark the trail. Be advised the trail is overgrown and not well marked and may prove challenging to novice hikers.

CLARK STATE FOREST

AB

←N — 1 mile —

Bowen Lake Trail

Bowen Lake

Knobstone Trail

See Knobstone Trail Map

5

160

148

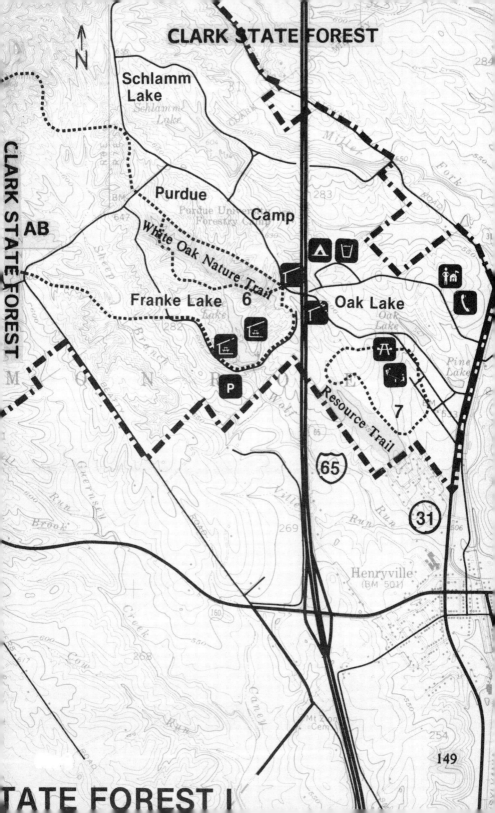

CLARK STATE FOREST

Schlamm
Lake

Purdue

Camp

White Oak Nature Trail

AB

Franke Lake

6

Oak Lake

7

Resource Trail

P

65

31

CLARK STATE FOREST

Henryville
(BM 501)

149

TATE FOREST I

The trailhead is located at the registration box of White Oak Nature Preserve across the I-65 crossover on the main forest road north of Franke Lake. The Boy Scout Trail follows 0.2 miles through the preserve, then heads north on a narrow foot trail to cross over the paved forest road (1 1/4 mile) and heads sharply uphill to Summit Knob (968 feet elev.). The trail follows the up and down of the knob ridge and saddle east to a firelane, then south to the gravel forest road which the trail follows about 2.5 miles downhill along Pigeon Roost Creek to Wilcox Lake. Once at the lake and the "T" road turn left to Bowen Lake. Retrace your steps from Bowen Lake to nearby Wilcox Lake. From Wilcox Lake continue uphill on the gravel road, sometimes closed in winter, to the right to the "Y" crossroad at the public service and radar tower. The trail continues on the gravel road to the right. A segment of the Knobstone Trail runs alongside the road on the left for nearly a mile before crossing the road and heading north.

Continue a 2.5 mile trek to the crossroads and crossing of SR 160, then proceed 2 miles to an old stone quarry and the Knobstone Trail, south of the first contact segment. Go north on the Knobstone Trail and cross SR 160 again and continue to the graveled forest road and the radar and tower installation once more. Between SR 160 and the gravel road, the Knobstone Trail passes through the southwestern portion of the Virginia Pine-Chestnut Oak Nature Preserve, a state nature preserve on state forest land.

Turn right or east on the gravel forest road and continue walking to the climbable fire tower. The trail crosses over to the south side of the road and the picnic area. It then heads nearly straight downhill following a power line swath. This is the most dangerous part of the hike and there is plenty of poison ivy. Once downhill on level land the trail continues through the forest and group selection harvest or clear cut areas back to Franke Lake and the White Oak Nature Preserve parking area.

Property Manager
Clark State Forest
Henryville, IN 47126
(812) 294-4306

Cottontail

17. DEAM LAKE STATE RECREATION AREA

Borden, IN/Clark County
USGS MAP(S): Speed 1:24,000
TRAIL(S) DISTANCE: 4 trails total 4.6 miles
ACREAGE: 1,000 acres
ACTIVITIES: hiking, picnicking, shelterhouses, playground, beach
   swimming, seasonal lifeguards, bathhouse, fishing, hunting, non-
   motorized boating, Class A camping, camp store, dumping station,
   boat rental, nature interpretive center
FEE(S): entrance, camping, rowboat rental

Deam Lake State Recreation Area is nestled in a scenic hollow at the
base of Waggoner Knobs and the south tip of Clark State Forest. The
former Clark State Forest land is still administered by the Division of
Forestry. The recreational area is named in honor of Charles C. Deam,
former state forester and author of <u>Flora of Indiana</u> and other native
plant books. In addition to the 4 short nature trails, the southern
terminus of the Knobstone Trial is found east of Deam Lake.

Trail 1 is a 1/3 mile easy loop trail that may also be called the
"Gatehouse Loop" since the short forest path begins and ends at the
campground entry gatehouse. The rolling terrain supports numerous large
white oaks. Wooden benches have been provided for comfort and
leisurely nature observation.

Trail 2 begins and ends at the main campground between F-1 and D-13
campsites near the pit toilet. The linear trail begins and ends also at
the parking lot off Knob Road, the main forest road, near Deam lake
close to the campground. The moderately rugged trail follows the eroded
overused banks of Stone Branch Run to a wooden bridge crossing and a
white pine plantation. Hazel bush and sweet gum are common in the wet
bottoms adjacent to Deam Lake.

Trail 3 is a rugged overgrown service road that connects the main
campground to the Knobstone Trail south terminus. The trail begins/ends
at the main campground A-13 campsite. The firelane may be wet in
places and definitely overgrown by summers end. You may decide to hike
the Knobstone Trail which is marked with white blazes. Head south at
the junction on the Knobstone Trail a short ways to the "Y" fork and
bear right on a old service road along the near east shore of Deam Lake
unless you want to follow the Knobstone to the south terminus trailhead.
You may also want to consider hiking north a few miles for a good day
hike on the Knobstone Trail towards Jackson Road Trailhead. Trail 3
"T's" at a paved county road where you walk along the roadside west to
the Deam Lake entrance gate or head through the woods to the earthen
dam and crossover back to the main park road and Trail 2 to the
campground.

Trail 4 or the Lake Vista Trail is the premier nature hike at Deam
Lake SRA. The 2 mile loop is forested with vistas of Deam Lake. The
trailhead begins immediately northeast of the campground gatehouse at
the visitors parking lot. The trail proceeds north across a creek and
lowland area to steadily climb Waggoner Knobs with overlooks 400 feet
above Deam Lake. Near the rocky, slightly overgrown summit the trail
becomes steep going. The knob is studded with Virginia pine and
chestnut oak.

The vista is nearly overgrown in summer. The trail returns descending a ridge through the 9 acre Demonstration Timber sale area with 20 interpretive stations that provide examples of forestry harvesting procedures. The Lake Vista Trail ends at the campground gatehouse visitors parking lot where it started.

To reach Deam Lake SRA from I-65 exit west on SR 60 at Hamburg and drive 7.5 miles to Carr Road and turn north. Drive 1/2 mile on Carr Road to Deam Lake SRA entrance gate. The entrance is 8 miles north of Hamburg.

In addition to the hiking trails, you may want to visit the new nature center. The nature center opened the spring of 1989 and is in operation during the summer season only (Memorial to Labor Day). It is located along the main forest road directly across from the property office.

"Indian Directional Tree", Trail 1, Deam lake

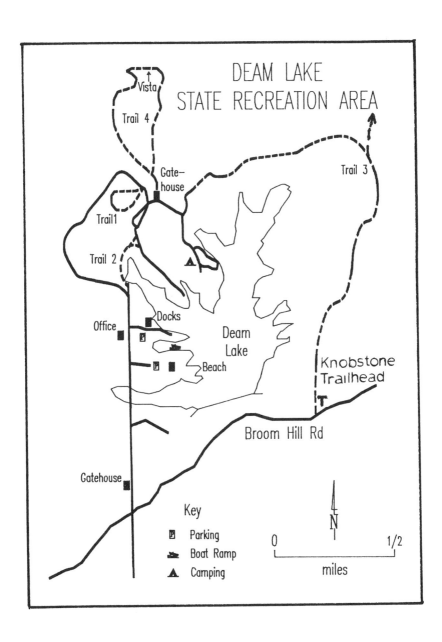

DEAM LAKE
STATE RECREATION AREA

Vista

Trail 4

Gate-
house

Trail 3

Trail1

Trail 2

Docks

Office

Deam
Lake

Beach

Knobstone
Trailhead

Broom Hill Rd

Gatehouse

Key

▣ Parking

⛴ Boat Ramp

▲ Camping

0   1/2

N

miles

18. KNOBSTONE TRAIL: OVERVIEW

The Knobstone Trail is a 50 plus mile hiking trek, over, down, and around a long chain of "knobs" or rock chestnut oak covered high ridges that rise abruptly above farmed valleys. Various divisions within the Indiana Department of Natural Resources and The Nature Conservancy are responsible for the establishment of the trail right-of-way through remote public lands of Clark State Forest, Elk Creek State Fish & Wildlife Area and Jackson-Washington State Forest as well as former private lands. The Youth Conservation Corps constructed several miles of the pathway. Volunteers help the DNR's Streams and Trails Crew maintain the trail.

The Knobstone Trail has the distinction of being the longest hiking trail in southern Indiana and it is sometimes referred to among hikers as the "Little Appalachian Trail". Beginning from the north terminus at Spurgeon Hollow and/or Delaney County Park, east of SR 135 in Washington County to the south terminus at Deam Lake State Recreation Area north of SR 60 in Clark County, the Knobstone ascends steep slopes to scenic vistas and descends to lush cool forest ravines and valley bottoms. Experienced backpackers may complete the trail in 3 days, however it is recommended that 5 days be taken for leisurely enjoyment. Dayhikers may car shuttle from trailhead to trailhead or back track to starting point. For safety sake, hikers should register at one of these stations: Clark State Forest Office at Henryville, Deam Lake SRA entry gatehouse, Starve Hollow SRA Office near Vallonia, Jackson-Washington State Forest Office near Brownstown and Delaney Park gatehouse, a Washington County facility.
5 suggested Day Trips:

Day 1: Spurgeon Hollow JWSF south to Elk Creek SFWA, 13-15 miles
Day 2: Elk Creek SFWA south to Leota Trailhead, 7 miles
Day 3: Leota Trailhead south to New Chapel Trailhead, 9 miles
Day 4: New Chapel Trailhead south to Jackson Road Trailhead 13 miles
Day 5: Jackson Road Trailhead south to Deam Lake SRA, 5 miles

Guiding white blazes appear both ways at eye-level on trailside tree trunks. Two white blazes together signal trail directional change. Initialed "KT" golden letters appear on black posts at trailheads, entrance roads and information signs at unattended trailhead parking areas. Overnight camping is permitted on state public lands, "at least one trail mile away from all roads, recreation areas and trailheads, and out of view from the trail and lakes". Good off-trail campsites are not always easy to locate when you need one at sunset especially in greenbriared and poison ivy steep hillsides, so plan ahead. Packing or placing your water at trailheads is important for the overnight backpacker. Limit campfires and burn dead windfallen wood. Contain your litter and bury only organic wastes. Be advised the fall hunting season coincides when hiking is at its best. Future plans are being made to possibly expand the trail northwest to Morgan-Monroe State Forest and eventually to culminate at Dunes State Park on Lake Michigan's shore, a state wide trail similar to Ohio's Buckeye Trail and Vermont's Long Trail.

The Knobstone Trail may be reached from I-65 at west bound exits: Uniontown exit SR 250 west to Brownstown and Jackson-Washington State Forest Office, Scottsburg exit SR 56 to Salem, Henryville exit SR 160 to Salem and the Hamburg exit to Deam Lake SRA.

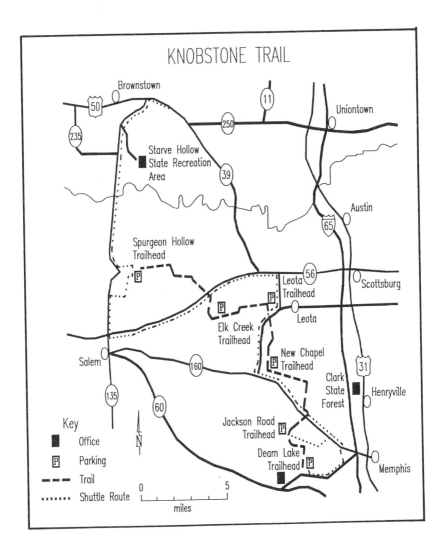

Knobstone Trail: North Portion
Day 1: Spurgeon Hollow JWSF south to Elk Creek SFWA
USGS MAP(S): Kossuth, Little York 1:24,000
TRAIL DISTANCE: approximately 13 miles or 15 miles optional

The hike from Spurgeon Hollow to Elk Creek Trailhead requires a full day's trek particularly during the dwindling daylight hours of fall and winter. Scenic sections include Spurgeon Hollow to first gravel road crossing and Nowling Hollow west of Elk Creek Reservoir. Negative aspects include 6 road crossings, recent clear cut logging areas and power line corridors the trail follows.

The Knobstone Trail begins on the northwest shore of Spurgeon Lake (fishing permitted) next to a spacious gravel parking area. The trail heads east with level easy walking through the hollow or narrow valley on a firelane trail 3 miles to the first road crossing. Knee high waters from Spurgeon Lake may cover portions of the trail in springtime but look for white blazes.

One mile east to the first gravel road the trail turns south for about 1/4 mile to a second road crossing. The path continues to head south 3 miles to Bane Hollow and 3 road crossings and 2 1/2 more miles to SR 56 (4th road). Exercise caution crossing. From SR 56 to Old SR 56 it is another mile. From Old SR 56 to Nowling Hollow (6th road crossing) and Elk Creek Trailhead is about 3 miles.

The Knobstone junctions twice with the Delaney Park Loop section. Junctions occur at 1/2 mile and 3 miles and the loops are 8 miles or 3 1/2 miles in length (see Delaney Park Loop, Trip 6). Indian-Bitter Nature Preserve is about 2 miles south of the first road crossing, south of Spurgeon Hollow. A natural stand of cucumber magnolia thrives in the protected ravine (see Indian-Bitter NP, Jackson-Washington SF, Trip 4).

Spurgeon Hollow Trailhead and parking area are located northeast of Salem, Washington County seat, one mile south of Delaney Park. Drive north of Salem on SR 135 about 4 miles and turn east and follow the paved unmarked county road. Turn north and drive 1 3/4 miles to the Crossroads Church and road and turn east right and jog immediately left/north. Continue just over a mile to a KT marked gravel road entrance on the east side of the county road. The gravel lane leads to the parking area, Spurgeon Hollow, Lake, and trailhead at the white pine plantation. Parking is unsupervised. Delaney County Park, 1 mile north of Spurgeon Hollow has fee supervised parking for overnight backpackers. Elk Creek Trailhead and parking are located 1.5 miles south of SR 56, 10 miles northeast of Salem. Follow directional signs.

Knobstone Trail
Day 2: Elk Creek SFWA south to Leota Trailhead
USGS MAP(S): Little York 1:24,000
TRAIL DISTANCE: approximately 7 miles

This section of the trail is considered one of the best of the Knobstone because of its remoteness and scenery. The surroundings are fairly natural and undisturbed. There are one or two minor road crossings. Dayhikers will find both ways enjoyable hiking if deciding to backtrack without car shuttle.

156

Ridge at Elk Creek Reservoir

The Elk Creek Trailhead is south of the parking area and boat ramp at Elk Creek SFWA. Camping sites are in the woods south near the trailhead. The Knobstone follows the scenic coves and hollows for 1 mile along the 48-acre lake's south shore. The trail rises uphill at one point between Garrett Hollow and Smith Hollow. The trail then heads uphill from McKnight Hollow and the lake following a power line swath through an open area providing views. The trail continues eastward 4 miles up ridge and down hollows to swing north to Vic Swain Hill. From here the trail heads southeast about 2 miles to Leota Trailhead and Clark State Forest.

Trailhead at Elk Creek, Knobstone Trail

Elk Creek SFWA trailhead and parking are located 1.5 miles south of SR 56, 10 miles northeast of Salem. Follow the directional signs. Leota Trailhead and parking are located 2 miles west of Leota, 4 miles south of SR 56, 14 1/2 miles east of Salem. From SR 56 turn south on West Road and drive 2 1/4 miles to Leota. Follow the Leota Road west from town 1 mile and turn on to a gravel road and drive southwest one mile to the Leota Trailhead and parking at the hilltop. A trailhead parking area near a power transmission line.

Knobstone Trail
Day 3: Leota Trailhead south to New Chapel Trailhead
USGS MAP(S): South Boston, Henryville 1:24,000
TRAIL DISTANCE: approximately 9 miles

This 9 mile section offers enjoyable backcountry hiking within Clark State Forest. The Knobstone is especially scenic in the long and narrow North Branch Valley.

The starting point, Leota Trailhead begins at the trailhead parking area 2 miles due west of Leota and the Leota Road atop a near 1,000 foot knob. Crossing the road, the south bound trail climbs downhill and uphill about 3 miles before descending into the North Branch. The stream has eroded cuts and exposed vertical sandstone bluff faces. Young tulip poplar is very common in the sunny open bottoms. After a mile along North Branch the trail turns due west to follow a tributary ravine. About another mile the trail heads south climbing out of the ravine along switchbacks to the ridgetop. The trail follows the forested ridge along the Washington and Scott County line nearly 2 miles before entering an open field and woodland border that extends the last 2 miles to the New Chapel Trailhead spur.

To reach New Chapel Trailhead and parking area from I-65, exit onto SR 160 west and continue 5 miles to New Liberty. From New Liberty continue west on SR 160 1/3 mile to the first unmarked paved county road to the north. Proceed 0.4 mile to the New Chapel Trailhead and parking area on the east side of the road.

Knobstone Trail
Day 4: New Chapel south to Jackson Road
USGS MAP(S): Henryville 1:24,000
TRAIL DISTANCE: approximately 12 miles

The Knobstone Trail winds within a few miles west of the Clark State Forest developed recreational sites north of SR 160 along this long segment. Virginia pine becomes a more common feature of the upland forest. The 1,000 foot climb up and down Round Knob is the main experience south of SR 160, a mile or so north of the Jackson Road trailhead and parking area.

The New Chapel Trailhead is easily accessible from SR 160 15 miles east of Salem and just over 5 miles from Henryville and I-65. Go 1/3 mile west of New Liberty and north on an unmarked paved county road 0.4 mile to the parking area on the east side.

Follow the trailhead spur to the main trail and turn right/east. The trail goes uphill following the South Branch a short distance northeast and then due east following ridgetops for about 2 miles. Dropping south and southeasterly 2 miles more. The trail descends to skirt alongside the base of knobs and ravine bottoms of Bowen Run (another possible site for trail parking). Climbing uphill, the trail crosses a main forest gravel road and follows alongside it east for about a mile to the microwave tower. Turning due south at the tower, the trail descends downhill a mile to SR 160. The trail enters the 24 acre Virginia Pine-Chestnut Oak Nature Preserve just south of the main forest road. The Clark State Forest Boy Scout Trail also shares this segment of the Knobstone (see Clark State Forest Trip 3).

The Knobstone crosses SR 160 climbing steep steps uphill to continue south following portions of an old forest road. Two county roads are crossed in the next 2 miles, Pixley Knob Road and the Bartle Knob Road. The next 2 miles feature ravine crossings and hill climbing in the Right Drain Creek area before the trail follows alongside the east side of Jackson Road. The trail heads southeast to Round Knob and its impressive vistas then descends to the Bartle Knob Run. The final leg is uphill to the paved county road. At the county road go right/west 1 mile to the gravel Jackson Road north to the trailhead parking area on the west/left side of the road. The New Chapel trailhead lies directly north just over 4 "crow" miles of the Jackson Road trailhead.

To reach Jackson Road trailhead from I-65 exit west at exchange 16 near Memphis, and the first exit south of SR 160 and Henryville. Go west on Blue Lick Road to the village of the Blue Lick and turn right on Reed Road. Follow Reed Road 4.2 miles bearing right on Reed Road to the junction with Jackson Road. Follow Jackson Road 0.4 mile to the signed trailside parking area.

Overhang Shelter, Knobstone Trail

Knobstone Trail: South Terminus
Day 5: Jackson Road south to Deam Lake SRA
USGS MAP(S): Henryville, Speed 1:24,000
TRAIL DISTANCE: approximately 5 miles

The shortest segment of the Knobstone also provides good hiking but no outstanding natural features. Access to more trails, camping and other recreation is provided at Deam Lake State Recreation Area at the trail's southern terminus.

The Jackson Road trailhead is located 4.2 miles west of Blue Lick, 0.4 mile north of the junction with Reed Road and Jackson Road. From I-65 exit at exchange 16, go west on Blue Lick Road and drive to the village of Blue Lick and turn west on Reed Road. The trailhead parking area is 1/2 mile from the main trail. Walk south on Jackson Road .3 mile to the paved county road and turn east/left 0.1 mile to the main trail crossing.

The Knobstone heads southeast up a steep hill to the top then rising and falling with the Bartle Knobs ridgeline for about 2 miles. For about a mile the trail drops down to cross Bowery Creek then curves sharply west to cross Reed Road. Once across Reed Road the trail points south for the next 2 miles of rolling forested terrain not far from the Deam Lake shore. The trail intersects at two points on the right with Trail 3 to Deam Lake campground and a second spur that is a south continuation of Trail 3. Follow the blazes and stay left to Deam Lake trailhead terminus. Trailhead parking is limited and not well supervised. It is recommended that overnight backpackers leave their vehicles at Deam Lake SRA headquarters parking area, one mile west of the trailhead.

The Deam Lake trailhead and parking area may be reached by exiting I-65 at Hamburg and driving west on SR 60, 7 miles and turning north and continuing one mile to the Deam Lake SRA entrance. Before the entrance road turn right/east on Wilson Switch Road and drive one mile to the trailhead. Watch for directional signs.

DAY 6: Delaney Park Loop
USGS MAP(S): Kossuth 1:24,000
TRAIL(S) DISTANCE: 2 loops total approx. 12 miles

Open year around, Delaney Park is a 353 acre Washington County Park that offers camping, fishing, non-motorized boating on a 88 acre lake, moor and docks, beach swimming, beachhouse, seasonal lifeguards, picnicking, shelterhouse, playfields, cultural arts program and overnight parking for backpackers on the Knobstone Trail. The park is an outdoor active park in a scenic knob and lake hollow setting.

The Delaney Park loop trail makes a fine day or overnight hike. There are 3 loop options of varying distance along the figure "8" like trail: North Loop 3.5 miles, South Loop 7 miles and both loops or the Delaney Park loop of approximately 11 miles. All 3 loops are marked and begin and end east of the beachhouse along a service road.

The North Loop is the shortest. At the bar gate head north or left uphill from the lake and over the 800 foot knob down to Mundy Hollow and up again following a ridgetop north curving east and then dropping south along the forest boundary along the base of high knobs and ravines to arrive at a east-west "T" trail junction. Go right/southwest and follow the ridge slope down to Clay Hill Hollow and a second trail junction. Go right and follow the service road along the north lakeshore back to the bar gate and the starting point.

The South Loop turn also begins at the bar gate 1/4 mile east of the beachhouse. Follow the service road south/right along the north shore of the lake and inlet backwaters to the trail junction or "Y". Go right/south uphill to the ridge slopes heading west to the next trail fork or "Y". Go right on the Spurgeon Hollow overlook spur 1/4 mile to the vista point and retrace your steps. Bear left/south at the "Y" and the trail descends to Spurgeon Hollow, Lake and trailhead. Head left at the "T" with the Knobstone Trail and follow it upstream along Spurgeon Hollow to its junction with the Delaney Loop trail just a short ways before the first county road crossing. Turn left/north curving northwesterly along ridgetops, down Clay Hill Hollow and up ridgetops to curve due west and the trail junction with the North Loop. Bear left/southwest down the ridge to Clay Hill Hollow and the lake and the first trail junction. Go right/north along the north shore of the lake on the service road to return to the bar gate.

The 3rd loop, the Delaney Park Loop is both the North and South Loop without the middle spur shortcut. Follow the same South Loop trail but continue on to the right and the North Loop instead of following the middle connecting spur. The blazed trails may be hiked in either direction.

To reach Delaney Park, 10 miles northeast of Salem and 2 miles east of Plattsburg, take SR 135 north 4 miles and turn right/east following the directional signs to Delaney Park. Follow the paved county road about 2 miles and turn north/left and drive to Crossroads Church. Turning right at Crossroads Church turn immediately north again at the jog and continue to the Delaney Park entrance, 1 mile north of the Jackson-Washington SF, Spurgeon Hollow Trailhead entrance.

Fees are charged for day-use entrance, boat rental, boat launch, cabin rental, Class A and C camping and shelter reservations.

Striped Skunk

KNOBSTONE TRAIL

⊢— 1 mile —⊣

N

LANEY PARK
(ashington County)

P

AB

Backcountry Area

Knobstone

Trail

Jackson-Washington

State Forest

163

J-W S.

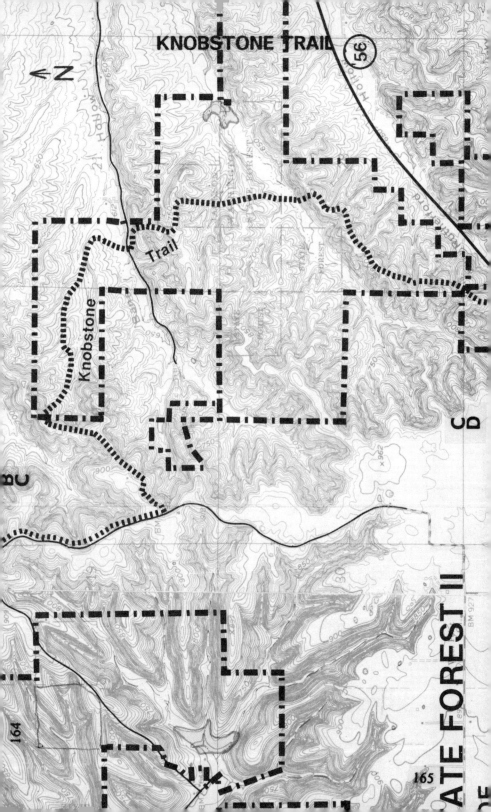

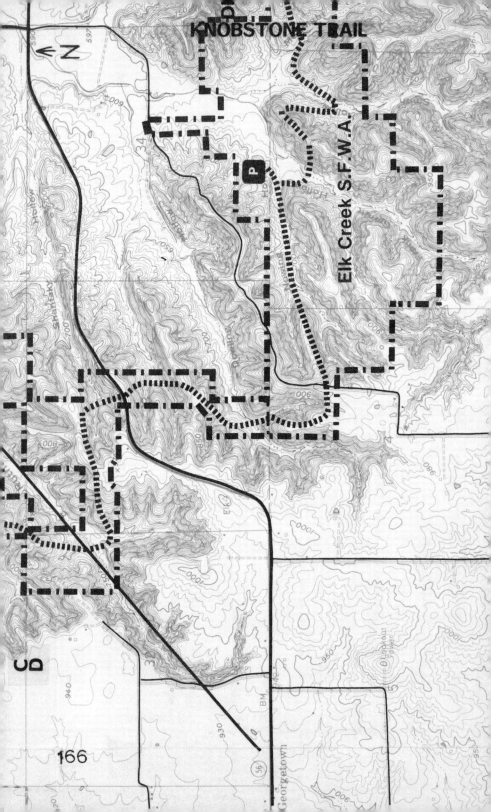

KNOBSTONE TRAIL

Elk Creek S.F.W.A.

166

KNOBSTONE TRAIL

←N

1 mile

Elk Creek
Fish & Wildlife Area

167

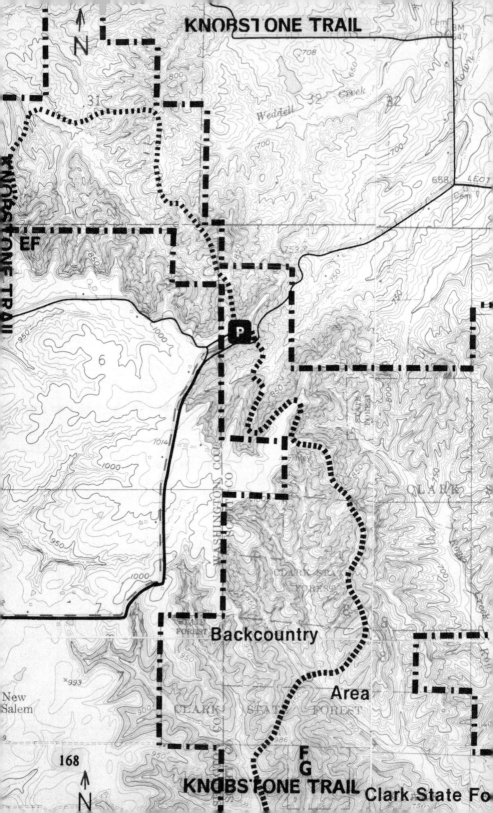

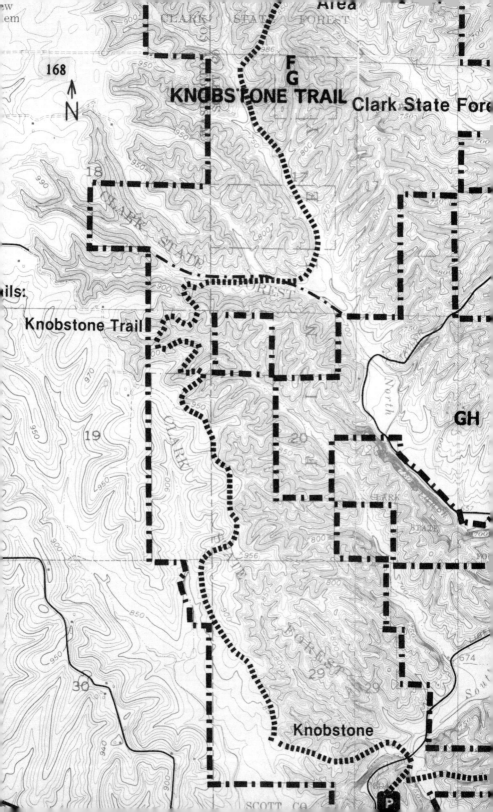

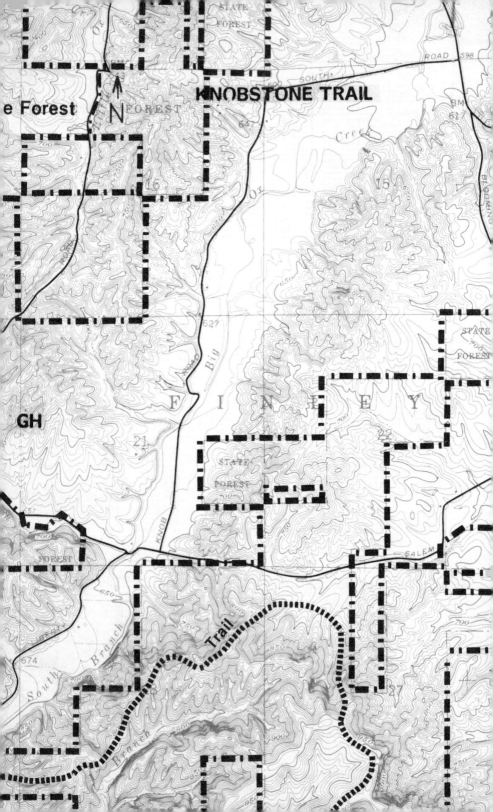

KNOBSTONE TRAIL

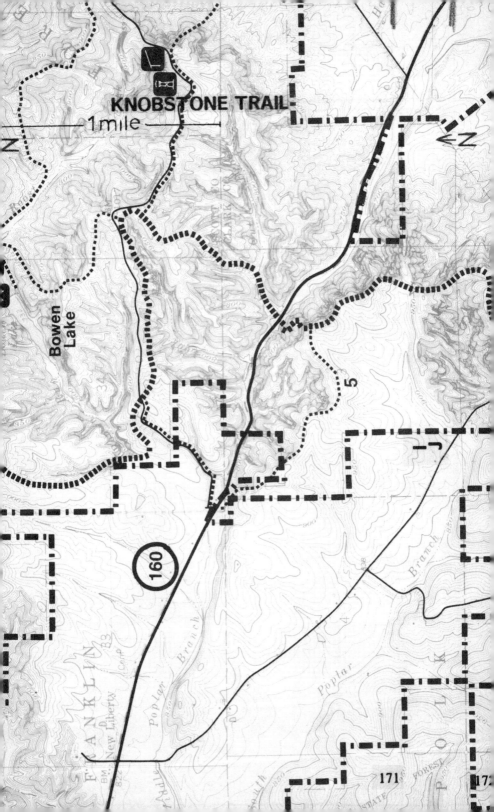

KNOBSTONE TRAIL

— 1 mile —

N

Bowen
Lake

160

171

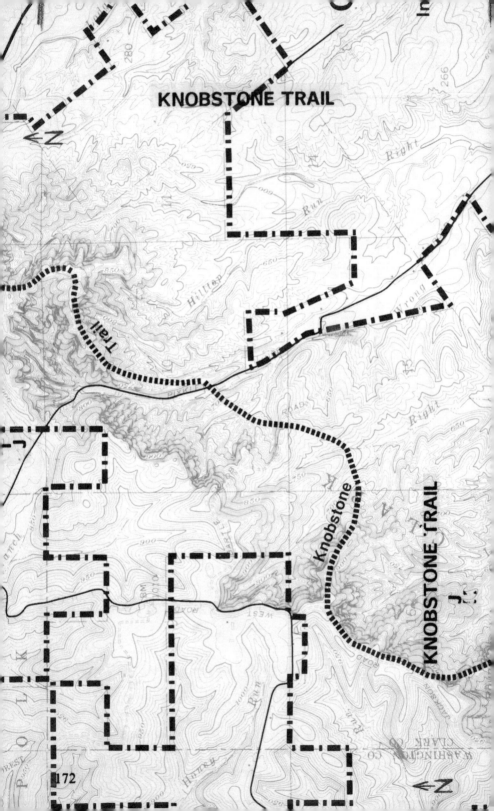

KNOBSTONE TRAIL

KNOBSTONE TRAIL

172

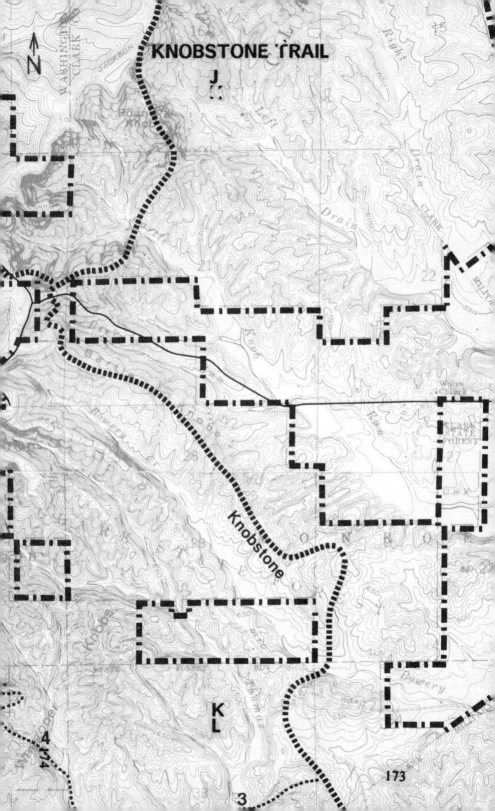

KNOBSTONE TRAIL

J

Knobstone

K

173

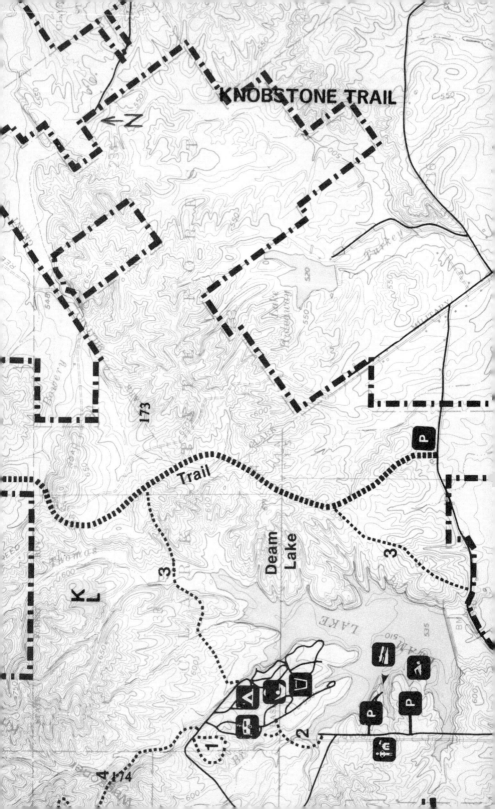

KNOBSTONE TRAIL

19. Brock-Sampson Ridge
New Albany, IN/Floyd County
USGS(S): Lanesville 1:24,000
TRAIL(S) DISTANCE: trails and parking not yet est. (Permission
  requested, contact Ind. Div. of Nat. Preserves)
ACREAGE: 442 acres
ACTIVITIES: hiking, nature study

Brock-Sampson Ridge Nature Preserve overlooks the Ohio River valley 6 miles southwest of New Albany near the Floyd and Harrison County line. Two long and narrow hollows flank 800 foot high Sampson Ridge. Several other ridge segments are found also on both sides of Sampson including part of Rock House Ridge. Loop trails are being planned that will traverse the dry glades, narrow canyons and upland oak forests of the steep rocky knobs. The property was acquired by The Nature Conservancy and is now owned and managed by DNR's Division of Nature Preserves.

From I-64 exit SR 62 southwest at Edwardsville (last exit west in Floyd County). Turn south on SR 11 and drive to Farnsley Knob Road south of the Antioch Church and Cemetery. Take Farnsley Knob east to Seven-Mile Road at a "T". Turn left/north and continue about 1/2 mile to a road pullout just beyond the first curve right. The preserve is on the left side of the road. White and black lettered property signs.

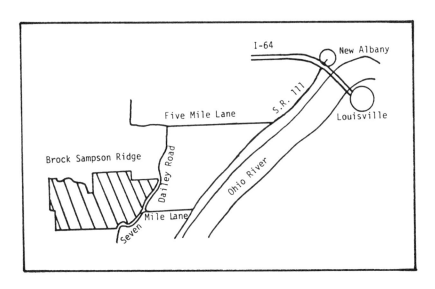

20. McCORMICK'S CREEK STATE PARK

Spencer, IN/ Owen County
USGS MAP: Gosport 1:24,000
TRAIL(S) DISTANCE: 8 trails totalling 16 miles
ACREAGE: 1,833 acres
ACTIVITIES: hiking, nature study, nature center/museum, naturalist
    programs, camping (Class A, primitive, rally, group), cabins, Canyon
    Inn, picnicking, saddle barn, swimming pool, tennis courts,
    playgrounds, various rentals, concessions
FEES: entrance, camping, swimming, rentals

McCormick's Creek State Park is the "granddaddy" of the Hoosier state park system. During the centennial statehood celebration in 1916, the land was purchased and named in honor of John McCormick, a pioneering Virginian who established a homesite in the vicinity of the canyon in the 1820's. Hilly and densely forested with old mixed woods, the park is known for its interesting geological features especially the mile long canyon and waterfalls.

Hiking is a popular activity at this premier of Hoosier parks. The maintained eight trails may be traversed in one day but allow yourself two days for leisurely walking. With the exception of Trail 6 and 8, all trails begin near the Canyon Inn. Day visitors may have some difficulty on busy days parking at the limited trailheads. Canyon Inn parking is for registered guests only.

Several of the trails were established by the Civilian Conservation Corps in the 1930's. Most of the trails involve hill walking with stairways on the steepest stretches to control erosion. The surface of the trails are limestone fines and wood chips. In time, all trails will be wood chip for comfort and quietude. It would be nice if the trails had names as well as numbers. All designated trails interconnect at some point in the park. Ask for a trail map at the entrance gate.

Trails 1-2-3 and 7 begin at Trailside Shelter just north of the recreation center near the Canyon Inn. Parking is available for about ten cars at the trailhead for day visitors. Trail 1 is a moderate 2 1/4 mile walk that nearly loops back to the trailhead. Trail 1 forks from the 2-3-7 trails when it descends down along the south green banks of McCormick's Creek. Spring wildflowers are abundant and birds, especially the pileated woodpecker may be observed. Plant life abounds on the low-lying Mississippian rocky bluff. The trail turns sharply uphill to the family cabins where the trail goes straight across to rejoin the trail. The rest of the walk is a hill and dale loop that ends at Friendly Shelter. Continue east on the paved park road past Maple Grove Shelter to Trailside Shelter parking.

Trail 2 forks north and descends into the canyon. At the canyon's edge is a late 19th century limestone quarry filled with water. A large portion of the stone was sent by railroad to Indianapolis to construct the Statehouse Capitol. The "Statehouse" quarry failed because stone removal proved economically unfeasible. The tressel across the White River collapsed twice, resulting in the closure of the quarry.

Trail 2 crosses the creek and ascends the north bluff and follows the canyon's edge, where it ends at Trail 5. Trails 3, 7, and 5 interjoin.

Trail 3 or Canyon-Falls Trail is the most scenic and involves a fair share of rockhopping. Once leaving Trailside Shelter it descends into the canyon and follows the boulder studded stream bottom to the falls. Millions of years ago, McCormick's Creek was a tunneled shaped, underground stream. Eventually eroding away, the roof of the tunnel collapsed and the canyon was created. The walk is two miles long and Trail 3 has parking available also at the falls. The trail loops back to Canyon Inn, a short ways from Trailside Shelter. Trails 2, 7, and 5 intersect.

Trail 7 departs from Trails 1-2-3 and goes over and down and across the canyon creek to ascend the north bluff after crossing Trail 2 and skirting the main campground. The trail then descends along the White River's West Fork. Along the river bottom, the trail leads the walker through an alluvial forest of sycamore, red elm, cottonwood, box elder maple and large stands of stinging wood nettle. There are open "windows" to view the White River. The trail loops back alongside McCormick's Creek to intersect with Trail 2.

Trail 4 is a 1 7/8 mile firetower and ravine walk. Trailhead parking is available for about six cars just south of Canyon Inn. The views at the firetower (climb at your own risk) are the highest in the park and open to west and south. Between the park road, the trail passes brookside in a shady ravine lined with pawpaw, christmas fern, spicebush, jewelweed and an occasional redbud. Recross the paved park road, pass the sinkholes to the swimming pool at the Canyon Inn.

Trail 5 to Wolf Cave Nature Preserve is the longest trail. It is a rugged three mile loop that begins at the Canyon Inn. It passes thru the Camp Outpost cabin area and descends down a wooden staircase and crosses the creek to ascend the north bluff. Parking for 10-15 cars is available at this point where the trail takes off thru beech-maple forest. Funnel or bowl-shaped sinkholes of good size are a common feature of the karst topography, characteristic of the Mitchell Plain of south central Indiana. Sinkholes are created when weak acidic rain percolates down into the soil and dissolves the limestone.

Wolf Cave, named for the last wolf to be seen in the area in the 1850's, was once a part of a local underground streambed. It is passable via the one small, 40 ft. passageway. The small tunnel opens up at Twin or Litten Natural Bridges, stone formations created when a section of the cave's roof tumbled down, leaving an arch. Most to the trail follows the Litten's Branch. The trail loops back to nearly rejoin the original trail at the northside bluff of McCormick's Creek. Retrace the trail, recross the creek and canyon, and return to Canyon Inn.

Trail 6 is actually a 1 1/4 mile camper's trail that leads from the primitive and rally campgrounds to the main campground (where it becomes confusing) and on to join with Trail 2 and other canyonside trails.

McCormick's Creek State Park

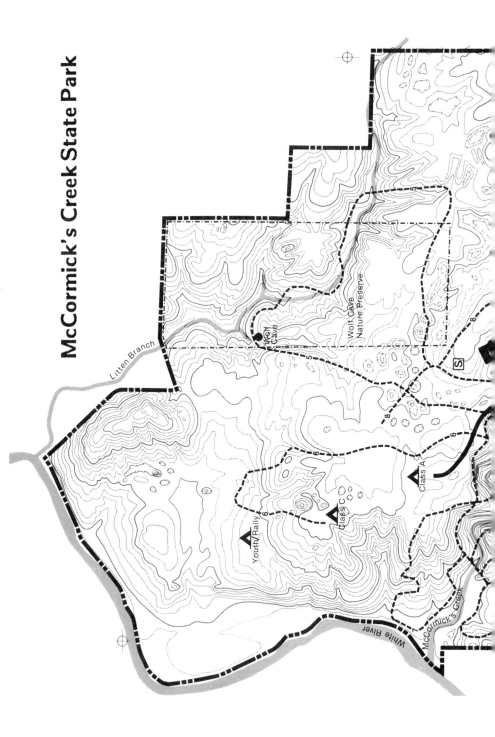

Litten Branch

Wolf Cave

Wolf Cave Nature Preserve

S

Class A

Class C

Youth/Rally

White River

McCormick's Creek

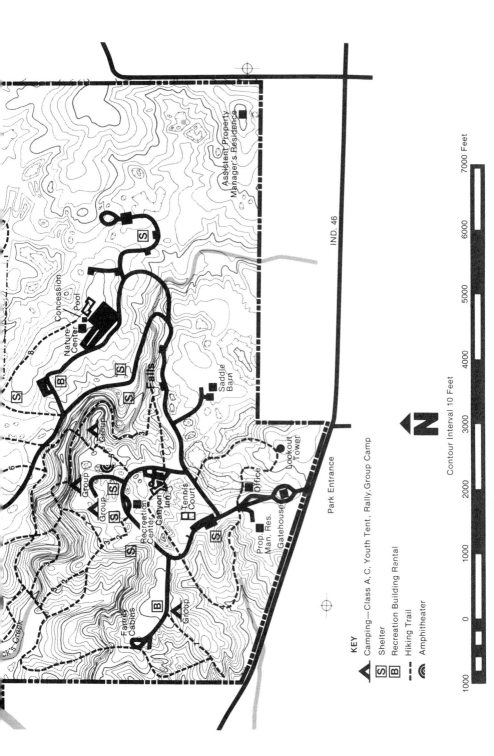

KEY

▲ Camping—Class A, C, Youth Tent, Rally, Group Camp
Ⓢ Shelter
Ⓑ Recreation Building Rental
- - - Hiking Trail
◉ Amphitheater

N

Contour Interval 10 Feet

1000   0   1000   2000   3000   4000   5000   6000   7000 Feet

Park Entrance

IND. 46

Assistant Property
Manager's Residence

Concession
Pool
Nature
Center

Saddle
Barn

Lookout
Tower

Office

Prop.
Man. Res.

Gatehouse

Canyon Inn

Tennis
Court

Recreation
Center

Group

Group

Group

Group

Family
Cabins

Falls

Dr's Creek

179

Trail 8 is a 1/4 mile, asphalt paved, all-weather trail that connects the main campground with the modern nature center, swimming pool and playground. There is a ten minute Habitat Enhancement Trail just outside the back door at the nature center. The brief but informative wood chipped trail is designed to educate how to go about attracting wildlife. There are numerous brochures available that describe the flora, fauna and geology of the park. The nature center has many natural history exhibits and games. It is open year around.

Besides nature walking, there is other recreational fare at this family-styled state park to enjoy. McCormick's Creek State Park entrance is two miles east of Spencer, on the north side of SR 46.

McCormick Falls and Canyon, McCormick's Creek State Park

21. BLOOMINGTON, IN/NATURE PLACES

USGS MAP(S): Bloomington 1:24,000
TRAIL(S) DISTANCE: 1/2 mile Cascades/ 1/3 mile Griffy Lake
ACREAGE: 213 acres Cascades/1200 acres Griffy Lake
ACTIVITIES: Lower Cascades; picnicking, playground, shelterhouses, short trails, Upper Cascades; picnicking, playground, shelterhouse, lighted softball field, 18 hole golf course, Griffy Lake; hiking, picnicking, nonmotorized boating, boat launch, fishing, boat rental
FEE(S): boat rental and boat launch fee at Griffy Lake

Anyone who loves nature and beauty will enjoy a visit to Bloomington's natural parks located on the city's northside. Bloomington residents and visitors are fortunate in having these natural woodland remnants preserved with the minimum of development in one of the fastest growing urban areas in Indiana.

One time dubbed the "Gateway to Bloomington" and the first city park, Cascades Park and in particular Lower Cascades Park attracts many outdoor enthusiasts who enjoy warm weather picnicking in the impressive canyon. Much longer than it is wide, the flat narrow valley is walled in on both sides by precipitous bluffs. Here, Cascades Creek, cascades alongside specimens of tall sycamores in a series of waterfalls. Cascades Falls highlights the scenic semi-natural area. Situated in a densely wooded cove near the upper reaches of the park on the west bluff, a short trail treks along the rise to the 20 foot waterfall. The lip of the falls extends beyond the base where erosive action has created an undercut. (People erosion is a problem at the falls especially along the bank.) Retrace your steps or follow the overgrown brook bank back to the grassy open area. Upper Cascades Park is found by turning left/west at the north boundary of Cascades Park Road that drives up out of the canyon to the flat ridge above. Golfing is the main activity here but there is a wooded picnicking, shelter, and playground area.

To reach the park from the downtown Monroe County Courthouse drive north on Walnut Street and turn west/left at the Howard Johnson motel and proceed across College Avenue onto Old SR 37. Follow Old SR 37 north under the overpass directly into the Cascades Park canyon.

Nearby Griffy Lake is bordered by upland mixed forest and provides acres of terrain to explore either by foot or boat. A self-guiding Canoe Trail is a popular activity on the 125 acre reservoir lake and a relaxing alternative to the feet weary. A self-guiding interpretive loop trail, 0.3 miles, begins near the park office at the parking area. The trail brochure identifies the flora, fauna and forest ecology of the 1,200 acre sanctuary. The defined wide path ascends the steep slope to wind along the ridgetop interspersed with open brushy meadowlands to descend to the lakeshore and east end of the parking area. Be alert for glimpses of wildlife. Raccoons, squirrels, chipmunks and pileated woodpeckers are often seen along the foot trail. There are other well worn undesignated footpaths that encompass the lake and its many coves and it is difficult to get lost. A second more challenging trail follows the north shore and heads west at a staircase just north of the parking area on the west side of the paved road. The 1 mile long one way, poorly marked trail follows the ridge, slope, ravines, coves and shoreline to the dam. Retrace your steps.

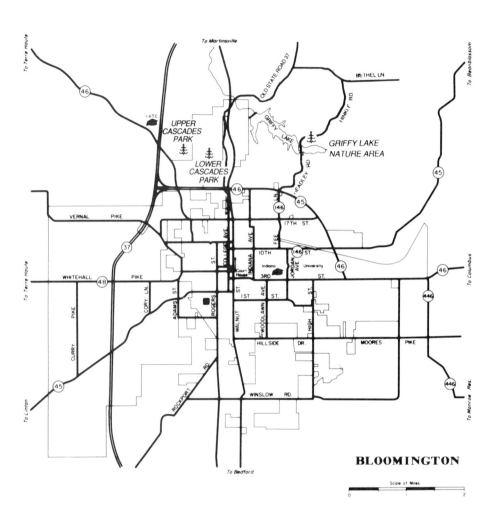

BLOOMINGTON

Scale of Miles

22. INDIANA UNIVERSITY CAMPUS WALK

Bloomington, IN/Monroe County
WALKING DISTANCE: approx. 2 to 5 miles or more depending on visitor
ACREAGE: 3,000 acre campus
ACTIVITIES: walking, tree and plant identification, tours, campus
museums, landmarks and other facilities

The campus of Indiana University is one of the most beautiful in the nation. The visitor will enjoy a nature walk on the all-weather pathways through the natural woodlands that contain trees as old as the university and the exotic semiformal landscaped grounds of the recently constructed and designed arboretum. Native maple, beech and tulip poplar are the most commonly encountered trees. The original woodlands are filled with spring wildflowers such as violets and spring beauty. The edible fruits of summer mulberries and fall persimmons bless the open sunny areas. Exotic tree specimens include English oak, ginkgo, Japanese pagoda and chestnut, paulownia, Chinese cork tree and metasequoia or dawn redwood. North American and north Asian flowering trees such as yellowwood, redbud, dogwood, Japanese magnolia, sophora and silk trees grace the forest understory and clearings. The main walking areas are bound on the north by 10th Street, east by Jordan Avenue, south by 3rd Street and west by Indiana Avenue, 7th Street and Woodlawn Avenue. Special inviting "islands of green" include Dunn Woods and Meadow, Jordan River, Forest Place and the Hoosier Arboretum.

There are free walking tours of campus starting from the Admissions Building and Student Services Building, Monday through Friday at 2:00 pm. However if you want to be self-guided obtain a free copy of The Woodland Campus of Indiana University by Paul Weatherwax, a former professor emeritus of botany, from the visitor center. This work of love identifies 80 trees and shrubs by their scientific and common names and their location on campus by a numbered map. The publication also lists over 70 Class Trees by year and their location, the flowering sequence of conspicuous trees (from magnolias to witch hazel), basic botany or how-to-identify trees by the shape of their leaves especially oaks, and a general background history of the campus flora and fauna. Furthermore, Dr. Weatherwax "leads" you around the grounds describing the trees and their natural and social significance. The booklet is a helpful reference to have along to enhance your appreciation of the green surroundings.

In addition to the scenic landscaping there are university facilities to visit. The Fine Arts Plaza at East 7th Street includes the Showalter Fountain and the sculpture of "The Birth of Venus" designed by the late Ralph Laurent; the Lilly Library features permanent displays, a special exhibition gallery, portrait gallery, a 15th century facsimile of a handprinting press, Lincoln Room and more, and the Indiana University Art Museum designed by I.M. Pei has galleries of Western, Ancient, Asian, African, Oceania, Americas and special exhibits.

Along the east edge of Dunn Woodland near Kirkwood Hall is a campus landmark, the Well House. Beneath the floor is the old cistern that contained the campus drinking water years ago. Near the south edge of the wood is the Kirkwood Observatory and its 12" refractor telescope that is accessible to the public one night a week. The Grove of All

Faiths thrives on the grounds of Beck Chapel and Dunn family pioneer cemetery. The individual trees represent separate religions that draw their nourishment from the same earth. This spiritual sanctuary is located between Indiana Memorial Union and Ballantine Hall.

Jordan Hall greenhouse contains interesting and exotic plant life from around the world. A self-guiding tour brochure is available. The greenhouse is located at the corner of 3rd and Hawthorne Streets.

Hilltop Garden and Nature Center is located on the east edge of Indiana University's campus, behind Tulip Tree Apartments, off Tenth Street. The facility is open to day visitors who may be interested in viewing landscaping displays of plants that thrive in south central Indiana. Besides landscaped areas, Hilltop offers workshops and classes, academic courses, outdoor education, a junior garden program and a Spring Garden Festival.

The Hoosier Heritage Complex shelters two museums of history, anthropology, and folklore. The Mathers Museum has an exhibit pool of 20,000 artifacts from around the world to display and the adjacent Glenn A. Black Laboratory is devoted to Great Lakes and Ohio Valley Archeology, displaying prehistoric Indian artifacts. The Hoosier Heritage Complex is situated between 9th and 8th Streets with the entrance on Fess Street.

Established in 1970, the 91 foot tall Metz Carillion, the 5th largest carillion in the United States, produces musical beauty with its 61 cast bells during concerts on Sunday afternoons. The Metz Carillion is located at Linglebach and Jordan Avenue.

These free public facilities are the major ones to visit yet there are exhibits and tours available of other departments and buildings. For further information regarding hours and tours contact the Indiana University Convention and Visitors Bureau located at 2855 N. Walnut. To reach the facility from the north exit at College Ave. off of Hwy 37 from the south, follow Walnut St. north. The center is located 1 mile north of the Holiday Inn. The Administration and Student Services Building information center is located at the corner of Kirkwood and Indiana Avenues.

Hourly parking is permitted at the Poplars garage, two Indiana Memorial Union lots, the 10th and Fee Lane lot and the Atwater garage. At 10th and Fee Lane lot and the Atwater garage the hourly rate is charged from 7:00 am to 6:00 pm. The Jordan Avenue meter lot, the 10th and Fee Lane lot and the Atwater garage are available for free weekend parking.

Young
Chickadee

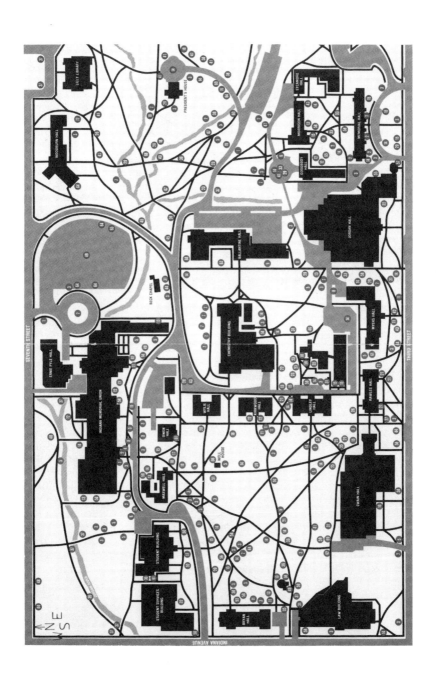

23 AVOCA FISH HATCHERY

Avoca, IN/Lawrence County
USGS MAP(S): Oolitic 1:24,000
TRAIL(S) DISTANCE: 1.5 mile loop and intersecting trails
ACREAGE: 70 acres
ACTIVITIES: hiking, nature study, picnicking, shelterhouse, Spring fish
   hatchery tours.
FEE(S): shelterhouse rental

Constructed in 1924, the Avoca Fish Hatchery is a warm water hatchery for bluegill, redear and especially largemouth bass. The hatchery's 13 old style, "drain and seine" ponds contain 5.6 acres of spring waters and rear 200,000 to 500,000 fish annually.

The 53 degree spring water is derived from the adjacent hillside spring cavern that measures at least 700 feet. The spring water is pooled by a concrete CCC built dam and piped to the outlying ponds. The excess water cascades over the lip adding a scenic touch. Historically, the spring provided water for a 1819 grist mill powered by turbine water wheels. The spring was also a inspiration for the community's place name. A Dr. Foote, pioneer doctor and founder of the Lawrence County limestone industry, visited the spring often and its beauty inspired him to quote often the "Sweet Vale of Avoca" by the Irish poet, Thomas Moore (1779-1852).

The nature trail begins at the wooden stairs just east of the first pond and nearby hatchery building. There are yellow arrow markers posted to guide your walk. The numbered signs identify trees, shrubs and herbaceous plants. Diamond-shaped signs identify plants for a second time to test your ability to recognize them. A trail guide is available at the hatchery building and trailhead box.

The trail goes uphill into a thick growth of mixed hardwoods to a lookout of the pool and dam. Continue uphill along the property's south boundary to the service road and turn left or north to the shelterhouse. Pine plantations and a shallow sinkhole are the natural features along the service road. A spur trail midway to the shelterhouse leads to a family cemetery. At the shelterhouse turn west and follow the ridgeside back to the steps or head downhill to the Daphnia rank pool and just east of pond 6 just south of Goose Creek Bridge. The genus Daphnia are minute freshwater branchipods crustaceans or water fleas. Rest assured you won't get lost in the small hilltop woods.

Avoca Fish Hatchery is a pleasant day visit from 7:30 am to sunset year around. Hatchery tours are given in April. Call for group reservations. Picnicking is pleasant at the pond-overlook shelterhouse. The Avoca Fish Hatchery is located approximately one mile west of SR 37 on SR 54 & 58, 5 miles northwest of Bedford, the county seat of Lawrence County.

Plants identified at Avoca Fish Hatchery Nature Trail:

1. Red Elm (Ulmus rubra)
2. Ohio Buckeye (Aesculus glabra)
3. Sugar Maple (Acer saccharum)

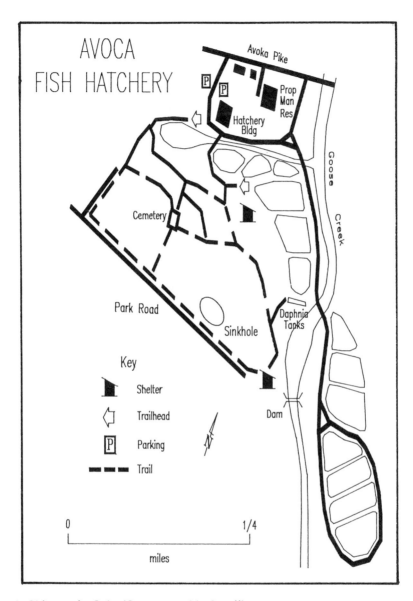

4. Chinquapin Oak (Quercus muhlenbergii)
5. Wild Ginger (Asarum canadense)
6. American Beech (Fagus grandifolia)
7. Shagbark Hickory (Carya ovata)
8. Bitternut Hickory (Carya cordiformis)
9. Pignut Hickory (Carya glabra)
10. Black Oak (Quercus velutina)
11. White Oak (Quercus alba)
12. Red Oak   (Quercus rubra)

Avoca State Fish Hatchery

13. American Hornbean (Carpinus caroliniana)
14. Sassafras (Sassafras albidum)
15. Poison Ivy (Rhus radicans)
16. Redbud (Cercis canadensis)
17. Dogwood (Cornus florida)
18. Shingle Oak (Quercus imbricaria)

19. Black Walnut (Juglans nigra)
20. Boxelder (Acer negundo)
21. Slippery elm or Red Elm (Ulmus rubra)
22. Multiflora Rose (Rosa multiflora)
23. White Pine (Pinus strobus)
24. Black Cherry (Prunus serotina)
25. Black Locust (Robina pseudo-acacia)
26. Tulip Poplar (Liriodendron tulipifera)
27. Paw Paw (Asimina triloba)
28. Basswood (Tilia americana)
29. Green Ash (Fraxinus pennsylvanica)
30. Sycamore (Platanus occidentalis
31. Adam's Needle (Yucca filamentosa)

Garold Spoonmore
Hatchery Manager
Avoca, IN 47420

24 BLUESPRING CAVERNS
Bedford, IN/Lawrence County
USGS MAP(S): Bedford West 1:24,000
BOAT TOUR DISTANCE: 1 1/4 mile
ACTIVITIES: cave boat tour, hospitality center, gift shop, picnicking,
    group camping, winter weekend group camp
FEE(S): cave boat tour, group camping by reservation only

The present day access to Bluespring Caverns was discovered in 1940 when a karst sinkhole-pond suddenly drained and revealed access to a subterranean stream. The exploration that followed found that the cave has the country's longest underground navigable river and is one of the longest documented caves (15th) in the United States. To date over 20 miles of passageways have been mapped, but there is additional unexplored branching.

Bluespring Caverns were formed by underground streams cutting through and down into the limestone to reach the level of the East Fork of the White River beginning approximately one million years ago. It was later altered by the influence of melting glaciers. The deep stream water in the cave flows into the White River. This opening on the river was a former 19th century entrance before nearby dam construction flooded the entry. Besides boating, the deep water provides a suitable habitat for cave faunal life. Bluespring Caverns has the distinction of having one of the largest and northernmost populations (2,000-3,000) of the rare and endangered northern cave blindfish.

The tour begins with a ticket purchase at the hospitality center gift shop. Tours leave every hour or more often and the last tour of the day leaves at 5 pm. There are uncrowded weekdays when you may enjoy a personal tour of the caverns. A sweater will be necessary since the cave is cool year around 52 degrees. The tour is 'natural' and not contrived show business with colored lights.

Once entering the sinkhole cavern entry you descend a staircase to awaiting johnboats with electric motors. There are few formations in the relatively young cave. Elephant Head, Devil's Backbone and the Quarry Room are the most notable. It is possible to see blind cavefish, blind crayfish, cave salamander and an occasional bat. The informative guide continues past the Rock of Gibraltar 600 feet and turns the boat around just beyond the Diamond Flowstone, a glittering crystalline formation.

Bluespring Caverns is open daily 9 am to 6 pm May 1st to September 30th. The cavern tour is also open weekends during the months of April and October. Group rates are available. To reach Bluespring Caverns drive 1/2 mile southwest on US 50 after its intersection with SR 37 south of Bedford. Turn right or west at Hartleville onto Stumphole Bridge Road 450S and drive 1/2 mile west to the entrance drive.

If adventuresome, continue on Stumphole Bridge Road 450S west to the "T" road and turn right and then left across the Stumphole Bridge and the East Fork White River to the town of Williams and the Williams Dam State Fishing Area. The area to walkabout is small but there is a boat launch and boat rentals, swimming, fishing, primitive camping and of course the dam which is especially popular with fishermen. Approximately 1.5 miles west of Williams straddling the White River fork is Williams Covered Bridge, the longest Indiana covered bridge in use that you may still cross in a vehicle. Built in 1884, the bridge is worth seeing while in the area.

If you return to US 50 from Bluespring Caverns instead and were considering visiting Martin State Forest stop at Tincher Pond enroute. This national forest property is just off the US 50 highway near halfway between Bryantsville and the junction of US 50 and SR 60 on the right or north side of the road. There is a inconspicuous circle driveway that allows parking for 2 or 3 cars. Tincher Pond, a local fishing spot, is just west of the circle drive and there is a fisherman's path that encircles the pond. Tincher Pond makes an ideal place to stretch your legs.

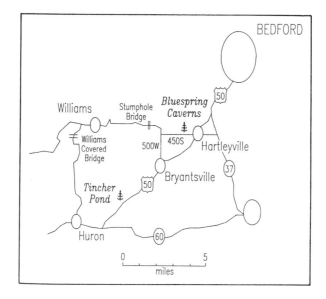

25. SPRING MILL STATE PARK

Mithchell, IN/Lawrence County
USGS MAP(S): Mitchell 1:24,000
TRAIL(S) DISTANCE: 5 moderate to rugged trails total 6 3/8 miles
ACREAGE: 1,319 acres
ACTIVITIES: hiking, nature study, picnicking, shelterhouses, nature
    center, naturalist programs, cave tours, nature preserves, saddle
    barn, bridle trails, boating (electric), canoeing, fishing, olympic
    swimming pool, bathhouse, playgrounds, tennis courts, cultural arts
    program, Class A & C, youth, and group camping, dumping station,
    camp store, concessions, restored Pioneer Village, Spring Mill Inn,
    Virgil I. Grissom Memorial
FEE(S): entrance, shelterhouse rental, rowboat, canoe and paddleboats
    rental, horse rental, Twin Caves boat tour, pool fee, camping,
    Spring Mill Inn

Founded in 1927, Spring Mill State Park is rich in natural and social
history. Five day hikes connect the restored 1817 "living history" pioneer
village of Spring Mill, Spring Mill Lake and Inn, Donaldson Cave and
Woods Nature Preserves, Twin Caves, Bronson Cave and the Virgil I.
Grissom Memorial.

Trail 1 is a 3/8 mile short loop that is seemingly designed for the
guests and visitors at the Spring Mill Inn to access Trails 4 and 5. The
marked trailhead begins on the west side of the Inn and descends to join
with Trail 4 at the hillside bottom. While Trail 4 heads to the Wilson
Memorial and Donaldson Cave, Trail 1 heads north or right and follows
alongside Donaldson branch and Spring Mill Lake. The trail turns uphill
to return to the Inn where it joins the main park road and Trailhead #5
around Spring Mill Lake.

Trail 2 is a moderate 1/2 mile linear ridgeside trail that connects Pine
Hill picnic shelter, the nature center and boat docks with the Pioneer
Village parking area. The trail surface is wood chipped and well
maintained.

Trail 3 is a 2.5 mile rugged hike that loops around the most natural
section of the park. This nature walk may be accessed on the south side
of Spring Mill Inn parking garage, the Twin Caves parking area, and/or
Donaldson Picnic parking area. Be advised there are several park road
crossings.

Starting at the Twin Caves parking area you may head down the
limestone steps (WPA erected) to Twin Caves where cave boat tours are
conducted April thru October. A narrow, flat-bottomed, square-ended
john-boat is hand maneuvered by the park guide up the stream into the
limestone cavern 500 feet to view formations and faunal life. This is a
fine trip with children on a hot summer day.

Follow Trail 3 downstream past Bronson Cave since it may be only
explored with a park naturalist. The trail continues on through a young
wooded section to arrive at the park road just north of the gatehouse.
Cross over and follow the trail north through beech-maple woodland
about 1/4 mile to the Virgil I. Grissom Memorial. Actually the trail does
not connect here but the Memorial is hardly out of the way. Virgil or
"Gus" Grissom, 2nd astronaut in space, is a Mitchell born native who

Mill, Spring Mill State Park

enjoyed many boyhood hours at the state park. In 1967, he and two other astronauts, were killed in a fire aboard Apollo I, the first manned Apollo flight. The Memorial, open 9 am to 5 pm daily, contains his personal memorabilia including the "Molly Brown" Gemini III space capsule.

Continue north recrossing the park road from the Memorial through the woodland, crossing over the park road once more to the Donaldson Cave Overlook. From there follow the ridgebluff north towards the Inn. The trail curves east and crosses the park road twice before reaching Donaldson's Woods. Sinkholes abound in this area. The nature preserve is a 67 acre virgin mixed forest of beech-maple and oak-hickory. The forest is considered a classic example of primeval Indiana and recognized as a National Natural Landmark. The State Tree, tulip poplar is the largest and the white oak is common. Trail 3 ends at the Twin Caves parking area.

Trail 4 is a rugged 2 mile loop that begins at the Donaldson's picnic parking area. Go west past Hamer Pioneer Cemetery and descend the wooden stairs to Hamer Cave, the water source that powers the pioneer village grist and sawmill. Follow the cascading Mill Creek streamside to the 1817 pioneer village where the numerous log buildings shelter a carpenter shop, tavern distillery, nursery mill office, blacksmith shop, apothecary shop, post office, springhouse, several homes, and the grist and sawmill and pioneer museum. A authentic pioneer herb and flower garden has also been reconstructed in the Virginia landscape style. Corn milled from the grist-mill and loom products from the Sheeks House are for public sale.   Pioneer products can be purchased at the Vigil I. Grissom Memorial gift shop.

Trail 4 continues past the restrooms turning right at the Munson log cabin, heading uphill alongside the ridge.   Continue alongside the ridge past Butternut Grove Shelter and concession area, past Sycamore Shelterhouse to curve south to join with Trail 1 to the Inn.   Continue walking upstream along the Donaldson branch to the fence enclosed Alexander Wilson Monument that was erected by George Donaldson in 1866 to honor the "Father of American Ornithology".   Continue up the ravine gorge to Donaldson's Cave Nature Preserve (6 acres).   Donaldson Stream flows freely from the large scenic cave entrance where on the sloping hillside above, prairie wildflowers thrive.   You may enter and explore the dry portion of the cave but further exploration is permitted only with the park naturalist. Indiana University Professor Dr. Eigenmann conducted his renowned blind cave fish studies here.   The trail climbs up and out of the gorge to return to the Donaldson's picnic parking area.

Trail 5 is a mile of moderate walking that encircles the 30 acre Spring Mill Lake.   Spring wildflowers abound on the east and north lakeshore. The nature center, boat dock (rental), and picnic area are located on the west shore.   The trail connects with Trail 2 to the Pioneer Village parking area.   The trailhead begins just south of the main park road bridge over Spring Mill Lake.

Spring Mill State Park is located 3 miles east of Mitchell on SR 60.

Dogwood Berries

Spring Mill State Park

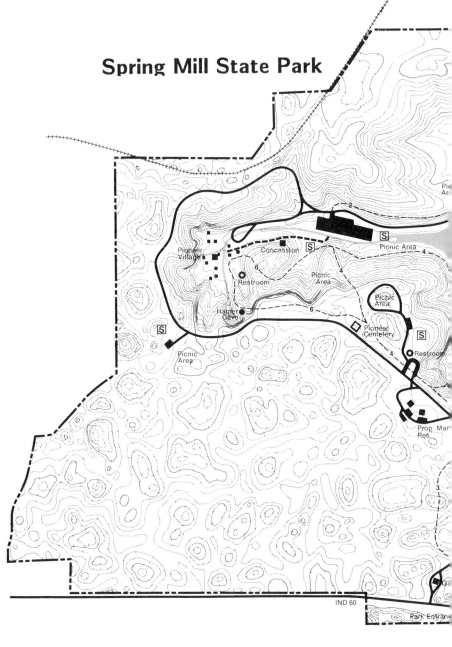

Pioneer Village

Concession

Picnic Area

Picnic Area

Restroom

Picnic Area

Hamer Cave

Picnic Area

Pioneer Cemetery

Restroom

Picnic Area

Prop. Mar. Res.

IND 60

Park Entrance

N

Contour Interval 10 Feet

1000　　0　　1000　　2000　　3000　　4000

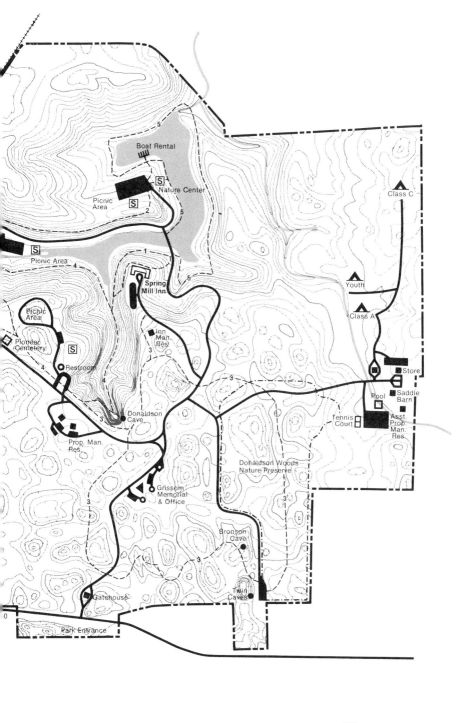

Boat Rental

Nature Center

S

Picnic Area

S

2

5

5

Class C

Picnic Area

S

4

1

Spring Mill Inn

Youth

5

Class A

Picnic Area

Pioneer Cemetery

S

Inn Man Res

3

Store

Restroom

4

3

Saddle Barn

Pool

4

Donaldson Cave

3

3

Tennis Court

Asst. Prop. Man. Res.

Prop. Man. Res.

Donaldson Woods Nature Preserve

Grissom Memorial & Office

3

3

Bronson Cave

3

Gatehouse

Twin Caves

0

Park Entrance

4000   5000   6000   7000 Feet

26. ORANGEVILLE RISE OF LOST RIVER
Orangeville, IN/Orange County
USGS MAP(S): Georgia 1:24,000
TRAIL(S) DISTANCE: no est. trails
ACREAGE: 3 acres
ACTIVITIES: nature study

The Orangeville Rise of the Lost River is a 100 foot wide artesian spring. This tributary of the Lost River "rises" or resurges once again after several miles of subterranean passage to surface at the base of a low limestone cliff in the village of Orangeville. The Lost River is a classic example of karst topography, a geologic name derived from Karst, Yugoslavia, where such irregular limestone features were first studied. Solutions or sinkholes have dissolved into the soft limestone streambed allowing the stream waters to flow or "dive" into a sink and tunnel underground for several miles. Twenty-two miles of meandering streambed has been left dry and now the underground river flows nearly due west, a much shorter route.

Although the Orangeville Rise is a tributary draining a 30 square mile area, the "true" or "main" rise is "found again" about a mile southwest of Orangeville on private property. After emergence the tributary flows southwest to merge with the main channel. This National Natural Landmark was purchased by The Nature Conservancy in 1972 and became a dedicated state nature preserve in 1975. No trails are available at this geological point of interest. At one time there was a proposal to create a Lost River National Monument that would have included swallow holes, dry stream beds, caverns, sinks, windows, rises and gulfs. These interesting karst topographical features would have been connected by scenic roads and nature trails.

The Orangeville Rise of Lost River is located on the south side of Orangeville along a county gravel road. Orangeville is located 5 miles northwest of Paoli and 7 miles west of Orleans in Orange County. From Paoli follow US 150/SR 56 west and turn north on Ames Chapel Road 550W. Follow 550W to 200N to 500W and proceed to Orangeville. From Orleans proceed south 3 miles on SR 37 and turn west on 500N or the Wesley Chapel Road and continue to Orangeville.

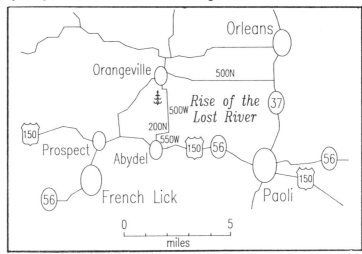

27. MARENGO CAVE PARK

Marengo, IN/ Crawford County
TRAIL(S) DISTANCE: 1 mile nature trail, 1 1/3 mile cave tours
ACREAGE: 120 acres
ACTIVITIES: nature trail, guided cave tours, swimming pool, horseback riding, shelterhouse, picnicking, canoeing, group buildings, primitive and RV camping, dumping station, gift shop, concessions, special group activities and packages
FEE(S): cave tours, camping, horseback trail rides, canoe rental, pool fee

Marengo Cave was discovered in 1883 by two children, Oris and Blanche Hiestand. Shortly thereafter, the cavern was explored and opened as a commercial "show" cave. Nature walkers will enjoy the underground Dripstone Trail and Crystal Palace Tours as well as the above ground nature trail that passes through a woodland over the caverns. It has been designated a National Natural Landmark.

The Crystal Palace Tour is a 1/3 mile long, 40 minute guided tour along level lighted walkways past massive formation filled rooms such as Queen's Palace and Rock of Ages. Near the end of the tour, a special subterranean pageant is featured in the Crystal Palace Room. There are plenty of stalagmites, stalactites, columns and speleotherms.

The Dripstone Trail is 1 mile in length and the guided tour requires about 70 minutes to complete. The huge dry corridors lead visitors past nearly ageless, delicate formations. Of special interest are the rimstone pools, "soda straws" and draperies such as the Indian Blanket. Orchestra bands once performed in the vastness of Musical Hall. Both guided tours are arranged 20 to 30 minutes apart. The marked, self-guiding, one mile above ground nature trail loop features interpretive markers of geological and botanical interest.

Marengo Cave Park is open all year except Thanksgiving and Christmas Days. The park hours are from 9:00 am - 6:00 pm, Memorial Day to Labor Day. The rest of the year the hours are from 9:00 am to 5:00 pm. Be advised the cave is a cool 52° degrees year around. Sweaters and light coats will help make your visit comfortable. To reach Marengo Cave Park from I-64 exit north via SR 66 to Marengo and turn east and drive one quarter mile to the park entrance on SR 64.

Manager, Marengo Cave Park, POB 217, Marengo, IN 47140

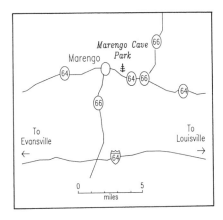

197

28. BUFFALO TRACE PARK

Palmyra, IN/Harrison County
U.S.G.S. MAP(S): Palmyra 1:24,000
TRAIL(S) DISTANCE: 1/8 mile loop
ACREAGE: 146 acres
ACTIVITIES: hiking, nature study, picnicking, swimming, boating,
  fishing, biking, orchard, athletic fields & courts, concessions,
  primitive, modern and group camping
FEE(S): entrance, swimming, boat rental, reservation fee, camping

This north Harrison County Park offers a variety of activities in addition to hiking. A short loop nature trail is located in the campground. The forest trail encircles a wooded ridge with 10 plant identification stations. The wood chipped trail begins and ends across from Campground A's picnic shelter, restroom and parking lot. In addition walking around the grassy shore of the 29 acre lake makes a good half hour ramble. This park even has a orchard located between the main picnic shelter and athletic courts. The park is historically named for the former herds of buffalo who wore a trail or trace just south of SR 150.

From I-64 exit north at Corydon exit onto SR 135 and proceed to Palmyra. Buffalo Trace Park entrance is located 0.5 mile east of Palmyra.

29. HAYSWOOD NATURE PRESERVE

Corydon, IN/Harrison County
USGS MAP(S): Corydon West 1:24,000
TRAIL(S) DISTANCE: 3 miles total
ACREAGE: Hayswood 150 acres/Indian Creek Woods 116
ACTIVITIES: hiking, nature reserve, nature study, picnicking,
  shelterhouses, playground, lake and stream fishing, non-motorized
  boating
FEE(S): boat rental at 9 acre Hayswood Lake

The main features of this unique Harrison County day-use park are the 877 foot Pilot Knob, and the gorge and bluffs of Indian Creek. The forested north half of the Hayswood surrounding Pilot Knob has state of Indiana nature preserve status. The other half of the reserve is mowed grassy open spaces for general recreation. Located just west of Corydon, the land was a gift to the county from Samuel P. Hays.

Three interconnecting loop trails ascend the wooded rock slopes and summit of the rounded isolated hill and adjacent floodplain of Indian Creek: Woodland Trail, Geology Loop and the Conservation Trail.

The Woodland Trail is a 1/4 mile paved loop that begins at the first parking lot with a picnic shelter and information sign. The all-weather surface is accessible to handicapped visitors. Numerous hardwood trees are sign identified by common name. Halfway, the Woodland Trail intersects with the Geology and Conservation Trails.

The Geology Trail heads uphill to Pilot Knob through an immature forest with limestone rock outcrops and vistas of Corydon. There are also bluffside views into Indian Creek several feet below. The unmarked overgrown trail loops down the west slope to the Woodland Trail or retrace your original uphill steps downhill.

The Conservation Trail features various labelled species of pine and hardwood plantations and demonstration plots along the west bank of Indian Creek. The 1/2 mile moderate trail begins at the second parking lot beyond the entrance facing east. The earthen path proceeds down along the hillside to an open abandoned field that is revegetating. The obvious unmarked trail leads uphill though the forested slope to join the Geology and Woodland Trails. Another obvious spur follows the forest-field edge to Indian Creek. The trail follows the creek north a short ways before it dead ends. Watch for poison ivy. Retrace your steps.

The Harrison County Parks and Recreation Department also owns 116 acres on the east side of Indian Creek, also a gift from Samuel Hays. The steep wooded bluffs make access from Hayswood Nature Reserve nearly impossible. Access may be attained from south Corydon via Lincoln Road.

Besides walking there is picnicking, playgrounds, boat rental and canoeing. Hayswood Nature Reserve is open year around from 8:00 am-dusk. The reserve entrance is located one mile south of SR 135 from the stop light at the junction of SR 135 and SR 62 at Corydon. From I-64 exit south on SR 135 and drive 2 1/2 miles to the entrance on the east side of the highway.

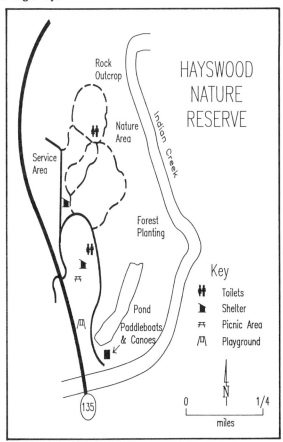

199

30. BATTLE OF CORYDON PARK
Corydon, IN/Harrison County
USGS MAP(S): Corydon West, Corydon East 1:24,000
TRAIL(S) DISTANCE: 1/4 mile trail loop
ACREAGE: 5 acres
ACTIVITIES: nature walk, historical site

This small historical Harrison County park is situated on the south edge of Corydon and is listed on the National Register of Historical Places. Besides Gettysburg, the only other Civil War battle fought in the northern states was the Battle of Corydon.

A log cabin dating from the 1860's sets in the middle of the deciduous wooded park. The wide grassy easy pathway begins and ends at the cabin. Mature oak, hickory, black walnut and elm comprise the forest stand that is gradually being surrounded by suburban development.

Interpretive markers have been placed near the cabin that describe the battle. On July 8th, 1863 John Hunt Morgan and 2,500 calvary men crossed the Ohio River into Indiana. The Confederates were met by 500 men of the Corydon Home Guard just one mile south of town the next morning but were easily defeated by the sheer number of "Morgan's Raiders". After 18 days of giving chase, Morgan and his horse soldiers surrendered to Federal cavalry troops near New Lisbon, Ohio.

The park is open to motor vehicles from April 1st to October 1st, but visitors may park at the locked gate where room is available for 2 or 3 cars. It is about a 60 yard walk to the cabin and trail.

The Battle of Corydon park is located one mile south of Corydon on Old SR 135. While near town other historical landmarks of interest include the Constitutional Elm Memorial (actually only an enclosed stump of the former tree), the first Indiana Capitol Building and the Governor William Hendrick residence where a 19th century herb and flower garden beautifies a small courtyard.

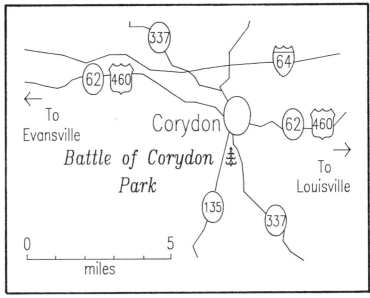

31. SOUTH HARRISON PARK
Elizabeth, IN/Harrison County
USGS MAP(S): Laconia 1:24,000
TRAIL(S) DISTANCE: 2 miles of moderate trail loops
ACREAGE: 220 acres
ACTIVITIES: hiking, nature study, picnicking, shelterhouses,
    playground, swimming pool, bathhouse, concessions, miniature golf,
    ballfields, tennis courts, shuffleboard, basketball courts,
    horseshoe pit
FEE(S): gate entrance, swimming, mini-golf, shelter reservation, ball
    diamond and pool reservation

First opened in spring of 1980, South Harrison Park is basically an
active facility park within a passive natural setting. Wide, well worn
trails wind through the mixed hardwood forest south and west of the
picnic shelter. Several woodland paths interconnect throughout the
wildlife sanctuary. Birding is good because of the meadow edge and
forest habitats. Trail signs exist but are unmarked in places. Be
venturesome. The park's woods is bordered by playfields and on the
south by Rehoboth Road. South Harrison Park is a fine Harrison county
facility that is open to motor traffic from April 1st to November 1st.
Foot traffic always welcome.
    The park is located 4 miles southwest of Elizabeth on SR 11. Follow
the directional signs to the entrance. Trailhead parking has been
provided at the two picnic shelterhouses parking lots.

32. SQUIRE BOONE CAVERNS AND VILLAGE
Corydon, IN/Harrison County
USGS MAP(S): Mauckport 1:24,000
TRAIL(S) DISTANCE: 1/2 mile cave tour, 1 mile nature trail
ACREAGE: 110 acres
ACTIVITIES: group cave tours, nature trail, picnicking, shelterhouse,
    playground, petting zoo, concessions, seasonal grist mill, seasonal
    pioneer village stores
FEE(S): seasonal entrance, cave tours

Squire Boone would probably never have dreamed his land and caverns
would someday become a commercial tourist attraction. Hunter, explorer,
trail blazer, Indian fighter, Baptist minister, and brother of the more
renowned Daniel Boone, Squire first discovered the caverns on a hunting
expedition in 1790. Leaving Kentucky in 1804, he remembered the large
spring that flowed from the cave and settle there to build a grist mill
and raise a family, the first in Harrison County. In 1815 he died of
dropsy and was buried in a small cave on the property where he once hid
to escape an Indian war party.
    Like all the other 500 Indiana caves, Squire Boone Caverns were
formed by erosion of the limestone bedrock. The informative tour guide
points out various formations or speleotherms as stalactites, stalagmites,
soda straws, flowstone, cave pearls, helictites, columns, draperies,
refection pools, blind crayfish, an underground river, waterfalls, and

rimstone dams. The 2,400 foot long cave has the largest rimstone formation in the world. Special areas of the caverns include the Lunar Terrace, Fountains of the Deep waterfalls, the Grand Canyon, Rock of Ages column, and the Rotunda Cathedral room. The final steps of the tour ascend a stairwell to emerge at the gift and souvenir shop starting-point-of-departure.

Squire Boone Caverns are open to the public for one hour cave tours that leave every 20 minutes during season, and at 10:00 am, 12:00 noon, 2:00 pm, and 4:00 pm during off season. The hours from May to October are from 9:00 am - 6:00 pm. March, April, November and December hours are from 9:30 am - 5:00 pm. During January and February 10:00 am-5:00 pm. Memorial Day, July 4th, and Labor Day weekends are from 9:00 am - 7:00 pm. The caverns are closed Christmas and Thanksgiving Days.

Probably the most interesting building for natural historians is the Indian Relic Museum that displays historical dioramas and artifacts of the first inhabitants on the land. Additional places of interest to visit include the restored 1804 water-powered grist mill, petting zoo and rock shop. There is plenty of food available. Picnic tables, shelterhouse and playground are provided. The Village is opened from Memorial Day to Labor Day 10:00 am - 6:00 pm. During the months of September and October weekends only from 11:00 am - 5:00 pm.

The Squire Boone Trail loop begins at the north side of the rock shop yard at the Village. Special natural features along the one mile easy to moderate marked trail are Squire Boone and Jing a Ling waterfalls, and the original Squire Boone burial cave and memorial stone. To reach Squire Boone Caverns and Village drive south on SR 135 from Corydon past the village of Central to Boone Cavern Road. Turn east onto Boone Cavern Road and proceed to Squire Boone Cavern Road and the village entrance. Look for the rustic humor directional signs along the county road east of SR 135.

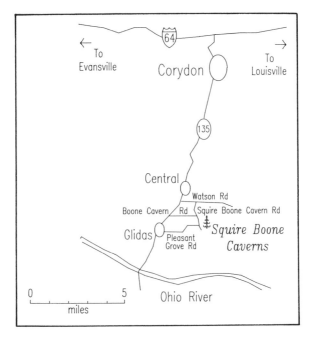

Squire Boone Grist Mill

33. FERN CLIFF
Reelsville, IN/Putman County
USGS MAP(S): Reelsville 1:24,000
TRAIL(S) DISTANCE: trails to be est., follow old roads
ACREAGE: 115 acres
ACTIVITIES: hiking, nature study. photography

Fern Cliff is a declared National Natural Landmark recognized for its botanical treasures of ferns, mosses and liverworts that are found thriving on steep sandstone blocks and cliffs adjacent to Snake Creek. A service road begins at the locked gate and mini-parking lot. Follow the service road downhill past the old house, keeping on the now obvious trail. Less than a 1/4 mile is Fern Cliff. Views looking downward into the bowl-shaped canyon are breath-taking. A former sandstone quarry is situated to the immediate west.

Follow the ridge trail down to the stream bottom to access the cliff and quarry. Other parts of the property include immature mixed wooded ravines that slope northeast to Snake Creek. Retrace your steps.

From I-70 about 10 miles east of Brazil exit SR 243 north and drive about 3 miles to the junction with US 40/Old National Road. Go west and drive 6.5 miles to Pleasant Gardens. Turn north at Pleasant Gardens and go 1 mile and turn right/north at the "Y" onto 625W and travel nearly 2 miles to a "T" road, 500S. Go right/east 1/4 mile to a 2nd "T". Turn left/north and drive 2.2 miles looping west to the preserves's gate entrance across from a farmhouse. State nature preserve markers line the property en route.

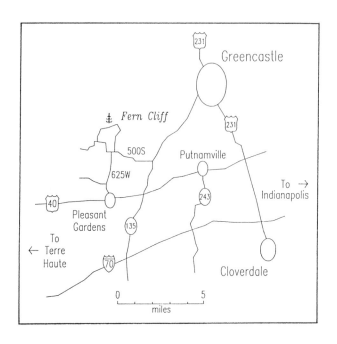

34. CATARACT FALLS & RICHARD LIEBER SRA / CAGLE MILL LAKE

Cataract, Cunot, Cloverdale, IN/ Owen and Putnam Counties
USGS MAP(S): Cataract, Poland, Reelsville, Cloverdale 1:24,000
TRAIL(S) DISTANCE: Cataract Falls; 1 mile one-way
ACREAGE: 8,283 land, 1,400 water
ACTIVITIES: nature study, swimming, Hulman Beach, lifeguard, bathhouse, marina, boating, boat ramp, water skiing, year around fishing, hunting, picnicking, shelter-houses, playground, grocery store, Class A-B-C, youth, rally camping, dumping station, wild food foraging
FEE(S): entrance, camping, boat mooring, boat rental

There are no established hiking trails in this vast state recreation area, however, Cataract Falls, Cagles Mill Spillway and Dam are two sites the nature walker will enjoy visiting.

Located at the eastern end of the reservoir on Mill Creek, Cataract Falls has the unique distinction of being the largest waterfall in Indiana. The word cataract is given to waterfalls of considerable size and are typical of young valleys. Actually there are two falls. The upper and lower falls are highly scenic year around and easily accessible either by driving or on foot.

Upon entering the Cataract Falls State Recreation Area a parking lot is situated on the west bank adjacent to the upper falls. An observation point has been established for viewing the larger picturesque upper falls, however, you can climb down past the old mill race to the bottom of the falls for closer inspection. From here or from the bank above, proceed downstream one mile alongside the riparian shore and through the white pine plantation to the lower falls. The unmarked path has been trodden by numerous hikers and has good surface and no brushy obstructions.

Historically, the Ten O'Clock Line Treaty of 1809 passes directly thru the middle of the lower falls. North of the line was Indian Territory and south of it three million acres opened up to American pioneer settlement. If the water level is low, inspect the stream bottom where the cascading waters have over time carved troughs in the limestone. Below the lower falls is the beginning of the 1,400 acre Cagles Mill Reservoir. Retrace your steps to the upper falls and the parking area. Picnicking and fishing are also popular activities at Cataract Falls.

Cagles Mill Spillway and Dam are located at the western end of the reservoir. The spillway acts as an emergency passageway for surplus flood waters. This ten acre spillway cut exposes outstanding Pleistocene and Pennsylvanian geological fossils, especially on the north side. Remnants of giant scale trees that grew up to 100 feet high over 230 million years ago have been preserved, such as stigmaria and lepidodendron. Various forms of gastropods or snails, coal seams, glacial till and other geological wonders are abundant. Two ancient stream channels have carved their passage in the coarse grained Mansfield sandstone. The spillway cut and its geological treasures of the past is considered to be of regional significance to professional geologists.

Dogwoods in Bloom

Near the south side of the dam a paved road veers left and descends to the bottom tailwater of the earthen and concrete impoundment and Mill Creek. A picnic area and the lovely St. Genevieve Ravine are located at this site. The heavily shaded and damp ravine provides a suitable habitat for an abundance of mosses, fungi and ferns. Worthy of exploration, there are waterfalls, rapids, riffles, and ample second growth forest cover. Rare ferns, liverworts, spleenwort and aquatic mosses have been discovered here. About 1/2 mile downstream is the original Cagles Mill building and its damsite that is now a general store. Above, on the Dam road is an observation overlook of Cagles Mill Lake.

The main recreation area near Cunot SRA does not have designated hiking trails but there is camping, swimming, boating and other active recreational activities.

To reach Cataract Falls SRA from Interstate 70 exit at Cloverdale and drive south on SR 231 approximately 10 miles and turn west onto Owen County Road 1050N. Continue driving west for about 1.5 miles to the "T" road and turn left, or south, until arriving at the historic Covered Bridge built in 1876. The entrance is just beyond the Covered Bridge.

To reach the main recreation area from I-70 exit south from Cloverdale on SR 231 and turn west after 3 miles onto SR 42. Continue west on SR 42 to Cunot and turn north onto SR 243 and drive about 2 miles to the marked entrance on the west side of the road.

To reach Cagles Mill Spillway and Dam Site continue the drive west on SR 42 to 830W and follow the signs northward. (For map, see Owen Putnam State Forest).

Upper Cataract Falls

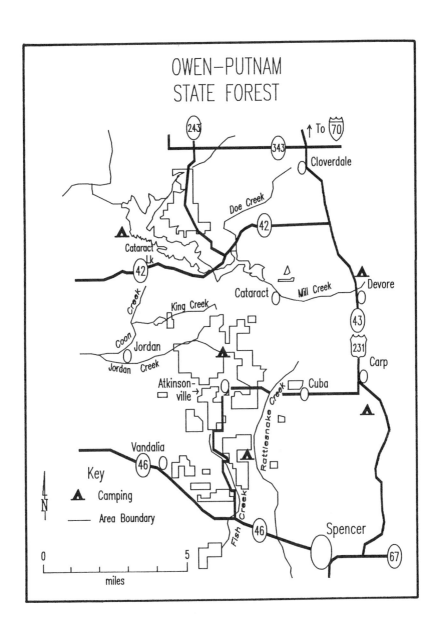

OWEN–PUTNAM
STATE FOREST

243

343 ↑ To 70

Cloverdale

Doe Creek

42

Cataract
Lk

42

Cataract

Mill Creek

Devore

43

231

Carp

Creek

King Creek

Coon

Jordan

Jordan   Creek

Atkinson-
ville →

Cuba

Rattlesnake Creek

Vandalia

46

Key

N

Camping

Area Boundary

Spencer

67

Fish Creek

0   5

miles

35. OWEN-PUTNAM STATE FOREST

Vandalia, IN / Owen County

USGS MAP(S): Cataract, Spencer, Poland, Patricksburg, Cloverdale
    1:24,000

TRAIL(S) DISTANCE: 15 miles firelanes, 1/2 mile Poplar Top Trail

ACREAGE: 6,462 acres

ACTIVITIES: hiking, bridle trails, nature study, picnicking, fishing,
    wild plant foraging, hunting, primitive camping, horse camp

FEE(S): camping

Established in 1947, the broken tracts of Owen-Putnam State Forests are found mainly north of Vandalia and south of Cunot in north central Owen County. There are approximately 15 miles of interconnecting loops, easy-to-rugged trails that follow logging and fire service roads. These trailroads have been designated bridle trails and hikers may also use them. Those willing to explore these public multiple use lands will need a compass, topographical maps and/or property map. Unmarked bridle trails begin and end near the horsemens campground.

The Fish Creek Road campsites have water and the 1/2 mile Poplar Top foot trail. The moderate loop heads up between campsite #9 and #10. The grassy firelane trail encircles plantations of yellow poplar and pine and young mixed woods with plenty of dogwood. Wildlife ponds have been constructed and stocked. Foot bridges and water bars have been placed along the trail. There are many pine species of red, white, pitch and scotch. European larch and cypress have been planted.

Entrance to the Fish Creek primitive campground and horsemens camp is north of SR 46, 5 miles west of Spencer. Just before Vandalia on SR 46 west of Spencer, go north on Fish Creek Road/CR 450 about 1/2 mile to the campground. Horsemens camp is further north on Fish Creek Road. Follow the black and gold directional signs. October to January is the main hunting season when deer, turkey, quail, rabbit, and squirrel are taken.

Property Manager, Owen-Putnam State Forest
RR 4, Box 214, Spencer, IN 47460, (812) 829-2462

36. GREEN'S BLUFF

FREEMAN, IN/OWEN COUNTY

USGS MAP(S): Freedom, 1:24,000

TRAIL(S) DISTANCE: old woods road .5 mile one-way

ACREAGE: 115 acres

ACTIVITIES: hiking, nature study, photography

A delightful place to visit year around, Green's Bluff provides some of the best scenery in southern Indiana. The place name, "Green's Bluff", refers to James Green who built a mill along Raccoon Creek just upstream from the bluff in the 1840's and whose foundation may still be seen. The place name may as easily be applied to the evergreen grove of large eastern hemlock trees that thrive on the cool north facing sandstone bluffs. Smaller hemlock are also found in the understory of the south facing bluffs where oak, hickory and several sizeable red cedars thrive. Rare and endangered Indiana plants include the hay-scented fern, goldenseal, pinesap, spotted wintergreen, mountain spleenwort and eastern hemlock. Easy to identify, the eastern or Canadian hemlock (Tsuga canadensis) has delicate bell-shaped, light-brown cones that have at twig's end and needles with silver undersides. Rich in wildlife, a variety of animals make their home here amidst the undisturbed surroundings.

The trailhead or woodland road begins near the parking area adjacent to Hedding Cemetery. Follow the gradual grade of the old logging road to the right as it winds down to the bottom of Raccoon Creek and Green's Bluff. The surface of the road is clay and can be very muddy and slick after a rain or a winter's thaw. There are other sidetrails or spurs that will also lead down to Raccoon Creek through the woodland. A power line swath more or less marks the east and south boundaries. The boundaries of the preserve are marked by yellow oak leaf signs of The Nature Conservancy, who owns and manages the land. Please remember the preserve is protected for all to enjoy. The hemlock relict forest was once common in Indiana 10,000 years ago when surroundings appeared more like the Upper Peninsula of Michigan.

To reach Green's Bluff from Bloomington, drive west on SR 48 to the village of Whitehall and then northward on SR 43 to Freeman. Continue driving north through Freeman and turn west onto the first road past the Clay Township fire station or the Sherfield Road/CR 525S. Drive approximately 2 miles to the "T" road and turn left on 75E and proceed about 0.5 mile to the Hedding Cemetery. You will see the wooden nature preserve sign of The Nature Conservancy and parking area just beyond the cemetery.

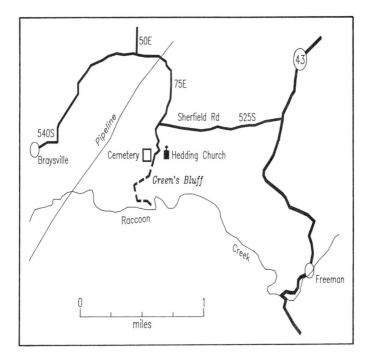

Red Cedar, Green's Bluff

37. CEDAR BLUFFS
Harrodsburg, IN/Monroe County
USGS MAP(S): Clear Creek 1:24,000
TRAIL DISTANCE: approx. 1 mile
ACREAGE: 23 acres
ACTIVITIES: hiking, nature study, photography

Cedar Bluffs aptly describes this highly scenic botanical and geological rich preserve that is owned by The Nature Conservancy. Windblown and sculptured by the elements, eastern red cedars dominate the 100 foot high and narrow Mississippian limestone bluffs that overlook the Clear Creek valley. The unmarked but well worn trail begins at the wire fence across from the Ketcham Road shoulder pullout where there is limited parking for 3 to 5 cars.

The trail briefly passes through an open herbaceous meadow to the north bank of Clear Creek. Follow the rock strewn path downstream along the sloping north bank at the base of the bluffs to the confluence of Clear Creek and a unnamed tributary stream. Over the past 1,000 years or so, these two streams have downcut the soft limestone rock and created the present day valley and half canyon bluffs. At the confluence the trail swings upwards along the tapered eastern point of the promontory to the flattop summit. The bonsai appearing cedars appear to be growing out of the weathered rocky outcrops. From this inspiring point, the spacious vista presents a sweeping panorama of photogenic western skies and sunsets. Several oak species thrive there as well as a smattering of redbud and ash trees. The path continues west along the crescent-shaped, widening ridgetop and the preserve's property boundary, and ends a few yards before the power transmission line swath. Although it would be natural to follow the grassy road lane west to Ketcham Road, it crosses private property. Please follow the preserve trail winding down the steep hill.

To reach Cedar Bluffs from Bloomington drive south on SR 37 and exit west on Ketcham Road. Proceed west on Ketcham Road to the preserve just before crossing Clear Creek and the Monon railroad track. Available parking is alongside the road. The preserve is 11 miles south of the Bloomington courthouse and 2.5 miles northwest of Harrodsburg.

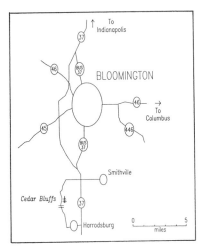

211

38. MARTIN STATE FOREST: OVERVIEW

Located 4 miles northeast of Shoals, the Martin County Seat on US highway 50, Martin State Forest was established in the 1930's from overexploited farmland. Open all year, the 6,000 plus hilly and rugged acres are mostly forested and serve as a timber, recreational and educational public resource. The visitor may discover hiking, nature studies, wild foraging, hunting, picnicking, shelterhouses, playgrounds, 26 Class C primitive campsites, canoeing or trolling and fishing on the 3 small lakes of Pine, Hardwood and Martin.

For the hiker there are four short and varied day trips and 20 miles of unmarked firelanes to explore. Ideally it is best to visit for a weekend and camp overnight. The Woodland Education and Arboretum trails are informative short distance trails with excellent trail surface. The 2 mile Three Lakes Trail that connects Pine, Hardwood, and Martin Lakes follows maintained firelanes and requires some uphill/downhill walking. The 3 mile Tank Spring is the premier hiking trail of the property with its scenic cliffside boulder breakdown and social history of the spring. Firelanes #18 and #12 traverse a ridge near a river bend of the East Fork of the White River. Firelanes #6 and #19 are also recommended for hiking. Firelane #17 north leads to Old Man's Nose along the riverbluff but crosses private property. There are additional property tracts north of the previously described main tract and east of the village of Trinity Springs. Maps and brochures of the state forest and further information is available from the forest office between Martin and Hardwood Lakes. The main entrance is on the north side of US 50 four miles east of Shoals.

TRIP 1: MARTIN STATE FOREST

Hoosier Woodland Arboretum
USGS MAP(S): Shoals 1:24,000
TRAIL(S) DISTANCE: 1,200 feet
ACREAGE: 3 acres
ACTIVITIES: nature study, tree identification

Created in 1981, the Hoosier Woodland Arboretum provides an informal representation of over 50 common Indiana woodland trees in a compact natural setting. This easy self-guiding loop trail is located just south of the state forest office adjacent to the main park road. Parking for 5 or 6 vehicles is situated across the road from the trailhead or available at the nearby park office.

Oak and hickory tree species predominate and there are several pine species. Eventually the arboretum will be planted to include nearly 50 additional woodland specimens. The east boundary of the arboretum borders the Woodland Education Trail making it easy access if you care to continue walking.

The arboretum includes the following woody species:

Chestnut Oak	Cherrybark Oak
Red Pine	Swamp Chestnut Oak
Osage Orange	Black Willow
Shingle Oak	Ohio Buckeye
Jack Pine	Boxelder Maple
Virginia Pine	Flowering Dogwood
White Pine	Bald Cypress
American Elm	Paw Paw
Red Cedar	Sycamore
Red Mulberry	Hackberry
Sassafras	Black Oak
Sugar Maple	Scotch Pine
American Beech	Red Maple
White Ash	Bitternut Hickory
Redbud	Pignut Hickory
Black Walnut	Shagbark Hickory
Sweet Gum	River Birch
Green Ash	Basswood, American
Burr Oak	Devil's Walking Stick
Swamp White Oak	Red Oak
Silver Maple	White Oak
Shumard Oak	Ironwood
Black Gum	Black Oak
Blue Beech	Yellow Poplar
Black Locust	American Holly
Honey Locust	

TRIP 2: MARTIN STATE FOREST

Woodland Education Trail
USGS MAP(S): Shoals 1:24,000
TRAIL DISTANCE: 1 1/4 mile
ACTIVITIES: nature study, photography, woodland management practices, plant identification

Developed by the Young Adults Conservation Corps (YACC), the Woodland Education Trail is a easy self-guided loop trail well marked by yellow arrows blazed on posts and interpretive signs. Besides being enlightened about forestry, this is a fine way to explore on foot the provided forest facilities such as the firetower, picnic shelterhouse, playground and campground.

The trailhead and parking area is located at Martin Lake. The first half of the earth surfaced trail skirts south past Martin Lake, a Walnut Demonstration Plot and the Hoosier Arboretum to the base of the climbable Willow Valley firetower. The second half of the trail winds back north across the forest road, past Tower Hill Picnic Area, playground and campground to Martin lake. Information signs along the trail describe woodland forestry management practices such as timber stand improvement (TSI), site index, epicormic branching, fire cost, multiple stems, multiple use and wolf trees.

A booklet is available that identifies 24 tree species that are listed below:

Eastern White Pine (Pinus strobus)
Largetooth Aspen (Populus grandidentata)
Persimmon (Diospryros virginiana)
Sassafras (Sassafras albidum)
Eastern Red Cedar (Juniperus virginiana)
Black Willow (Salix nigra)
Pignut Hickory (Carya glabra)
Black Cherry (Prunus serotina)
Shagbark Hickory (Carya ovata)
Sugar maple (Acer saccharum)
Black Gum (Nyssa sylvatica)
American Elm (Ulmus americana)
Black Walnut (Juglans nigra)
American Beech (Fagus grandifolia)
White Ash (Fraxinus americana)
American Sycamore (Platanus occidentalis)
Flowering Dogwood (Cornus florida)
Redbud (Cercis canadensis)
Red Oak (Quercus rubra)
Black Oak (Quercus velutina)
White Oak (Quercus alba)
Tulip tree (Liriodendron tulipifera)
Scarlet Oak (Quercus coccinea)
Paw Paw (Asimina triloba)

TRIP 3: MARTIN STATE FOREST

Martin/Hardwood/Pine Lakes Trail
USGS MAP(S): Shoals 1:24,000
TRAIL DISTANCE: approx. 2 mile
ACTIVITIES: hiking, nature study

An enjoyable hike that ties together the 3 property lakes begins and ends at Martin Lake where trailhead parking is available for several vehicles. A fishermans path encircles each lake but most of the trail follows firelanes. Go south to north around Martin Lake and then follow the main park road north a short ways to the Hardwood Lake parking area. Descend 100 yards north across the dam of Hardwood Lake on firelane #5. Turn left or west at the junction with firelane #8 and continue past the numerous firelane access roads approximately 0.5 mile until you reach firelane #11. Go south 200 yards on firelane 11 to the northeast shore of the lake. Encircle the white and red pine shoreline of Pine lake. Retrace your steps and return to Hardwood lake. For the more adventurous, follow firelane #11 north and cross firelane #12 onto firelane #17 "out" to the Old Man's Nose rock outcrop along the East Fork of the White River. This crosses private property.

Once returned to Hardwood Lake follow the trail north around Hardwood Lake to firelane #6 and descend the hillside until the firelane nearly dead-ends with US 50. Turn right onto the conspicuous unmarked trail into woodland and head and follow it 100 yard to the "T". Turn right at the "T" and follow the trail to the Woodland Educational Trail, which will return you to Martin Lake. The trail is confusing in this section but if you happen to stray off the path continue to head uphill to the Tower Hill picnic and campground that are closely situated to Martin Lake.

TRIP 4: MARTIN STATE FOREST

Tank Spring Hiking Trail
USGS MAP(S): Shoals and Huron 1:24,000
TRAIL DISTANCE: 3 miles
ACTIVITIES: hiking, nature study, geology, social history

Labelled moderately rugged, the marked and well worn Tank Spring Trail was established in 1979 and expanded to its present day length in 1981 by the Young Adult Conservation Corps (YACC). Midpoint along the ridgeside trail is Tank Spring, a year-around flowing spring whose cool waters formerly filled a holding tank for steam powered engines of the Baltimore & Ohio locomotives at the Willow Valley stop. Today the spring waters flow freely into Beaver Creek.

The posted trailhead adjacent to a gravel county road has limited parking for about 3 vehicles. The trail heads uphill about 60 yards on a firelane road then follows along the ridgeside northeast thru mixed woods and ravines. After a easy 1 1/2 mile hike, the spring site is reached. Boulder outcroppings are outstanding along the steep hillside and streambottom. Continue uphill on the steep rocky trail to the ridgetop for a bird's eye view of the plant covered rock formations and the entire north slope cove. Follow the ridgetop southward across ravine and stream, thru pine and hardwoods, past wildlife ponds to the same firelane, turning right and descend the hill to the parking lot.

Tank Spring trailhead and parking lot is located approximately 2.5 miles southeast from the state forest office. From the main entrance at US 50 go directly across the road to SR 650 and descend the hill and turn left at the stop sign and the US Gypsum Plant. Go 1/4 mile on the gravel road and turn right or east and drive 1/2 mile to the posted trailhead parking lot on the left side of the gravel road.

Property Manager
Box 290
Shoals. IN 47581
(812) 247-3491

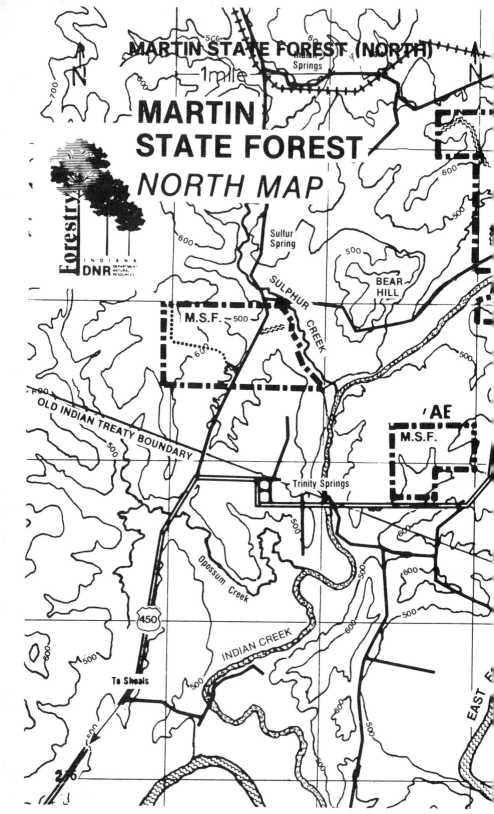

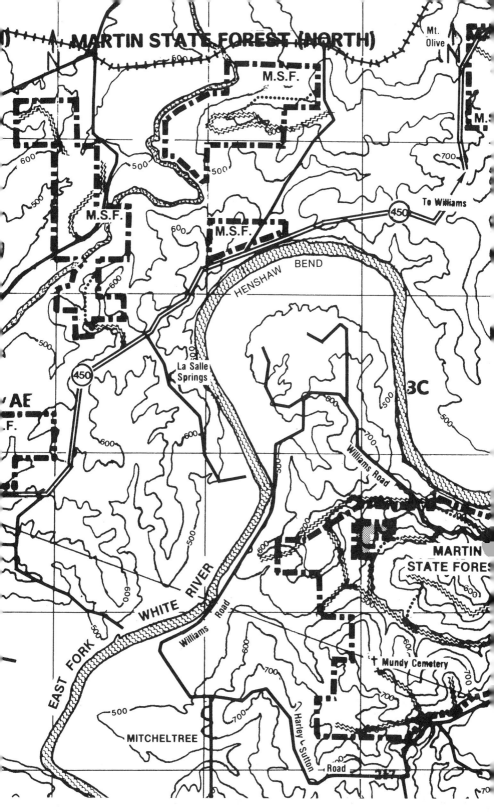

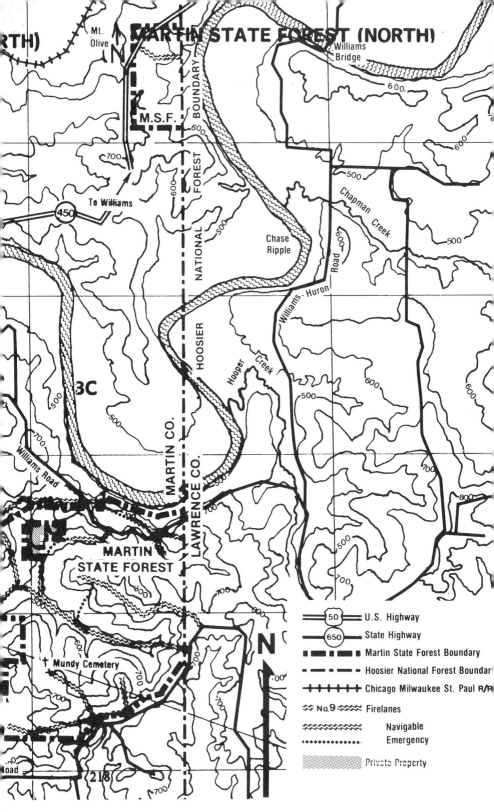

MARTIN STATE FOREST (NORTH)

	U.S. Highway
50	
650	State Highway
	Martin State Forest Boundary
	Hoosier National Forest Boundary
+++++++	Chicago Milwaukee St. Paul R/R
∼∼ No.9 ∼∼	Firelanes
∼∼∼∼∼	Navigable
∙∙∙∙∙∙∙∙∙	Emergency
	Private Property

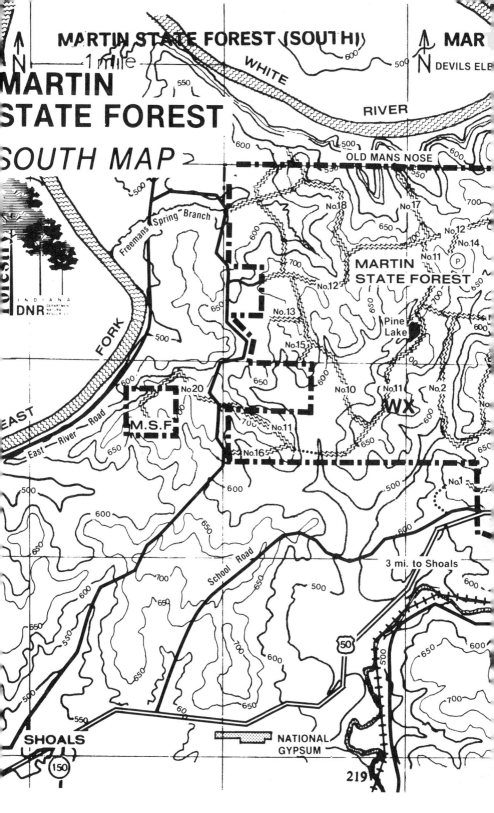

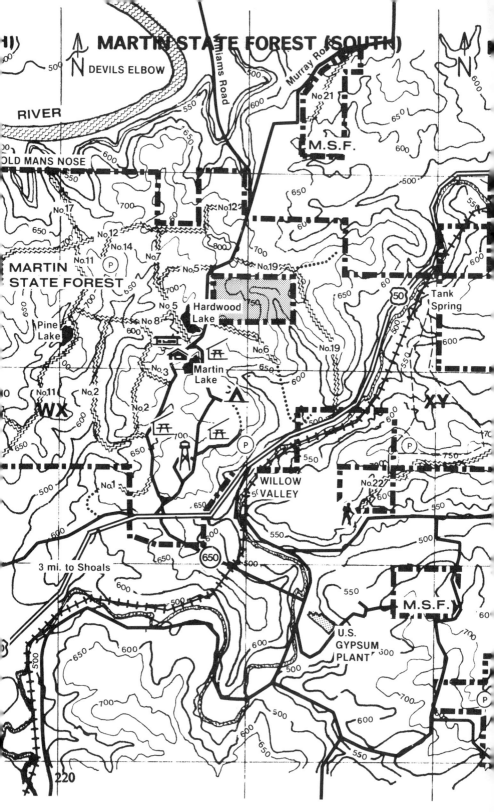

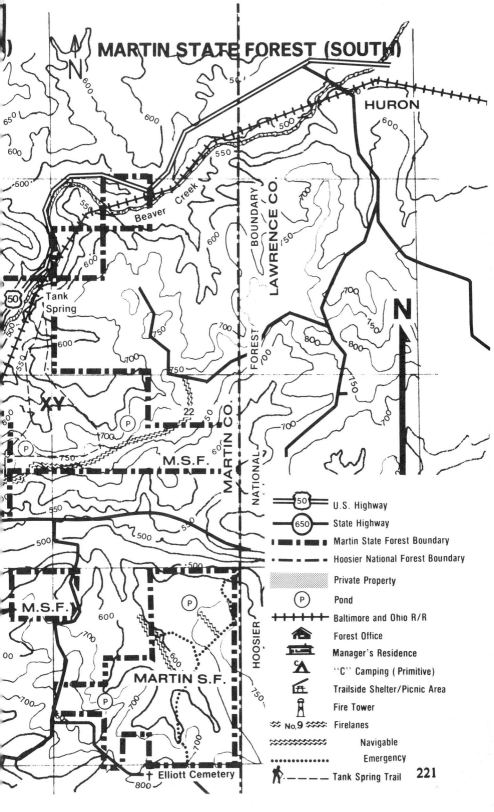

MARTIN STATE FOREST (SOUTH)

HURON

LAWRENCE CO.

BOUNDARY

FOREST

Beaver Creek

Tank Spring

50

XY

22

M.S.F.

MARTIN CO.

NATIONAL

HOOSIER

M.S.F.

MARTIN S.F.

† Elliott Cemetery

50	U.S. Highway
650	State Highway
	Martin State Forest Boundary
	Hoosier National Forest Boundary
	Private Property
P	Pond
+++++	Baltimore and Ohio R/R
	Forest Office
	Manager's Residence
"C"	"C" Camping (Primitive)
	Trailside Shelter/Picnic Area
	Fire Tower
No.9	Firelanes
	Navigable
	Emergency
	Tank Spring Trail

221

39. JUG ROCK & THE PINNACLE
Shoals, IN/Martin County
USGS MAP(S): Shoals 1:24,000
TRAIL(S) DISTANCE: no est. trails
ACREAGE: 34 acres
ACTIVITIES: hiking, nature study

Jug Rock and The Pinnacle are geological rock formations along a cliff overlooking the East Fork of the White River at Shoals, the Martin County seat. Both formations were acquired by the Indiana Division of Nature Preserves.

Jug Rock, a massive 60 foot high sandstone formation may be viewed and walked to along a 60 yard woodland path from the roadside turnout west of Shoals on US 50. The roadside turnout is on the north side of the highway about 200 yards downhill from the Shoals Overlook Rest Park. The standing rock is capped with **a massive** flat vegetated stone resembling a giant jug or vase which is the remains of a large sandstone cliff reduced by erosion.

Until a short 1/4 mile trail is built to connect Jug Rock with The Pinnacle, take US 50 downhill to Shoals and turn north onto Poplar Street, the first street left before the White River bridge crossing. Turn immediately right off Poplar Street to West River Road and proceed about 1/2 mile to a roadside pullout where the road curves. Walk uphill along a conspicuous path past a waterfall to the summit. Views at the top are worth the hike.

The following description was written of The Pinnacle in the <u>History of Martin county</u> under Natural Environment:

> *"The Pinnacle is the front part of the original massive*
> *sandstone formation that was eroded to form the Jug Rock. The*
> *broad ridge gradually becomes narrow until it is no wider than*
> *a wagon track and finally terminates with an almost perpendicular*
> *descent of over 200 feet. The cliff is more spectacular because*
> *of the Cyclopean boulders that have catapulted from its top and*
> *lie between its base and White River which flows 300 feet away.*
> *The magnitude and unusual summit of the rocky peak accounts for*
> *the name Pinnacle."*

-Page 8, <u>History of Martin Co.</u>

Jug Rock and The Pinnacle are located on the northwest edge of the community of Shoals between US 50 and the West River Road.

Jug Rock

40. HINDOSTAN FALLS PUBLIC FISHING AREA
Hindostan Falls, IN/Martin County
USGS MAP(S): Rusk, Shoals 1:24,000
TRAIL(S) DISTANCE: no est. trails
ACREAGE: 135 acres
ACTIVITIES: nature study, canoeing, boating, boat ramp, fishing,
picnicking, Class C primitive camping, pit toilets

Although there are no designated walking trails existing at this state
fishing area, the site is worth visitation to view the low wide waterfall,
camp, and to learn the social history of the former village Hindostan
Falls, the first county seat of Martin County.

It is recorded a "plague" (possibly milksickness) during the early 1820's
eliminated 600 or 1/2 of the 1,200 residents of Hindostan Falls and the
trading outpost village of Greenwich, directly across the East Fork of the
White River. The survivors hastily buried their dead and moved upstream
to nearby Mt. Pleasant. Historical markers are located alongside
Hindostan Road between SR 550 and the campground and falls; an Indiana
"ghost town" that has left little proof of its being.

Pronounced "Hin-daw-stan" locally, the falls are a disappointment to
most who view them for the first time due to their lack of "water fall"
(only 7 feet drop) which is so evident at Cataract Falls, Owen County,
Anderson Falls, Bartholomew County or Clifty Falls, Jefferson County.
What the falls lacks in height it makes up in width since the White River
is 429 feet across. The falls are best viewed in late summer to mid-
autumn when rainfall is low making the waterfall and ledge more
conspicuous. Below the falls there is a wide flat sandstone shelf that
was the site of a former mill during the original early 19th century
settlement. Across the road from this scenic site is a grassy parkland
meadow where primitive camping is permitted.

It should be mentioned a Hindostan Falls Hiking Trail was jointly
planned and marked by BSA troop local 484 and the Martin County
Historical Society in 1964. The 16 mile trail somewhat re-traces the
historical stagecoach trail of the early 1800's that passed thru the
southern half of Martin County from Vincennes. The trail follows town
streets, state highways and country roads from the corner of North Line
and East Main Streets from Loogootee to the Shoals historical museum.
Currently no effort is being made to maintain the old wooden yellow
diamond-shaped markers that are still erect. The trail passes by a former
brick kiln, over Boggs Creek, thru Mt. Pleasant Village, over the East
Fork of the White River, along Hindustan Falls, atop Gomerly Bluffs, the
Shoals County Courthouse, the Archer Gang Hanging Trees, Shoals
Overlook Park, Jug Rock, and ends at the Martin County Historical
Society Museum, Shoals. This same route may be travelled in a motorized
vehicle. A route booklet is available free from the Martin County
Historical Society.

To reach Hindostan Falls from Loogootee and US 50 turn south onto
SR 550 and drive 4 miles east to Hindostan Church and turn right or
south at the next road or Hindostan Road. The falls and campground are
approximately 0.3 mile from SR 550.

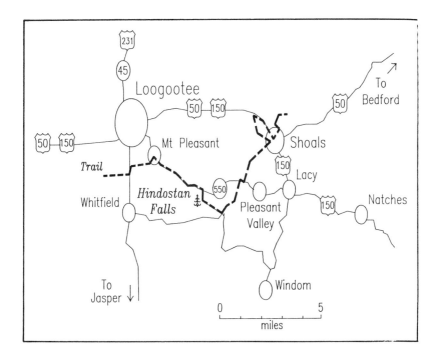

A Further Note About Martin County's Natural Features:

Martin County is rich in natural areas such as caves, springs, rock formations, streams and cliffs but most holdings are in private ownership and requires permission for entry. Bear, Cale, Tow's, Dover Hill and Rattlesnake are the major caverns within the county. LaSalle and Elliotts springs are located along the East Fork White River as are many rock formations and outcrops such as McBrides Bluffs, Bluffs of Beaver Bend, Gomerly Bluffs, Great Stone Face or Old Man's Nose, The Pinnacle, various Rock Houses, Duzan Rock, Mile Rock and Norman Rock. Plaster Creek Seeps is a Nature Conservancy natural area that is home to many northern plant species. Southwestern Martin County contains various tracts of the Lost River Purchase Unit of the Hoosier National Forest.

Jug Rock, a massive 60 foot high sandstone formation may be viewed from the roadside turnout west of Shoals on US 50 along the right or north side of the highway about 200 yards east or downhill from the Shoals Overlook Rest Park. West River Road, the first road right west of the White River bridge at Shoals off of US 50 is excellent for seeing House Rock, The Pinnacle and other formations.

41. PATOKA LAKE / NEWTON-STEWART SRA

Wickliffe, IN/Dubois, Orange, & Crawford Counties
USGS MAP(S): Cuzco, Greenbriar, Birdseye, Taswell 1:24,000
TRAIL(S) DISTANCE: 3 trails total about 9 miles
ACREAGE: total 25,583/8,880 lake/4,564 Newton-Stewart SRA
ACTIVITIES: hiking, nature study, solar interpretive center,
   amphitheatre, naturalist, picnicking, shelterhouses, playground,
   beach swimming, bathhouse, concessions, motorized & non-motorized
   boating, launch ramps, fishing, water-skiing, marina, campstore,
   fisherman's camp, backcountry camping, Class A & C camping, bicycle
   trail, dumping station
FEE(S): camping, entrance, row boat rental

Patoka Lake is Indiana's second largest reservoir. It was initially completed in 1980 by the U.S. Army Corps of Engineers. The reservoir is the result of damming the waters of the Patoka River and its many tributaries of DuBois, Crawford and Orange Counties. Of all the access areas that surround the enormous lake, Newton-Stewart State Recreation Area has the most facility development. All established trails begin and end at the visitor's solar center: Main Trail, Wildlife Management Demonstration Trail, and Garden Rock Trail. A trail map depicting all 3 trails is available from the visitor's center.

The maintained Main Trail is a self-guiding 6.5 mile loop that encircles the 1,000 acre peninsula north of the visitors center. The scenic uplands include mixed woods, rock shelters, stone outcroppings, pine plantations, abandoned farm fields, and fine vistas of Patoka Lake. The trail is considered rugged and requires about 3 to 4 hours or longer to hike. The trailhead begins at the west side of the parking lot directly behind the solar interpretive center. The trail is marked by white metal blazes set at eye level and regular intervals. Totem Rock, approximately 1 mile from the visitors center trailhead, is of special interest. The sandstone rock overhang sheltered early Indians. Turtle carvings were found on rocks and trees. Early settlers utilized Totem Rock for picnic gatherings and even as a corral for cattle. South of Totem Rock is Rocky Point, a large outcropping of sandstone along a ridge slope. From Rocky Point the trail heads across an abandoned field to follow the ravines and hillsides of the west side of the peninsula.

At the overlook are spectacular views north and east of Patoka Lake. An additional trail spur, Bird Watchers Spur, junctions with the Main Trail at the overlook. The linear trail heads north to the end and back. Bird Watcher's Spur is approximately 1 1/2 mile in length. Patoka Lake is one of the best places to see bald eagles during the winter months when cold weather forces the birds south in search of unfrozen waters. A second overlook provides similar lake views shortly beyond the junction with Bird Watcher's Spur. The Main Trail continues to follow wooded hillsides the rest of the way back to the visitors center. Short cuts on old service roads back to the visitor's center may be taken at their junction with the Main Trail. Refer to the map for details.

The Wildlife Management Demonstration trail is a self-guiding 2 mile loop with 17 numbered interpretive stations that correspond with the available trail booklet. Wildlife diversity, habitat, food plots and periodic burning are some of the subjects discussed along the marked trail that begins and ends at the visitor's center.

The Garden Rock loop trail is a short 3/4 mile trail that begins just east of the visitors center across from the parking area. This hilly trail features rock overhangs and "vases", and pine plantations. Select trees are identified by metal markers. The trail descends the ridge and returns uphill to the visitor's center.

Additional areas of interest surrounding **Patoka Lake Reservoir** include the following:

Dam and Tailwater - picnicking, fishing, restrooms, drinking water and overlook.
Jackson SRA - picnicking, shelter, boat ramp, restrooms, drinking water
Lick Fork SRA - boat ramp, picnicking, marina
Tillery Hill SRA - threatened primitive area
Little Patoka - restrooms, overlook, boat ramp
Painter Creek - restrooms, picnicking, boat ramp
Walls Lake - restroom, picnicking, boat ramp
South Lick Fork - overlook, boat ramp
SR 164 Overlook - picnicking, overlook, marina, camping

To reach Newton-Stewart SRA at Patoka Lake from I-64 at the SR 145 exit in Perry County, drive north to Birdseye. Turn right onto SR 64 and proceed to the junction with SR 145 and continue north to SR 164. Turn west on SR 164 and drive to Wickliffe. Turn north at Wickliffe and follow the directional signs to the gatehouse and visitor's center.

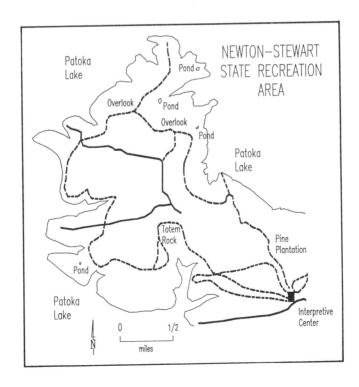

42. FERDINAND STATE FOREST

Ferdinand, IN/ Dubois County
USGS MAP(S): Saint Anthony, St. Meinrad, Birdseye 1:24,000
TRAIL(S) DISTANCE: several miles of firelanes
ACREAGE: 8,000 acres, 46 a. lake
ACTIVITIES: hiking, nature study, picnicking, shelterhouse, non-
    motorized boating, boat rental, boat launch ramp, fishing,
    playground, hunting, Class C camping, dumping station, swimming
FEE(S): camping, row boat rental

Ferdinand State Forest is a multiple-use forest whose main
recreational area is located 3 miles east of Ferdinand in Dubois county.
No established trails exist, however 6 firelanes are cleared of vegetation
spring and fall and provide hiking access to the many ravines and ridges.
Firelane Description:

#1 - Begins northeast of campground and follows along the base of a
slope to a wooded ravine. Extends from main forest road to Property
Office safety zone.

#2 - The first firelane from the forest entrance on the south side of
paved forest road. Park along the road on pullout. Firelane follows
ravine to wildlife pond curving westward.

#3 - Begins on north side of forest road at the west tip of Ferdinand
Lake. Firelane goes north uphill and downhill, through ravine, open
meadow and large stand of trees. Firelane #3 also winds south from dam
at the east end of lake near old fish hatchery to county road.

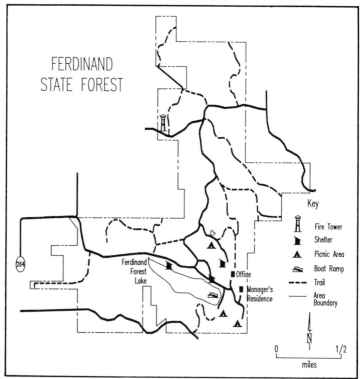

#4 - Begins at the north end of forest at the junction of main forest road and fire tower road. Wooded ridgetop trails descend to wildlife pond.

#5 - Begins at firetower next to pit toilet. Firelane loops back east to the main forest road.

#6 - Also at the north end of property off of main forest road. Follow the level ridge and ravine north to property line.

Firelanes are numbered and linear in design and tend to be overgrown despite clearances. The areas near the lake are the best to explore.

To reach Ferdinand State Forest from I-64 exit SR 162 north to the community of Ferdinand. From Ferdinand proceed east on SR 264. The marked entrance to the area is at the junction of SR 64 and SR 264.

RR #2, Box 649, Ferdinand, IN 47532   (812) 367-1524

43. SAALMAN HOLLOW
Branchville, IN/Perry County
USGS MAP(S): Branchville 1:24,000
TRAIL(S) DISTANCE: No est. trails
ACREAGE: 100 acres
ACTIVITIES: hiking, nature study, photography

The Nature Conservancy is responsible for preserving Saalman Hollow, a dedicated state nature preserve. The 100 acre picturesque hollow is botanically significant with its sandstone cliffs and overhang communities that support such rarities as French's shooting star and mountain laurel along the cliff tops. The wide box canyon narrows walking upstream to "end" at a water slide. Several waterfalls, caves, overhangs, and canyon walls are interesting features found in Saalman Hollow which on some maps is also called Rich Cave Hollow.

Access to Saalman's Hollow begins at the Saalman's residence near Branchville. Introduce yourself or selves and follow the signs to the hollow. The stream bottom is easy to follow but be advised there are thorny greenbriar and multiflora rose.

To reach Saalman Hollow from I-64 exit south at Saint Croix on SR 37, 5 miles to the Branchville Road. Turn east on the Branchville Road, 1.4 miles through Branchville and turn left on the first county road before the Oil Creek bridge. Drive north on the gravel road 1.3 miles to the dead end and the Saalman's residence and trailhead for Saalman's Hollow.

44. YELLOW BIRCH RAVINE

Taswell, IN/Crawford County
USGS MAP(S): Taswell 1:24,000
TRAIL(S) DISTANCE: no est. trails, old roads (permission requested, contact Indiana Division of Nature Preserves)
ACREAGE: 441 acres
ACTIVITIES: hiking, nature study

Primarily a tree of the cool moist uplands of northeastern North America and the Appalachian mountain chain, the Yellow Birch occurs locally in the north central United States. This persistent isolated remnant of a once abundant species was the main focus of preservation at Yellow Birch Ravine, now a state dedicated nature preserve. In addition to yellow birch trees, eastern hemlock and mountain laurel are found thus making the preserve the only place in southern Indiana where all 3 botanical rarities occur together.

Within the property's perimeter dry oak-hickory forest are found in the uplands while steep sandstone cliffs descend 100 feet to the moist, rocky "Y" shaped ravine bottoms of the interior. The branched scenic box canyon ravines feature several wet weather (not spring-fed) waterfalls, caves, rock overhangs, boulders and natural bridges. Most of the yellow birch trees are found along the rim of Yellow Birch Bluff on the east edge of the preserve. No designated trails exist at the preserve but the best way to explore is to follow the bottoms upstream to their source. Please contact the Division of Nature Preserves before visitation. (317) 232-4052.

To reach Yellow Birch Ravine Nature Preserve from Taswell on SR 64, turn south on the first paved road that goes under the Southern Railroad track. The road turns east/left. Continue along the road from the railroad viaduct a short ways and turn south at the curve and drive downhill to roadside pulloffs and access the property via the stream bottoms and old roads. This road divides the property into east and west sections. Note the nature preserves boundary signs. The preserve is open from sunrise to sunset. From Taswell, distance is 1 mile.

Debra Wickerson

45. HARRISON-CRAWFORD WYANDOTTE COMPLEX: OVERVIEW

Administered by the Indiana Division of Forestry, the Harrison-Crawford Wyandotte Complex is comprised of three separate areas: Harrison-Crawford State Forest, Wyandotte Woods State Recreation Area and Wyandotte Caves Area. All three areas offer outstanding hiking opportunities for day use or overnight backpacking.

Harrison-Crawford State Forest was the first area set aside of the three beginning in 1932 from abandoned farmlands of Harrison and Crawford counties. Today the 24,000 acre state forest is 8 times the size of its original purchase. Besides timber management harvesting, there is little development of these wild lands. Hikeable nature preserves have been dedicated in the state forest.

Nearly all of the trails are located at Wyandotte Woods and Wyandotte Caves Areas. These special areas were created from the state forest lands and all trails were developed in 1976-1977 through federal financial assistance. All trails are well marked and well used.

The 2,100 acre Wyandotte Woods State Recreation Area is so popular with outdoor recreationists that there is pressure for it to become a state park. The scenic recreation area offers picnicking, shelterhouses, swimming pool, forestry interpretive center, naturalist service, horse bridle trails, playground, fishing in the Blue and Ohio Rivers, hunting, canoeing, launch ramps, Class A campground, youth tent area, group camp, and horsemens campground. The numerous trailheads are well identified by overhead signs that note trail name, mileage and difficulty. All have colored round metal blazes and several of the trails interconnect. Horse trails are being rerouted to reduce intersection with foot trails. Only in a few places do they still intersect. Fees are required for entrance, swimming and camping.

The Wyandotte Caves Area offers hiking and fee-charged cave tours of the Little and Big Wyandotte Caves. Other activities included in this 200 acre site are guided spelunking tours of Big Wyandotte, fishing, picnicking, shelterhouse, and visitors center. Hiking to Wyandotte Spring is pleasurable. There is pressure for this area to become part of the state park system and join Wyandotte Woods complex.

Harrison-Crawford Complex is located south of I-64 between Leavenworth and Corydon on SR 62. Wyandotte Woods State Recreation Area is situated at the end of SR 463 via SR 62 about 10 miles west of Corydon. Wyandotte Caves Area is just off SR 62 three miles east of Leavenworth and 12 miles west of Corydon.

TRIP 1: HARRISON-CRAWFORD WYANDOTTE COMPLEX
Wyandotte Woods SRA/Campground Area Trails
TRAIL(S) DISTANCE: 3 trails total 4.9 miles
USGS MAP(S): Leavenworth, Corydon West 1:24,000

The Rocky Ridge Trail is one of four short trails found at the main Class A campground. The rugged 2 mile trail loop begins and ends between campsite #111 and #35. Day visitors may park at the campground entry gate visitors parking lot. The trail is indeed rocky and follows ridge tops and slopes to deep ravines near the Blue River. Blue blaze buttons identify the trail.

Sleepy Hollow Trail is a one mile horseshoe loop trail that is also rugged. Red blazed buttons on posts guide the hiker. The marked trailhead begins near a firelane gate just before the campground entry gate across from a cemetery. It ends further down the firelane about 100 yards. The high point literally is a picnic tabled overlook of the Blue River valley.

The third developed trail is the 0.5 mile rugged and steep Tulip Valley Trail. The trailhead begins between campsite #278 and #254 just east of the comfort station restroom. The trail is marked by orange-brown metal button blazes. It descends to the Hickory Hollow Forestry Interpretive Center. All three trails may be easily hiked in one day.

TRIP 2: HARRISON-CRAWFORD WYANDOTTE COMPLEX
Wyandotte Woods SRA/ East Property Trails
TRAIL (S) DISTANCE: 5 trails total 4 miles
USGS MAP(S): Leavenworth, Corydon West 1:24,000

The east property trails are located near the main entry gate and the active recreational facilities area. The CCC Camp Trail begins and ends near the Group Camp entrance and ends/begins at the swimming pool parking area. The 1.5 mile rugged loop is marked by orange round metal blazes set on knee-high posts. The woodland trail intersects a heavily used horse trail. The best section is the west ridgetop that leads down and up alongside a steep deeply wooded ravine. Other connecting trails are the Flowertop Trail and the Tulip Valley Trail. The Tulip Valley Trail is a 0.5 mile in distance and leads from the group campground to Hickory Hollow Forestry Interpretive Center (see Trip 1).

Flowertop Trailhead

The Flowertop Trail is a one mile moderate loop marked by blue blazes that begin just south of the picnic shelter, south of the swimming pool parking area and ends at the adjacent volley ball court. The short trail follows a black locust tree covered rocky hillside of exposed West Baden bedrock and lichen covered Blue River limestone.

The 0.2 mile Wyandotte Trail is a rugged path guided by orange buttons. The brief trail begins just north of Wyandotte firetower. The trail crosses a horse path and travels through wooded ravines, a wildlife pond and white pine plantations. The final leg of the trail follows a firelane to return to the firetower and picnic area.

A stones throw across the Cold Friday Road into Harrison-Crawford State Forest is the Post Oak-Cedar Nature Preserve. A easy self-guiding 0.8 mile loop encircles a prairie opening or "barren" or "glade". The thin rocky soils support several prairie flowering plants and an impressive stand of post oak, red cedar and hardwoods such as chestnut, white, black, blackjack and scarlet oaks. A trail brochure is available at the trail registration box at the trailhead alongside the gravel road. Twenty five marked stations describe the flora, fauna and geology of the dry south facing open slope. Stunted post oaks are estimated to be 300 years old. The south portion of the dedicated nature preserve borders Potato Creek. Post Oak-Cedar Nature Preserve is located alongside Cold Friday Road, one mile south of the property office.

TRIP 3: HARRISON-CRAWFORD WYANDOTTE COMPLEX
Wyandotte Woods SRA/South Property Trails
TRAIL(S) DISTANCE: 2 trails total 3.2 miles
USGS MSP(S): Leavenworth, Corydon West 1:24,000

These two out-of-the-way trails along and near the Ohio River offer some of the best hiking experience at Wyandotte Woods SRA. The 1.7 mile rugged Cliff Dweller loop trail begins and ends behind the re-constructed pioneer cabin. Parking is permitted at the pullout near the pioneer cabin along the main SRA road. Orange-brown metal buttons line the trail. Cliff Dweller Trail traverses a variety of scenic terrain along ravines, stream bottoms and atop bluffs. A short segment of the wooded path follows the Adventure Trail (see Trip 4). One section of the trail offers a choice of trails along a face of a cliff or its blufftop.

White-tail Deer Trail follows blue blazes 1.5 miles along a loop overlooking the south bank of the Ohio River. The trail begins at the service road gate immediately west of the Ohio River blufftop picnic shelter parking area. The path curves along the wooded bluff with the wide Ohio River below. The trail ends or begins at the picnic and playground area. A cedar ridge segment provides fine vistas of the river valley and Kentucky.

Post Oak Cedar Nature Preserve

TRIP 4: HARRISON-CRAWFORD WYANDOTTE COMPLEX
Wyandotte Woods SRA/Harrison-Crawford SF
TRAIL(S) DISTANCE: Adventure Trail 30 mile loop/4 day hikes
USGS MAP(S): Leavenworth, Corydon West 1:24,000

Declared a National Recreation Trail, the Adventure Trail is an easy to very rugged 30 mile loop that passes through all three areas of the Harrison-Crawford Wyandotte Complex. For backpackers on overnights,

Trail Shelter, Adventure Trail

the trail requires 3 to 4 days at 8 to 10 miles a day due to the hilly terrain. Day hikers may explore long trail segments without being weighed down with gear but will have to back track or car shuttle. Overnight hikers should register at the gate house at Wyandotte Woods SRA.

Blazed in both directions, neon green painted stripes appear on numbered posts (1-21) and serve as orientation landmarks as "cairns" do in treeless mountains. Post 1 is found near the main SRA road at the Ohio River parking area. There is a good deal of hiking uphill along ridge tops and slopes as well as descending into ravines and stream bottoms. From Post 17 to 21, the trail follows the bluff tops of the Ohio River and nearby tributaries providing some of the best hiking on the Adventure Trail. Lack of mature forest, clearcut areas and considerable horse usage are negative aspects about the trail. Car shuttles for day trips or overnights would work fine. A trail map is available from the park office and entry gate.

ADVENTURE TRAIL

DAY 1: Post 1 to Post 7
TRAIL DISTANCE: 7 miles

This segment of the Adventure Trail leads from the Wyandotte Woods SRA at the Ohio River and follows the ridge uphill to the picnic shelter and playground overlooking the river valley. From here the trail follows ridge lines and slopes to the bridge crossing and parking area on the Blue River and SR 62. Crossing SR 62 is dangerous due to high speed traffic and hidden curves, use caution. You have now entered Harrison-Crawford State Forest. The trail climbs up to ridgetops and slopes then heads west to Wyandotte Lake and Wyandotte Spring. An open shanty overnight camping shelter has been established near the flowing perennial spring, the source of water for Wyandotte Lake. Parking is available at Wyandotte Lake.

Day 2: Post 7 to Post 13 and Stage Stop Campground
TRAIL DISTANCE: 7 miles

From the Wyandotte Lake parking area head north on the Buckeye Trail around the east edge of the lake. On the north end of the lake, go north on a conspicuous unmarked spur once crossing the inlet creek formed from the Wyandotte Spring. Go uphill through wooded slopes crossing the Wyandotte Cave Road. Follow the trail downhill along the ridge slopes to a narrow valley then uphill again to Post 10, the point that comes the closest to I-64. This section of the trail may be confusing especially when the leaves are down in late fall, but rely on the trail blazes. Recent clearcutting has been extensive in this area and the trail has been re-routed in sections. The trail follows ridgetops and rocky slopes descending to SR 62. Use caution for this dangerous road crossing. The trail follows the Blue River upstream northeast a short distance to cross over the SR 462 bridge over Blue River. The trail then turns southwest through abandoned meadow alongside the Blue River and Post 13. The trail goes uphill to the top and slopes to Stage Stop Campground. There is no bridge but the stream is shallow enough to wade across. Camp in the fee charged primitive campsites. A car shuttle is recommended from Wyandotte Lake to Stage Stop Campground, just over 2 miles via SR 62.

DAY 3: Stage Stop Campground to Post 17
Trail Distance: 8 miles

From the scenic Blue River setting the trail heads southeast slowly climbing a ridge through old fields, pine plantations, to cross SR 462. Across SR 462 the trail enters a pinery then follows a gravel road a brief ways before crossing into a young mixed forest along an old service road. The trail follows the old service road several miles along ridgetops then enters a scenic tributary ravine of Indian River. An established open front shanty shelter is found uphill on a high point not far from Indian River. Day visitors must either retrace their steps back to Stage Stop Campground parking area or if daylight allows, continue on to the Ohio River parking area and Post 1.

Wyandotte Spring

DAY 4: Post 17 to Post 1
Trail Distance: 8 miles

The segment of trail along the Ohio River blufftop is considered the most scenic section of the Adventure Trail. Post 17 is one of two overnight shelters or open face shantys. From here the trail heads downridge to ravine bottoms and then uphill along ridge slopes to ridgetop to descend once again to ravines following a ravine southwest to the Ohio River. The trail heads uphill to the blufftop following the ridge to descend alongside a small stream to connect with the Cliff Dweller Trail and Post 21 and the main park road. The trail follows alongside the east side of the main SRA road to the Ohio River parking area and Post 1.

Adventure Trail Access Parking Areas:
Ohio River Post 1/main SRA road at Wyandotte Woods SRA
Pioneer Cabin pullout/main SRA road at Wyandotte Woods SRA
SR 62 at Blue River/3 miles east of Leavenworth
Wyandotte Lake parking area/SR 62
Wyandotte Caves Area/north of SR 62
Stage Stop Campground/south of SR 62
Property Office parking area at Wyandotte Woods SRA/SR 46.

TRIP 5: HARRISON-CRAWFORD WYANDOTTE COMPLEX
Wyandotte Caves Area
TRAIL(S) DISTANCE: 2 cave tours and 1 nature trail total 2.85 mile
USGS MAP(S): Leavenworth 1:24,000

Acquired by the state of Indiana in 1966, the Wyandotte Caves Area is one of the most interesting 1,174 acres in Indiana due to its limestone caverns of the Big and Little Wyandotte and Wyandotte Spring. According to geologists, the caverns had their origins 2 to 3 million years ago when the limestone was slowly being dissolved by the acidic groundwater. The most common speleotherms are stalactites and stalagmites. Jackets or warm clothing are recommended on cave tours since the temperature is a cool 52-54 degrees year around. The well-lighted caverns are very safe. Fees are charged for the guided cave tours.

Modern Cave Tours:
Little Wyandotte (30-45 min.)
    summer, 9:00 to 5:00, every hour
    winter, 8:00 to 4:00, even hours only
Historic Tour (1 hour)
    summer, 9:30 to 4:30, every hour
    winter, none
Monument Mt. Tour (2 hour)
    summer, 10:00 to 4:00, every hour
    winter, 9:00 to 3:00, odd hours only
Spelunking Cave Tours:
Pillar Tour (4-5 hours)
    summer, 10:00 am, Mon., Wed., Fri., Sat., and Sun.
    winter, 10:00 am, Sat. and Sun.
All Day Tour, (7-8 hours)
    summer, 9:30 am (Tues., Thurs., Sat. & Sun.)
    winter, 8:30 am (Sat. & Sun.)
Junior Spelunking Tour (2 1/2 - 3 hours)
    summer, 10:45 am, Sat. and Sun.
    winter, 10:30 am, Sat. and Sun.

Wyandotte Caves were first discovered by prehistoric Indians 3,000 years ago. The original Americans utilized the caves for shelter, food storage, a source of flint and other minerals, and burial of their dead. The first documented visitation to the cave by Euro-Americans was a F. I. Bentley, a fur trapper who assisted a Wyandotte Indian brave. It wasn't until 1856 after Indian removal to the West that the caves were "re-discovered" by American settlers.

The 2 hour guided 1.6 mile tour of Big Wyandotte Cave is an underground nature walk viewing unique formations along lengthy passageways and large rooms. Washington Avenue is a 400 foot long passageway near the cave's entrance. Rothrock's Cathedral Room, the setting for Monument Mountain the world's largest underground mountain, is vast with its 360 foot long and 135 foot high "room". The Garden of Helictites features one of the best displays in the world. Stair climbing and narrow passageways are part of the tour but for the most part it is dry moderate walking through level spacious passageways.

Monument Mountain, Wyandotte Cave

Big Wyandottes's shortest trip is the Historical Tour which lasts one hour. New developments in old sections like "Rugged Mountain" allows visitors to see parts of the cave not open since lantern tours were conducted. This tour is only available during the summer.

For the more adventurous there are 2 rugged spelunking cave tours of the Big Wyandotte. The Pillar of the Constitution is a 5 hour tour, the all day tour is an 8 hour tour, and the Junior Spelunking Tour is about a 3 hour tour. Reservations are required for these tours and lanterns are provided. Correct clothing suggested include bluejeans, sweats, hiking shoes, knee pads, hard hats and knapsack.

Little Wyandotte Cave guided tour is 1/2 hour long and 1/4 mile in distance. Unlike its bigger counterpart, Little Wyandotte is a wet, smaller cave with narrow passageways and stairwells. The entire cave is rich in formations. Like the Big Wyandotte, it has one of the largest collections of helictites in the United States.

Southwest of the caves about 1/2 mile is Wyandotte Lake and Wyandotte Spring. The 1 mile Buckeye Trail encircles the lake created by the year around flowing waters of Wyandotte Spring. The natural spring rises at the base of a hill immediately north of Wyandotte Lake just beyond the Adventure Trail camp shanty shelter. Follow the obvious well worn path north after crossing the second bridge over the inlet stream to the spring. The Buckeye Trail is an easy hike through oak-hickory woodland. Red buttons on posts guide the trail. Picnicking and fishing are also popular. Wyandotte Lake and parking area are located on the north side of SR 62 east of Leavenworth just before the turn to Wyandotte Caves.

TRIP 6: HARRISON-CRAWFORD STATE FOREST
Leavenworth Barrens Nature Presure
USGS MAP(S): Leavenworth 1:24,000
TRAIL(S) DISTANCE: no est. trails

The 119 acre Leavenworth Barrens is similar in terrain and flowering plants as the Post Oak - Cedar Nature Preserve at Wyandotte Woods SRA. Both of these "barrens" are south facing slopes with a large number of prairie type plants. The grassy openings are best seen in late summer and early fall when the coneflowers, black-eye susans and prairie dock are in bloom.

To reach Leavenworth Barrens Nature Preserve go north on a county road on the east side of Leavenworth 500 feet west of a cemetery. Drive one mile north and just before the "Y" shaped junction the preserve will be on the west side of the road. There are no established trails. Three other separate parcels of the nature preserve are found nearby but access is restricted by automobile due to the terrain.

Property Manager, Harrison-Crawford State Forest
7240 Old Forest Road
Corydon, IN 47112
(812) 738-8232

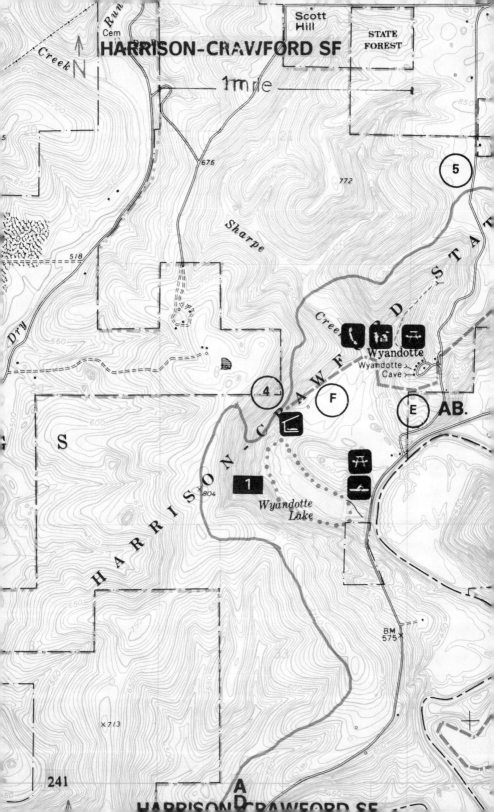

HARRISON-CRAWFORD SF

Scott
Hill

STATE
FOREST

Run

Cem

Creek

N

1mile

675

772

(5)

Sharpe

518

Creek

Dry

550

(4)

Wyandotte

Wyandotte
Cave

(F)

(E) AB.

550

S

600

1

804

Wyandotte
Lake

×713

BM
575×

241

A

HARRISON-CRAWFORD SF

Fountain Ch.

BLUE

S P E N C E

Harr

HARRISON—CRAWFORD
STATE FOREST

64

R

RIVER

553

Gaging Station

Scout
Mtn

Hick

HARRISON
CRAWFORD
STATE FOREST

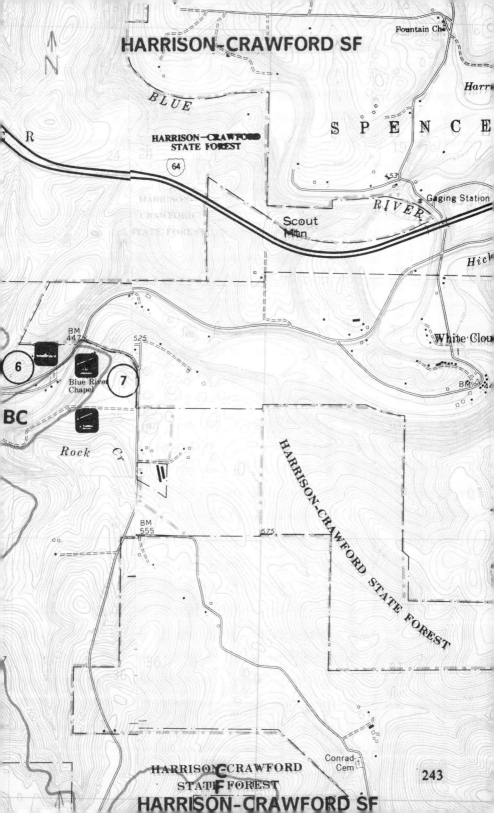

BM
447

525

White Clou

6

7

BM

Blue River
Chapel

BC

Rock   Cr

462

BM
555

675

HARRISON-CRAWFORD STATE FOREST

7

Conrad
Cem

HARRISON-CRAWFORD
STATE FOREST

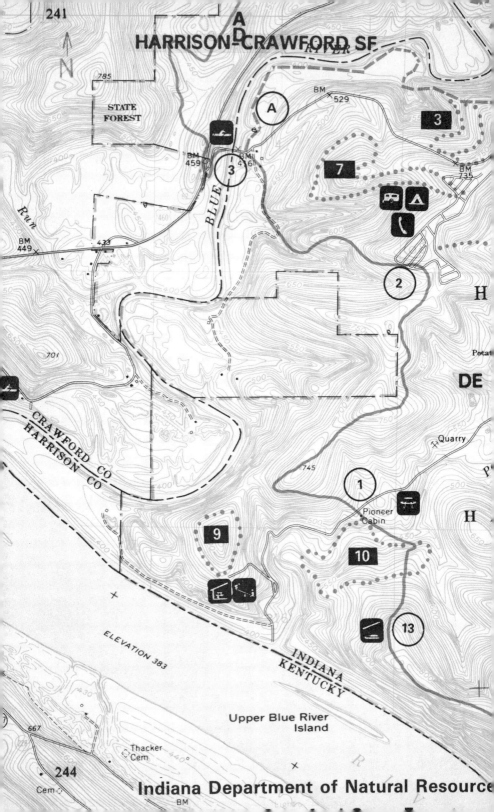

N

HARRISON-CRAWFORD SF

STATE
FOREST

785

BM
459

BM
456

3

A

A

3

7

BM
529

BM
735

BM
449

433

460

2

H

DE

Potat

701

Quarry

745

1

Pioneer
Cabin

H

P

9

10

CRAWFORD CO
HARRISON CO

ELEVATION 383

13

INDIANA
KENTUCKY

Upper Blue River
Island

667

Thacker
Cem

Cem

Indiana Department of Natural Resource

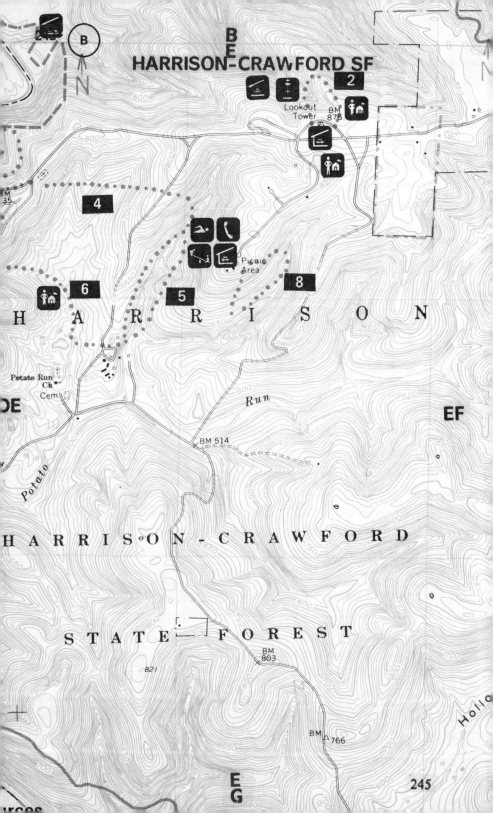

HARRISON-CRAWFORD SF

2

Lookout
Tower
BM
875

4

Picnic
Area

6

5

8

H A R R I S O N

Potato Run
Ch
Cem

DE

Run

EF

BM 514

Potato

H A R R I S O N - C R A W F O R D

S T A T E   F O R E S T

BM
803

821

BM △ 766

Hollo

rces

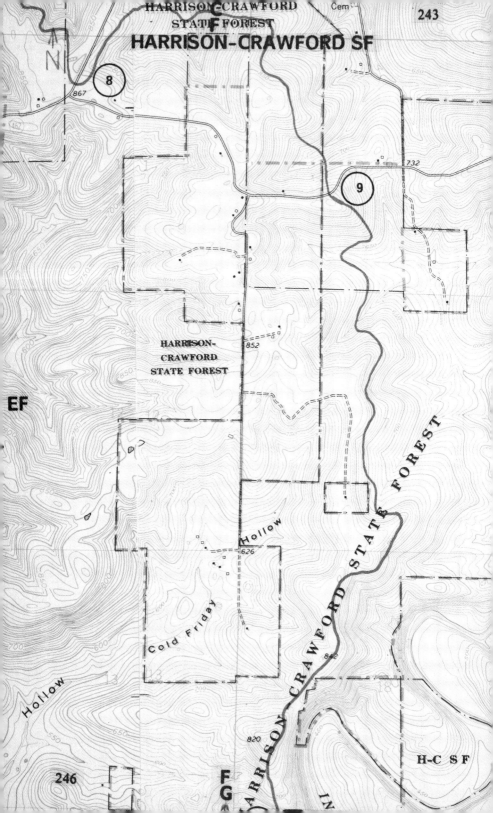

HARRISON-CRAWFORD SF

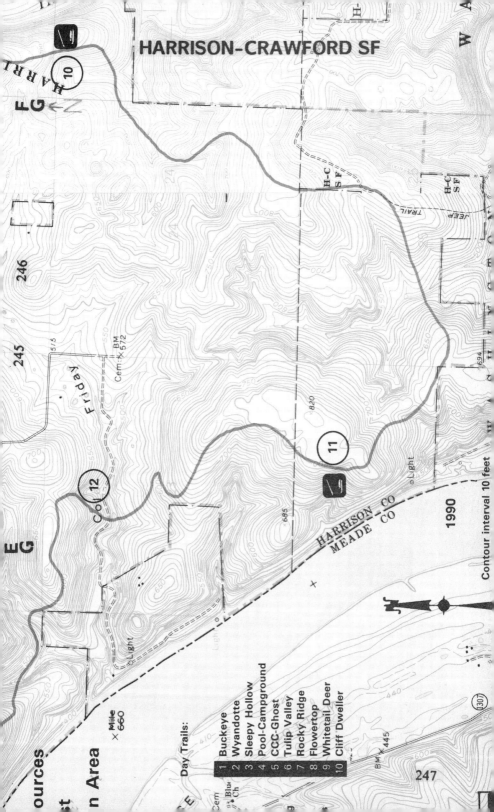

Day Trails:

1	Buckeye
2	Wyandotte
3	Sleepy Hollow
4	Pool-Campground
5	CCC-Ghost
6	Tulip Valley
7	Rocky Ridge
8	Flowertop
9	Whitetail-Deer
10	Cliff Dweller

Contour interval 10 feet

HARRISON CO
MEADE CO

1990

NATURE WALKS IN THE SOUTHWESTERN LOWLANDS

School Group, Dobbs Woods

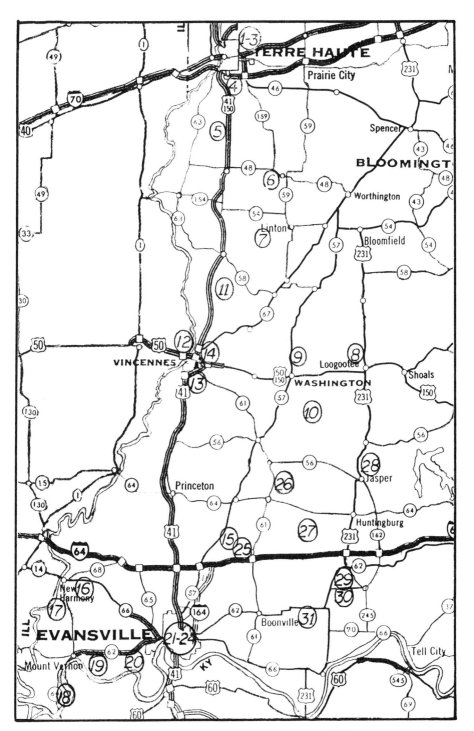

SOUTHWESTERN LOWLANDS

SOUTHWESTERN LOWLANDS: OVERVIEW

The Southwestern Lowlands is a large region bordered by the Ohio River on the south and the Wabash River on the west. The vicinity of Terre Haute marks the northwestern corner. The lowlands boundary runs essentially east along SR 46 to Spencer and the West Fork of the White River. The eastern line roughly follows SR 67, US 231, and SR 56 south to Jasper, then southeast to the Anderson River. The northern 3/4 of the region was glaciated and is characterized by low relief and rolling plains and valleys. The unique riparian areas include oxbows, bayous, and sloughs found mainly along the Wabash and Ohio Rivers. Twin Swamps, Hovey lake, Goose Pond Cypress Slough, Harmonie State Park and Beall Woods in Illinois are fine representatives. Bald cypress and pecan trees are found here and are more indigenous in the southern United States. Oak and hickory forests predominate and excellent examples may be found at Dobbs Memorial Grove, Hemmer Woods and Wesselman Woods.

The major river cities of Terre Haute, Vincennes and Evansville offer urban nature spots to explore. Angel Mounds and New Harmony are special with their natural and social history. Coal strip mines have and will continue to provide parklands in the region. Fowler Park and Wilderness, Shakamak State Park, Greene-Sullivan State Forest, Lynnville Park, Scales Lake and Patoka Fish and Wildlife Area were former strip mines.

1. TERRE HAUTE, IN/NATURE PLACES
ACTIVITIES: observatory, planetarium, city park, herb farm

The city of Terre Haute offers nature oriented facilities and properties that are worthy of visitation. The Astronomical Observatory provides telescopic stargazing on clear evenings, Tuesday and Friday nights 7:00 pm to 10:00 pm. The observatory is located at the corner of 6th and Chestnut atop the Science building in the downtown campus of Indiana State University. For further information call (812) 237-3294.

Built in 1931, the Allen Memorial Planetarium features a Spitz model A4 Planetarium projector that displays the solar system and other heavenly bodies on the overhead 30 foot diameter aluminum dome. Spring and fall programs are held during the school year and the public is also invited to visit 9:00 am to 3:00 pm during school days. The Allen Planetarium is located at Terre Haute South High School, just south of I-70 and US 41 exit. Telephone (812) 238-4272, 3737 South 7th Street for further information.

The 145 acre Fairbanks Park offers a sunken garden, picnicking, playground, exercise course, boat ramp, fishing, a musical theatre, fountain, and river promenade plus excellent views of the Wabash River. The relocated home of composer Paul Dresser who penned the state song, "On The Banks Of The Wabash" in 1913 is located on Dresser Drive and South 1st Street at the park entrance. The home is open to visitation May thru September, Sundays only 1:00 pm to 4:00 pm. Admission is free. Another renowned Terre Haute native was U.S. labor leader and Socialist Presidential candidate, Eugene Debs. A memorial flower garden is located at the Debs home at 451 North Street near the Indiana State University campus. The hours are Wednesday thru Sunday 1:00 pm to 4:30 pm. There is a nominal admission fee to the home.

Deming park is 160 acres of active and passive recreational activity in a woodland setting. Exercise course, picnicking, shelters, playground, fishing, swimming, tennis, archery, mini-train ride and concessions are some of the activities. The city park is situated west of Dobbs Park on Poplar Avenue.

Briarpatch Herb Farm, located at 2000 South Fruitridge Avenue in Terre Haute, grows some 150 varieties of herbs. Visitor accomodations include a restaurant that utilizes the home grown culinary herbs, a reconstructed vinegar barn, potting shed, gift shop, individual and/or group tours, herb lectures, and seasonal plant sales.

2. DOBBS PARK MEMORIAL GROVE

Terre Haute, IN/Vigo County
USGS MAP(S): Seelyville 1:24,000
TRAIL(S) DISTANCE: 4 trails total 3 miles
ACREAGE: 105 acres
ACTIVITIES: hiking, nature study, naturalists, nature center with bird
observation windows, cross country skiing, ice skating, lake
(1.5 a.), fishing, publications, programs, picnic shelters,
caboose, butterfly and hummingbird gardens

Dobbs Park Memorial Grove is exceptional in the fact it preserves a virgin forest on the edge of an encroaching urban area. The primary purpose of this city park is environmental education which is carried out by naturalists who conduct guided walks, lectures, and slide shows at the nature center. Live animal displays and other nature exhibits are featured at the nature center including programs, workshops and classes.

The day visitor will enjoy the maintained and easy trails that begin and end at the nature center. Nature Preserve Trail is a one mile footpath along the edge of virgin and old second growth mixed woods and a tulip poplar plantation. 25 acres of the forest was dedicated in 1975 as a state nature preserve. A 14 acre section is considered outstanding for its diverse giant trees. The self-guiding trail is in the northwest portion of the preserve where 20 marked stations correspond to a trail brochure available at the nature center. A 0.9 mile trail explores the concepts of forest ecology and identifies several trees and plants of the preserve. The 0.7 mile Pinewoods Trail includes the 0.3 mile Deer Path loop in the eastern edge of the property. The trail passes thru a mixed pine plantation and an immature deciduous forest. This trail and other segments of the other trails may be wet and muddy at certain times of the year due to the low lying elevation. The nature center is open year around. For seasonal hours call (812) 877-1095.

Dobbs Park Memorial Grove is located on the east side of Terre Haute. From I-70 exit north onto SR 46. Turn left/west at the junction of SR 46 and SR 42 or Poplar Street. The entrance is on the right/north side of the road.

Vigo County also includes 3 nature preserves that are open to the public with visitation by permission only: R. Kermit Flesher Memorial Woods, Little Bluestem Prairie, and Kieweg Woods.

The 36 acre R. Kermit Flesher Memorial Woods is a dedicated state nature preserve that is owned and managed by the Vigo County Parks Department. Just over a mile from the Wabash River, the floodplain forest includes silver maple, green ash, shellbark hickory, swamp white oak and burr oak. The most notable feature of the woods are pecan trees that reach their northernmost point in Indiana. There are no established trails. Permission from the Vigo County Park Department is necessary for access. Their address and telephone number is Room 40, Vigo County Courthouse, Terre Haute, Indiana 47802 (812) 238-8391.

The Little Bluestem Prairie Nature Preserve consists of 8.5 acres of dry prairie overlooking the Wabash River floodplain. This remnant includes Indian plume grass, bush clover, flowering spurge, hoary puccoon, big bluestem and pearly everlasting.

Dedicated as a state nature preserve, the property is under the ownership of Indiana State University. For visitation permission call or write the ISU Department of Life Sciences, Terre Haute, Indiana 47809 (812) 232-6311 ext. 2435 or 232-6211 ext. 2636.

The 42 acre Kieweg Woods is also under the ownership and management of Indiana State University, Department of Life Sciences. The exceptional beech-maple forest is located near the western limits of where this type of forest meets the Illinois prairie. The preserve is open by appointment to visitors by contacting the Department of Life Sciences.

3. HAWTHORN PARK

Terre Haute, IN/Vigo County
USGS MAP(S): Seelyville 1:24:000
TRAIL(S) DISTANCE: 5 trails total 3 miles
ACREAGE: 271 acres
ACTIVITIES: hiking, picnicking, shelterhouses, playgrounds, playfield, beach swimming, fishing, boating, boat ramps, canoe and rowboat rentals, Class A camping, concessions
FEE(S): shelterhouse reservation, canoe and rowboat rentals, camping

Directly north of the Rose-Hulman Institute of Technology campus lies Hawthorn Park, a Vigo County facility. Surrounded by oak-hickory forest, 15 acre Burns Lake is the center of recreational activities. Encircled by footpaths, Trail 3 follows the west and south shoreline next to the campground. Trail 4 skirts the north shore adjacent to the picnic area. A portion of Trail 1 completes the walking route around the lake on the east side next to another picnic area.

Further east of this busy waterfront is the 61 acre J. I. Case Wetland Wildlife Refuge. Highly productive in wildlife, the refuge is home to herons, ducks, geese, grebes, muskrats, cattails and other birds, mammals and plants. Spring and fall draws the migratory waterfowl. Unfortunately the south, east and north shores are not protected by woodlands as the west shore. Trail 5 provides feeder spurs to and from the parking area on the high ground between the two water bodies. Trail 1 also provides woodland spurs from Burns Lake. In addition Trail 1 follows a service road along and between the wet shore swamp forest and the more upland forest to the west. This is the ideal wood duck habitat. Connecting Trail 1 and Trail 3, Trail 2 passes along the south levy next to a railroad track and continues around the shoreline to complete the refuge loop.

To reach Hawthorn Park from I-70 exit north at the SR 46 exchange and go north to the "T" and US 40/Wabash Avenue. Turn right/east and proceed past Rose-Hulman and turn left/north onto J.P. Hunt Road. Follow J.P. Hunt Road north to the nest crossroads and turn left/west onto Hanker Road. Follow Hanker Road to the park entrance on the left/south side of the road.

4. FOWLER PARK & WILDERNESS AREA

Pimento, IN/Vigo County

USGS MAP(S): Lewis, Pimento 1:24,000

TRAIL(S) DISTANCE: 1.5 mile Fowler Park; 3 mile Wilderness Area

ACREAGE: 140 acre Fowler Park/300 acre Wilderness Area

ACTIVITIES: hiking, backpack camping, nature study, fossil collecting, picnicking, shelterhouse, horseback riding, fishing, non-motorized boating, boat ramps, boathouse, beach swimming, concessions, Class A and primitive camping, covered bridge, Pioneer Village, Pioneer Day's Festival

FEE(S): camping and shelterhouses

Fowler Park and Wilderness Area consists of two separate property tracts divided by Bono Road and private property. The terrain of each consists of reclaimed coal strip mines and the main recreational activities and hiking is centered around the small, narrow, north to south lake pits.

Fowler Park is the scene of all the active recreational pursuits. Hiking is available on the west portion of the property beyond the main lake.

Muskrat Den, Hawthorn Park

The unmarked but conspicuous loop trail encircles a hour-glass shaped strip pit along the top of spoil banks. Pine tree plantations are common and so is poison ivy. The extreme west open area has several prairie plant species such as prairie dock and big bluestem grass. A short cut spur bisects the middle of the lake if you decide not to hike the entire loop. Mined in the 1950's, the trees have yet to reach their maturity. Time will do much for the improvement of this hiking area.

The Wilderness Area entrance is less than 1/2 mile south on Bono Road from the Fowler Park entrance. The trailhead lies between the north and south parking lots. The south parking lot includes a boat ramp for non motorized boating on the 18.6 acre strip pit lake. Supposedly this is one of the best Indiana locations for fern fossils. The trail or old road proceeds north along the west shore through pine and Chinese chestnut plantations. The trail curves east around the north tip near Old Mine Road. Spoil mounds are common and devoid of vegetation in this area. The trail continues south into the forested east portion of the Wilderness Area. Grassy service roads interlace the strip pitted area and serve as trails. Backpack camping is permitted here. The shoreline trail does not loop but ends 1/4 mile north of the boat ramp on the opposite west shore. Retracing your steps is necessary. Formerly the trail continued on to connect Mine Road and 111th Drive.

To reach Fowler Park and Wilderness Area from Terre Haute drive south on US 41 to Cox Road (Stuckey's restaurant on corner) and turn left/east. Follow Cox Road east across the railroad tracks and turn right/south onto Bono Road and proceed 1/2 mile to the Fowler Park entrance. The Wilderness Area entrance is just beyond Fowler Park on Bono Road on the left/east side of the road.

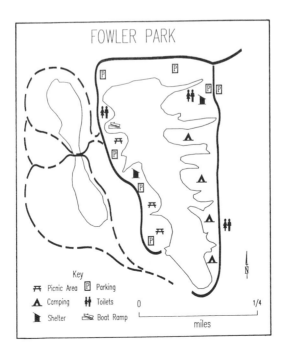

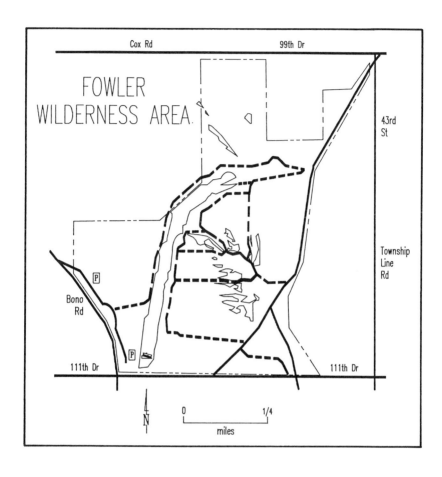

5. PRAIRIE CREEK PARK
Prairie Creek, IN/Vigo County
USGS MAP(S): Pimento 1:24,000
TRAIL(S) DISTANCE: 2 miles
ACTIVITIES: hiking, nature study, picnicking, shelterhouses,
    playground, playfields, tennis courts, swimming, fishing,
    non-motorized boating, boat ramp launch, sugar camp tours,
    Class A camping
FEE(S): shelterhouses, camping

A Vigo County park, Prairie Creek Park is situated in a natural woodland setting. A small lake has been formed from dammed tributaries of Prairie Creek which provides fishing, boating and swimming. This pleasant isolated area offers passive as well as active outdoor amenities for all age groups.

There is one trail that winds and loops throughout the woodland and along the lakeshore. The main trailhead begins beside the park road just south of the campground and north of Maple Picnic Shelter. Huge maple trees dominate the Miami Nature Area. From February to March, 400 sugar maple trees are tapped for their watery sap. The trail crosses the park road south of Maple Shelter to join two other trail spurs that lead north of the campground and south to the lake. Both trails loop back to the original trail. Be advised the trail is overgrown, unmarked in places, and suffers from general neglect. The trail receives low priority in regard to maintenance, however the parkland deserves exploration due to its picturesque natural state.

To reach Prairie Creek Park from Terre Haute drive south on US 41 to SR 246 and turn right/west to Prairie Creek. Turn north on CR 35S/Byrd Road and proceed to CR 21W/Rynerson Road and turn right/east. The park entrance is 1/2 mile on the right side of the road.

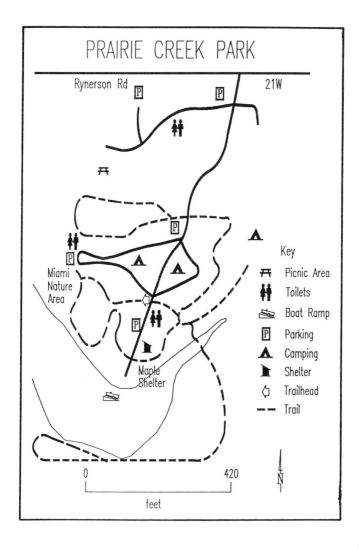

Sugar Maple Giants, Miami Nature Trail
Prairie Creek Park

6. SHAKAMAK STATE PARK
Jasonville, IN/Greene, Clay and Sullivan Counties
USGS MAP(S): Jasonville and Hymera 1:24,000
TRAIL(S) DISTANCE: 4 trails total 7 miles
ACREAGE: 1,766 land acres/400 acres water
ACTIVITIES: hiking, nature study, swimming beach, lifeguard, beach house, picnicking, shelterhouses, hiking, biking, playground, tennis, year around fishing, non-motorized boating, boat ramps, boat rentals, paddleboats, bridle trails, saddle barn, nature center (Apr.1 - Nov.1), naturalist (May-Aug), recreation building, concessions, Class A tent and electrical camping, group camping, family cabins
FEE(S): entrance, camping, recreation building rental, boats, horses

Shakamak is a Delaware Indian word for the nearby Eel River. The Algonquian name "Schack-a-mak" was given in reference to the snake-like eels (Anguilla rostrata) or "slippery long fish" that inhabit the river waters and were considered a choice wild food source by the native Americans. Like Greene-Sullivan State Forest located approximately 20 miles south of the state park, Shakamak was created from abandoned coal mines. A few years after the land was donated to the state of Indiana it was developed by the Civilian Conservation Corps during the early 1930's. Three easy to moderate trails that traverse the lake shores and wooded spoil banks offer a varied and impressive evidence of how strip mines can be successfully converted into recreational areas.

Trail 1 is 3.4 miles long, that begins and ends near the beach area. Parking is available at the beach area just west and east of the causeway dam. The trail provides an easy opportunity to view Lake Shakamak and its native shoreline flora such as buttonbush, arrowwood viburnum, waterlilies and arrowhead and related waterfowl. The route is easy to follow as it weaves in and out of the fingerlike inlets of Lake Shakamak. The trail loop ends near the beach and bathhouse.

Connecting Trail 1 is Trail 2, 1.4 miles in distance. The trail is neither difficult or too long. The walker will experience some ups and downs over the spoil banks and ravines that are wooded with oak, hickory, spicebush and white pine plantings. Insects can be a nuisance and the trail is never far from the sound of highway and park traffic. Parking is at the beach parking lot or north of the beach area near the cabins on the east side of the road where a spur trail joins with Trail 2.

Trail 3 begins just east of the Saddle Barn parking lot south of the gatehouse. The one mile loop trail enters a white pine plantation and arrives shortly at the park office drive and open area and continues on through the woods to skirt the north shore of Lake Lenape and Oven Shelterhouse. The trail continues to wind northeast through the oak-hickory forest to arrive again at the Saddle Barn.

Trail 4 connects with Trail 3. It is 1.5 miles long and features a modern walk along the shoreline of Lake Lenape, which is "real men" in the Delaware Indian language. The trail ends in the campground. It connects the campground with the beach.

To reach Shakamak State Park from I-70 exit SR 59 south about 12 miles to SR 246, then east 9 miles to SR 159. Turn south on SR 159 and drive to the park entrance located 3 miles northwest of Jasonville.

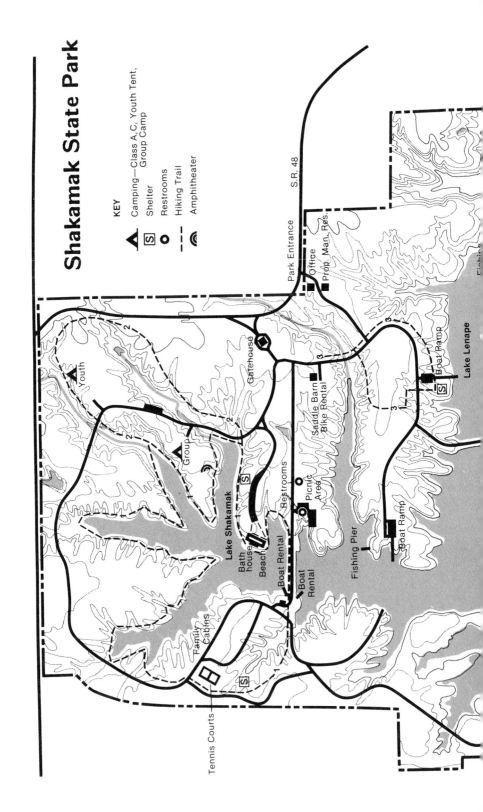

Shakamak State Park

KEY

▲ Camping—Class A,C, Youth Tent, Group Camp

Ⓢ Shelter

● Restrooms

- - - Hiking Trail

◉ Amphitheater

S.R. 48

Park Entrance

Office

Prop. Man. Res.

Gatehouse

Youth

Group

Saddle Barn
Bike Rental

Lake Lenape

Boat Ramp

Ⓢ

Boat Ramp

Lake Shakamak

Ⓢ

Bath house

Beach

Boat Rental

Restrooms

Picnic Area

Boat Rental

Fishing Pier

Family Cabins

Ⓢ

Tennis Courts

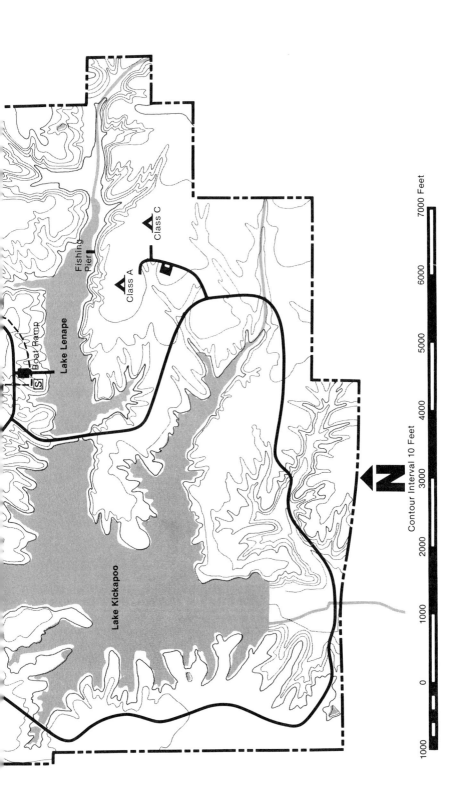

Lake Lenape

Lake Kickapoo

Boat Ramp

Fishing Pier

Class A

Class C

N

Contour Interval 10 Feet

1000   0   1000   2000   3000   4000   5000   6000   7000 Feet

7. GREENE-SULLIVAN STATE FOREST

Dugger, IN/Greene & Sullivan Counties
USGS MAP(S): Dugger, Linton, Bucktown, Sandborn 1:24,000
TRAIL(S) DISTANCE: 30 miles of firelanes
ACREAGE: 6,764 land, 1,500 water
ACTIVITIES: hiking, fishing, camping, picnicking, hunting,
  non-motorized boating, canoe trail, photography, bridle
  trails, and nature study
FEE(S): camping, firewood, private boat rental nearby

Situated west of the hill counties, Greene-Sullivan State Forest was created from reclaimed strip mined coal lands. The first of these lands was donated to the state of Indiana in the 1930's. The Division of Forestry is still obtaining land and has doubled in size. The landscape is dotted with over 100 artificial lakes, all stocked with panfish. Lakes range from 5 to 200 acres. Between the lakes is an abundance of small conical "mounds" of spoil banks. A few lakes are acidic and cannot support fish life. Currently, a hundred acres of land and water are being reclaimed.

Hikers and horsemen share firelane trails that weave and intersect throughout the environs. Some of these trails are wet and muddy and overgrown with brush in sections. Despite this, short and long hikes with map and compass in this unique man altered surrounding is recommended.

Some of the best walking is found in the developed areas of Reservoir #26 and nearby Wampler Lake. Camping sites and picnic tables are located at these largest of lakes within the state forest. Additional picnic tables may also be found at other lakes throughout the forest.

There is a wide variety of wildlife due to the wide range in habitats. One might easily see in an early morning or late afternoon song birds, waterfowl, squirrels, deer, hawks, muskrats and beaver. There are also many types of wild flowers. Many of these can be found along the roadsides as one drives through the forest. These are in bloom throughout the spring, summer, and fall. Rock hounds will find fossils in the rocky outcrops around the lakes. A firetower and rock house are located south of Pleasantville.

Wheelchair ramps are located at Airline, Reservoir #26, and Wampler Lakes. Canoeists will discover the Ledgerwood Canoe Trail to be of special interest. The canoe trail is a two day trip with portages and campsites. Hikers should exercise caution when visiting the property during the fall hunting season as there are many hunters scattered throughout the forest.

To reach Greene-Sullivan State Forest from I-70, take US 41 at Terre Haute south to Sullivan and drive east on SR 54 to Dugger, turn south on SR 159. The property manager's office is located on the east side of SR 159 about 1 1/2 miles south of Dugger. One may also get to Dugger by driving south on SR 67 to SR 54 west at Switz City. The state forest lies between SR 159, 54, and 59 southwest of Linton.

The Department of Natural Resources has also leased from the AMAX Coal Company, 12,500 acres in Sullivan County west of Dugger. This area is known as the Minnehaha Fish and Wildlife Area and is presently the largest fish and wildlife area in the state. The property is also open to hiking and picnicking besides hunting and fishing. Walking the grass covered upland terrain is very prairie-like and includes lakes. Twin Lakes near the property's center is probably the nicest area.

Minnehaha Fish and Wildlife Area is located east of Sullivan on SR 54. For further information regarding this property, visit the check-in station before entering this area on SR 54 just west of Dugger.

Property Manager
Green-Sullivan State Forest
R.R. 1, Box 382
Dugger, IN 47848
(812) 648-2810

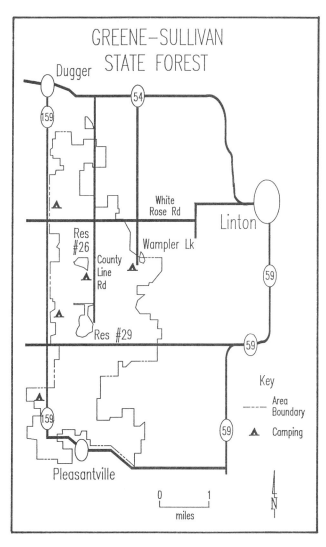

8. WEST BOGGS PARK
Loogootee, IN/Martin and Daviess Counties
USGS MAP(S): Loogootee, Odon 1:24,000
TRAIL DISTANCE: approx. 1 mile
ACREAGE: 600 land and 622 water
ACTIVITIES: hiking and exercise trail, picnicking, shelterhouses, beach, swimming, water skiing, windsurfing, fishing, boating, boat ramp, athlete field, tennis, basketball, volleyball, ballfields, shuffleboard, horseshoes, Go-Kart track, amphitheater, flower garden, Amish restaurant, special events, Class A camping, cabins, regulation 9 hole golf course and mini golf bait and fishing license, arts and crafts, Country Store
Fee(s): entrance, boating fees and rental, beach, shelterhouse rental, gazebo rental, camping, cabin rental

The West Boggs Nature trail is a rather tame and short loop trail that passes through woodland and along lakeshore. The well marked and maintained earthen trail is a fine walk especially with children. It begins and ends about 1/2 mile south of the park office and entry gate next to a seldom used Go-Kart track where parking is available for several vehicles.

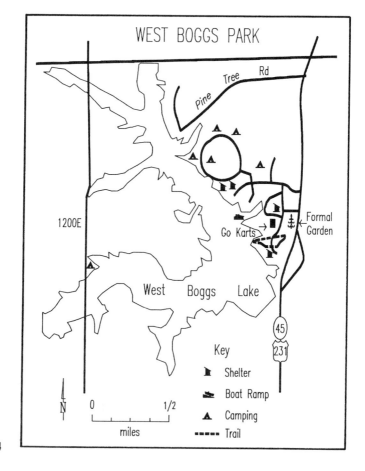

At first the trail descends along the wooded lakeshore pass wood duck box nesting houses and birdfeeder observation sites. The trail continues thru white pines to the playground and picnic area. Crossing the park road where restrooms and parking are located, the trail enters young woods where several trees are labelled. The trail crosses the main park road once more to the parking lot. In the summertime, you may decide to continue your walk north along the park road to the nearby Alex Dyer Formal Garden where there are many home horticultural ideas displayed.

With its rich recreational menu to choose from, hiking alone would not be the only reason to visit this year around quality park.

To reach West Boggs Park entrance drive four miles north of Loogootee on US Highway 231/SR 45.

Superintendent, West Boggs Park
P.O. Box 245, Loogootee, IN 47553, (812) 295-3421

West Boggs Nature Trail

265

9. THOUSAND ACRE WOODS

Washington, IN/Daviess County
USGS MAP(S): Washington, Montgomery 1:24,000
TRAIL(S) DISTANCE: no est. trails, old roads present
ACREAGE: 1,075 acres
ACTIVITIES: hiking, nature study

Thousand Acre Woods is just that plus 75 acres. Drained by Prairie Creek, the seasonally wet woodland is surrounded by miles of rolling and flat open fields. This huge block of bottomlands is the largest acreage of any Indiana Nature Conservancy property. East to west, the property is 2.5 miles long and 0.5 mile wide north to south. Water retaining clay soils support hickory, elm, cottonwood, sycamore, maple, ash, sweet gum, pin oak and swamp white oak. Best months to hike are the bug-free ones from fall to early spring. To explore the woods on foot will require a full day's tramp since there are no established trails.

From Washington, the Daviess County seat, drive north on SR 57, four miles and turn right/east on CR 400N just past the Sugarland Church. Continue one mile east past the curve fork directly towards the woods and park alongside the gravel road. Topographical maps are useful.

The east road access may be found by driving south from the west access at the curve fork CR 75W 0.5 mile. Turn left/east on CR 350N and continue 1.8 miles to CR 250E. Go north/left on CR 250E and travel 0.9 mile to CR 450N and turn right/east to CR 300. Proceed north one mile and the preserve is on the left. You are never out of sight of the woods driving along the country roads enroute west to east.

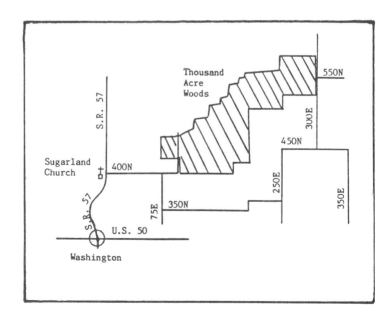

10. GLENDALE STATE FISH & WILDLIFE AREA

Montgomery, IN/Daviess County
USGS MAP(S): Glendale 1:25,000
TRAIL(S) DISTANCE: several miles of firelanes and old roads, undesignated trails
ACREAGE: 8,020 acres includes 1400 acre Dogwood Lake
ACTIVITIES: hiking, nature study, birdwatching, fish hatchery tour, picnicking, year-around fishing, ice-skating, wild food foraging, hunting, motorized and non-motorized boating, river and lake boat launch ramp, boat rental, archery range, Class A-B camping, special events
FEE(S): camping, boat rental, hunting waterfowl, pheasant release

Although there are no marked trails there are several easily accessible natural areas to explore in this abandoned farmscape. Uplands, woodlands, wetlands and 18 small ponds in addition to the well stocked 1400 acre Dogwood Lake, harbor a variety of wildlife.

Just northeast of the visitors center and campground beginning at I1 and I2 parking areas is a overgrown country lane that leads east and then southward along a finger like peninsula that extends out into Dogwood Lake. Other peninsular walks are located west of Catfish Pond and the F1 parking area, south of Wern Pond and E2 parking lot, and north of the dam and J2 parking lot. Fisherman's paths encircle most of the small ponds such as Wren, Little and Big Piney, Bluebird and Goose where birding is fair to good.

South of the reservoir dam is the warm and cool water East Fork Fish Hatchery where there is a self-guiding tour (map and brochure available) from 8 am to 4:30 pm Monday through Friday. The hatchery has 45 earth ponds dotted over the 80 acres where hybrid striped bass, tiger muskie, walleye and channel catfish are reared. Just east of the fish hatchery is a 2 mile long nature walk that follows old roads and a levee to the East Fork of the White River bottoms. Canada geese and other waterfowl nest in this area. Another good hike on the west side of Dogwood Lake begins at the picnic area of the H3 parking lot. Follow the service road to Retriever Pond and continue north to Coyote Pond. Retrace your steps.

Upland game and waterfowl hunting is a popular recreational activity at Glendale, so use caution during season. Pointing and retriever dog field trials are usually held in springtime. Be advised that ticks are especially common in the spring about grassy herbaceous areas.

To reach Glendale State Fishing Area entrance, 10 1/2 miles southeast of Washington, take SR 257 south from US 50 to CR 600S or CR 500S to the village of Glendale. The fish and wildlife area entrance is 1 mile east of Glendale on SR 600S.

Ruby-throated Hummingbird

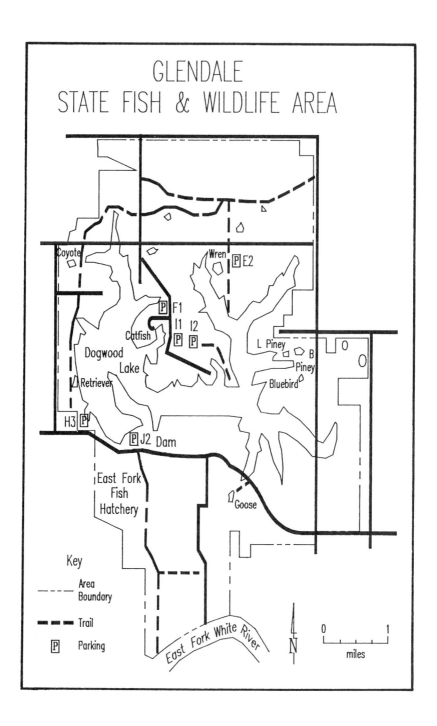

GLENDALE
STATE FISH & WILDLIFE AREA

Coyote

Wren

P E2

P F1

I1 I2

Catfish

P P

L Piney

B
Piney

Dogwood
Lake

Bluebird

O

O

Retriever

H3 P

P J2 Dam

East Fork
Fish
Hatchery

Goose

Key

Area
Boundary

Trail

P Parking

0   1

N

miles

East Fork White River

11. GEORGE HARRISON HOKE WILDLIFE HABITAT TRUST AREA

Oaktown, IN/Knox County
USGS MAP(S): Oaktown, Bicknell 1:24,000
TRAIL(S) DISTANCE: no est. trails
ACREAGE: 60 acres
ACTIVITIES: walking, nature study, wild food foraging

Named in honor of a mid-nineteenth century landowner, this oak-hickory forest is currently under the management of the Indiana Division of Fish and Wildlife as a Wildlife Habitat Trust Area. Even though there are many large trees, the woods shows recent evidence of being grazed and logged. Studies are being carried out to determine the ecological succession following the agricultural and timbering disturbance.

There are no established trails and a large portion of the woods is difficult to walk through due to the new understory growth particularly near the small stream that divides the property. However in the area near the entrance large oaks and maples provide a fairly open understory where paw paw trees are abundant. Spicebush and wildflowers are common. Hawthorn surrounds the forest border along with redbud, wahoo, elm, hackberry, ash, walnut and sycamore. Unfortunately pig pens border the north and east boundary. Yet this protected woodland is a survivor surrounded by an agricultural sea.

To reach George Harrison Hoke Wildlife Habitat Trust Area from Vincennes drive north on US 41 to Oaktown. At Oaktown go east/right on CR 1000N for approximately 2 miles to CR 400 E and turn right/south one mile to CR 900N. Turn east/left and proceed 0.3 mile and go left at the crossroads and travel northeast 1/2 mile to the memorial woods which is marked by a property sign. Parking is limited for 2 to 5 cars at the gate entrance.

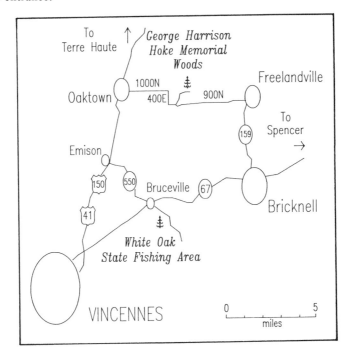

Approximately 10 miles south of George Harrison Hoke Wildlife Habitat Trust area is White Oak State Fishing Area which is also managed by the Division of Fish and Wildlife. Fisherman trails and old roads provide access to the wooded south shore of the first lake (one of two) along the main road. The oak-hickory forest has not been disturbed for several years. The acreage is large enough to invite exploration without any thoughts of getting lost.

White Oak SFA is located northeast of Vincennes off SR 67, 1 mile south of Bruceville. Follow the directional signs.

12. OUABACHE TRAILS PARK/FT. KNOX II HISTORICAL PARK
Vincennes, IN/Knox County
USGS MAP(S): Vincennes, IN-IL, Frichton, IN-IL
TRAIL(S) DISTANCE: 4 miles
ACREAGE: Ouabache 254 acres/Ft. Knox II 34 acres
ACTIVITIES: hiking, nature study, social history, picnicking,
    shelterhouse, interpretive nature center, naturalist walks,
    playfields. playgrounds, Class A tent and trailer camping,
    activities and programs
FEE(S): camping

These two separately administered parklands adjoin each other on the east bluffs of the Wabash River, 3 miles north of Vincennes. Ouabache Trails Park provides outdoor recreation while the south bordering Ft. Knox II is a historical interpretive site. The Louisville & Nashville railroad "divides" the properties from the Wabash River and poses a possible danger. With this in mind the Park Board will develop the trail system to pass under the railroad.

Ouabache Trails is a Knox County park with four miles of interconnecting woodland foot trails that lead from the interpretive center/office and picnic area to Ft. Knox II and from the picnic area north through the forest to the campground. There is an additional loop trail in the wooded floodplain north of the campground. All trails are maintained, easy to moderate, and wood chipped. "Ouabache" is a French translation of the Miami Indian word "Wab-bah-shik-ki" or Wabash. The original French Settlers of Vincennes called the park and fort area, "Le Petit Richer", or "The Little Rock" in reference to the sandstone outcrops visible along the river. The park is open daily 8:00 am to dusk.

Ft. Knox II historic site is owned and managed by the Indiana Historical Society. The exact site of where the fort was erected was determined by the late Dr. Glenn Black, Indiana University archaeologist, who also excavated at Angel Mounds near Evansville, Indiana. Named in honor of the first Secretary of War, Henry Knox, the fort served as a defense for Vincennes and a staging base for Gen. Harrison's attack of Prophetstown at the Battle of Tippecanoe. Ft. Knox II served American military interests from 1803-1813 and was abandoned for reasons it was no longer significant in the defense of Vincennes.

Today, visitors may walk about the 3 foot posts that outline the old fort and read the 15 self-guiding interpretive markers that describe the history of Ft. Knox II. Open hours are: daily 10:00 am to 5:00 pm.

To reach Ouabache Trails and Ft. Knox II from the US 50 Bypass in north Vincennes exit US 41/North 6th Street south and turn right/west at Executive Boulevard, the first right. Follow Executive Boulevard west curving north under the US 50 Bypass and turn left/west onto Old Fort Knox Road. Proceed on Old Fort Knox Road to Ft. Knox II entrance. To reach Ouabache Trails turn right/north at the "T" where Old Fort Knox Road and Ft. Knox Road intersect. There are directional signs.

13. SONOTABAC PREHISTORIC INDIAN MOUND & MUSEUM
Vincennes, IN/Knox County
USGS MAP(S): Vincennes, IN-IL 1:24,000
TRAIL(S) DISTANCE: 100 yards
ACTIVITIES: archaeology museum, prehistoric Indian mound, group
    tours, gift shop
FEE(S): nominal admission

Sonotabac Prehistoric Indian Mound has the distinction of being the second oldest and largest Early Woodland Mound in North America. The inverted cone-shaped ceremonial temple mound rises several feet above the surrounding Wabash Valley floodplain and was constructed by the Hopewell Indians about the time of Christ. It is believed repeated flooding of the river ended the Woodland Peoples occupation. A stairstep trail leads from the base of the mound to the apex and a fine southwestern view.

The first stop is the interpretive center, a converted house, which shelters the museum and gift shop. Arranged in historical sequence, the dioramas and exhibits display prehistoric and historic Indian artifacts primarily of the Lower Wabash Valley and include ceramic arts and crafts, implement tools, and weapons especially projectile points. Sonotabac of "Son of Tabae" was a Piankeshaw (a Miami Indian band who lived along the banks of the Lower Wabash Valley) Indian Chief who assisted George Rogers Clark in the American defeat of the British in early 1779.

Sonobac Prehistoric Indian Mound and Museum are open daily May 1st to September 30 including October weekends from 10:00 am to 4:00 pm and Sunday 1:00 pm to 4:00 pm.

To reach the site at 2401 Wabash Avenue in east Vincennes from US 41 Bypass exit Hart Street south one block and turn right/west onto Veteran's Drive. Proceed on Veteran's Drive west to Wabash Avenue and turn left/south and drive to the parking lot entrance on the right/west side of the street at the "Y" with SR 61.

Red Billed
Woodpecker

271

14. VINCENNES, IN/NATURE PLACES
ACTIVITIES: historical sites, planetarium, river park

While at Vincennes consider visiting other nature oriented locations such as the George Rogers Clark Memorial and grounds, Dunseth Planetarium and Harrison Historical Park on the campus of Vincennes University, and Kimmel City Park on the banks of the Wabash River.

The 26 acre George Rogers Clark Memorial is a national historic park located south of the Lincoln Memorial Bridge by the Wabash River. Gen. Clark and his soldiers captured Ft. Sackville from the British on this site in February 1779 and secured the Northwest Territory during the American Revolution. The visitors center has exhibits, displays, a bookstore and a film of Clark's military conquest. Inside the memorial is a rotunda painted with murals and a bronze statue of Clark. The landscaped grounds offer views of the river, several statues, and adjoins the Old French Cathedral Complex. Located at 401 S. 2nd Street, the memorial and visitor center is open daily 9:00 am to 5:00 pm except Thanksgiving, Christmas, and New Year's Days.

Ten blocks north on N. 2nd Street at the campus of Vincennes University is the Dunseth Planetarium. Public planetarium lecture demonstrations are given the last Sunday of the month from September to May at 2:00 pm in the Dome Room. This "Theatre of the Heavens" is located on the east campus at the southwest corner of 4th and Center Streets. A nominal admission is charged.

Consider walking about the 87 acre landscaped campus of Vincennes University. Founded in 1801, the junior college is the oldest west of the Allegheny Mountains. Harrison Historical Park on Harrison Street south of the campus includes the Old Territorial Capitol, Western Sun Printing Office, Indiana author Maurice Thompson Home, and Grouseland, home of William Henry Harrison. A nominal fee is charge and tickets may be purchased at the Log Cabin visitor center nearby.

The 16 acre Kimmel Park is north and west of downtown and Vincennes University along the Wabash River. This city park offers picnicking, shelterhouse, play courts, fishing, boat ramp, boating and pleasant surroundings. The park is located along Oliphant Drive.

Hemmer Woods Nature Preserve

15. HEMMER WOODS
Buckskin, IN/Gibson County
USGS MAP(S): Lynnville 1:24,000
TRAIL(S) DISTANCE: 0.7 mile
ACREAGE: 72 acres
ACTIVITIES: hiking, nature study

Formerly owned by the Hemmer family since 1870, Hemmer Woods was acquired by the state of Indiana in 1974. It was dedicated as a state nature preserve as well as a National Natural Landmark. This "living museum" of old growth hardwoods is a rarity in southwestern Indiana and a pleasure to visit.

The Upland Nature Trail, a self-guiding loop, begins and ends at the registration box where a trail brochure is available. The 25 numbered stations match the trail brochure and identify the arboreal residents and the ecology of the predominantly oak-hickory forest. The upland portion of the woods harbors white, black, and red oaks, shagbark and pignut hickories, white ash, sassafras, dogwood and pawpaw on the slopes and ravines.

Hemmer Woods is located 2.5 miles east of Buckskin. Take CR 900S east 2 miles to CR 1050E (fourth intersection after the Buckskin railroad tracks) and turn left/north and drive 1/2 mile to the marked parking lot across from an abandoned farmhouse. Buckskin is located north of Evansville and I-64 on SR 57.

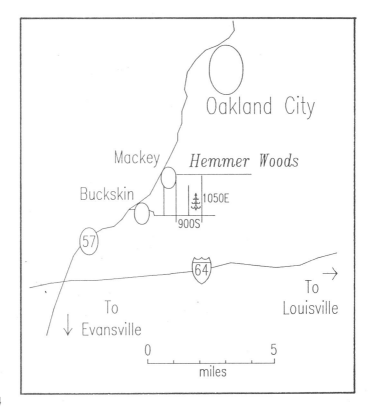

274

16. NEW HARMONY, IN/NATURE PLACES

ACTIVITIES: walking tour, gardens, parks, natural history exhibits, fossil site, Historic New Harmony Tours, social history, cultural arts, camping

FEE(S): tours, Murphy Park camping, entrance fee to Old Dam site

Recognized as a state and national historic landmark, the community of New Harmony is known for its restoration as well as a present day cultural arts and education center. Many of the buildings and gardens of two short lived early 19th century utopian experiments in communal living have been authentically restored. Moved by a modern day philanthropic spirit, newly established contemporary buildings and gardens continue to "make" history with their progressive designs. Walking is a pleasure in this refreshing small river town. Emphasis is placed on the natural history rather than the social history on this described tour. Tour tickets may be purchased at the Atheneum Visitors Center or separate admission may be paid at individual historic homes and buildings.

The Atheneum Visitors and Community Center at the intersection of Arthur and North Streets should be the first stop. This architectural wonder of aluminum, steel and glass, appears ship-like as if moored on the banks of the Wabash River. Of particular interest is the outdoor amphitheater and the roof top observation promontory.

Immediately east of the Atheneum on North Street is the 1822 David Lenz House and restored garden of "old fashioned" flowers and herbs. The home and garden portray an example of how residential life was for the Harmonists. The first commune which was highly religious in outlook under the guidance of George Rapp (1819-1824). There is a fee to tour the home however the tour of the garden is free.

Continue walking east on North Street past the intersection of West Street and in the middle of the next block on the south side is the Carol Owen Memorial Garden. The wooden board fenced garden retreat is densely shaded by Bradford pears. Gravel paths are outlined by an extensive ground cover of lily-of-the-valley. A Fountain of Life is the central focal point of the peaceful garden and benches have been well placed for rest and meditation.

Across the street is the Roofless Church, an interdenominational place of worship that commemorates New Harmony's religious heritage. The grounds and interior of the open air chapel are enhanced with plantings of flowering crab apples, hackberry, yews and golden rain trees. The golden rain tree was first introduced to the United States via Mexico to New Harmony by William MacClure, a geologist and naturalist of the second social but secular experiment of Welsh industrialist Robert Owen. A pine shingled canopy at the west end of the open space is, according to the architect Phillip Johnson, "shaped like a upside down rosebud that casts the shadow of a full blown rose".

At the corner of Main and North Street walk north to Tillich Park. Mounded evergreen spruces and spiritual inscriptions carved into large boulders line the short loop pathway. The thought provoking inscriptions were selected from the writings of Paul Tillich, a 20th century German theologian who is buried here (see page 5).

David Lenz House, New Harmony

Retrace your steps back to North Street and continue walking eastward to the corner intersection with Brewery Street. On the southeast corner is the 1824-1825 Hop House and Distillery of the Harmonists which produced as much as 500 gallons of beer a day. A garden demonstration of hop vine cultivation may be seen on the grounds. The twining vines of the Mulberry Family yielded ripe dried catkins used by the Harmonists to impart flavor to their malt brews. Although not seen today, the original avenue plantings included mulberry trees, and beds of flowers and herbs between walks and curbs.

Proceed south on Brewery Street two blocks and turn east onto Church Street. In the middle of the block across from Thrall's Opera House is the 1829 John Beal House. Inside are several natural science exhibits of William MacClure, Thomas Say, and Charles-Alexandre Lesueur. These 3 men were scientists from the "Boatload of Knowledge" of Robert Owen's social experiment. An admission fee is charged.

After viewing the exhibits head west down Church Street and walk south onto Brewery Street once more. Follow Brewery Street one block south to Tavern Street and go west to mid-block and the 1820 George Keppler House, the second house on the right side of the street. David Dale Owen's geological collection is housed within. This was the site of Owen's (son of Robert Owen, founder of the 2nd social experiment) geological laboratory where he conducted surveys that opened up the Old Northwest to development. There is an admission fee.

Continue walking west on Tavern Street to the Lichtenberger Building at the northeast corner of Tavern and Main Streets. The building quarters the Maxmilliam and Bodmer collections of the Upper Missouri River explorations.

Four blocks south from the Lichtenberger Building on Main Street is Murphy Park, the main city park. Camping is available as well as picnicking. Three more blocks south of Murphy Park is the Labyrinth or the Harmonist's "Path of Life". Maintained and owned by the Indiana Division of Heritage Preservation/DNR the re-created Labyrinth is situated just south of the original garden. Pruned English privet shrubs form living walls that separate the numerous circular-shaped paths from each other and all but one leads to blind alleys or cul de sacs. The right path leads to a central temple that is inscribed with biblical verses. The mystic maze symbolizes life's difficult choices and the right path of God leads to harmony and salvation.

If you really feel like walking, the last stop is the Old Dam on the Wabash River, an additional 2 mile round trip hike. Historically, 19th century New Harmony residents enjoyed leisurely Sunday picnic outings to this scenic natural rock ledge that becomes a series of rapids during dry periods. More importantly, the shale, siltstone and Pennsylvanian limestone was and is fossil rich and from 1840-1870 the New Harmony scientists made important paleontological discoveries. Fossils obtained from the Old Dam site are today found in geological museum collections throughout the United States. The Old Dam is privately owned but opened to the public for fishing and visitation for a small fee.

To reach the Old Dam from New Harmony turn right at the Maple Hill Cemetery from south Main Street just past the Labyrinth onto gravel road 540N. Follow 540N south about 1/2 mile and turn right/west onto the Old Dam Road/435N. Follow the Old Dam Road/435 west about 1/3 mile, and turn right/north at the road curve onto a gravel road lane. The Old Dam site is about 100 yards from the road.

Owen Garden, New Harmony

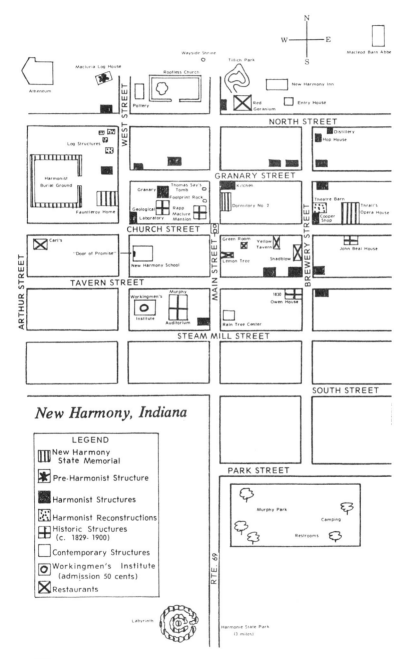

New Harmony, Indiana

LEGEND

New Harmony State Memorial

Pre-Harmonist Structure

Harmonist Structures

Harmonist Reconstructions

Historic Structures (c. 1829- 1900)

Contemporary Structures

Workingmen's Institute (admission 50 cents)

Restaurants

17. HARMONIE STATE PARK

New Harmony, IN/Posey County
USGS MAP(S): Solitude 1:24,000
TRAIL(S) DISTANCE: 6 trails total 7.5 miles
ACREAGE: 3,465 acres
ACTIVITIES: hiking, nature center, seasonal naturalist, picnicking, shelterhouses, playground, swimming pool, lifeguard, playfields, bicycle trail, Hoosier Hills Bike Route, fishing, bridle trails, camp store, youth, rally, Class A campgrounds, dumping station, cultural arts program
FEE(S): entrance, pool fee, shelter reservation, bike rental, camping

Established in 1966, Harmonie State Park borders the Wabash River a few miles south of New Harmony, Indiana. The level to rolling landscape was acquired from oil companies whose "rights" are still evident to visitors by the over 100 active oil wells. The 6 maintained trails do not lead to any outstanding physical features such as caves, rock formations, high hills, or scenic vistas or even along the Wabash River. However they do meander thru shady forest and ravines with a chance to see wildlife.

Trail 1 is a moderate one mile long loop that begins and ends at the Youth and Rally camping area. The grassy trail rapidly descends into a ravine then gradually ascends the slope to a level open area close to the main park road. The trail wanders past one of the park's largest pecan trees. Pecan hickory trees usually bear heavily every 3 to 5 years and prefer the inundated habitat of river bottoms of the Wabash and Ohio River in Indiana.

Trail 2 is a moderate 1.5 mile loop that connects with Trail 4. It begins at the main campground campsites 194-195 and follow a service road to a meadow opening. The trail continues across a small stream curving east along an old county road uphill back to the campground's main entry station. An access trail spur to Trail 4 is on the right just before the bridge and the trek uphill.

Trail 3 is an easy one mile loop that begins near the Poplar Grove Picnic area near the park entrance. The trail connects a service road to the water tower and crosses Bend Run and heads uphill back to the picnic area. This path can be muddy and wet.

Trail 4 is a moderate 2.5 mile loop and is considered the best hiking trail in the park. There is no designated trailhead but access to the trail is available from Walnut Ridge, Sycamore Ridge and Cherry Hill picnic areas as well as from the main campground and trail 2. From Walnut Ridge to Cherry Hill picnic areas the trail follows a grassy mowed service road alongside the main park road. The trail crosses the road just northeast of Cherry Hill picnic areas and gradually descends into a scenic ravine. Go left up and down and old county road towards Walnut Grove. A right turn would lead to the Trail 2 campground loop.

Trail 5 is a easy 3/4 mile near-loop that begins at the campground gate and heads north skirting 2 wildlife ponds and the park's bicycle trail before curving back south to the campground and campsites 94-95.

Trail 6 is a short 3/4 mile loop that begins at Cherry Hill picnic shelter and heads down the ridge and curves back to the shelterhouse.

Harmonie State Park is located 4 miles south of New Harmony and 12 miles north of Mt. Vernon on SR 69. Visitor hours: 7:00 am-11:00 pm.

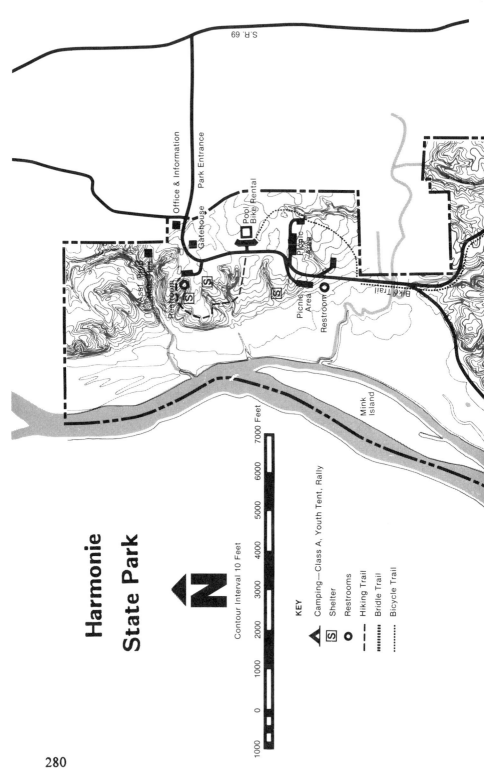

Harmonie
State Park

Contour Interval 10 Feet

KEY

▲ Camping—Class A, Youth Tent, Rally
Ⓢ Shelter
⊙ Restrooms
— — Hiking Trail
▪▪▪▪ Bridle Trail
⋯⋯ Bicycle Trail

S.R. 69

Office & Information

Park Entrance

Gatehouse

Pool/Bike Rental

Picnic Area

Restroom

Picnic Area

Restroom

Bike Trail

Mink Island

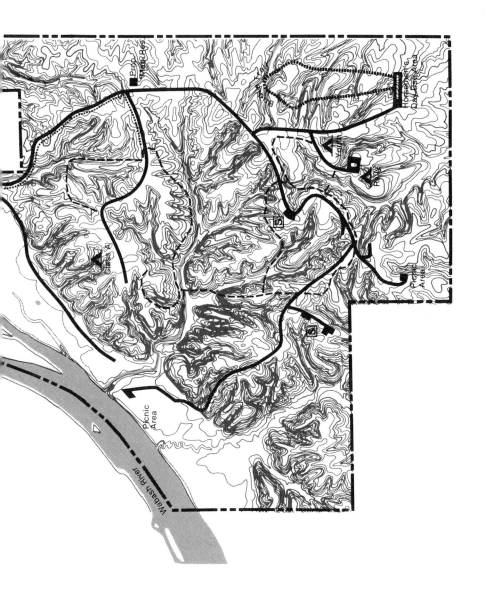

18. HOVEY LAKE STATE FISH & WILDLIFE AREA
TWIN SWAMPS NATURE PRESERVE

MT. Vernon, IN/Posey County
USGS MAP(S): Uniontown 1:24,000
TRAIL(S) DISTANCE: Hovey Lake SFWA no est. trails/300 ft. boardwalk
    Twin Swamps NP
ACREAGE: 4,400 land, 1,400 lake HLSFWA/600 acre TSNP
ACTIVITIES: hiking, nature study, birdwatching, wild food foraging,
    picnicking, fishing, hunting, boat ramp, canoeing and boating, Class
    C primitive camping. Twin Swamps Nature Preserve allows hiking and
    nature study only
FEE(S): camping and boat rental at Hovey Lake

Geographically and botanically, Point Township, Posey County is about as "southern" as one can be in the Hoosier state. A number of plant species found at these two Lower Wabash and Ohio River state properties belong to the flora of the Mississippi Valley and find their northern limits in this area. These southern affinities make the visit unique and somewhat out of the ordinary in comparison to other parts of Indiana.

Hovey Lake, named in honor of former Governor Alvin P. Hovey of Mt. Vernon (1889-91), is a 500 year old oxbow lake that was created when the Ohio River short cutted across a horseshoe bend. Pecan, southern red oak, swamp privet, mistletoe, water lotus and bald cypress, some over 200 years old, are part of the southern floral types growing along the lake border and surrounding swamplands.

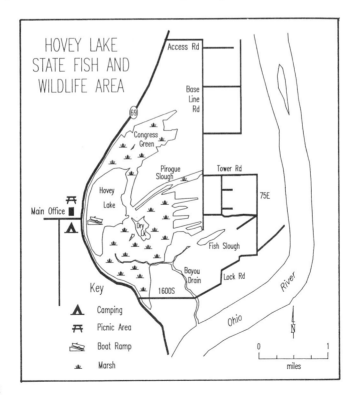

The large lake provides an ideal habitat for resident and migratory waterfowl such as herons, cormorants, white ibis, and bald eagle, osprey, ducks, and geese.

The primary purpose of the state fish and wildlife area is to provide quality hunting and fishing however hikers are welcome although there are no established trails. Much of the surrounding land is under water during the winter and spring months making it seemingly more ideal for canoeists than hikers and insects can be a problem during the warm season. The months of October to April are considered the best months to visit Hovey Lake. This time of year offers a insect free opportunity to see unique migratory birdlife heading south and north along the Mississippi flyway. It is also the wintering grounds of thousands of ducks and geese.

The best areas to explore on foot are the old county and service roads, closed to unauthorized vehicles, on the north, south, and east sides of Hovey Lake which is home to the swamp rabbit and pecan trees. Hovey Lake State Fish and Wildlife Area is located at the end of SR 69, approximately 9 miles southwest of Mt. Vernon.

Twin Swamps is a dedicated nature preserve approximately 2 miles west of the Hovey lake entrance at the end of SR 69 on CR 1500S. The preserve, the largest of the state nature preserves, was previously owned by Oakland City College, Oakland City, Indiana. Oil wells frequent the edge of the preserve but the interior of the property is undisturbed. From 1500S follow the service road north into the swampland. A mile long loop trail leads from the parking lot to a 300 foot boardwalk that juts out into the center of the most easterly of the two bald cypress swamps or sloughs. The preserve also harbors an abundance of overcup oak as well as post, laurel, pin, and Shumard's red oaks. Sugarberry, pecan, sweet gum, swamp cottonwood, buttonbush and trumpet creeper are also part of the flora. The rare eastern mud turtle, active from April to October, finds refuge in the swamps.

Gray Woods, which is adjacent south of Twin Swamps, was recently acquired by The Nature Conservancy. This 370 acre cypress and bottomland hardwood forest does not have accessible foot trails but access may be provided in the future.

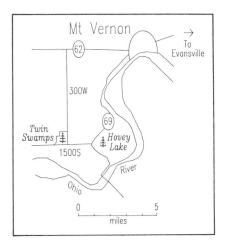

19. GOOSE POND CYPRESS SLOUGH
MT. Vernon, IN/Posey County
USGS MAP(S): Caborn, IN-KY 1:24,000
TRAIL(S) DISTANCE: no est. trails
ACREAGE: 60 acres
ACTIVITIES: walking, nature study

Posey County is home to the largest number of public accessible natural stands of bald cypress remaining in southwestern Indiana. More bald cypress swamps were destroyed in the original 5 county range by drainage and logging than exist today. The geologist Collett in 1874 estimated that 20,000 acres of trees covered southwestern Knox County in an area known as Little Cypress Swamp and today only remnants remain.

Goose Pond Cypress Slough is a prime example of a bald cypress slough or swamp. This 3 mile long backwater pond and marsh area was at one time part of the river channel for the evershifting Ohio River that now flows just over a mile to the south. There are no established trails or boardwalks but the remote gravel road that runs alongside the preserve will provide good views of the cypress and Goose Pond especially at the bridge. The bald cypress is a deciduous member of the Redwood Family (Taxodiaceae) and reaches its northwest range limit in southwestern Indiana. Conspicuous features of the trees are the cone-shaped knees, the enlarged trunks near the base and the light green delicate foliage that turns brown in autumn. The oldest trees in eastern North America are the bald cypress growing in the Big Cypress Swamp of southern Florida. Mosquitoes can be pesky during the warm summer months. The property is under the ownership of The Nature Conservancy.

To reach Goose Pond Cypress Slough drive east from Mt. Vernon on SR 62 approximately 3.5 miles and turn right/south onto 500E. Follow 500E south nearly 3 miles to the preserve which is just north of the curve and bridge along the left/east side of the road.

Cypress Tree, Goose Pond

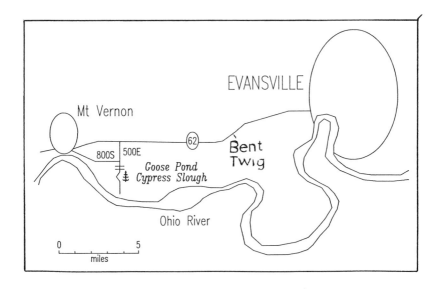

20. BENT TWIG OUTDOOR LEARNING ENVIRONMENT
Evansville,IN/Vanderburgh County
TRAIL(S) DISTANCE: 8 self-guiding trails total 2 miles
ACREAGE: 25 land acres, 7 acre lake
ACTIVITIES: hiking, nature study, fishing

Located adjacent to the 300 acre campus of the University of Southern Indiana, 5 miles west of Evansville just off SR 62, Bent Twig Outdoor Learning Environment is a small woodland interspersed with connecting foot trails that traverse runs, ravines, and alongside the watery borders of Reflection Lake.   Twenty species of hardwood trees have been identified by markers. Developed by the Westwood Garden Club and aided by the Boy Scout Troop #371, Bent Twig is an inviting place to learn about lake, marsh, riparian and woodland life. The 8 short trails explore all the diverse habitats of the outdoor learning area.

Trail Descriptions:
A. Border Trail--woodland and ravine, interconnects with many trails
B. Meditation Point Walk--scenic waterfall area, fairly level trail
C. Mandrake Walk--woodland walk, moderate
D. Fern Walk--moist slope supports abundant and diverse fern life
E. Lake Shore Walk--views of USI campus from Reflection Lake
F. Ridge Trail--brushy young woodland growth
G. Columbine Walk--lake cove walk
H. Marsh Plant Walk--wetland habitat in prairie-like opening

The Bent Twig main trailhead begins just west of the tennis courts and parking area.   A large entrance sign features a map of the trails. The trails are hikeable from sunrise to sunset and are open to the general public.

21. MESKER PARK ZOO
Evansville, IN/Vanderburgh County
WALKWAYS DISTANCE: 1.5 miles
ACREAGE: 67 acres
ACTIVITIES: zoo tour, party decks, group tours, train tour,
pedalboats, snack bar, gift shop, educational programs, zoological
society, gift shop, support group
FEE(S): admission, party shelter rental, pedalboat rental, train
rides, stroller rental, group rates and advance ticket sales
available

Mesker Park Zoo is virtually a "living museum collection" of over 700
native and exotic animals. The gently rolling 67 acres are well
landscaped and wooded with natural plantings. The 22 acre lake and
smaller ponds are surrounded by all weather, handicapped accessible
walkways, and instead of fences, many of the exhibits are separated from
visitors by moats for ideal observation. This regional zoological parkland
features indigenous North American mammals such as Arctic fox, black
bear, bobcat, and wolves. African zebra, elephant, giraffe and lion,
Australian kangaroo, emu, and wallaby, Asian tiger, leopard,. and deer are
some exotics. The zoo is arranged not only by specimen but
geographically: Asian Valley, East African Plains or Veldt, and Tropical
Americas. A children's petting zoo is a pleasant experience for children
and adults.
Open all year, the zoo's hours are from 9:00 am to 4:00 pm daily.
The zoo is closed Christmas and New year's Day.
To reach Mesker Park Zoo at St. Joseph and Bement Avenues in
Mesker Park, northwest Evansville, take I-64 exit south on US 41 and
drive approximately 12.5 miles to SR 66/Diamond Avenue. Turn west onto
SR 66/Diamond Avenue and proceed 3.5 miles to St. Joe Avenue and turn
left at the second intersection onto Bement Avenue. Follow the
directional signs to the parking area.

Public Relations, Mesker Park Zoo
Bement Avenue, Evansville, IN 47712
812-428-0715

22. EVANSVILLE MUSEUM OF ARTS AND SCIENCE
Evansville, IN/Vanderburgh County
ACTIVITIES: science, anthropology, history, art collections,
planetarium, cultural programs, guided tours, lectures, classes,
museum memberships
FEE(S): planetarium admission, special programs

Overlooking the Ohio River in downtown Evansville's Sunset Park is
the Museum of Arts and Science. Of special interest to nature
enthusiasts are the natural history exhibits of the Koch Science Center
and Science Discovery Forest. The 2nd Level Anthropology Gallery
features displays of North and South American Indian life from 13,000
B.C. to modern times. In addition the Koch Planetarium on the 3rd upper

level presents a series of multi-media astronomy programs and lectures throughout the year. Showtimes are Saturday at 1:00 pm and 2:00 pm, Sunday at 2:00 pm and 3:30 pm. Daily shows are presented during the summer. The museum hours are Tuesday through Saturday 10:00 am to 5:00 pm and Sunday 12:00 noon to 5:00 pm. An outdoor Sculpture Garden provides fine views of the Ohio River.

The Evansville Museum of Arts and Science is located at 411 Southeast Riverside Drive. From I-64 exit south onto US 41 and drive south approximately 17 miles to Veterans Memorial Parkway. Turn west and proceed about 2.5 miles to the museum parking lot on the south or river side of the road.

Public Relations
The Evansville Museum of Arts and Science
411 Southeast Riverside Drive, Evansville, IN 47708

23. WESSELMAN WOODS NATURE PRESERVE & NATURE CENTER

Evansville, IN/Vanderburgh County
TRAIL(S) DISTANCE: 8 self guiding trails total 4 1/2 miles
ACREAGE: 200 acres
ACTIVITIES: hiking, environmental education, interpretive center,
amphitheater, gift shop, general public programs, field trips,
library, prairie reconstruction, butterfly garden, pond

Only minutes from downtown Evansville, Wesselman Woods Nature Preserve and Nature Center encompasses one of the finest virgin hardwood forests in southern Indiana. Dedicated a National Natural Landmark, this urban woodland of 200 acres is owned by the city of Evansville and is open to the public year around. The nature center is the first place to visit before walking the marked trails. The modern rustic facility offers indoor natural history displays, a bird observation area, library, classrooms, a bookstore, and the administrative offices. A butterfly garden is located near the building. A self-guiding trail map and flora and fauna brochures are available.

Ten trails traverse the flat, poorly drained woodland. The magnificent stand of large trees include Shumard's red oak, sweet gum, pin oak, green ash, swamp white oak, red elm, tulip, red maple, white oak, black gum, wild black cherry, sassafras, and big shellbark hickory. The woods has state nature preserve status. The seven acre adjoining field contains a freshwater pond, wildlife plantings, and a reconstructed prairie.

The nature center is open Tuesday through Saturday 8:30 am to 4:30 pm and Sunday 12:00 noon to 4:00 pm and closed Mondays, year round.

Wesselman Park Nature Center and Preserve is located at 551 North Boeke Road in northeast Evansville. To reach the facility from I-64 exit US 41 south and drive to Evansville and turn east on the Lloyd Expressway. Take the Bocke Road exit and go north. Go past the Roberts Stadium entrance to the main park entrance. Follow the park road all the way to the back. Parking is available next to the nature center.

Director
Wesselman Woods Nature Preserve and Nature Center
551 North Boeke Road
Evansville, IN 47711
(812) 479-0771

Great Horned Owl

Debra Wilkerson

24. ANGEL MOUNDS STATE HISTORIC SITE

Evansville, IN/Vanderburgh & Warrick Counties
USGS MAP(S): Newburgh 1:24,000
TRAIL(S) DISTANCE: self-guiding 2 mile interpretive loop walk
ACREAGE: 103 acres
ACTIVITIES: archeological history walk, interpretive center, exhibits,
   displays, slide program, book store, group tours

Once an important religious, political and trade center, Angel Mounds is one of the best examples of Middle Mississippian Indian culture and one of the best preserved sites in the United States. From 1250 to 1450 A.D., prehistoric native Americans lived here on the banks of the Ohio River. It is estimated 1,000 to 3,000 villagers cultivated food crops, built homes, defense fortifications, and various types of mounds.

Artifacts and exhibits of the people are displayed at the interpretive center along with a video presentation. Through the back door of the center and over and beyond the wooden bridge lies the partially reconstructed prehistoric town. Interpretive markers are placed at key points along the grassy paths that lead past a portion of the reconstructed stockade, several thatched home dwellings, 11 mounds of which the most significant are the Central Mound and Temple Mound. There are several theories why this prosperous thriving site was abandoned such as climatic change, depletion of natural resources, revolution, disease and war but its decline remains a mystery.

The present day historic site was purchased by the Indiana Historical Society from the Angel family in 1938 and was transferred to the state of Indiana in 1947. Under the direction of Glenn A. Black, Indiana University archaeologist, the site was excavated from 1938-1964, thereby providing much of our present-day knowledge about the Middle Mississippian cultural site (so named because their culture was first discovered along the Mississippi River between St. Louis and Memphis). The 63 acre Ashumbala (Choctaw Indian word for cottonwood tree) Nature Preserve lies immediately east, adjacent to the Angel Mounds State Historic Site. Access is by permission only to the wooded floodplain that stretches one mile in length along the Ohio River.

Angel Mounds State Historic Site is open free every day but Monday and most major holidays (open Memorial Day, July 4th and Labor Day). The hours are 9:00 am to 5:00 pm. Wednesday thru Saturday and 1:00 pm to 5:00 pm Sunday and Tuesday. To reach Angel Mounds at 8215 Pollack Avenue 7 miles east of Evansville, exit I-64 onto US 41 and drive south to Evansville. Continue approximately 2 miles south past SR 66 to Riverside Drive. Turn south east on Riverside Drive 3 blocks to the intersection with Pollack Drive and turn east. Proceed about 4.5 miles to the entrance of Angel Mounds State Historic Site.

Of further interest to hikers is the *Muskhogen Trail, a flood control grassy levee that spans 10 linear miles from Angel Mounds Historic Site to downtown Evansville's Riverfront Park. The levee was constructed in 1937 by the Army Corps of Engineers. The Boy Scout Troop #301 was responsible for designating the levee as a foot path. The trail is safe and scenic along the Ohio River from Riverfront Park until it reaches the US 41 highway crossing which is very dangerous. Once across US 41 the levee is intersected by numerous street and road crossings. The last 2 miles are the least congested. The levee ends just west of Angel Mounds near Chicksaw Drive. Parking for day-users of the trail is best at Angel Mounds parking area or the downtown Sunset Park area just west of Riverfront Park. A car shuttle is advised for those who plan to walk the entire length.

*(Since this writing the trail has been rerouted).

Historic Site Curator, Angel Mounds State Historic Site
8125 Pollack Avenue, Evansville, IN 47708
(812) 853-3956

25. LYNNVILLE PARK & SCALES LAKE PARK

Lynnville & Boone, IN/Warrick & Gibson Counties
USGS MAP(S): Lynnville, Boonville 1:24,000
TRAIL(S) DISTANCE: no est. trails
ACREAGE: Lynnville 1100a./Scales 477a.
ACTIVITIES: Lynnville: beach swimming, boating non-motorized
    picnicking, shelterhouse, concessions, cabin rental, camping,
    observatory, coal museum. Scales lake: picnicking, playground,
    swimming, boating non-motorized, fishing, concessions, camping
FEE(S): admission, camping, cabin rental, fishing fee, swimming fee,
    shelterhouse reservation

Closely situated, both of these water oriented parks were created from former strip mined coal pits. Peabody Coal Company donated to the Town of Lynnville a 1,100 acre tract with 275 water acres for use as a recreational area and city water supply in 1964. There are no established hiking trails but the service roads especially Mid, West and Fire Roads

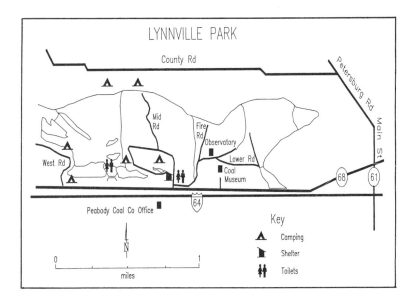

enter the remote areas of Lynnville Park. Waterfowl and other wildlife are attracted to the numerous ponds. The "compact" landscape contains many now wooded slag heaps that appear as small hills. Several miles of trail could be constructed to follow the "ridges" alongside the ponds. Of special interest to stargazers is the Wahnsiedler Observatory which shelters one of the largest telescopes in Indiana. Operated by the Evansville Astronomical Society, the observatory has special hours for public viewing and group tours. For hours and group tour information (10 or more) call (812) 922-5681. Usually the observatory is open the first Saturday of each month at 7:30 pm. The Museum of Coal Industry is currently under construction.

Lynnville Park is open all year. To reach Lynnville Park from I-64 exit SR 61 at Lynnville and drive north less than a mile to SR 68 and turn west. Drive 2 miles on SR 68 to the park entrance.

Scales Lake, a Warrick County park, is located 10.5 miles south of I-64 Lynnville exit on SR 61 just north of Boonville. The strip mined area, given as a gift to the state of Indiana by the owner of the same name, was formerly a state forest and state beach recreation area before its return to Warrick County. The 73 acre man constructed lake was built during the 1930's. Formerly at the foot of the dam, the Division of Wildlife (DNR) maintained a fish rearing pond. The 3 acre beach includes a bathhouse and non-motorized boat launch ramp. Unmarked trails lead through the mostly wooded park.

To access Scales Lake County Park from SR 61 take the Boonville Road north or the Tennyson Road on the north edge of Boonville.

26. PIKE STATE FOREST

Winslow, IN/Pike County
USGS MAP(S): Augusta, Winslow, Velpen, Otwell 1:24,000
TRAIL(S) DISTANCE: 1/2 mile Tree Identification Trail, 15 miles of
    firelanes, 7 miles of horse trails
ACREAGE: 2,914 acres
ACTIVITIES: hiking, nature study, picnicking, shelterhouses, fishing,
    playground, bridle trails, hunting, firetower, forest management
    tours, horsemens camp, Class C camping
FEE(S): camping

Land acquisition for Pike State Forest began in the 1930's and has continued to the present day. The WPA went to work during the depression and early WW II days to construct the property's buildings using oak trees from native stands. The terrain varies from hilly forested upland (40%) to the low bottomlands (60%) along the Patoka River. The proposed 28,000 acre Patoka River National Wildlife Refuge would extend along the "Hartwell Bottoms" of the river throughout Pike County and would provide necessary habitat for waterfowl and other wildlife especially wood duck. Surprisingly in an area of intense coal production, only 3 acres of the state forest has been strip-mined. Like all state forest lands, a multiple use policy is in effect (timber, wildlife, watershed and recreation). Pike State Forest is named in honor of General Zebulon M. Pike.

Designated hiking trails are nearly non-existent yet horse bridle trails are blue blazed and found throughout the forest and are hikeable. A self guiding 1/2 mile Tree Identification Trail (18 trees) extends from the picnic shelter and playground area to a parking pullout along the main park road near the river. The "hill-ravine-hill" trail is situated just east of the camping area. In addition numerous firelanes and horse trails provide access to all areas of the state forest. Firelane #12 follows alongside Hog Branch Ravine and begins just north of the service area and property office where parking is available. The blue blazed horse trails that follow alongside the west bank of the Patoka River are scenic but tend to be popular and "horsed-out" for hikers. Mosquitos and poison ivy are common in the river bottoms. The Patoka is a steep and muddy banked stream however rare sandstone outcroppings are found south of the main river access road east of the property office. In short, Pike State Forest is oriented more to horsemen and not the hiker but this "out-of-the-way" state forest is worthy of visitation and exploring on a quiet week day. Be advised of the hunting season from mid October to mid December.

Pike State Forest entrance is located 6 miles south east of Winslow on SR 61 to SR 364 east in Pike County.

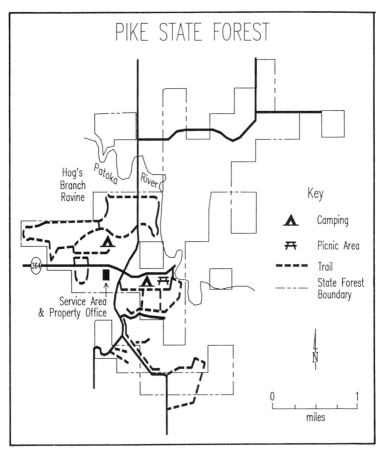

27. PATOKA FISH & WILDLIFE AREA

Winslow, IN/Pike & Warrick Counties
USGS MAP(S): Augusta, Oakland City, Winslow, Folsomville 1:24,000
TRAIL(S) DISTANCE: foot trails around lakes/service roads
ACREAGE: over 6,889
ACTIVITIES: hiking, nature study, picnicking, canoeing, fishing,
    primitive camping
FEE(S): camping

Patoka Fish and Wildlife Area is undergoing a contest for a new name
to avoid confusion with Patoka Lake. It consists of 6 separate landholdings located primarily within Pike County but also includes portions
of adjacent north Warrick County. Nearly half of the properties are
comprised of reclaimed strip-mining pits 33 acres and smaller, some dating
over 100 years old, leased from 2 coal companies. The other property
half has remained rugged rolling forest and fields.
Developed for sportsmen and not hikers, designated hiking trails are
limited at Patoka FWA. Aside from overgrown shoreline fishing trails
constructed by the YCC at several pits, it is entirely service road walking
or cross country compass-venturing. Hikers are advised to use caution
during the hunting seasons.
Area I consists of 929 acres and is located 2 miles west of Winslow
along access Sugar Ridge Road 150S from SR 61. Picnicking, non-
motorized boating, boat ramps, trap range, and camping facilities are
provided. Besides service roads, well used fishermen paths exist along
the shores of West, Twin, East Twin, Dog Leg Pits and Lotor Lake.
Area II lacks the facility development of Area I but is popular with
fishermen and hunters. The 768 acres have several strip-mined pits of
which the largest are Pigeon and Whitney. Area II is located 2 1/2 miles
southwest of Winslow off SR 61 on Number 7 Road/550S.

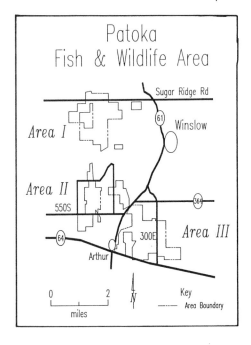

Area III is developed with picnicking, primitive camping, boat ramp, rifle, and archery range. Across from the camp ground is Ashby Pit which features an overgrown Shoreline Trail. To reach Area III drive 2 miles south of Winslow on SR 61 to SR 364 and turn east. Follow SR 364 past Patoka SFWA headquarters to 300 East and turn south to Area III.

Area IV is 600 acres centering around a 33 acre lake which although is very picturesque does not contain water quality good enough to support fish life. The area has a good balance of hardwoods and pines. There are no facilities in the area. It is located 3 miles east of SR 61 on SR 364 then 0.6 miles south on 450E.

Area V is located in north central and eastern Warrick County, east of Lynnville 6 miles and west of Selvin, 3 miles north of SR 68 on 300E. The undeveloped 1,465 remote acres are nearly inaccessible. The area is not recommended for exploration except by compass and topographical maps only. Be further advised the vegetation of strip-mined areas consists largely of greenbriar, poison ivy, brambles and briars making access difficult.

Area VI is located south of SR 64 and west of Stendal and SR 257. Haul Road, between 900S and 1150S, accesses most of the pits of this area. Besides boat ramps there is little facility development in Area VI's 2,609 acres. An overgrown Shoreline Trail exists at Bethel Pit that was constructed by the YCC in 1979.

Although designated hiking trails are nearly non-existent at the present time, future plans call for additional trails to be constructed. The potential of strip mining areas for recreational hiking is enormous.

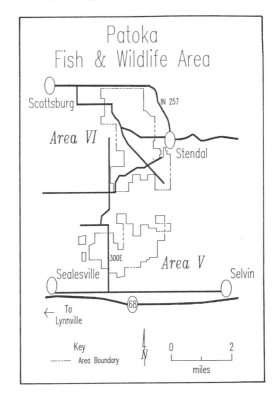

Patoka Fish and Wildlife Area

28. BUFFALO FLAT

Jasper, IN/Dubois County
USGS MAP(S): Jasper 1:24,000
TRAIL(S) DISTANCE: no est. trails
ACREAGE: 375 acres
ACTIVITIES: hiking, nature study

Buffalo Flat was purchased by The Nature Conservancy in 1984, and is now administered by the Indiana Division of Nature Preserves. The area is noted for its botanical and historical significance. Andre Michaux, French botanist and naturalist, noted in his journey along the Buffalo or Vincennes Trace in 1795 that "the buffalo had settled down for the night on their journey southeast to the salt licks in Kentucky on a hillside overlooking Buffalo Flat". He also noted, "in this swamp, Virginia willow, American snowbell, crossvine and Louisiana sedge occur together as in the most familiar swamps of the Carolinas". These rare plants Michaux mentioned 200 years ago are found at Buffalo Flat and are now protected.

Situated just north of the Patoka River, Buffalo Flat occupies a floodplain swamp forest surrounded by farm fields. Near the center of the property is a pond that harbors several of the endangered plants. Minimal use of this area is requested. No trails have been established but the visitor is free to explore on foot knowing poison ivy is abundant as well as mosquitos in warm weather. Mid to late fall, winter or early spring are suggested times for pest free visitation.

Buffalo Flat lies about 2 miles northeast of Jasper. From US 231 in Jasper turn east on 15th Street and drive 0.6 mile to the Jasper-Kellersville Road located at the crossroads of the Kimball Headquarters. Turn north on the Jasper-Kellersville and proceed northeast about a mile to the property. There is limited parking alongside the road near the river and at an abandoned farm.

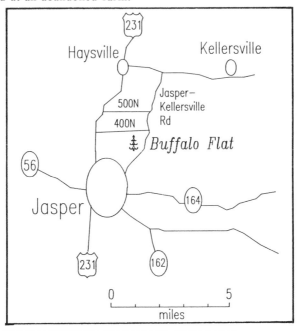

29. LINCOLN BOYHOOD NATIONAL MEMORIAL
Lincoln City, IN/Spencer County
USGS MAP(S): Chrisney, Santa Claus 1:24,000
TRAIL(S) DISTANCE: 2 trails total 2.0 miles
ACREAGE: 200 acres
ACTIVITIES: hiking, memorial visitor center, bookstore, films,
    museum, library, living historical farm, historical sites
FEE(S): admission

In 1816, Thomas Lincoln moved his family from Kentucky to Indiana just across the Ohio River near Little Pigeon Creek in hopes of a better life. Abraham Lincoln was 7 years old at the time his father chose the 160 wooded acres of government surveyed land for a homesite. It was here in southern Indiana that Abe Lincoln "grew up". During his formative years his mother, Nancy Hanks Lincoln died of milk sickness (1818), and his father re-married (1819). He received most of what little formal education he had (age 11-16), and worked hard at building the family farm. In 1830 the Lincolns moved to the fertile prairies of Illinois. Abe was now 21 years old and for the next 30 years of his life he would be claimed as a son of the state of Illinois, where he would reach his final destiny as the 16th President of the United States.

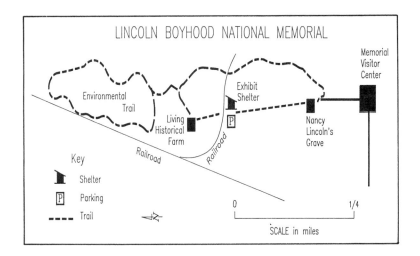

LINCOLN BOYHOOD NATIONAL MEMORIAL

Memorial
Visitor
Center

Exhibit
Shelter

Environmental
Trail

Living
Historical
Farm

Nancy
Lincoln's
Grave

Railroad

Railroad

Key

Shelter

P   Parking

- - - - Trail

0   1/4

SCALE in miles

Administered by the National Park Service, Lincoln Boyhood National Memorial is Indiana's tribute to Abraham Lincoln and his family. The visitor center, constructed of native timber and stone, has two halls joined by a "cloister" or hallway. Public information, bookstore, museum, library and auditorium are located at the center.

To the north of the visitor center is an "allee" or walkway that leads to the gravesite of Nancy Hanks Lincoln. From there a trail winds to the Living Historical Farm of the early 1800's period. Farm "residents" in costumed character greet visitors at the working homestead that features a log cabin, out buildings, animals, gardens and crop fields in the wooded clearing. Pioneer demonstrations and activities may be seen and experienced from mid April through October.

The Trail of Twelve Stones begins at the Lincoln family cabin site near the Living Historical Farm. The twelve stones were brought from significant places associated with Lincoln's life. Descriptions are inscribed in bronze markers and are placed near each of the stones. A self-guiding brochure is also available. Benches have been provided for leisurely meditation along this historical 1/2 mile gravel pathway.

Along the Trail of Twelve Stones, about 60 yards east from of the Living Historical Farm, is the junction of the Boyhood Nature Trail. The 1.0 mile level grassy trail encircles a regenerating meadow and woodland. The self guiding pathway has numbered stations that correspond to a brochure available at the trailhead box. Ecological plant succession, plant identification and pioneer usages of the native flora for food, medicine and construction are described.

The trails are open year around during daylight hours. The visitor center is open daily 8:00 am to 5:00 pm CST/CDT except Thanksgiving, Christmas and New Years Day. The Living Historical Farm is accessible daily, year-around, but it is only staffed 8:00 am to 5:00 pm CST/CDT mid April through October.

Lincoln Boyhood National Memorial

To reach Lincoln Boyhood National Memorial from I-64 use exit 57, drive south on US 231 about 6.5 miles, then east on SR 162 about 2 miles. Follow signs to "Lincoln Parks". The 1,727 acre Lincoln State Park, with 11.5 miles of hiking trails, is directly south of the memorial. Lincoln State Park is also the home of the Young Abe Lincoln Musical Outdoor Drama.

30. LINCOLN STATE PARK
Lincoln City, IN/Spencer County
USGS MAP(S): Santa Claus, Chrisney 1:24,000
TRAIL(S) DISTANCE: 4 trails total 11 1/2 miles
ACREAGE: 1,747 acres, 58 acre lake
ACTIVITIES: hiking, nature center, picnicking, shelterhouses, historical sites, swimming beach, bathhouse, playfields, playgrounds, bike trail, non-motorized boating, boat launch ramp, fishing, tennis court, firetower, amphitheater, cultural arts program, group camp, youth tent, family cabins, Class A & C camping, dumping station, 1500 feet roofed amphitheater
FEE(S): entrance, shelter reservation, canoe & boat rental, cabin rental, firewood

Lincoln State Park lies directly south of Lincoln Boyhood National Memorial. The Civilian Conservation Corps developed the park which was established in 1932. The recently constructed outdoor amphitheater is unique in the fact that it is covered by a roof, the only "under roof" amphitheater in the United States. It serves as home for the "Young Abe Lincoln" Outdoor Musical Drama.

Four short and long easy to moderate trails traverse the forest covered parkland. Trail 1 (Lake Trail) is an easy 3 mile hike that starts and ends at the boat dock and nature center on the west shore of Lake Lincoln. The well used trail leads around the south shore of Lake Lincoln crossing Trail 3 and continues uphill via firelane to the firetower. You may either retrace your steps back to the lakes south shore and continue on the Trail 1 loop or take a short cut spur to the family cabin area on the east lakeshore. The longer Trail 1 loop connects Trail 2 on the east park boundary where it follows a firelane instead of the lakeshore. The trail continues past the north shore and the bathhouse and lakeside shelter.

Trail 2 (John Carter Trail) is a moderate 2.5 mile hike that begins east of the gatehouse and follows the north and east park boundary to connect Trail 1 near the family cabins. The trail passes through old and young forest areas of red cedar, white ash and dogwood and follows a firelane alongside a railroad track, strip mine, an old homesite and meadow. A complete loop may be walked by following Trail 1 to the lakeside shelter and then following Trail 4 north to Trail 2.

Trail 3 (Noah Gorden Trail) is the shortest hike within the park of 1.5 moderate miles. The hike begins west of the old church just south of Trail 4. Sarah Lincoln Grigsby, Abe's only sister, is buried in the pioneer churchyard and her ridgetop homestead is further along the trail. Following a graded climb uphill along a firelane, the trail also goes near the Noah Gorden Mill and Home site. Trail 3 connects Trail 1 near the south shore of Lake Lincoln.

Trail 4 (James Gentry Trail) is a moderate 4.5 mile trek that begins at the lakeside shelter and goes west and north of the old church near Trail 3. Undesignated trail spurs lead around Weber Lake and north through young woods to connect Trail 4. The forest path heads north past the newly constructed picnic area, amphitheatre and youth tent area to head west across the Southern Railroad tracks. The trail then gently rolls along a power line cut north of Weber Lake to eventually cross a county road and SR 162 (be careful of crossing) to the James Gentry historic homesite. The trail continues between a field and SR 162 to re-cross SR 162 under the highway via a railroad cut underpass. The trail re-crosses the railroad tracks and leads to the gatehouse crossing the main park road at the junction with Trail 2 and heads south through Oak Grove picnic area to eventually return to the Lincoln Lake picnic shelter.

From I-64 exit SR 162 or US 231 and drive south to the park. Lincoln Boyhood National Memorial lies directly north of the state park.

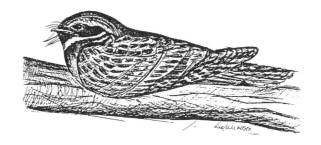

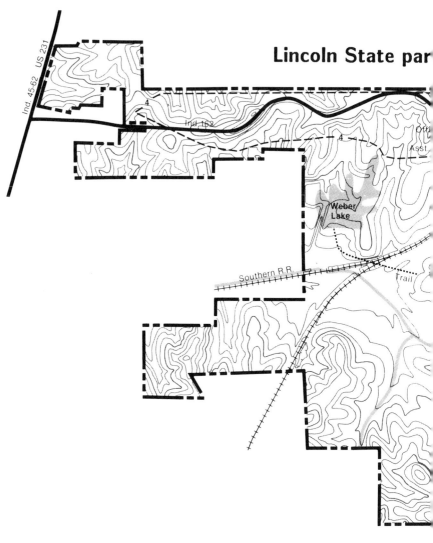

Lincoln State par

Weber Lake

Southern R.R.

US 231
Ind 45-62
Ind 162

N

Contour Interval 10 Feet

| 1000 | 0 | 1000 | 2000 | 3000 | 4000 | 5000 | 6000 | 70 |

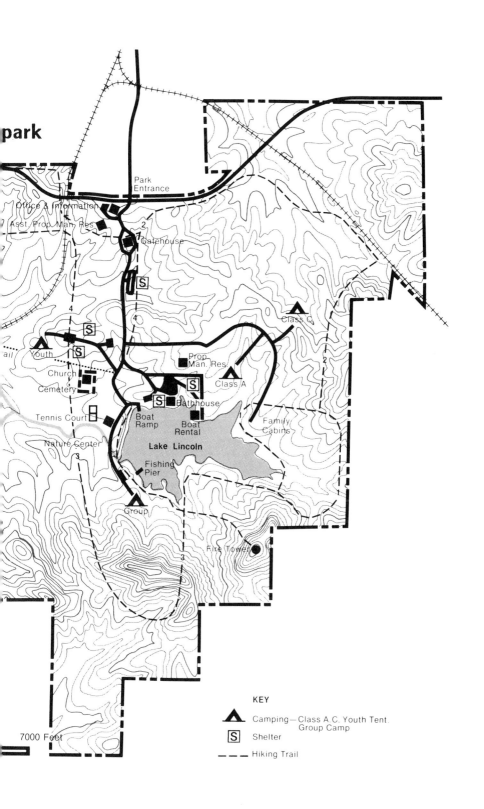

park

Park
Entrance

Office & Information
Asst. Prop. Man. Res.
2
Gatehouse

S

4

4

S

Class C

Youth

S

Prop.
Man. Res

2

Church

Class A

Cemetery

S

Bathhouse

S

Tennis Court

Boat
Ramp

Boat
Rental

Family
Cabins

Nature Center

Lake Lincoln

3

Fishing
Pier

Group

3

Fire Tower

KEY

Camping—Class A.C. Youth Tent.
Group Camp

S Shelter

Hiking Trail

7000 Feet

31. POST OAK BARRENS
Chrisney, IN/Spencer County
USGS MAP(S): Chrisney 1:24,000
TRAIL(S) DISTANCE: no est. trails
ACREAGE: 466 acres
ACTIVITIES: hiking, nature study

The Nature Conservancy purchased Post Oak Barrens in 1985 to preserve rare botanical species and plant communities. Post oak in Indiana is fairly restricted to the southwestern counties where it is sometimes called "Iron Oak", for its wood is tougher than white oak. The leaves suggest a cross or crucifix and the wood is used for crossties or posts and other construction. The word "barrens" is a term used by early pioneers to designate seasonally wet and dry level prairies that support an inferior growth of trees and several prairie herbs and grasses. The flat, poorly drained property is located a short distance southeast of Little Pigeon Creek and the East Fork of Chrisney Creek, near an area called High Banks. The hard light clay soil also supports white, black and pin oaks, cork or winged elm, and mockernut hickory as well as 8 other threatened and endangered species. Poison ivy and mosquitos are plentiful.

To reach Post Oak Barrens from I-64 in Spencer county exit US 231 south to Gentryville and continue south to the junction of SR 62 and US 231. Go west on SR 62 and drive about one mile and turn south (at the second road) of 100W. Drive south approximately one mile on 100N and turn west on 1050W and proceed to the junction or turn off 1050W and 225W and park at the pullout curve. On foot follow the farm lane north past the house trailer to the woods. Notice The Nature Conservancy golden signs. The farm lane follows the property boundary to the west and north.

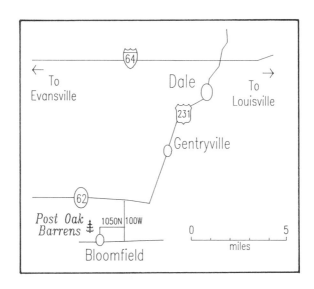

HOOSIER NATIONAL FOREST

Up the Trail

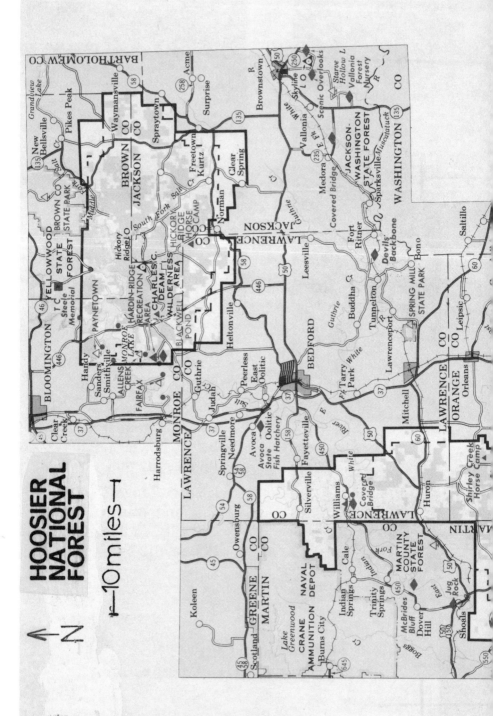

HOOSIER NATIONAL FOREST

N

⊢10miles⊣

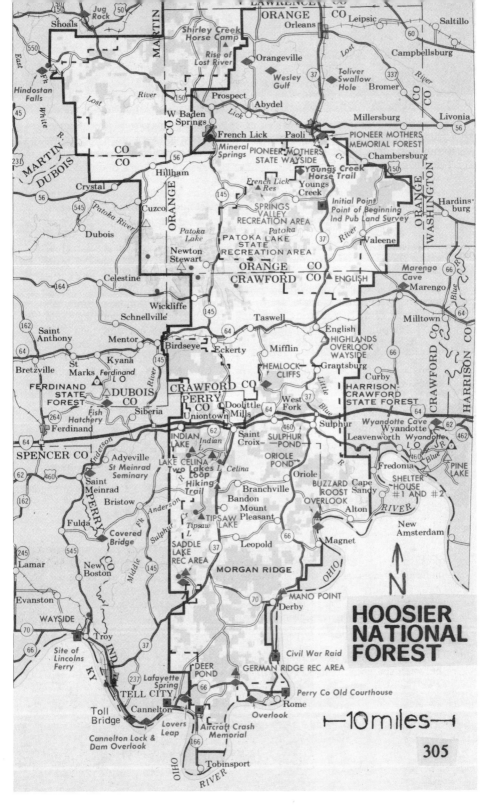

HOOSIER NATIONAL FOREST

├─10 miles─┤

305

HOOSIER NATIONAL FOREST: OVERVIEW

From Lake Monroe south to Buzzard Roost along the bluffs of the Ohio River, the 188,000 acre national forest lands in scenic southern Indiana provide miles of superb hiking opportunities. Administered by the US Forest Service, Department of Agriculture, much of the Hoosier National Forest is interspersed with privately owned farmlands and homes however there are large block tracts of public forest land. The Hoosier is managed under the multiple use concept which includes timber, range, wildlife, watershed and outdoor recreation.

The national forest is divided into 4 areas or units managed by the supervisor headquarters at Bedford and two out-lying district offices at Brownstown and Tell City. The four areas are Pleasant Run, Lost River, Little Africa and Tell City. The forest service has done a fine job of establishing miles of hiking trails, although more trails in special areas could be added and existing trails could be improved. Unmarked trails should not be attempted without a map and compass. Besides trails, the forest service has developed recreational sites that offer picnicking, swimming, boating, bridle trails, hunting, fishing, points of interest, historical sites, lake boating, seasonal naturalist programs, camping, wild food foraging and more. Existing special areas are not described here due to restricted access and rarity. Abbots, Bear and Slick Rock Hollows, Goblin Rocks, Jublin Creek, Fuzzy Hole, Tar Springs, Hominy Mortar, Wells Cave, and Big Creek-Sam's Creek are a few of the many special areas within the national forest that may be more public accessible in the future.

TRAIL TIPS:

-Hikers are advised to arrange water supplies. Carry, stash, or purify water on the trail since there is no potable water available on most trails.

-If hiking off established trails, do so at your own risk. Map and compass are suggested.

-Backpacking is permitted on national forest lands. Camping and fire permits are not necessary, but exercise caution when making a fire and none at all during dry weather months. Backpacking stoves recommended.

-You may camp 14 days in a row in developed campgrounds.
8 people and 2 vehicles limited to a site.
Water usually available and flush toilets closed during winter.

-Use picnic sites, swimming beaches, and other day use areas only between the hours of 6:00 am - 10:00 pm

Backcountry Camper

Be advised certain Perry County forest sites have the introduced southern Lone Star tick commonly called "deer", "seed", or "turkey" tick. This minute tick was accidentally introduced to Perry County in the 1930's from Missouri white-tail deer restocking. Difficult to see, the tiny tick is commonly found in open grassy or brushy places from early June to October frost, about the same time span as the insidious chigger-mite season. It is believed cold weather is a major factor in keeping the Lone Star tick localized. For maps and further information contact:

Forest Supervisor
Hoosier National Forest, 1615 J. Street
Bedford, IN 47421, (812) 275-5987

Located in Bedford NE of the crossroads of SR 37 and SR 450 & 458.

Brownstown
North District Ranger Office:
Hoosier National Forest
608 West Commerce Street
US 50
Brownstown, IN 47220
(812) 358-2675

Tell City
South District Ranger Office:
Hoosier National Forest
15th and Washington Streets
Tell City, IN 47586
(812) 547-7051

Paoli Office
262 NW Court St., Paoli, IN 47454
(812) 723-5368

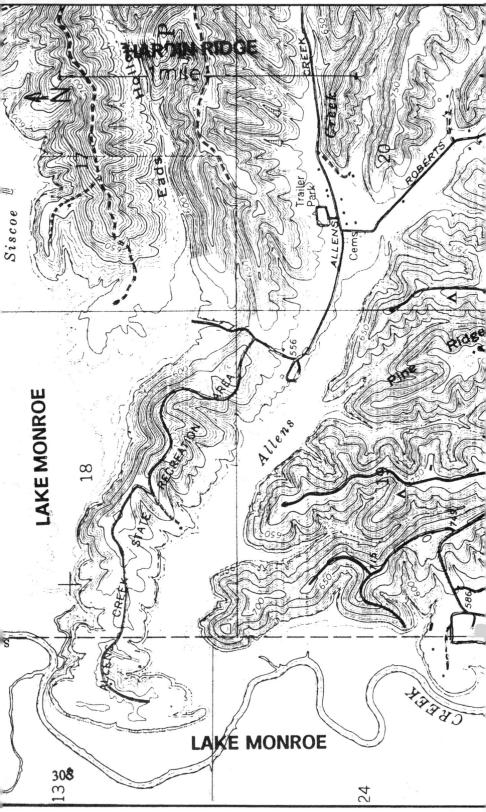

HARDIN RIDGE

LAKE MONROE

HOOSIER NATIONAL FOREST: PLEASANT RUN AREA
TRIP 1: Hardin Ridge Recreation Area
USGS MAP(S): Allen's Creek 1:24,000
TRAIL(S) DISTANCE: 2 trail total approx. 4 miles
ACREAGE: 1,200 acres
ACTIVITIES: hiking, nature study, visitor nature center, interpretive
   programs, outdoor amphitheater, picnicking, shelterhouses, swimming
   beach, bathhouse, concessions, boating, launch ramp, fishing,
   playfields, Class A camping, walk-in camping
FEE(S): camping, shelterhouse reservations

Hardin Ridge is the most popular recreational site in the Hoosier
National Forest. The forested ridge and ravines form the southeastern 19
mile shoreline of 10,750 acre Lake Monroe, Indiana's largest man made
lake. Two nature trails have been established and marked at Hardin Ridge.
   The Campground-Beach Trail is 1.5 mile one-way linear hike from Eads
campground to the beachfront. Eads campground is the first camp beyond
the entry gate on the paved main forest road. Staying close to the main
park road, the forest trail heads down Hardin Ridge to the beach area
connecting all 5 campgrounds and the Twin Oak Visitor Center. Wildlife
ponds exist at Blue Gill and White Oak campgrounds. This trail is not a
loop. You must retrace your steps.
   Directly behind the Twin Oak Visitor Center is the trailhead of a 2.5
mile interpretive loop and linear spur. Take time to read the Prayer of
the Woods marker at the outdoor amphitheater. The self-guiding trail
descends a staircase into a ravine following a small tributary with posted
stations describing the flora, fauna, and woodland ecology. Near the
point where the final leg of the trail loops uphill to the Twin Oak
Visitors Center, a linear trail spur follows the tributary to Allen's Creek
cove with views across the inlet of the state recreational site. No trail
markers are located along the conspicuous spur that dead ends at the
cove. Retrace your steps back to the loop trail and uphill to the visitor
center and parking area.
   While in the general area, you may want to visit Allens Creek State
Recreation Area and hike the service road that leads out onto a ridgetop
peninsula and Lake Monroe. Allen's Creek is one of the few places to
hike state recreation property surrounding Lake Monroe. The approximate
3 mile walk out and back begins uphill at the locked service road gate
from the boat ramp, pit toilets, picnic and primitive campground area.
The gravel service road follows the forested and open ridgetop with fine
views of Lake Monroe. Persimmons are plentiful. The road ends at the
lake edge, a former primitive state recreation site. Retrace your steps.
   Hardin Ridge Recreation Area and Allen's Creek SRA are located south
of Bloomington on the southwest shore of Lake Monroe. At the east side
of Bloomington, take SR 446 south across the causeway. Across the
causeway, the marked access gravel road to Allen's Creek SRA will be on
the right/west side of SR 446 at the 4th road. Approximately 1 mile
south on SR 446, the next road right is paved Chapel Hill Road. Take
Chapel Hill Road right and follow the directional signs to Hardin Ridge
for about 2 miles on the right/north side of the road.
   Both recreation sites are approximately 2 miles west of SR 446, south
of Lake Monroe's causeway.

HOOSIER NATIONAL FOREST: PLEASANT RUN AREA

TRIP 2: Charles C. Deam Wilderness Area
USGS MAP(S): Allen's Creek, Bartlettsville, Norman, Elkinsville
 1:24,000
TRAIL(S) DISTANCE: 75-100 miles of unmarked trails
ACREAGE: 12,953 acres
ACTIVITIES: hiking, nature study, backpacking, bridle trails, fishing,
 hunting, horsemens campground, camping

Established in 1982, the Charles C. Deam Wilderness Area is Indiana's only wilderness. The vast nearly 13,000 acres consists of numerous ridges deeply dissected by gullies, ravines, canyons, hollows, and valleys. The secluded wilderness is now undisturbed intervened only by day hikers, overnight backpackers, seasonal hunters, perennial fishermen, horsemen and other non-motorized visitors. The national forest wilderness is named in honor of Charles Clemon Deam (1865-1953), Indiana's foremost state forester, botanist and botanical author who travelled 100,000 miles in a custom model T "weed wagon" around Hoosierland for 50 years collecting and cataloging the native flora.

Basically the wilderness area is bordered on the north by Lake Monroe and the Middle Fork State Wildlife Refuge, on the west by SR 446, on the east the South Fork of Salt Creek and Maumee Road and Hunter Creek on the south. The wilderness includes 3 separate tracts: Grubb Ridge and Terril Ridge north of Tower Grove Road and Cope Hollow south of Tower Grove Road. Several small parking lots are located along Tower Ridge Road from Blackwell Pond to Hickory Ridge Lookout Tower. The mini-parking lots provide access to nearby old roads, horsetrails and the no longer maintained 20 mile Hickory Ridge hiking trail. The concept of wilderness, according to forest service means challenging, no-marked foot trails so that every hiker must learn on his own "the ways of the wood". For the hiker who intends to explore the wilderness, a topographic map and compass are essential. The DNR map office at Indianapolis has new maps available. Portions of the former road and trail system are well used by visitors and remain obvious and easy to follow. The Sassafras Audubon Group of Bloomington went to great lengths during the 1970's to compile a detailed account of the trails in the wilderness and Nebo Ridge. Unfortunately no longer available outside of libraries, the booklet describes a step by step detailed account of unmarked wilderness trails. The following briefly described wilderness trails are day hikes that require bringing water and other day use gear.

If the forest service would maintain one trail in the wilderness area it should be the former Hickory Ridge hiking trail, the trail that explores the Terril and Grubb Ridges. Fading blue diamond blazes are still evident on both sides of trees along the 20 mile trek over high ridges overlooking Lake Monroe, through pine plantations and beech-maple hollows, past abandoned fields, wildlife ponds, old homesites and cemeteries. Patton Cave was also included along the hike. The entire trail is located north of Tower Grove Road.

The Hickory Ridge lookout fire tower on Tower Ridge Road located about 6.2 miles east of SR 446 is the trailhead and parking area. The fire tower is enjoyable to climb with rewarding vistas of Browning Hill,

Terril Ridge, Grubb Ridge, Lake Monroe, Brown County State Park and Bloomington. The trail follows the service road north past the locked gate about 1/4 mile before descending east down a ridge to Sycamore Branch, a fine day hike area. An outstanding white pine plantation is situated along the lower branch before switching back uphill north to cross the abandoned primitive road. The trail curves west to follow Terril Ridge ridgetop, never far from the forementioned primitive road, crossing it twice and following it down Terril Ridge to Axsom Branch.

The trail then ascends John Grubb Ridge hiking west with vistas of Lake Monroe and the Middle Fork State Wildlife Refuge, a waterfowl migratory resting area. A spur-linear trail goes north to the tip of a peninsula jutting out into Lake Monroe. The loop trail continues south to ever popular Patton Cave. Horse use in this area is particularly heavy. An old road spur heads west to Patton Cave uphill from a finger cove of Lake Monroe. The trail descends the ridge to curve east up a ravine uphill to Frank Grubb Ridge. The Hickory Ridge trail crosses and re-crosses and follows a primitive road, ravines and ridges east back to the Hickory Ridge lookout tower. These basic trail descriptions are not intended for specific directional detail but as a general idea "map" of the former trail and the wilderness areas of the Terril and Grubb tracts. The Cope Hollow tract, the 3rd tract in the wilderness area lies south of Tower Ridge Road and is as easily accessed but less visited than the north tracts.

You may want to consider some of the following day hike alternatives in the wilderness area:

Sycamore Branch Loop- Begins and ends at Hickory Ridge Lookout Tower. Approximately 6 mile long moderate loop. Descends into scenic Sycamore Branch then uphill along old road and Terril Ridge, then south along primitive road back to lookout tower. Additional day hiking may include the rest of Terril Ridge descending into Axsom Branch following the primitive road back to Hickory Ridge lookout tower. Geodes and white pine plantations are fine.

Axsom Branch Loop- 5.3 mile loop west and north of Hickory Ridge lookout tower. Moderately difficult 3 hour hike with views of Lake Monroe. Head north on primitive service road from the Hickory Ridge lookout tower to Terril Cemetery. Descends old Hickory Ridge hiking trail into Axsom Branch. At the bottom, turn and follow the primitive road upstream to the ridgetop and original service road. Go right, back to the Hickory Ridge lookout tower.

Patton Cave Loop- 8 mile rugged loop. Trailhead begins 1.7 miles west on Tower Ridge Road from Hickory Ridge lookout tower at mini-parking pullout on north side of road. The trail follows an old service road to the Hickory Ridge hiking trail. The trail and the service road cross and recross each other along Frank Grubb Ridge. Trail descends into Saddle Creek Hollow that separates the Grubb ridges; John and Frank. This section can be very muddy and "horsed-out". Near the finger cove of Lake Monroe, the trail ascends John Grubb Ridge to a side road spur to Patton Cave . The wet limestone cave lies west of the Mt. Carmel Fault

Forest, Charles C. Deam Wilderness

line that runs north and south. The Hickory Ridge hiking trail loop continues along the John Grubb Ridge east descending south to connect an old road that leads to a wildlife pond and the original primitive entry road that returns to the trailhead parking.

Frog Pond Ridge- A shorter route to Patton Cave. The trailhead begins behind Todd Cemetery on the north side of Tower Ridge Road approximately 1.5 miles east from SR 446. Park at the 2nd or 3rd mini-parking lots. The trail follows and old north road now heavily used as a horse trail (a short distance east of Blackwell Pond horsemens campground). At ridge end the trail descends into Saddle Creek and a cove finger of Lake Monroe. At the southwest base of John Grubb Ridge, Patton Cave faces the west and the finger cove on the hillside. Follow the old road uphill or the old Hickory Grove hiking trail to the cave. You may want to continue north on John Grubb Ridge to the old Peninsula trail spur north to Lake Monroe. Be advised maps and compass are helpful. A good opportunity to learn orienteering.

Cope Hollow Tract- South of Tower Ridge Road between SR 446 and Hunter Creek Road. The triangular shaped, south wilderness tract is little used although a horse trail is present along Tanyard Branch. Park at mini-lots 11 or 12 on Tower Ridge Road for access to a former road that descends a ridgetop between Cope Hollow and Dennis Murphy Hollow to Mitchell Cemetery. Parking lot 6 leads to Cope Hollow. Parking lot 13 leads to Murphy Hollow. All hollows are tributaries of Hunter Creek draining south and west.

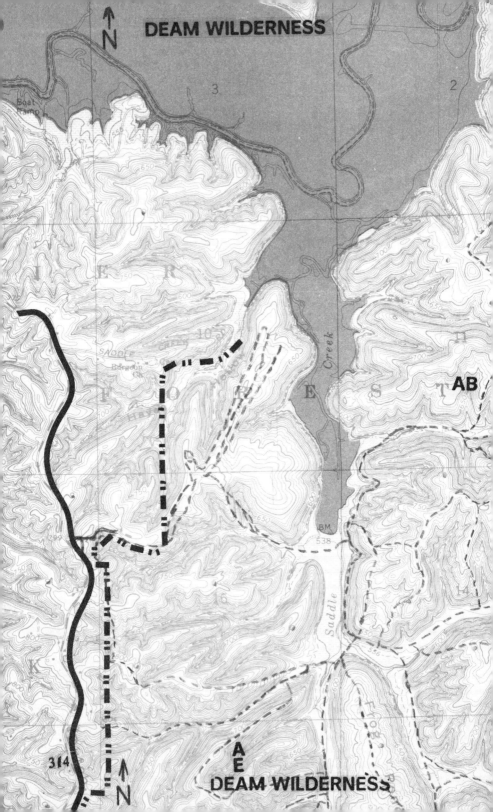

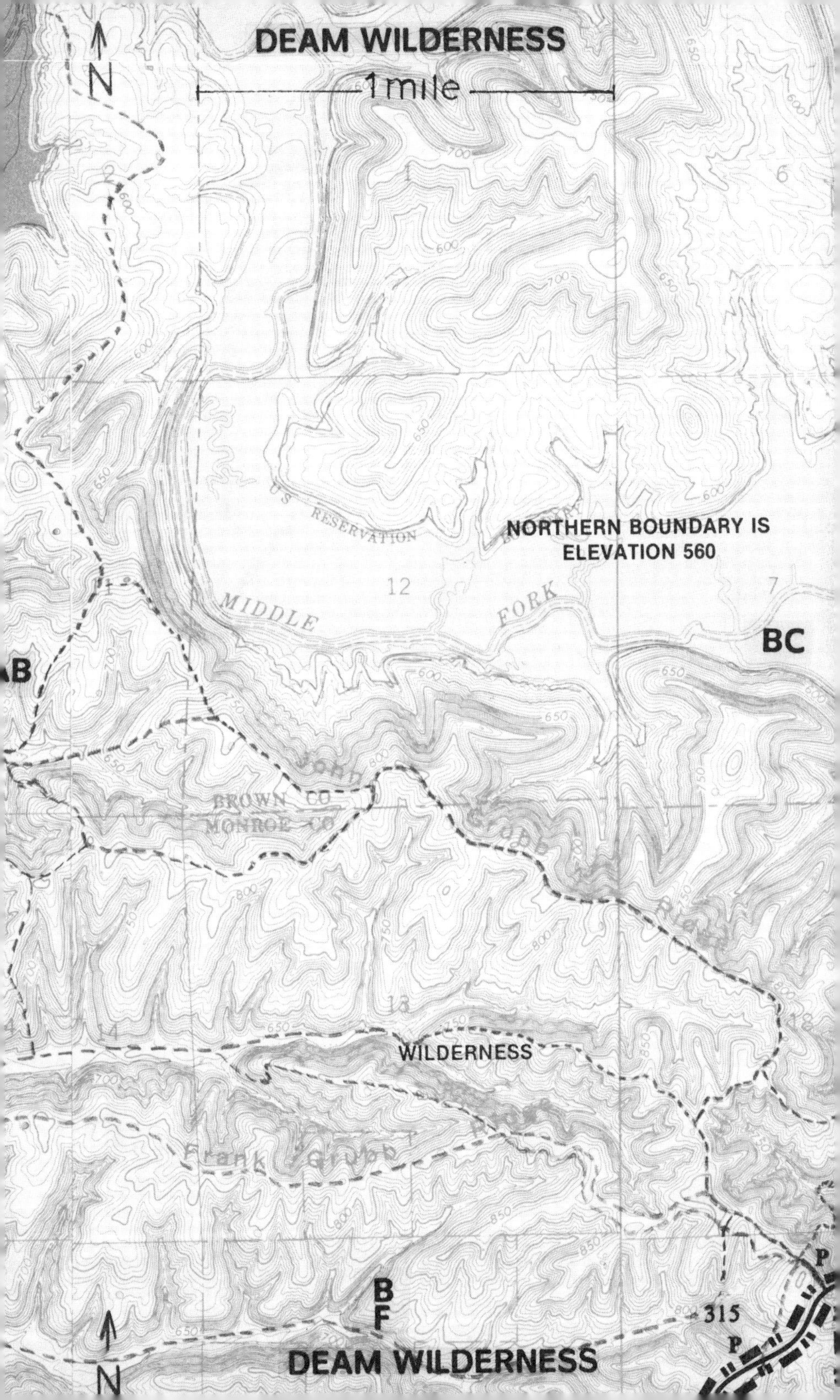

DEAM WILDERNESS

— 1 mile —

N

6

US RESERVATION

NORTHERN BOUNDARY IS ELEVATION 560

12

MIDDLE

FORK

7

B

BC

John

BROWN CO
MONROE CO

Grubb

Ridge

13

18

WILDERNESS

Frank Grubb

Fork

B
F

315

P
P

N

P

DEAM WILDERNESS

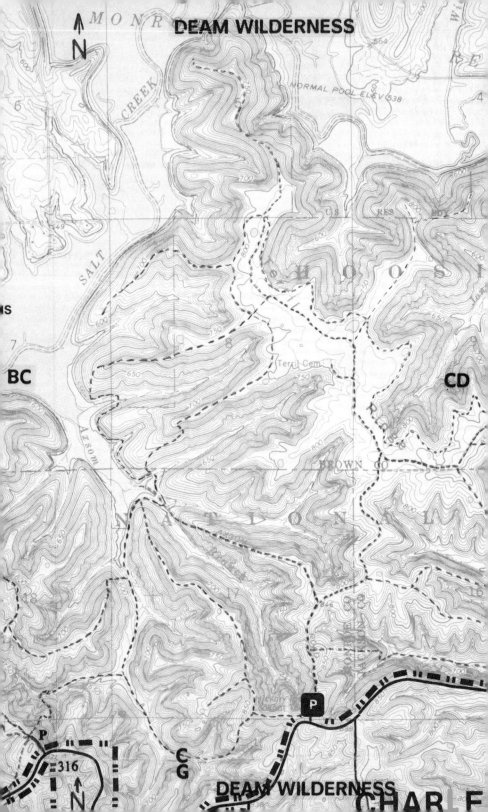

DEAM WILDERNESS

N

MONR

CREEK

DEAM WILDERNESS

NORMAL POOL ELEV 538

HOOSI

BC

CD

Teru Cem

BROWN CO

NATION L

P

P

316

N

CG

DEAM WILDERNESS

CHARLE

DEAM WILDERNESS

ES C. DEAM WILDERNESS

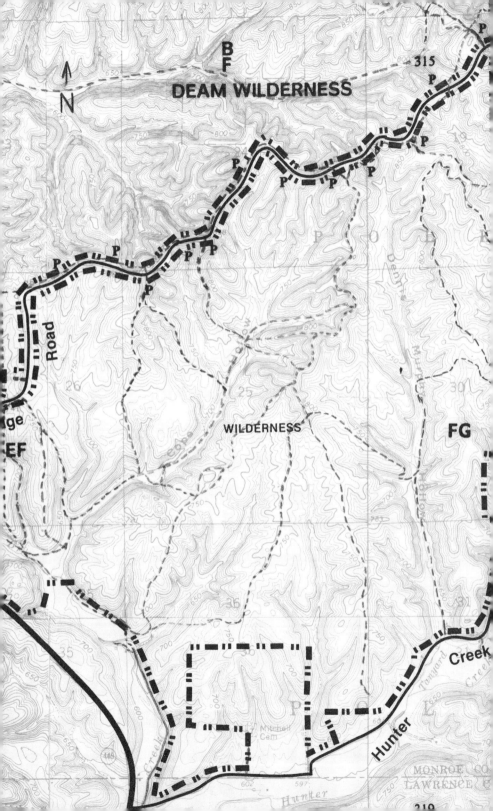

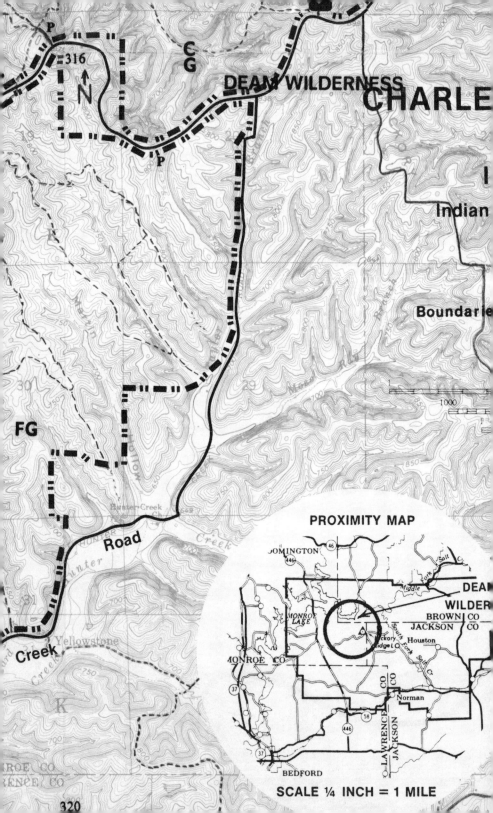

P

316

N

C
G

DEAN WILDERNESS

CHARLE

I

Indian

Boundarie

19

R

30

FG

1000

Hunter Creek

Road

Creek

Creek

Yellowstone

K

Creek

PROXIMITY MAP

LOOMINGTON 46
446

Middle Fork Salt

DEA
WILDER

BROWN CO
JACKSON CO

MONROE
LAKE

Hickory
Ridge

South Fork Salt

Houston

MONROE CO

37

58

Norman

LAWRENCE CO
JACKSON CO

446

37

ROE CO
RENCE CO

320

BEDFORD

SCALE ¼ INCH = 1 MILE

HOOSIER NATIONAL FOREST: PLEASANT RUN AREA
TRIP 3: Hickory Ridge Horse Trail
USGS MAP(S): Norman 1:24,000
TRAIL(S) DISTANCE: 20 miles
ACTIVITIES: hiking, nature study, bridle trails, horsemens camp
FEE(S): camping

As a general rule, horse trails are more rugged and not quite as scenic as hiking trails. However, hikers may find the moderately used Hickory Ridge horse trail a hiking option to the wilderness area to the near north. The entire 20 miles of trails are interconnecting. If the horseman trail marker is on the right you are going away from the horse camp. If the trail marker is on your left you are going towards the horse camp. All trails are marked and maintained and originate from the campground. The horse trail pass through a variety of terrain: wooded ridges, ravines, wildlife ponds, overlooks and rock outcrops, service firelanes, old forest roads, county road crossings, pipeline routes, Henderson Creek, Brannaman Branch, Starnes Branch and Hickory Grove Church. A trail brochure is available. It is a good area for a day hike.

Hickory Ridge horse trail camp and trailheads are located south of Lake Monroe and the Charles C. Deam Wilderness Area. At the yellow flashing light junction of SR 446 and SR 58 go east on SR 58 and drive to Norman. Turn north on a paved county road immediately northeast of Norman. Follow the curving paved and gravel road approximately 3 miles to the horse camp.

Snake Skin   321

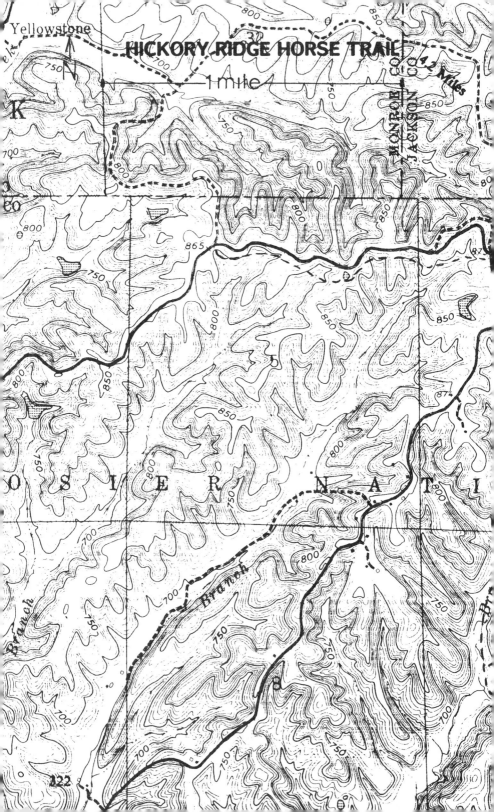

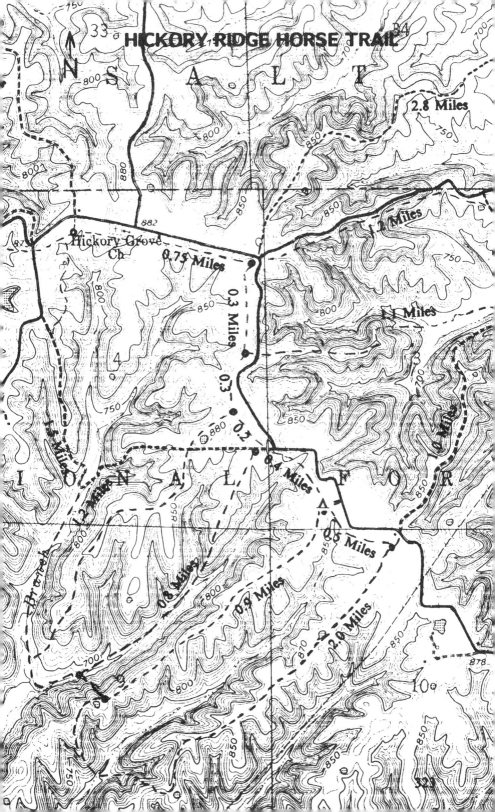

HICKORY RIDGE HORSE TRAIL

HICKORY RIDGE HORSE TRAIL

HOOSIER NATIONAL FOREST: PLEASANT RUN AREA
TRIP 4: Browning Hill
USGS MAP(S): Elkinsville, Story 1:24,000
TRAIL(S) DISTANCE: 2 approaches: Maumee 2 miles, & Elkinsville 3 miles
ACTIVITIES: hiking (undesignated FS trail), nature study

900 foot high Browning Hill is one of the highest points in the Pleasant Run Area of the Hoosier National Forest. Old service roads ascend the hilltop along ridges and provide access to the flat-top hillcrest. Scenic views in all directions are especially good after the leaves have fallen. There are 2 approaches to the summit. Be advised that the west tip of Browning Hill is private property.

The shortest, yet steepest approach is from Elkinsville. East of Nashville on SR 46, take SR 135 south to Story. Continue west through Story and stay on the paved Elkinsville Road to Elkinsville where the road will "T". Go left/east and park just beyond the house at the "T" alongside the road and Spanker Branch. Please respect private property. Follow the old road nearly straight up over 300 feet for about a mile to the summit of Browning Hill. Retrace your steps.

The longest approach is a gradual 300 foot climb from Combs Creek north of Maumee. Instead of going west through Story, stay on SR 135 south, turning southwest 1.5 miles at the Mt. Nebo Road. Go 1.6 miles west on the Mt. Nebo Road and turn right/west at Berry Road. Follow Berry Road past Nebo Ridge downridge to Houston and North Road. Go west on paved North Road about 4 miles to Maumee driving north 1.1 miles on Combs Creek Road to a parking area on the left side of the road just beyond the 2nd bridge.

The trail follows an old road uphill adjacent to the parking area all the way to Browning Hill. Follow the obvious main route avoiding spurs or side routes. One confusing fork occurs in the higher elevation overlooking Bad Hollow but stay to the right. You can see Browning Hill to the north, the highest ridge. The view is worth the climb. The 2,000 acre area includes mature climax forest. Compass and map are necessary for exploration of Bad Hollow.

(For map, see Nebo Ridge Topos).

HOOSIER NATIONAL FOREST: PLEASANT RUN AREA
TRIP 5: Nebo Ridge/Greenbriar Ridge and Hound Dog Ridge Trails
USGS MAP(S): Story 1:24,000
TRAIL(S) DISTANCE: 4 miles each loop
ACTIVITIES: hiking (undesignated FS trails), nature study

These two trails interconnect along Nebo Ridge making one fine day hike. The unmarked and somewhat overgrown trails begin and end on Berry Road 3.4 miles north of Houston and 4 miles south of Brown County State Park. Park alongside the pullout on Berry Road near the curve or off the narrow gravel road on the east side at an abandoned homesite near the two trailheads.

Greenbriar Ridge trailhead descends the ridge on the west side of the curve pullout (the highest point if coming from Maumee on Berry Road).

Once reaching the branch bottom the trail ascends the next ridge south to connect with Hound Dog Ridge Trail and Berry Road. The final leg follows Berry Road north to complete the 4 mile Greenbriar Ridge loop. The old service roads serve as overgrown trails. It is hard to believe up and down the ridge is four miles.

Hound Dog Ridge Trail begins about 1/4 mile south of the Greenbriar Ridge trailhead on the east side of Berry Road. The trail descends the ridge southeast from a clearing past a wildlife pond to intersect over a mile beyond with a pipeline swath. Go west/right following the pipeline up and down with the rolling ridge slope to cross Berry Road and descending and climbing another ridge before turning due north/right to follow the natural ridge slope and connect with Greenbriar Ridge Trail. Go north at the "T" trail junction 1/2 mile to join with Berry Road and turn left/north and return to the trailhead parking area on the east side of the road.

Besides driving north 3.4 miles of Houston on Berry Road to the high point at the curve, you may reach Greenbriar Ridge and Hound Dog Ridge (Nebo Ridge) from SR 135 at Story. Go south 1.5 mile on SR 135 from Story to interconnect with Mt. Nebo Road. Drive 1.6 mile south on Mt. Nebo Road and turn left/west on Berry Road and drive to the south bound curve.

Paper Hornet Nest

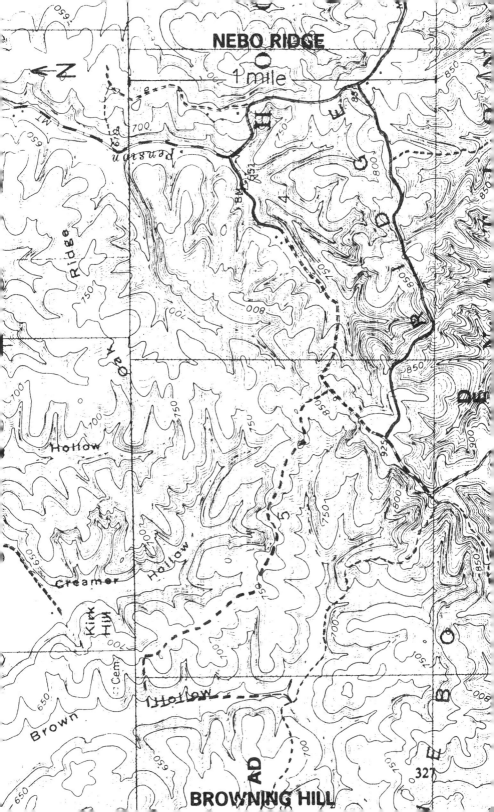

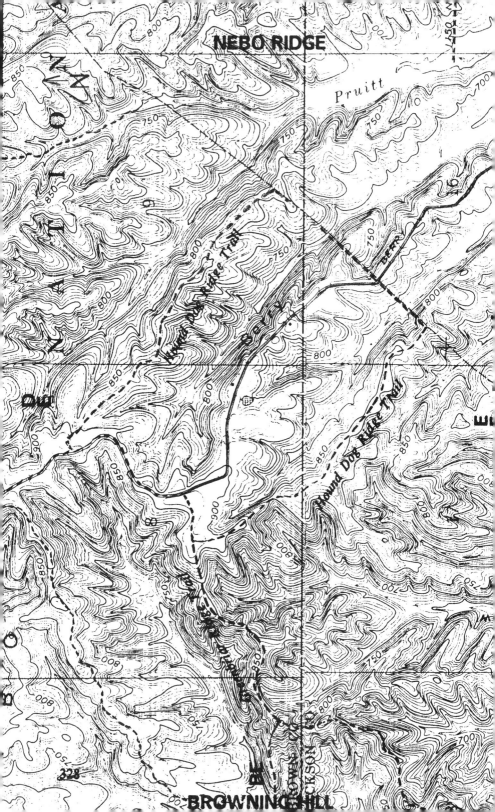

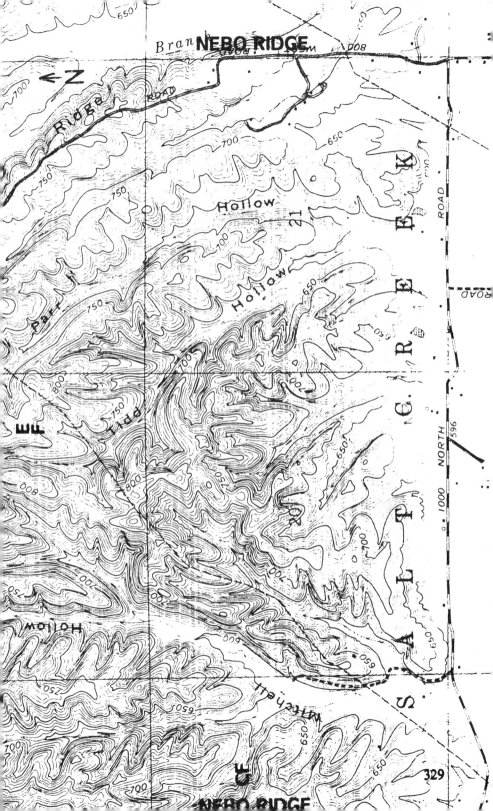

NEBO RIDGE

329

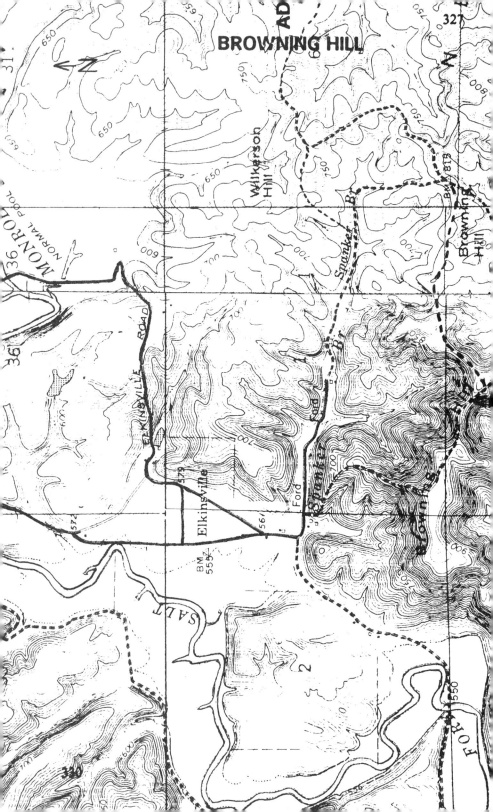

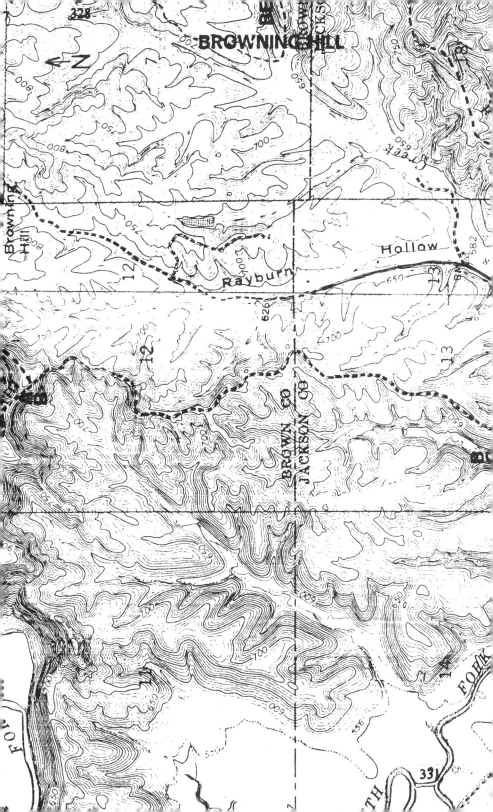

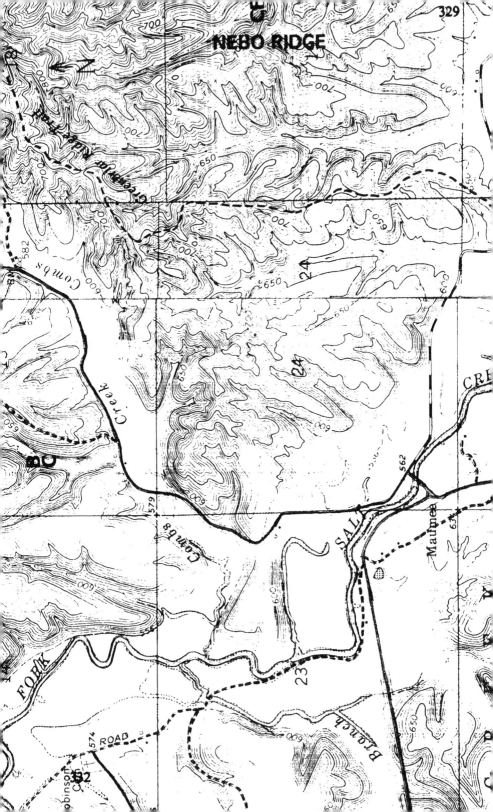

NEBO RIDGE

HOOSIER NATIONAL FOREST: LOST RIVER AREA
TRIP 6: Shirley Creek Horse Trail
USGS MAP(S): Georgia, Huron 1:24,000
TRAIL DISTANCE: 16 mile loop
ACTIVITIES: hiking, nature study, bridle trail, Class C camping,
   brochure available

Shirley Creek horse trail, although designed for horses, will equally suit the hiker. The blazed-marked wide trail is not overly used as are those at Blackwell Camp in the Charles Deam Wilderness. The day hike makes a 16 mile loop encircling 750 foot Luke Knob. Shirley Creek is the only maintained trail in the Lost River Unit, an area that includes portions of southeast Martin County, southwest Lawrence County and northwest Orange County. Most of the national forest lands in this unit are small parcels that do not form large consolidated acreage suitable for long distance hiking trails. There are special areas however in the Lost River Unit worthy of visitation such as Fuzzy Hole, Tar Springs, Trout Lily Valley and Box Canyon.

The trailhead begins at the campground although marked access points and pullouts are located along the gravel 775W road south of Hindostan. Two trail spurs lead from the east boundary of the horse camp to descend to Shirley Creek and the main trail heading north to northwest. The trail leads along ridge slopes through the forest to cross a paved road twice near Bonds Chapel and Cemetery. The trail then turns south on an abandoned county road 860W. Vistas of fields and distant hills are noticed along the abandoned road. The trail has occasional glimpses of Lukes Knob particularly during the descent into the open abandoned fields of Felknor Hollow. Turn northeast at the stream bottom and follow the trail up Felknor Hollow. The path turns into a climb of switch backs up the ridge to arrive at a logging road and the eventual re-crossing of the gravel road 775W just north of the horsemens camp. A trail spur winds alongside 775W north and south interconnecting the loop trail.

To reach Shirley Creek horse trail and camp from the town of Orleans, Orange County and SR 37, take Vincennes Street south of the town square, west and drive approximately 10 miles to Hindostan village, northwest of Orangeville. At Hindostan turn south/left at the abandoned old store onto 775W. Drive about 1.5 miles to the horsemens camp on the east side of the gravel road.

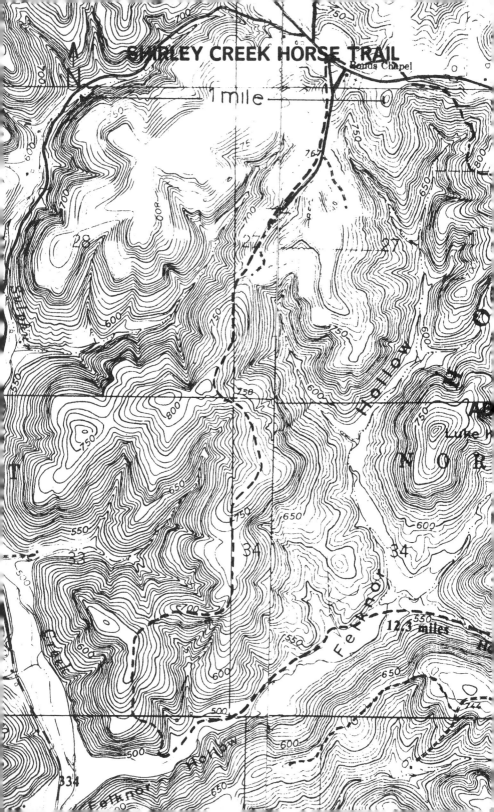

SHIRLEY CREEK HORSE TRAIL

Bonds Chapel

1 mile

12.3 miles

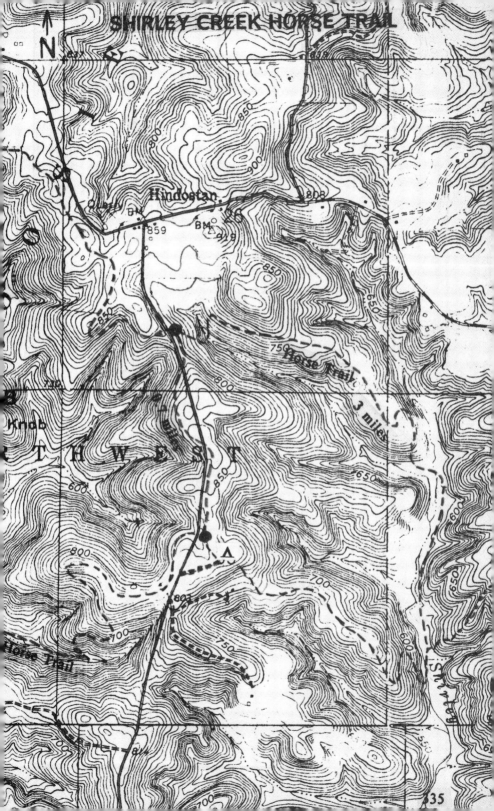

HOOSIER NATIONAL FOREST: LITTLE AFRICA AREA

TRIP 7: Pioneer Mothers Memorial Forest
USGS MAP(S): Paoli 1:24,000
TRAIL(S) DISTANCE: 1 mile trail (no longer maintained)
ACREAGE: 258 acres
ACTIVITIES: hiking, nature study, historical site, picnicking

Just southeast of Paoli, Pioneer Mothers Memorial Forest is a 258-acre, rich forest named in honor of women who helped to settle Indian-acquired lands of the Old Northwest. Refusing to saw down his grove of trees, the original (1818) owner Joseph Cox preserved one of the most exceptional mixed woodlands in southern Indiana today. 88 acres of virgin hardwood trees were designated a natural area by the forest service in 1944 and later dedicated as a Memorial Woods in 1955.

The property's terrain is a long north/south ridge with two slopes and coves facing southeast into Lick Creek that flows along the northeast boundary of US 150 near Paoli. The trail leads from the parking area access via US 150 uphill to the memorial wall and a 600 year old white oak. The trail then follows the ridge past several large specimens of black walnuts. The forest path also has a short 1/4 mile well used half loop connecting the main trail. Former trail sections further down the ridge have become overgrown. The trail ends at the SR 37 wayside rest area about 2 miles south of Paoli on the east side of the highway.

Trail users may also park at the SR 37 wayside rest area to hike the trail. The US 150 access is closed with a gate that reads "Foot Traffic Welcome". Parking would be acceptable for a few cars on the entry road shoulder but not in front of the gate. The closed US 150 entrance is located 1.5 miles southeast of Paoli. Turn right/south at Christ the King Church and park. Walk in on the paved entrance road to the parking area and trailhead.

Pioneer Mothers Memorial

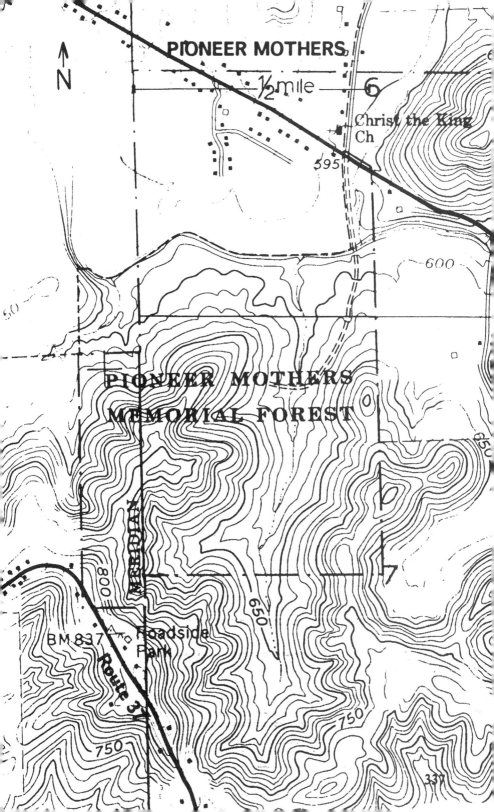

HOOSIER NATIONAL FOREST: LITTLE AFRICA AREA
TRIP 8: Young's Creek Horse Trail/Initial Point
USGS MAP(S): Valeene 1:24,000
TRAIL DISTANCE: 10 mile loop
ACTIVITIES: hiking, bridle trail, nature study, historical site,
primitive camping, brochure available

Initial Point was established in 1795 as the "point of beginning of the Indiana Public Land Survey". An unmarked but obvious trail leads from the parking area at Initial Point to the nearby monument and marker. Just southwest of the monument is the fenced-in Pivot Point Survey Marker. The point represents the intersection of the Baseline with the 2nd Principal Meridian and it is also a memorial to surveyors who died working on the frontier surveying the land. The trail is less than 100 yards at Initial Point but nearby is the 10 mile Young's Creek horse trail.

Initial Point and parking area is located 1/2 mile south of Pine Valley on SR 37 in south central Orange County. Turn west at the directional sign and drive 1/8 mile to the parking area.

Hikers will find the Young's Creek horse trail not so heavily used although there are well worn sections. The trail is marked but there are confusing places particularly in the eastern portion of the trail near Initial Point. The trail crosses an Indian Treaty Boundary and the Principal Meridian twice. The condition of the trail is rugged and is best hiked during the weekdays for the joys of solitude.

The established trailhead is north of Initial Point. To reach Young's Creek trailhead and campground from Initial Point drive north on SR 37 towards Pioneer Mothers Memorial Forest and Paoli. Follow the directional signs from Hwy 37. Take the first road south of Pioneer Mothers west, the paved Beech Grove Road. Proceed west on Beech Grove Road about 1 mile to 50W the first road left, and turn south and drive to the dead end and the campground and trailhead on the east side of the road. Volunteers maintain the site for picnicking with tables, primitive camping and a pit toilet.

Young's Creek horse trail is for the adventurous hiker. The rugged loop trail heads southwesterly descending a series of forested and open ridges arriving at CR 560S. The trail turns into roadway and goes west/right for a short distance to turn south at the next crossroads south CR 150W. The gravel road trail crosses over Young's Creek and heads uphill. Halfway uphill the trail turns due east through the woods on a rolling wide forest logging road. After approximately 2 miles the trail descends into a tributary of Holy Defeat Creek. The path crosses and climbs the ridge curving northwest. Initial Point is not far east of this area. The trail can be unmarked and also confusing here. Several unmarked trails venture off to Initial Point along the east segment of the trail. Follow the open ridge to re-cross CR 550. Continue northwest along ridgetops to descend and cross the graveled Burma Road (marked) The final segment continues uphill to the ridgetop then heads west along ridge and ravine back to the Young's Creek trailhead and campground.

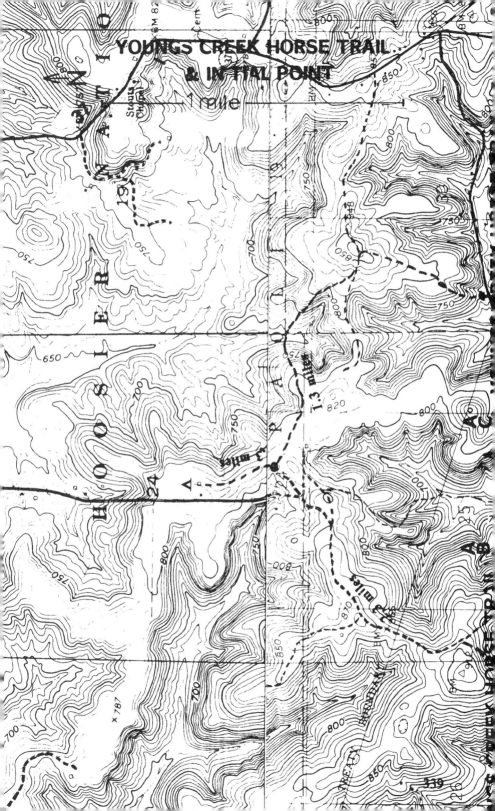

YOUNGS CREEK HORSE TRAIL
& INITIAL POINT

1 mile

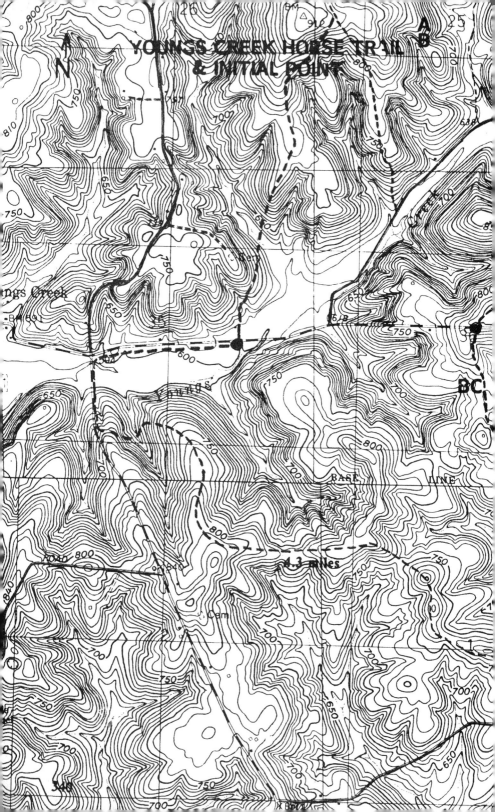

YOUNGS CREEK HORSE TRAIL
& INITIAL POINT

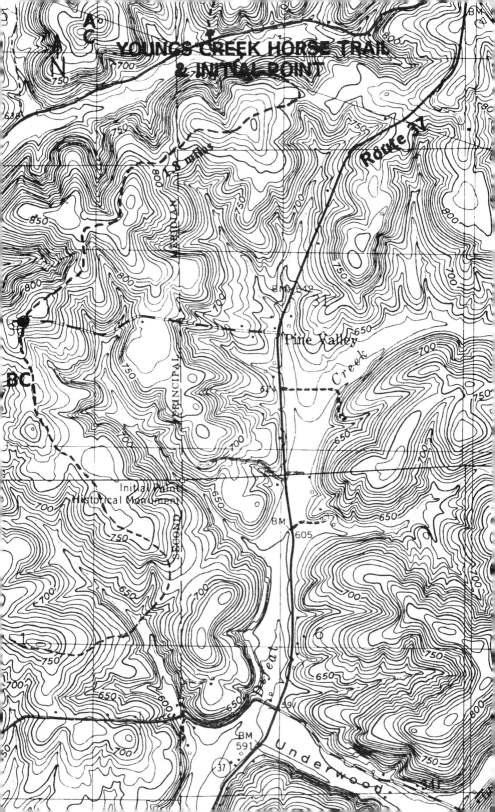

HOOSIER NATIONAL FOREST: LITTLE AFRICA AREA

TRIP 9: Springs Valley Recreation Area
USGS MAP(S): Greenbriar 1:24,000
TRAIL DISTANCE: 5.5 mile lake loop
ACREAGE: 1,205 acre, 150 acre Tucker Lake
ACTIVITIES: hiking, nature study, social history, picnicking,
fishing, non-motorized boating, launch ramp, hunting, Class C
camping

The 5 1/2 mile Buffalo Trace Trail around spring fed Tucker Lake is one of the finest day hikes in the Hoosier National Forest for its length, moderate difficulty, maintenance and scenery. The lakeshore and forest trail is guided by white blazes and follows a portion of the old buffalo salt route or "trace" from Vincennes to the Falls of the Ohio, crossing to the Kentucky "licks". This quiet Orange County beauty spot was acquired in 1985 in a property exchange with the Indiana Division of Fish and Wildlife.

The marked trailhead is located near a wooden foot bridge and the lake on the southwest shore next to the main property entrance road. Park in the level and spacious pullout next to the trailhead. The trail follows the scenic lakeshore northeast up a lake finger cove to a stream crossing. Cross the stream and continue uphill south to the level ridgetop going south, away from the lake through forest, pine plantations and abandoned fields. The path emerges on the lake with good views.

The trail then follows a second finger cove and French Lick Creek along an old road bed. This area of the trail was supposedly the route the buffalo herds came looking for salt licks. The trail crosses the creek and curves uphill to a blufftop and ravine forest segment on the southeast shore of the second finger cove. The trail heads through the woods to the third lake finger following the shoreline. The trail becomes more open as it draws closer to the dam. Cross over the dam and enjoy the vistas of Springs Valley. The trail follows the lake forest edge uphill to the campground road and downhill to the trailhead parking and lakeshore.

To reach Springs Valley Recreation Area, approximately 6 miles south of French Lick, take SR 145 south about 3 miles crossing French Lick Creek and turn southeast/left and jog onto Moore's Ridge Road. Follow Moore's Ridge Road east nearly 3 miles to the first paved right beyond Moore's Ridge Chapel. Follow the directional signs 3/4 mile to the lakefront and trailhead parking at Springs Valley.

Morning Mist on Tucker Lake

SPRING VALLEY–TUCKER LAKE

1 mile

SPRING VALLEY STATE FISH AND WILDLIFE AREA

French

Tucker Lake

HOOSIER NATIONAL FOREST: TELL CITY AREA
TRIP 10: Hemlock Cliffs Recreation Area
USGS MAP(S): Taswell 1:24,000
TRAIL(S) DISTANCE: 1/2 mile Hemlock Cavern, 1/2 mile Hemlock Falls
ACREAGE: 840 acres
ACTIVITIES: hiking, nature study, archaeology

Approximately 6 miles south of Taswell and Yellow Birch Ravine Nature Preserve lies Hemlock Cliffs, a narrow 150 foot deep sandstone canyon with waterfalls and caverns along its forested cliffs. Archaeological excavations at Indian Cave and Arrowhead Arch have discovered Indian occupation of the area since 10,000 B.C.   Two maintained and marked loop trails are a short walk from the parking area.

The "Old Trail", which is closed, proceeded from the parking area north downhill to a trail fork. The new, easier trail, leaves west/left and circles clockwise, crosses twice the Hemlock Cavern Trail loop on the left, and meets the "T" junction of the old closed trail. Continue ahead and the trail will take you 1/2 mile to Hemlock Falls and loop back to the parking area. The hike is moderately easy along the canyon to the 45 foot waterfalls that flow to Otter Creek. Snow brushed hemlock trees and mountain laurel and frozen falls make a fine winter scene.

The Hemlock Cavern Trail is a 1/2 mile loop to the left of the "new trail" prior to meeting the old trail "T" junction. Climbing uphill and underneath the recessed broad overhang, 45 feet high and 200 feet wide, the modern day visitor will gain some idea of what shelter and defense was to the earlier occupants especially during a summer cloudburst.

There are several shallow caves and shelters found throughout the boulder strewn canyon. A service road leads through the canyon curving left uphill to the parking area. Several spur roads connect with the canyon.

Gayle Gray Overlook

345

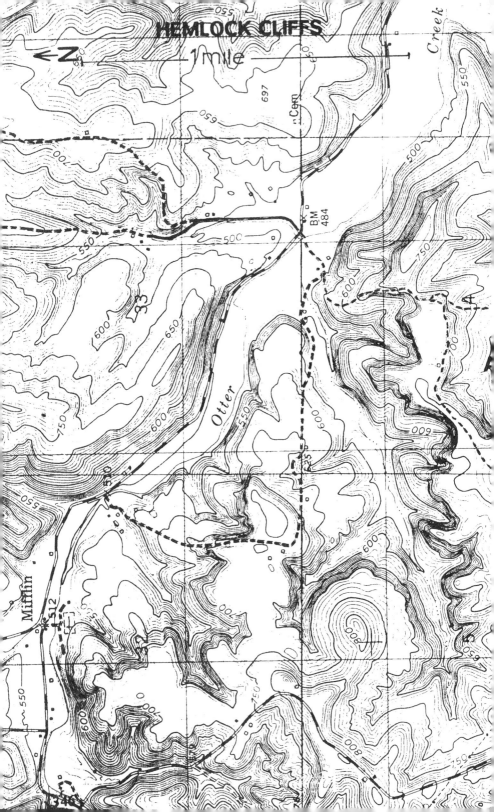

HEMLOCK CLIFFS

Hemlock
Cliffs Picnic Area

To reach Hemlock Cliffs Recreation Area turn west onto a county road 1 1/2 miles south of Grantsburg from SR 37 in Crawford County. Go west 4 miles and south to the forested entry road. Follow the directional signs.

Enroute to Hemlock cliffs, about midpoint from SR 37, is Gayle Gray Overlook, a point of interest worthy of climbing for the vista. The elevation of 890 feet above sea level provides panoramic views to the north. The former established trail from the road to the open grassy ridge top is now blurred by non maintenance.

Hemlock Cliffs

HOOSIER NATIONAL FOREST: TELL CITY AREA
TRIP 11: Carnes Mill
USGS MAP(S): English 1:24,000
TRAIL DISTANCE: 1.5 mile round trip
ACTIVITIES: hiking, natural and social history

The hike to Carnes Mill is a nature walk alongside scenic riparian beauty of the Little Blue River. Access to this historical mill site is limited to walking in on an abandoned county road or canoeing. The trailhead is located at a dead end on a maintained county gravel road. The road appears to end at a farmhouse and it does, so please be courteous and inform the owners that you plan to park and hike to Carnes Mill. Ownership of Carnes Mill is divided in several ways: National Forest Service, State Division of Nature Preserves, The Nature Conservancy, and private owners. The approximate 3/4 mile walk to the site follows the west heavily timbered and steep banks of the Little Blue River. Yellow Nature Conservancy signs appear en route to the site.

Arrival at the site is marked by a forest covered, sandstone Mississippian "backbone". Eastern hemlock, mountain laurel and bush honeysuckle are the more unique plants found on the mixed deciduous evergreen slopes. At the east tip of the backbone and the narrowest point of the horseshoe bend is the location of a natural rock tunnel and bridge through which downstream water "shortcuts" the horseshoe bend and flows underneath. With the aid of man the natural tunnel was enlarged to turn the grist wheels of a special mid 19th century grain mill. Supposedly the still operational dam was built further east at the bend to create more water flow.

The dam is the only man made obstruction on the free and wild Little Blue. The river is canoeable for 41 miles from English to about Alton on the Ohio River. 33 miles of the stream passes through the Hoosier National Forest.

The old county road continues east on the promontory point or peninsula between the stream to the dam. A fork to the left leads to a private property residence. Be advised poison ivy and stinging wood nettle are common in the off road bottoms. Retrace your steps.

Carnes Mill is located 1 mile south of Grantsburg near SR 37 in Crawford County. From I-64 exit north on SR 37 exit and drive 2.7 miles and turn right/east at the first paved road after leaving the interstate. Follow the paved road 0.8 mile to a gravel road on the right/south. Turn and drive 0.2 mile to the end of the county road at the farmhouse. Stop and ask permission to park. Continue to walk along the abandoned county road to Carnes mill. Until better access is provided, available parking room is limited to 2-3 vehicles.

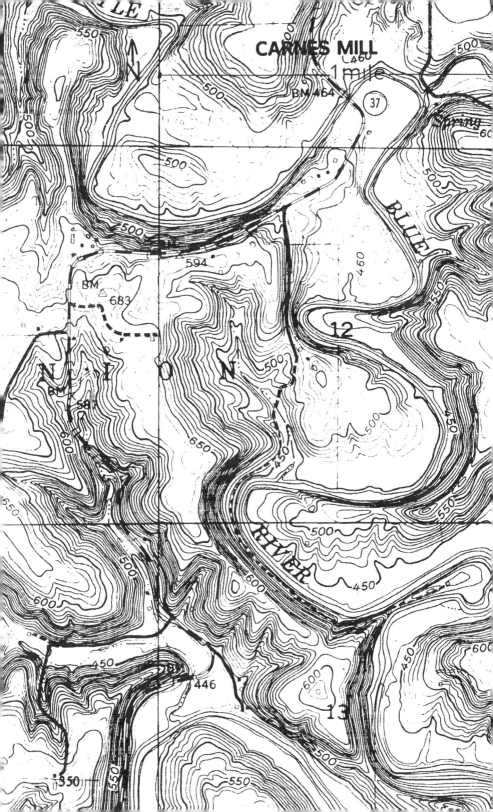

HOOSIER NATIONAL FOREST: TELL CITY AREA
TRIP 12: Celina and Indian Lakes
USGS MAP(S): Bristow, Branchville 1:24,000
TRAIL(S) DISTANCE: 3 trails: Two Lakes Loop 12.2 miles, Celina-to-Tipsaw Spur 4 miles one way no longer maintained, 0.5 mile Celina Interpretive Trail.
ACTIVITIES: hiking, nature study, historical sites, picnicking, non motorized boating, launch ramps, fishing, hunting, seasonal naturalist programs, outdoor amphitheater, Class A camping, brochure available.
FEE(S): camping

Lake Celina and Indian Lake are two of four dam impoundments constructed in the late 1960's along the Middle Fork of the Anderson River and its tributaries. Campgrounds and other development are along the ridges of the northeast shore of Lake Celina, the first lake west of SR 37, driving south from I-64. The 3 trails provide great outdoor experiences particularly along the lengthy and forested 12.2 mile Two Lakes Loop which was designated a National Recreation Trail in 1979.

The Two Lakes Loop skirts the eastern and south shore of Lake Celina and the southern and west shore of Indian Lake with miles between the two water bodies. Besides the connecting trail spur from the North and South Face Campgrounds, there are 7 trailhead parking lots marked with orange diamonds along the main forest road plus two boat ramp parking areas. The Two Lakes Loop Trail is marked with white painted, diamond-shaped blazes on trees and stumps.

The main trailhead is located at the 7th or last parking lot west on the south side of the main forest road enroute to Indian Lake from Lake Celina. However you may begin your hike at any of the connecting trailhead parking lots or from the campground at South Face site #18 and #19. One possible plan is to camp overnight and start the next morning early and be somewhat leisurely making the hike a full day's experience. Follow the 1/2 mile Celina Interpretive Trail beyond the Indian overhang rock shelters to the marked trail intersection with the Two Lakes Loop.

Continue to follow the mixed forested, east lakeshore around finger coves south and west to the Lake Celina dam. Just south of the dam crossing, remains of a linear trail spur, now removed, led southward to Tipsaw Lake (4 miles). Once across the open space of Celina dam, the trail continues through forest and open abandoned fields. Approximately mid-point, between Indian and Celina Lakes, enroute to the dam and the south shore of Indian Lake, there is a trail junction with the main connecting access trailhead and 6 other parking areas along the main forest road. The 12.2 mile loop trail may be shortcutted in half by hiking the connecting spur north and then looping back southeast to Lake Celina's boat ramp.

Before crossing over the Indian Lake dam there is a trail spur that leads north to end at the boat ramp and picnic area. The west shore of Indian Lake is well forested and remote. The trail continues east crossing streams and service roads, up and down ridgetops and slopes back to Lake Celina campgrounds and boat ramp.

Two Lakes Loop, Indian Lake

The Tipsaw Lake spur is no longer maintained due to vandalism. It heads south from Lake Celina approximately 1.5 miles from the Celina Interpretive Trail intersection. The marked forested ravine trail leads to open fields and up along a gravel county road that heads east then south to a "T" with a paved county road, a short distance from SR 37. Turn right/west at the trail sign and follow the county paved road about 1/2 mile and turn south 100 yards on a gravel road and walk southwest through a grassy abandoned field. The trail spur descends along Sulphur Fork, a main tributary of Tipsaw Lake. The trail crosses the main park road at Tipsaw Lake. In the open bottoms of Sulphur Fork, the trail forks with the Tipsaw Lake Loop. Bear right and follow the north shoreline to the Tipsaw boat ramp and beach area.

The Celina Interpretive Trail begins and ends at the Lake Celina boat ramp and parking area south of the campgrounds and the main forest road and entrance. The fenced off and unrestored old village of Celina's post office and stagecoach stop is the first stop along the 1/2 mile easy self-guiding trail loop. Other interpretive points of interest include Indian shelter rocks, plant succession, hardwoods and dead tree ecology. The trail connects the Two Lakes Loop trail at mid point. The Celina Interpretive Trail leads to the Rickenbaugh Cemetery and back to the old Celina post office and the boat ramp parking area.

The entrance to the Two Lakes, Celina and Indian area is located 3 miles south of I-64 and Saint Croix at the SR 37 exit.

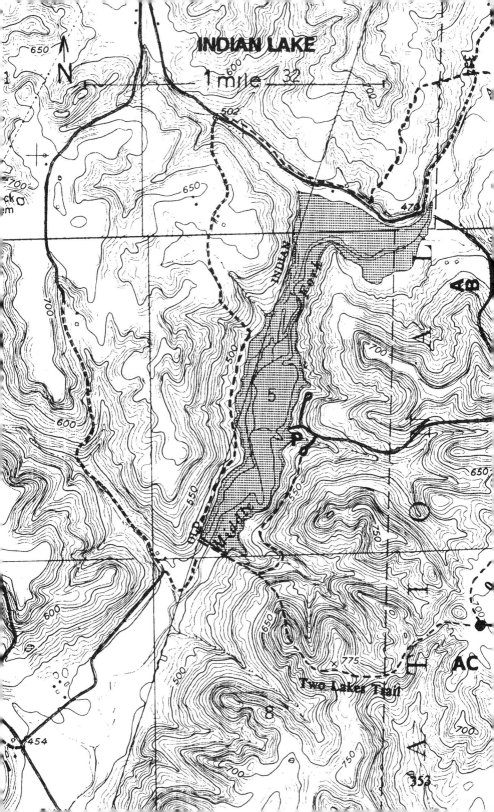

INDIAN LAKE

1 mile

Two Lakes Trail

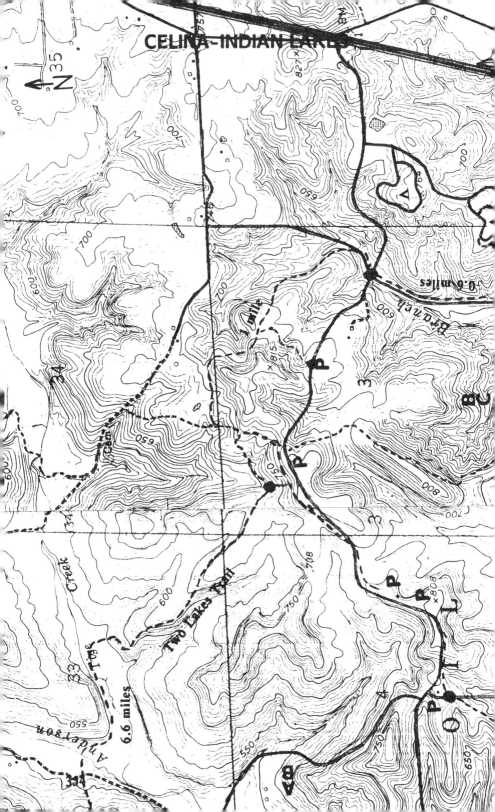

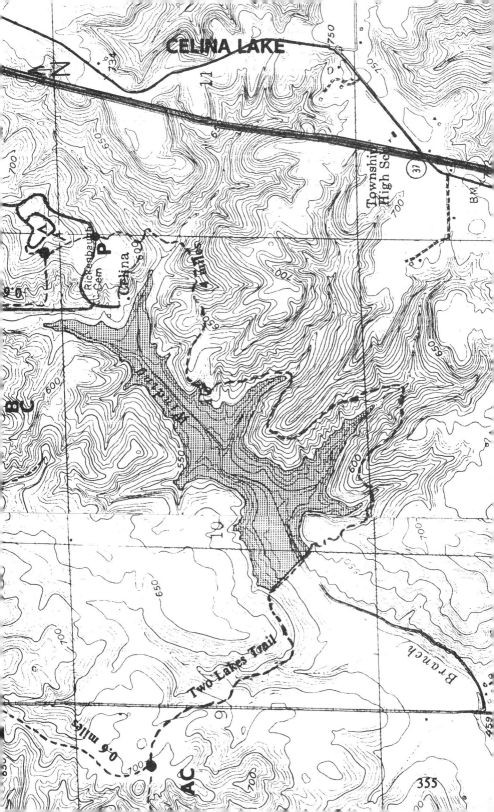

HOOSIER NATIONAL FOREST: TELL CITY AREA
TRIP 13: Tipsaw Lake
USGS MAP (S): Bristow, Gatchel 1:24,000
TRAIL(S) DISTANCE: 2 trails total 6.5 miles
ACTIVITIES: hiking, nature study, picnicking, shelterhouse, beach
swimming, bathhouse, fishing, non-motorized boating, launch ramp,
Class A camping
FEE(S): camping, brochure available

Tipsaw Lake is the middle lake of the 4 impoundments that the forest service has developed along the Middle Fork of the Anderson River in Perry County. Tipsaw's scenic waters are derived from Sulphur Fork Creek, Massey Branch, Snake Branch and other smaller tributaries.

The 4 mile Tipsaw-to-Celina trail spur connects the Two Lakes Loop Trail (see Trip 12). This trail is no longer maintained due to vandalism. The linear trail begins at the Tipsaw Lake boat ramp parking area and follows the northwest shoreline of Tipsaw Lake. In the bottomlands heading up Sulphur Fork, the mowed grassy service road trail forks with Tipsaw Lake Loop. Bear left and continue across the main forest road through abandoned meadows, woodlands, and plantations to a gravel road. Turn left/north and walk 100 yards to the "T" paved road and go right/east. Proceed about 1/2 mile east on the paved county road to a gravel road on the left side just before the junction with SR 37. Go left and follow the gravel road north and then west. The road becomes a forest trail to connect with Two Lakes Loop on the southeast side of Lake Celina east of the dam. The Tipsaw-to-Celina Spur to Two Lakes Loop Trail is 4 miles one way. Retrace your steps or possibly car shuttle.

The Tipsaw Lake Loop trail begins west of the beach area parking lot at the Tipsaw shore. The trail follows around the finger cove keeping close to the lakeshore along a forest trail to the dam. The open space of the dam area offers fine vistas of the lake-hill setting. On the south side of the dam the trail enters a meadow undergoing succession and around 2 more lake fingers on across the Snake Branch to an old road. The trail continues on the service road around the south lakeside through abandoned meadow and forested north facing ridgesides between the lake and the Lenmon Cemetery. The trail surface becomes a mowed, grassy, vehicle wide path as it levels out in the lush bottom land of Sulphur Fork to connect with the Tipsaw-to-Celina Spur. Bear left and follow the lakeshore of Tipsaw Lake instead of going straight north to Lake Celina. The trail ends at the beach area of Tipsaw Lake.

Tipsaw Lake entrance road is located 7 miles south of I-64 exit and Saint Croix on SR 37. From Lake Celina and Indian Lake entrance it is 4 miles south off SR 37. The Tipsaw Lake entrance road from SR 36 to the beach area is at least 2 miles.

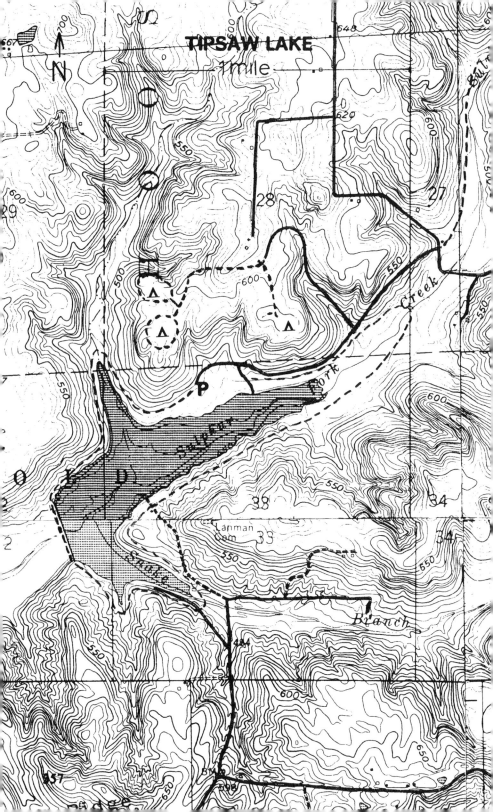

Trail Junction, Celina/Indian Lakes

HOOSIER NATIONAL FOREST: TELL CITY AREA
TELL CITY AREA
TRIP 14: Saddle Lake
USGS MAP(S): Gatchell 1:24,000
TRAIL DISTANCE: 3 mile lake loop
ACREAGE: 41 acre Saddle Lake
ACTIVITIES: hiking, nature study, picnicking, beach swimming, playground, fishing, non-motorized boating, launch ramp, limited primitive Class C camping
FEE(S): camping, brochure available

The compact Saddle Lake Recreation Area is the smallest and most southerly of the Middle Fork Lakes. Dammed freshwaters of Thesis Creek and hillside gullys form the 41 acre multi-purpose Saddle Lake. The three easy miles Lakeside Trail encircles the saddle shaped lake. The trail was erected in 1968 by the Branchville Civilian Conservation Center.

The trailhead begins at the beach and boat ramp parking area and may be hiked in either direction around the lake. The best portion of the trail is east of the beach along the ridge side and bottoms of Thesis Creek inlet and cove. The dam area is a fine picnic place. The west and south shore trail section is forested and level. There is a small creek fork at the most south finger, south of the boat ramp launch. A good portion of the trail is graveled with limestone fines.

Saddle Creek entrance road is located 12 miles northeast of Tell City off SR 37 at the north edge of Gatchel. From I-64, exit south at Saint Croix on SR 37 and drive about 20 miles to Saddle Creek's entrance.

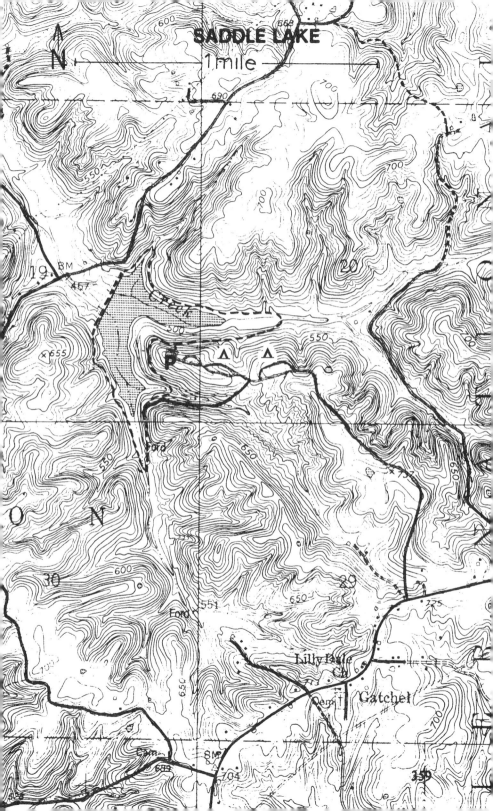

SADDLE LAKE

1 mile

HOOSIER NATIONAL FOREST: TELL CITY AREA
TRIP 15: Mogan Ridge
USGS MAP(S): Derby IN-KY 1:24,000
TRAIL(S) DISTANCE: no est. trail, Mogan Ridge Trail not maintained
ACREAGE: 7000 acres
ACTIVITIES: hiking, nature study, hunting

The 21 mile Mogan Ridge hiking trail is no longer maintained or marked except by old fading diamond shaped blue blazes. It may also be confusing due to the number of old roads and trails. There are however several accessible forest roads and map and compass trails. Mogan Ridge, Kuntz Ridge, and Rockhouse Hollow are mature forest natural areas worthy of visitation but require rugged backcountry hiking.

The Mogan Ridge area is currently managed for timber, wild turkey and other wildlife and not recreation. This large block of unbroken forest land is unfortunately for hikers, beset with chiggers and Lone Star ticks. Lone Star ticks, a mini-form of the wood tick, was introduced to Perry County from restocking deer herds from Missouri. Fortunately these abundant ticks are so far confined to Perry County locally and not all southern Indiana. At the junction of state roads 70 and 37 go north on old SR 37 about a mile on the east side of new SR 37 and turn east on a marked gravel road and drive to the pulloff parking sites south of the tower near the locked bar gate at Mogan Ridge entrance road.

Follow the primitive forest entry road to the "T" and turn east/left, bearing left 1.5 miles to Mogan Ridge road and trailhead. 3 miles from the entry gate the forest road connects an old 3 mile loop forest road of the Mogan Ridge Trail through Rockhouse Hollow. 5 miles further east of the entry gate the forest road connects Kuntz Ridge. The gravel road dead ends at the wildlife ponds near Clover Lick. Retrace your steps. Be advised to bring maps and compass when exploring offroad. Winter or early spring is the best time to explore Mogan Ridge.

Wildlife Ponds, Mogan Ridge

MOGAN RIDGE
─1mile─

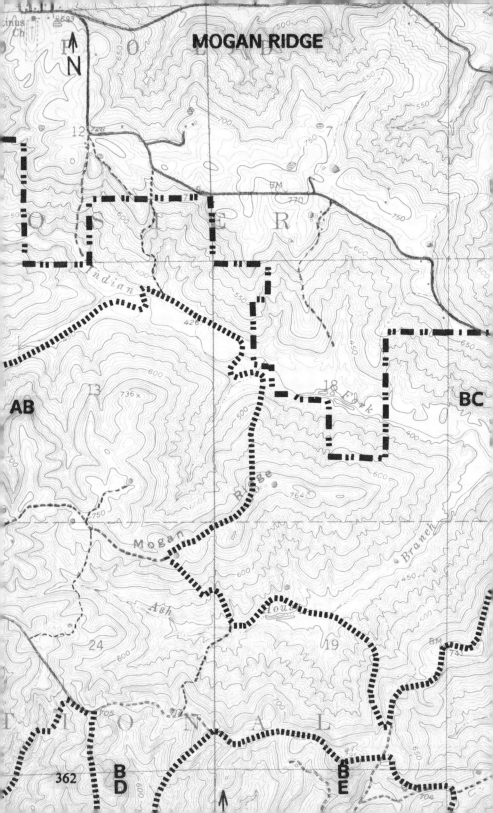

MOGAN RIDGE

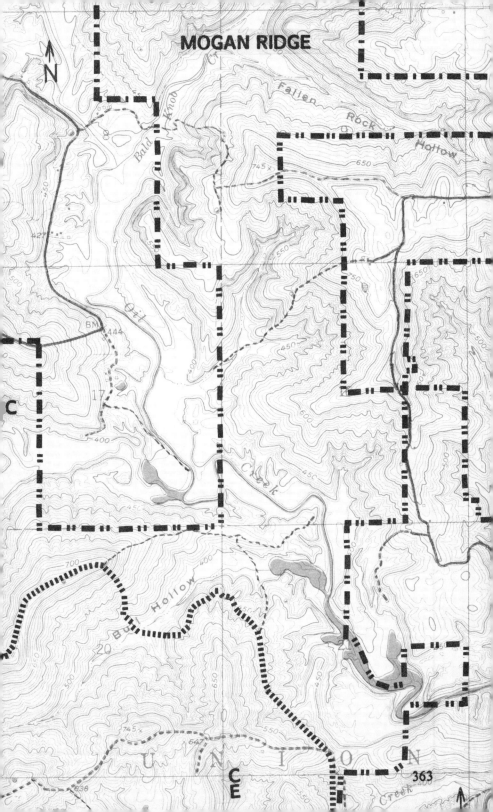

MOGAN RIDGE

363

MOGAN RIDGE

MOGAN RIDGE
(U.S. Forest Service)

1983

INDIANA HIKING GUIDE

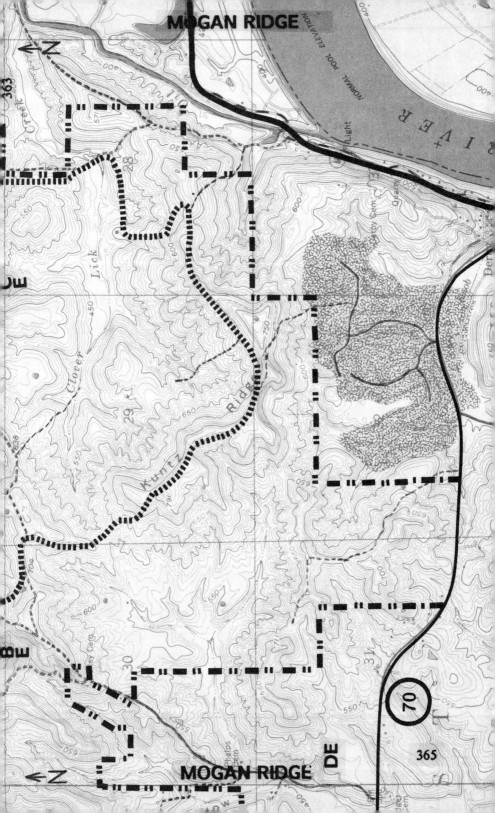

HOOSIER NATIONAL FOREST: TELL CITY AREA
TRIP 16: Buzzard Roost
USGS MAP(S): Alton, IN-KY
TRAIL(S) DISTANCE: 3/4 mile trail loop
ACTIVITIES: hiking, nature study, picnicking, Ohio River fishing,
Class C primitive camping

Buzzard Roost is a 300 foot high wooded bluff overlooking the Ohio
River between the river villages of Magnet and Alton. Buzzards or
turkey vultures (Cathartes aura) who soar freely above the landscape
looking for carrion, roost or nest in the rock outcrops high above the
river until migrating further south for winter.

The 3/4 mile Ohio River Trail, a moderately rugged loop, begins and
ends along the ridge at the picnic and campground area. Heading
north/upstream, the marked trail follows the ridgeline then descends
along switchbacks and stairs to the river bottom, portions which are not
maintained. Waterfalls are active after a rain along the vertical cliffs. 3
rest benches provide views of the river, and Magnet is seen 1.5 miles
downstream from the south bench. Barge traffic is often heard and seen.
Along the river trail, one bridge is washed out and requires a deep ravine
crossing. Walnut, silver maple, box elder maple, elm, sycamore,
cottonwood, ash, willow and pawpaw are some of the common riparian
trees. There are rugged rock outcrops along the south trail staircase.

To reach Buzzard Roost Recreation Area from SR 66, take the first
paved road east 1 1/2 miles south of the village of Oriole. Follow the
paved and graveled road CR 182, bearing to the right to the marked
entrance of Buzzard Roost. The recreation site is located on the
northeast county line of Perry and Crawford counties.

Oriole Pond, enroute to Buzzards Roost

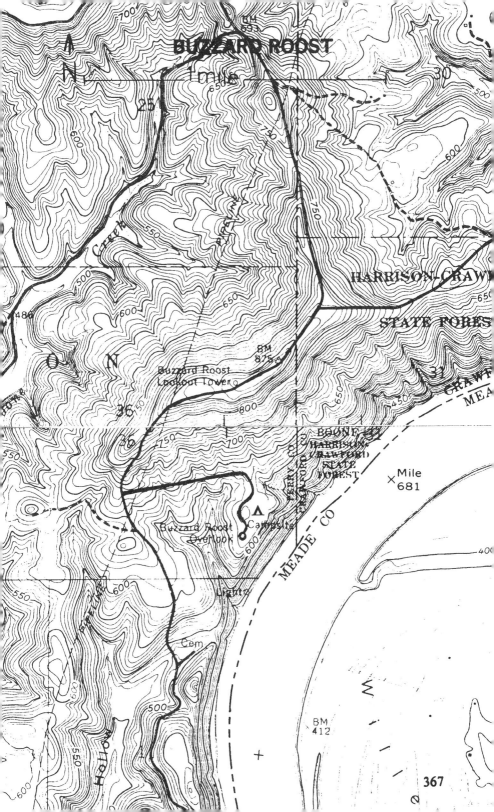

HOOSIER NATIONAL FOREST: TELL CITY AREA
TRIP 17: German Ridge
USGS MAP(S): Rome, IN-KY 1:24,000
TRAIL(S) DISTANCE: 3/4 mile Cliffside Trail Loop
ACTIVITIES: hiking, nature study, picnicking, shelterhouse, beach
  swimming, pond fishing, hunting, bridle trails, horse camp
FEE(S): camping

German Ridge Recreation Area was originally constructed by the Civilian Conservation Corps during 1939-40. Buildings were built and eroded fields planted to pine. The scenic ridge was the first developed national forest site in the Tell City Area. Unfortunately there are not more blazed trails along the ridge.

Cliffside Trail, German Ridge

The marked 3/4 mile Cliffside Trail is a lovely walk that passes through a massive moss covered boulder ridge between the campground and beach-lake area. The short, but sweet trail may also be accessed via a spur along the main forest road loop north of the campground and east of the beach-lake.

The former Woodland Management Resource Trail, no longer maintained by the forest service, is an old trail that is still relatively free of vegetation. The mile long loop begins and ends at the campground or parking area north of the campground. The forest trail follows an old service road north from the parking area to cross the county road to a shortleaf pine plantation and Shove Ridge. The trail re-crosses the road further east about 100 yards. The trail then passes through more plantations and a walk-in pond for fishermen. The trail heads west at the pond to the campground. The paved park loop road also makes an enjoyable hike and there are hikeable service roads along the ridge.

To reach German Ridge Recreation Area, northwest of Harding Grove and Rome from Tell City, go east on SR 66 12 miles, turn north on a paved county road. Drive 3/4 miles to the entrance road on the south/left side. You may want to stop at Deer Lake about 1.5 miles from the German Ridge turnoff along SR 66. The attractive lake has a fisherman's path encircling it.

Fishing Pond Trail, German Ridge

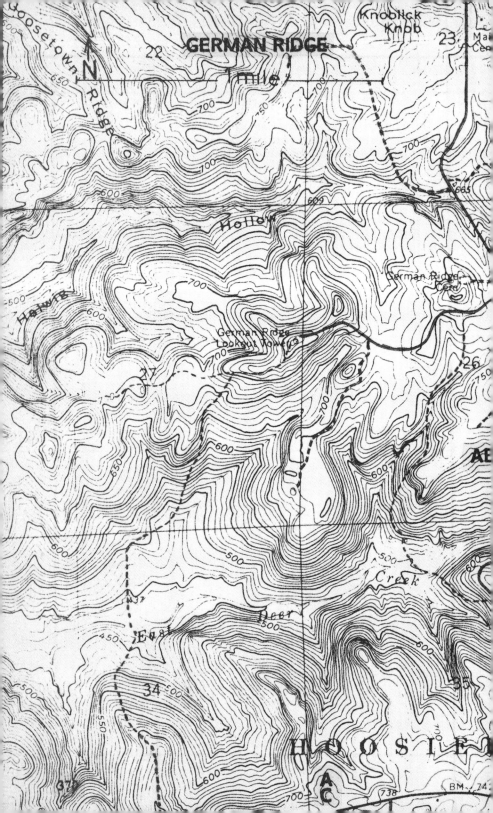

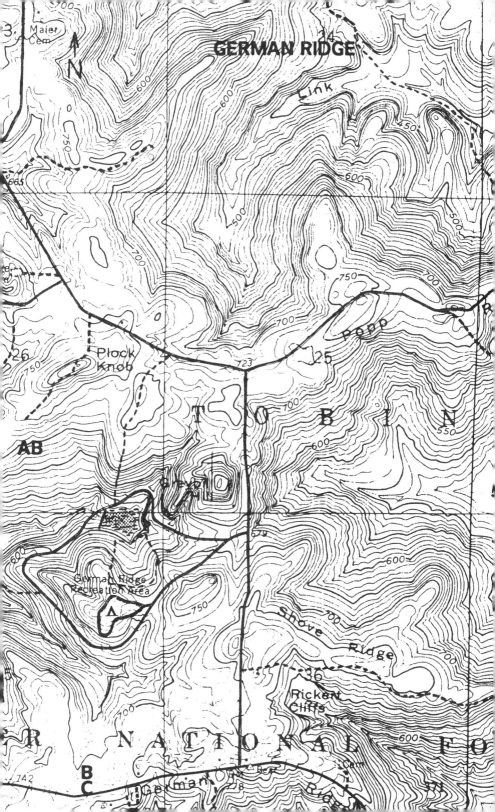

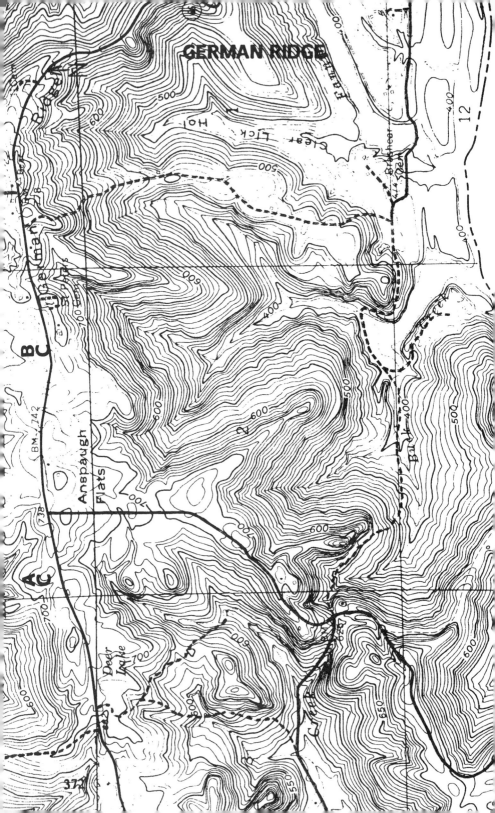

GERMAN RIDGE

INDIANAPOLIS NATURE WALKS

1. Indiana State Museum
202 North Alabama Street at Ohio Street
Indianapolis, IN 46203
Phone: (317) 232-1637

The museum collections include 700 items in 8 galleries. Exhibits of the natural and social history of Indiana are featured. There are group tours, special exhibits, lectures, programs, book and gift shop, and museum membership available.

Administered by the Department of Natural Resources, the state museum occupies the old Indianapolis City Hall building downtown, a fine example of neo-classic architecture. Located north one block of Market Square and the new City-County building.

Open Monday-Saturday 9 am - 4:45 pm   Donations accepted
Sunday 12 noon - 4:45 pm
Closed major holidays

2. Children's Museum of Indianapolis
30th and Meridian Streets
Indianapolis, IN 46208
Phone: (317) 924-5431

Natural science exhibits are displayed along the five levels of galleries of the largest children's museum in the world including a simulated southern Indiana limestone cave. The museum sponsors school group tours, special events, theater performances, a lending department, nature walks and classes. A restaurant and outdoor picnic area are also available.

From I-65 at downtown, exit north onto Meridian Street/US 31 and from I-465 exit south on Meridian Street/US 31.

Open Tuesday-Saturday 10 am - 5 pm   Admission Fee
Sunday 12 noon - 5 pm
Closed Mondays, September - May,
Thanksgiving, Christmas and New Year's Day

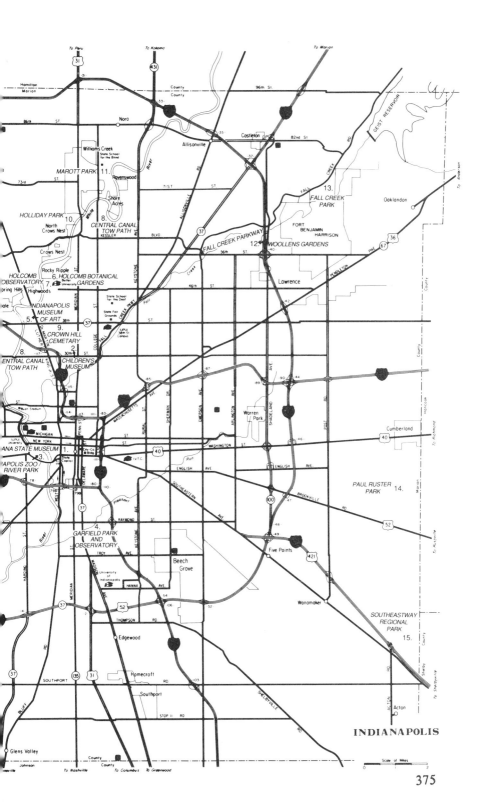

INDIANAPOLIS

Scale of Miles

375

3. Indianapolis Zoo/White River State Park
801 Washington Street west of downtown
Indianapolis, IN 46204
Phone: (317) 634-4567

Opened June 1988, the new 75 acre Indianapolis Zoo is located on the west bank at White River State Park. The zoo's theme, "River of Life" features 2,500 world-wide animals in four living areas or ecological biomes: Temperate and Tropical Forest, Grasslands, World's Waters and Desert, all within a botanical garden atmosphere.

A restored 1870 water pumping station serves as a visitor's center at White River State Park. The 250 acre urban state park includes the Eiteljorg, a museum of American Indian and western art, a sports fitness center, performing arts center, historic Military Park, and the world's second largest free standing tower (750 ft.). Planned is a family thematic amusement and aquatic park comparable to Tivoli Gardens in Copenhagen, Denmark. Be sure to explore the half mile one way Riverwalk Promenade along the White River adjacent to the zoo.

White River State Park, Daily 8:00 am - Sunset   Admission Fee
Indianapolis Zoo, Winter & Summer hours

4. Garfield Park and Conservatory
2450 South Shelby at Raymond and Garfield
Indianapolis, IN 46203
Phone: (317) 787-3044

There are 500 different plants from tropical and desert regions displayed at Garfield Park's conservatory, Indiana's largest tropical horticulture exhibit. Special seasonal flower shows, exhibits, guided group tours, conservatory function rental, and a gift shop are available. The 130 acre park also includes trails, sunken gardens, picnic shelters, playfields, tennis courts, swimming pool, and community center.

South of downtown. From I-65 exit west onto Raymond and drive one block to South Shelby.

Open 10 am - 5 pm Tuesday - Saturday   Nominal Admission Fee
Sunday 12 noon - 5 pm, Closed major holidays   No Charge Tuesdays

5. Indianapolis Museum of Art Grounds
1200 West 38th Street
Indianapolis, IN 46208
Phone: (317) 923-1331

Located on the grounds of the Oldfields Estate, former home of the Lilly family, the lovely 154 acres contains formal sculptures, fountains, greenhouses, botanical gardens, and nature trails. The landscaping of the 52 acre mansion grounds was designed by Frederick Law Olmsted, designer of New York's Central Park.

Seasonal flowers and plants are available for sale at the greenhouses. The Horticultural Society's study center is open Wednesday through Saturday, 1 pm - 4 pm. The "Garden on the Green" retreat adds the pleasure of dining outdoors during summer in formal surroundings from 11 am - 5 pm. Winter cross country skiing is permitted.

From I-65 exit north on Northwestern Avenue/US 421 and proceed to 38th Street. From I-465 exit south on US 421/Michigan/Northwestern Avenue to 38th Street. The entrance is on the north side of 38th Street before the White River bridge.

Open Daily, 11 am - 5 pm Tuesday - Sunday
except Monday, Thanksgiving, Christmas and New Year's Day

6. Holcomb Botanical Gardens at Butler University
North End of Clarendon Road at Central Canal
Indianapolis, IN 46208
Phone: (317) 283-9231

Established 1950 at the beautiful 232 acre Butler University campus, the James Irving Holcomb Botanical Gardens displays 500 different types of woody perennials. During May flowering trees such as hawthorn and flowering crabapple line the Central Garden Mall adjacent to the Central Canal. Lilac bushes are a garden specialty and 80 different varieties found throughout the world display their colors at springtime. Inscriptions from the Great Masters such as Plato and Shakespeare are carved on pathside stones for reflection. A pond and waterfall also grace the grounds. A carillon and reflecting pool are situated at the wooded knoll east of the gardens.

Holcomb Botanical Gardens are located to the north of main campus and the Holcomb Observatory and Planetarium. From I-465 exit south on US 31/Meridian Street and turn right/west on 46th Street.

Open Daily, Dawn to Dusk

7. Holcomb Observatory and Planetarium at Butler University
4600 Sunset Avenue
Indianapolis, IN 46208
Phone: (317) 283-9333

During the college year, group tours of the observatory's 38" telescope and planetarium shows are scheduled on weekends from 3 pm - 5 pm and 7 pm - 9 pm. Tours and shows begin at 4 pm and 8 pm. The World Time Clock Room is an additional attraction.

The facilities are located west of the Carillon and south of the Holcomb Botanical Gardens at Central Canal on the campus of Butler University.

Open September to July 31st   Special Program Fee
Saturday and Sunday 3-5 pm, 7-9 pm
Closed August and university holidays

8. Central Canal Tow Path
College and Westfield Boulevard to 30th Street
Indianapolis, Indiana
Phone: (317) 639-1501

This historic waterway provides nearly 7 linear miles of walkway from College Avenue near the White River at Broad Ripple southwest to Riverside Park and 30th Street. The best natural section is between 52th and 38th Streets. The dedicated American Water Landmark passes by Butler University's Holcomb Gardens and the grounds of the Indianapolis Museum of Art.

The Central Canal is administered by the Indianapolis Water Company. Only 8 miles of the Central Canal was completed when the Panic of 1837 brought an end to the feeder spur that eventually would have connected the Wabash & Erie Canal.

From I-465 exit south on US 31/Meridian Avenue or Keystone Avenue to 62nd Street and Broad Ripple.

Open Daily

9. Crown Hill Cemetery
700 West 38th Street
Indianapolis, IN 46208
Phone: (317) 925-8231

Established in 1863 on the highest natural point with 25 miles of roads in the Old City limits, Crown hill is one of the largest cemeteries in the nation. Tour maps and a self guiding handlist of over 100 trees and their location are available at the gatehouse for a small fee.

Entrance to Crown Hill Cemetery is along 38th Street between Meridian Street/US 31 and the Michigan Road/Northwestern Avenue north of downtown and east of the Indianapolis Museum of Art.

Open Daily, 8:30 am - 5 pm

10. Holliday Park
6349 Spring Mill Road and West 64th Street
Indianapolis, IN 46260
Phone: (317) 924-9151, (317) 924-7070

This popular 86 acre wooded metro park borders the West Fork of the White River in north central Indianapolis. 300 species of trees are labelled on the 50 acre arboretum grounds surrounding the "Ruins", an outdoor sculpture setting of fountains, pools and Grecian statues designed by Elmer E. Taflinger. Unmarked trails and old service roads are found in the forest area bordering the White river.

To reach Holliday Park drive west on 64th Street from Meridian/US 31 just north of the river bridge in Meridian Hills. From I-465 exit south on Meridian Street.

Open Daily, 7 am - 10 pm

378

11. Marott Park
7350 North College Avenue
Indianapolis, Indiana
Phone: (317) 924-7070, (317) 293-4827

This nature oriented, excellent bird watching, 80 acre metro park along the banks of White River and Williams Creek is half forest. Nineteen acres have been set aside as a state nature preserve. Also, self guiding nature trails, picnicking, shelterhouses, and playfields are available.

To reach Marott Park near Meridian Hills and Broad Ripple take Meridian/US 31 north to 75th Street and turn east and drive to College Avenue. Proceed south along College Avenue to the park entrance.

Open Daily

12. Woollens Gardens/Fall Creek Parkway
6800 East Fall Creek Parkway, North Drive
Indianapolis, IN
Phone   (317) 255-8134
        (317) 924-7070

The 125 acre, Woollens Gardens was donated as a nature preserve in 1909 by William Watson Woollen. Unmarked nature walks follow Fall Creek and nearby riparian bluffs and ravines. The parkway's roadside along Fall Creek Road may also be explored on foot.

From I-465 east side exit west onto 56th Street and drive to the intersection with Fall Creek Parkway just beyond the Fall Creek bridge. Turn right/north and proceed along Fall Creek Parkway to Woollen Gardens. Roadside parking is available at the curve near the intersection with Fall Creek Road. Skilles Test Park lies just north of Fall Creek Road adjacent to I-465.

Open Daily, Dawn to Dusk

13. Fall Creek Park
8725 Fall Creek Road
Lawrence, IN
Phone: (317) 549-4815

This City of Lawrence riverside park offers a 3/4 mile, self-guiding woodland trail, as well as picnicking and play areas.

To reach the park from I-465 east side exit 56th Street east at Lawrence and drive 2/3 mile to Boy Scout Road and turn left/north. Continue on Boy Scout Road north just over a mile to Shafter Road and turn left/west and proceed 1/5 mile to Fall Creek Road and turn right/east. Follow Fall Creek Road about 2 miles to the park entrance on the right/south side of the road.

Seasonal

14. Paul Ruster Park
11300 Prospect Road
Indianapolis, IN
Phone: (317) 924-7070

Besides forest trails along Buck Creek, the 80 acre, all season, natural park includes a shelter, playground, gazebo, ice skating pond and sledding hill. There are plenty of playfields and open space. The park is about 3 miles north of Southeastway Regional Park, also along Buck Creek.

From I-465 eastside exit US 40 or US 52 and drive east to the Marion-Hancock County Line Road. Turn south or north and proceed to Prospect Road and turn west to the park entrance.

Open Daily, Dawn to Dusk

15. Southeastway Regional Park
5624 Southeast County Line Road
Indianapolis, IN
Phone: (317) 861-5167, (317) 924-7070

One of four major regional parks outlying Indianapolis. Southeastway emphasizes outdoor recreation and environmental education. Wooded nature trails follow Buck Creek and there is a nature center. Additional recreational fare includes bicycle trails, timber form playlots, picnicking with shelters, basketball and tennis courts, and a community building.

Southeastway Park is accessible from I-74 at the Acton Road exit. Go southeast on Southeastern Avenue to County Line Road north to the park entrance.

Open Daily, Dawn to Dusk

16. Eagle Creek Park and Nature Preserve
7840 West 56th Street
Indianapolis, IN 46254
Phone: (317) 293-4828

The largest county park in Indiana offers 7.2 miles of hiking trails plus numerous other recreational activities all year long in a state park atmosphere. The 46 acre Eagles Crest Woods Nature Preserve has flat ridge tops and steep slopes covered with old second growth. The preserve's eastside shoreline is excellent for observing birdlife. Of special interest to the nature oriented is the nature center, arboretum, lakeside picnicking, canoeing and Daniel Boone's carving on a beech tree. Special cultural programs and events, recreational, and educational programs are offered.

Gatehouses are located at West 7840 56th Street and West 71st Street and Eagle Creek Parkway. Exit from I-465 exit interchange 19 north bound only and from I-65 West 71st Street.

Open Daily, Dawn to Dusk   Admission Fee, Gate and Museum

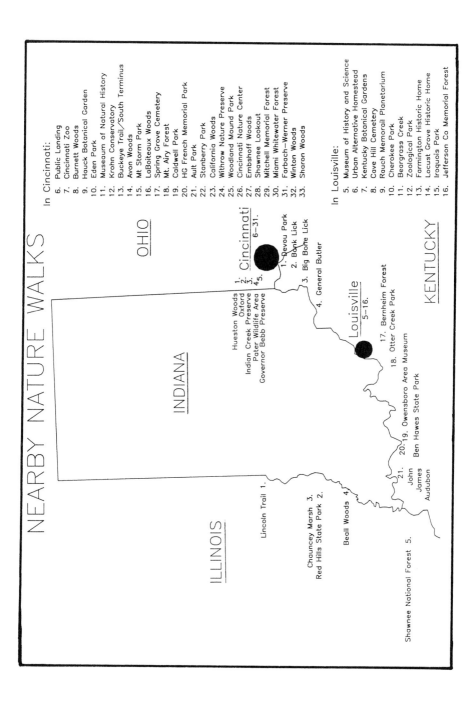

OHIO BORDERLANDS AND CINCINNATI

1. Hueston Woods State Park
Route #1, Ohio SR 732
College Corner, Ohio 45003
Phone: (513) 523-6347

Four of the twelve established trails at Hueston Woods crisscross a 200 acre virgin forest preserve that is considered one of the finest in Ohio. The nature center and museum have excellent wildlife exhibits and naturalists on duty year around. Acton Lake occupies 625 water acres and offers beach swimming, beach concessions, boat rental, boating, launch ramp, sailing, ice skating and ice fishing, ice boating and marina. Fossil collecting and cross country skiing are popular activities. Bridle trails, picnicking, shelters, camping, cabin rental, lodge, historic sites, Indian mounds, restaurant and golf course available.

Hueston Woods State Park is located 4.5 miles north of Oxford, Ohio on Ohio SR 732, one mile west of the junction of Ohio SR 732 and SR 177.

Open Year-Around   Admission Fee

2. Oxford, Ohio/Nature Places
Butler County, Ohio 45056

Self-guiding walks and campus tours are available of the beautiful Williamsburg-style campus of Miami University. A campus walking tour map and information are found at the Shriver Center between Patterson and Maple Avenues and Spring Street. The Conrad Formal Gardens are located at east campus. Goggin Ice Arena at Tallawanda Road and High Street is open to the public. The geology museum at Shiedler Hall is open weekdays for visitation. Entomological insect collections are displayed at Upham hall east of the Hub. The Hub, the central point of campus, has 50 stones from each of the 50 states embedded in concrete around the central green. Molyneaux-Western Bell Tower and the Ernst Nature Theatre are located at southeast campus. Oxford's Peffer Memorial City Park, located just off US 27 southeast of town, has a nature trail.

Oxford, Ohio is accessible from US 27, Ohio SR 73 and Ohio SR 732.

3. Indian Creek Preserve
Reily, Ohio
Phone: (513) 867-5835

Recently acquired by the Butler County Park District, this 132 acre preserve borders scenic Indian Creek. A short woodland loop trail leads to a prehistoric Hopewellian Indian mound. Picnic tables, shelterhouse and pit toilets are available.

The Indian Creek preserve entrances lie just north of the village of Reily, south of Oxford, Ohio along Ohio SR 732 and Springfield Road.

Open Year-Around

4. Pater Wildlife Area
Bunker Hill, Ohio

Two miles downstream from Indian Creek Preserve, Pater Wildlife Area offers 191 acres along Indian Creek for hiking and fossil collecting. The state property is also open to fishing and hunting.

West of Bunker Hill, turn south onto Garner Road and drive 1/4 mile to the entrance. The Pater Wildlife Area is ten miles west of Hamilton and then north of SR 129 and St. Charles.

Open Year-Around

5. Governor Bebb Preserve
Scipio, Ohio
Phone: (513) 867-5835

Two self guiding, short trails encircle the property at this Butler County Park which also includes picnicking, shelters, camping and cabins.

Visitors may also see the 1846 reconstructed birthplace of Governor Bebb, a covered bridge and pioneer village where special seasonal events are held.

The preserve is located along SR 126 between Scipio and Okeena, Ohio about 2 miles southeast of the Indiana-Ohio state line.

Open Year-Around

6. Cincinnati Public Landing/
Yeatman's Cove Park/Sawyer Point Park
River's edge of 2nd Street downtown between Broadway and Butler
Phone: Division of Waterfront, Cincinnati Parks Dept.

The new central riverfront is where the city began and now over 150 years later the site is a public modern day landing with landscaping, fountains and sculpture gardens. The public boat landing is also a steamboat landing for the Delta Queen, Mississippi Queen and Majestic Showboat.

Serpentine Wall at Yeatman's Cove serves as a sculptured amphitheater for public events. Sawyer Point is a performing arts center and recreational park. Special programs and festivals occur throughout the year.

Open Daily Year-Around

7. Cincinnati Zoo
3400 Vine Street
Cincinnati, Ohio 45220
Phone: (513) 281-4700

The 65 acre zoo is home to more than 2,500 animals, several rare and endangered. The zoo's many firsts include the first US world insect exhibit, an outstanding captive breeding program particularly with white Bengal tigers and lowland gorillas and the first to pioneer barless enclosures. It was also the last site of the now extinct passenger pigeon. The largest inland shark exhibit is a popular exhibit. There are educational programs, lectures, shows, animal rides, tram, guided tours, zoo membership, picnicking, restaurant and gift shops.

From I-75/Mill Creek Expressway exit east on Mitchell Avenue and proceed 1/2 mile to Vine Street. Turn south/right on Vine and continue to the intersection with Erdenbrecher and the main zoo gate for pedestrians. Continue south on Erdenbrecher to Dury Avenue and the main auto gate. Follow the paw print directional signs.

Open Daily

Summer 9 am - 8 pm, Closes 6 pm. Winter 9 am - 6 pm, Closes 5 pm

8. Burnet Woods
Brookline Avenue bordered by Bishop, Jefferson, Clifton,
and St. Clair Avenues
Cincinnati, Ohio 45202
Phone: (513) 751-3679

Burnet Woods is a 92 acre wooded urban park located across St. Clair Avenue north of the University of Cincinnati. Numerous nature paths cut through the forested parkland. Trailside Nature Center and Museum, the first children's nature center in the city, displays exhibits of local birds, mammals, insects and geology. There are weekend nature walks and programs the year around. Over 13,000 daffodils have been planted throughout the grounds. A 1,000 foot long lake is situated adjacent to the nature center.

From I-75 exit east on Hopple Street to Dixnyth Avenue to Clifton Avenue. The park road, Brookline Avenue is accessed from Jefferson and St. Clair Avenues.

Open Daily, Dawn to Dusk

9. Hauck Botanic Garden/Garden Center of Greater Cincinnati
715 Reading Road
Cincinnati, Ohio 45202
Phone: (513) 221-0981

Affectionately called "Sooty Acres" , the 8 acre landscaped garden was given as a gift to the city of Cincinnati by Cornelius J. Hauck. It is planted with tolerant plant species selected to survive in a polluted city environment. The collections include a herb garden, specimen trees and shrubs, ground covers, roses, perennials and a dwarf evergreen collection. Special events, meetings, and horticultural lectures occur throughout the year. A horticultural library is open to the public and members.

The garden lies just west of I-71 (no access) at the intersection of Reading Road and Taft Road about 10 blocks east of the University of Cincinnati. From I-75 exit Mitchell Avenue to Reading Road south to Taft Road.

Open Tuesday-Friday 9 am - 4 pm
Saturday 9 am - 3 pm
Closed Holidays

10. Eden Park
Gilbert Avenue between Elsinore and Morris Streets
Cincinnati, Ohio 45202
Phone: (513) 352-4086

The original owner, Nicholas Longronth cultivated grape vines and referred to his riverbluff property as a "Garden of Eden".

Today this lovely 186 acre city park has several natural points of interest: Krohn Conservatory, magnolia tree collections, numerous plantings of flowering dogwood, Museum of Natural History, Mirror and Twin Lakes and the stately Presidential, Heroes, Pioneer and Authors tree groves. A Guide to the Spring Flora of Eden Park is available at Krohn Conservatory.

Eden Park is located north of Mt. Adams east of downtown between I-71, Gilbert Avenue and Columbia Parkway/US 50.

Open Daily, Dawn to Dusk

11. Cincinnati Museum of Natural History and Planetarium
1720 Gilbert Avenue, Eden Park
Cincinnati, Ohio 45202
Phone: (513) 621-3889 Museum
      (513) 621-3336 Planetarium

Tracing its origins from the Western Academy of Sciences, this natural history museum is the oldest west of the Alleghenies, founded in 1835. Fossils, insects, spiders, reptiles, amphibians, rocks, minerals and shells are displayed including a male model Allosaurus dinosaur.

The "Wilderness Trail" depicts Ohio's animal and bird life of a marsh and deciduous forest during the four seasons of the natural year. The "Indian Path" shows dioramas of Paleo-Indian life and their native American successors. The world's largest man made cavern presents examples of cave formations and a 30 foot waterfall. There are group tours, programs, classes, workshops, publications, and special events. Visit the planetarium for a better understanding of our universe.

From I-71 downtown to Gilbert Avenue and Eden Park.

Open Tuesday-Saturday 9 am - 5 pm   Admission Fee
Sunday 12:30 pm - 5 pm   Museum and Planetarium
Closed Monday and major holidays
Planetarium hours:
September-Mid-June, Saturday & Sunday 1 pm - 3 pm
Mid-June-August Tuesday - Sunday 1 pm - 3 pm

12. Krohn Conservatory at Eden Park
950 Eden Park Drive
Cincinnati, Ohio 45202
Phone: (513) 352-4086
        (513) 421-INFO

The Krohn Conservatory, "Cincinnati's Horticultural Showcase Under Glass", displays 1,500 labelled exotic plant specimens from around the world. The 20,000 square feet is divided into four houses: Palm, Tropical, Desert and a Seasonal Floral Display House. A self guiding map is available and guided tours by reservation. There is a gift shop.

Eden Park is located north of Mt. Adams, east of downtown between I-71, Gilbert Avenue and Columbia Parkway/US 50.

Open Daily, 10 am-5 pm Monday-Saturday   Donations Accepted
Sunday 10 am - 6 pm
Special hours during Easter and Christmas

13. Buckeye Trail/South Terminus at Eden Park
Buckeye Trail Association
P.O. Box 254
Worthington, Ohio 43085

Maintained by volunteers, the Buckeye Trail is often called the "Walking History Trail of Ohio". Blue blazed both directions, the 1,200 mile loop trail encircles the interior of the state of Ohio and a large section of trail has been designated the North Country National Scenic Trail (New York to North Dakota). The free-to-all trail follows abandoned railroad right-of-ways, old canal towpaths, river banks, lakeshores, farmland and roadways.

The southwest terminus spur of the Buckeye Trail is located at the Murray Seasongood Bandstand Pavilion opposite the Cincinnati Historical Society headquarters and the Art Museum at Eden Park. Guide books and sectional maps are available from the Buckeye Trail Association. Write for information.

Eden Park is situated north of the Mt. Adams neighborhood east of downtown between I-71, Gilbert Avenue and Columbia Parkway/US 50.

Open Year-Around

14. Avon Woods
4235 Paddock Road
Avondale, Ohio 45229
Phone: (513) 861-3435

Established in 1970, this 114 acre outdoor education center has several self-guiding trails. The facility also includes day camping, programs, special events, mobile nature program and a nature gift shop.

The park is located 3 miles north of Cincinnati in Avondale west of the golf course on Paddock Road/ SR 4.

Open Monday-Friday 8:30 pm- 5 pm   Day User Fee

15. Mt. Storm Park
Lafayette north of Ludlow Avenue in Clifton
Cincinnati, Ohio 45202
Phone: (513) 521-PARK

Handsome formal gardens grace the grounds of Mt. Storm, a former "Clifton Baron" estate designed by landscape architect Adolph Strauch.

The Temple of Love situated at the park's entrance is a setting for many springtime weddings. There are no established trails. Picnicking under shelters and a playground are available.

The park borders the junction of I-75 and I-74. Exit I-75 at Ludlow Avenue and turn right/south and drive 1/4 mile to McAlpin Avenue and Lafayette Avenue. Turn left/east on McAlpin and turn left at Lafayette at the jog.

Open Daily, Dawn to Dusk

16. LaBoiteaux Woods
5400 Lanius Lane
College Heights, Ohio 45224
Phone: (513) 542-2909

Besides nature trails throughout the 50 acre wooded preserve, the outdoor education facility offers natural history museum displays, educational workshops, classes, guided walks, and a gift shop.
The park is located just off of Hamilton Avenue/US 127 adjacent to Spring Grove Cemetery northeast of Mt. Airy Forest. Exit north from I-74 to Colerain Avenue and turn east/right and continue straight on Blue Rock Street to Hamilton Avenue. Go north/left to park entrance.

Open Daily Tuesday-Friday 9 am - 5 pm
Grounds Open Dawn to Dusk

17. Spring Grove Cemetery and Arboretum
Between Winton, Gray, Grosbeck Roads and Hamilton
and Spring Grove Avenues
Cincinnati, Ohio 45202

Dedicated in 1845, the cemetery officials have planted 400 varieties of trees on the 733 acres and included a sculpture garden. Adolph Strauch, landscape architect of Mt. Storm park, also designed the Spring Grove Cemetery grounds. Guidebooks may be obtained from the visitors office. Horticultural staff members conduct tours of the cemetery grounds.
From I-75 exit Mitchell Avenue and turn left/west on Spring Grove Avenue and proceed to Winton Road to Gray Road or Spring Grove to Crawford Avenue right to Parker Woods Park.

Open Daily, 8:00 am - 6 pm

18. Mt. Airy Forest and Arboretum
5083 Colerain Avenue
Cincinnati, Ohio 45223
Phone: (513) 352-4094, (513) 541-8176

The 1,469 acre city park property was the site of the first municipal reforestation project in the United States in 1911. Today the city's largest park has 12 trails totalling over 10 miles in length. The 120 acre arboretum specialty garden collections consist of over 1,700 species including native hardwoods, rare and dwarf evergreens, lilacs, azaleas, rhododendrons, viburnums, quince, crabapple, ground covers, perennial and demonstration gardens. There are guided tours, lectures, publications and a horticulturist on duty to answer questions.
Mt. Airy is located 8 miles northwest of Cincinnati on US 27. From I-74, exit Colerain Avenue west, and drive north on Colerain to the forest entrance.

Open Daily, 7:30 am - Dark

388

19. Caldwell Park
430 West North Bend Road at Caldwell Drive
Hartwell, Ohio
Phone: (513) 761-4313

Approximately 4 miles of trails lead through the wooded areas of this outdoor education center including a National Recreation Trail. In addition there are guided walks, classes, and workshops conducted at the nature center and outdoor amphitheater.

From I-75 exit Paddock Road/Vine Street/SR 4 north to Caldwell Drive. Turn west on Caldwell and drive around one mile to the park.

Open Daily, Dawn to Dusk

20. H.G. French Memorial Park
Intersection of Ridge and Section Roads
Amberly Village, Ohio
Phone: (513) 521-PARK

This Cincinnati park has 275 acres of woods and open spaces for picnicking, shelters, vegetable garden plots, and the historic H.G. French home. Guided walks looking for fossils is popular.

From I-75 exit east on Seymour Avenue to Reading Road north/left one mile to Section Road. Go east/right 2.5 mile to the park entrance at Ridge and Section Roads.

Open Daily, Dawn to Dusk   Admission Fee, Historic Home Tour

21. Ault Park
East end of Observatory Drive at Hyde Park
Cincinnati, Ohio 45202
Phone: (513) 521-PARK

The city's third largest park features garden plots, specialty gardens and other educational display gardens. The "Trees for Your Yard" arboretum has 110 woody species planted for the home gardener or "yardener's" interest. One of the nation's ten Dahlia Test plots is here. Scenic views and short trails.

Ault Park borders Columbia Parkway/US 50. From I-71 exit south on the Red Bank Expressway to Erie Avenue to Observatory Drive east.

Open Daily, Dawn to Dusk

22. Stanberry Park
Oxford Avenue north of Corbly in Mt. Washington
Cincinnati, Ohio 45202
Phone: (513) 521-PARK

A National Recreation Trail follows the beautiful ravine, intersecting streams and steep sloped hillsides.

Wildflowers are especially abundant in spring thanks to the loving caretaker of this city park. Playfields, playgrounds, shelterhouse, picnicking, summer band concerts, and winter sledding are popular.

From Ohio SR 125 in Mt. Washington west of the Lunker Airport and the Little Miami River, go west on Corbly Avenue to Oxford Avenue.

Open Daily, Dawn to Dusk

23. California Woods Nature Preserve
5400 Kellogg Avenue
California, Ohio 45228
Phone: (513) 231-8678

California Woods was one of the first outdoor education centers in the United States and the oldest natural history museum in southwestern Ohio. The nature preserve harbors an undisturbed forest, steep hills, ravines and there are several trails to hike including the Trillium Valley Trail, a National Recreation Trail. Guided tours, workshops, and gift shop.

From I-275 exit north onto US 52. The preserve entrance is about 2 miles north of the interstate interchange on the east side of the highway.

Open Monday-Friday 9 am - 4:30 pm   Daily User Fee
Saturday-Sunday 12 noon - 5 pm

24. Withrow Nature Preserve
Five Mile Road near Sweetwine, Ohio
Cincinnati, Ohio
Phone: (513) 521-PARK

Recently acquired, the 273 acre Hamilton County Park District property is one of the finest spring wildflower preserves in the Cincinnati area. The 2 mile Trout Lily Trail has two short loops. Withrow also has a small lodge, informal outdoor amphitheater and naturalist office.

From I-275 in east Hamilton County exit south on Five Mile Road and drive to the preserve.

Open Year-Around   Motor Vehicle Permit Required

25. Woodland Mound Park
Old Kellogg Road/US 52 east
Phone:(513) 521-PARK

The one mile moderate Hedgeapple Trail overlooks the Ohio River as it passes through abandoned meadows. Opened in 1980, the 923 acre Hamilton County Park District also includes an outdoor amphitheater, ballfields, golf course, naturalist office, fitness trail, playground, concessions, frisbee golf and reservable lodge.

Woodland Mound Park is located east of downtown Cincinnati along the Ohio River just off US 52/Old Kellogg Road between Eight and Nine Mile Roads. From I-275 exit Five Mile Road south to US 52.

Open Year-Around   Motor Vehicle Permit Required

26. Cincinnati Nature Center
4949 Tealtown Road
Milford, Ohio 45120
Phone: (513) 831-1711

This nature center, a private non-profit outdoor educational organization, offers 755 acres of forested sanctuary with 12 miles of self guiding trails, an interpretive center that includes classrooms, offices, a library, gift shop and natural history bookstore. Workshops, meetings, field trips and a lodge are available to supporting members. The trails and grounds are restricted to members and their guests on Saturday, Sunday and holidays due to heavy park usage. Visitors are welcome Monday through Friday.

To reach the nature center from I-275 exit SR 32 east and drive to Glenest-Tealtown Road and turn north/left. Upon reaching Old SR 74 turn right and then turn immediately left at the next intersection onto Tealtown Road.

Open Grounds 7:30 am - 7:30 pm   Nominal Donation
8:30 pm during Daylight Savings Time   or Membership

Rowe Interpretive Building
9 am - 5 pm Monday - Saturday; 1 am - 5 pm Sunday

27. Embshoff Woods Nature Preserve
Cul de sac at Pauls Road
Cincinnati, Ohio
Phone (513) 521-PARK

Hiking trails allow easy exploration of the 226 acre natural area. Other facilities and activities include an outdoor amphitheater, fitness trail, picnic shelter areas, playfields, playgrounds, ice skating and sledding, frisbee golf and concessions.

The Hamilton County Park District preserve lies west of downtown Cincinnati. From Delphi Road go south on Mt. Alverno Road to Pauls Road.

Open Year-Around   Motor Vehicle Permit Required

28. Shawnee Lookout
Lawrenceburg and Browder Roads
Phone: (513) 521-PARK

This Hamilton County Park District 1,027 acre park is situated at the confluence of the Miami and Ohio Rivers. The park site is historically rich with former Native American Indian habitation. Three short self guiding loop trails lead from the museum to archaeological sites and overlooks of the river valleys. In addition to hiking, picnicking, playfields, fishing, boating and a golf course are available.

From I-275 near Cleves exit south on Kilby Road to US 50 and Cleves. Take Mt. Nebo Road or the Miamiview Road west from Cleves to the Lawrenceburg Road south to Shawnee Lookout.

Open year around   Motor Vehicle Permit Required

29. Mitchell Memorial Forest
Buffalo Ridge Road
Cincinnati, Ohio
Phone: (513) 521-PARK

William Morris Mitchell bequested 1,160 acres to the Hamilton County Park District system as a living memorial forest to his parents. Opened in 1978, the natural park includes the one mile Wood Duck Trail, picnic and memorial shelter, conservation pond, and scenic overlook. Plant and bird identity and forest ecology are the major focus of the hiking trail.

From I-74 Taylor Creek exit take Rybolt Road south to Wesselman Road and turn west/left. Follow Wesselman road and continue straight west on Zion Hill Road to Buffalo Ridge Road. Turn west/left on Buffalo Ridge Road to the park entrance.

Open Year-Around   Motor Vehicle Permit Required

30. Miami Whitewater Forest
Mt. Hope Road and Dry Fork Road
Harrison, Ohio 45030
Phone: (513) 521-PARK

Nearly bordering the Indiana State line, this 2,359 acre Hamilton County Park District forest has a wide array of recreation activities.

These include a nature program center and museum, outdoor amphitheater, and lake related activities. There are 4 easy to moderate self-guiding trails that total about 5 miles distance. The main park entrance is located at Harrison lake off I-74 at Dry Fork exit north. Park entrances are also at West Road and Dry Fork Road.

Open Year-Around   Motor Vehicle Permit Required

31. Farbach-Werner Nature Preserve
Colerain Avenue at 3455 Poole Road
Cincinnati, Ohio
Phone: (513) 521-PARK

Since 1972 this Hamilton County Park District outdoor education facility has been providing a good deal of recreation for its small 23 acres. Besides hiking the Pin Oak Trail, there are guided hikes led by the resident naturalist, a nature barn museum, visitors center, amphitheater, nut tree arboretum, outdoor programs, and a gift shop.

From I-275 in northwest Hamilton County exit US 27/ Colerain Road south 1.5 miles to the park entrance off Poole Road.

Open Year-Around   Motor Vehicle Permit Required

32. Winton Woods
10245 Winton Road
Cincinnati, Ohio
Phone: (513) 521-PARK

Winton Woods is probably the most popular of the Hamilton County Park District parks. The 2,133 forested acres are 80% undeveloped and provide excellent hiking opportunities. Appointments may be made with the naturalist to visit Winton Wood's 4 wildflower preserves that are registered as state of Ohio Nature Preserves. The county park district offices are located here. Boating, camping, bike trails, bike rental, lake fishing, golf, bridle trails, riding center, parcours physical fitness trail, outdoor education programs, picnicking, playgrounds, cultural events are other activities.

The park entrance is off Winton Road south of I-275.

Open Year-Around   Motor Vehicle Permit Required

33. Sharon Woods
Cincinnati, Ohio
Phone: (513) 521-PARK

Sharon Woods, the oldest park in the Hamilton County County Park District, was preserved by the Cincinnati Hiking Club in the 1930's. The Gorge Hiking Trail accesses Buckeye Falls, a dedicated natural area. An 1880 Ohio historical village may be toured from May to October.

Cross country skiing, boating, golfing, biking, playground, playfields, and picnicking are some of the activities that may be enjoyed on the 737 acres.

From I-275 at Sharonville exit south on Columbus-Cincinnati/US 42 to the park entrance near the intersection of US 42 and Reading Road, five miles north of downtown Cincinnati.

Open Year-Around   Motor Vehicle Permit Required

KENTUCKY'S OHIO RIVER VALLEY AND LOUISVILLE

1. Devou Park/William Behringer-Crawford Memorial Museum
Western Avenue/1600 Montague Road
Covington, Kentucky 41012
Phone: (505) 292-2281 Devou Park
       (505) 292-2297 Museum
       (505) 491-4003

    The Friends of Devou Park has established a 1/2 mile streamside trail in the 600 acre parkland of rolling pastoral hills over looking Cincinnati and the Ohio River Valley. Within Devou Park at 1600 Montague Road is the William Behringer-Crawford Memorial Museum. The collections include exhibits of the natural and social history of northern Kentucky. Wildlife, geology, prehistoric Indian artifacts and paleontology of the region are displayed. Devou Park also offers golfing, fishing, tennis, horseback riding, fitness course and picnicking.
    From I-71-75 in Covington, Kentucky exit west at Sleepy Hollow Road and Devou Park. Follow directional signs.

Devou Park Open Daily Daylight to Dusk   Nominal Fee
Wm. Behringer-Crawford Memorial Museum   or Donation
February-November Tuesday-Saturday   at Museum
10 am - 5 pm
Sunday 1 pm - 5 pm
Closed Monday, January, December and major holidays

2. Bank Lick Woods Park
Independence Station Road
Independence, Kentucky
Phone: (505) 431-4701

    Established in 1981, this Kenton County Park located just outside Covington, offers 8 miles of wooded trails winding throughout its 160 acres in the south county. Besides hiking, fishing, vita course ballfields, picnicking and shelters are available.

Open Year-Around

3. Big Bone Lick State Park
Rural Route 2, Box 92, 3380 Beaver Road
Union, Kentucky 41901
Phone: (606) 384-3522

Attracted to salt licks, prehistoric animals became mired in the quagmire, preserving their remains to the present day. The site became well known by early American paleontologists for its abundance and variety of Pleistocene animal bones that were delivered to museums world wide. A one mile, self-guiding interpretive walk leads through the salty marshlands of Big Bone Creek to a rare salt-sulphur spring. Dioramic models of a woolly mammoth, bison, and giant ground sloth stand life-like along the paved path. A 1.4 mile trail leads from the campground to the lake below, then continues to the museum. Other activities and facilities include a gift shop, picnicking, boating, fishing, swimming, tennis and Class A camping.

The Kentucky state park is located 20 miles southwest of Covington, KY. From I-71-75 exit west on KY 338 and drive to Beaver Lick. Turn north on KY 237 to Beaver Road and the park entrance.

Open Year-Around   Admission Fee to Museum

4. General Butler State Resort Park
Box 325, US 227
Carrollton, Kentucky 41008-4384
Phone: (502) 732-4384

Two short hiking loop trails begin and end at the base of the Butler Lodge. This resort state park offers winter snow skiing, ski rental, 18-hole golf course, mini-golf, lodge, dining room, gift shop, swimming beach and pool, fishing, picnicking with shelters, boating, boat rental, playfields, playgrounds, Class A camping, special events, the Museum of Ohio River Lore and the restored 1860 mansion of early resident General Butler, hero of the Battle of New Orleans, for whom the park is named.

From I-71 at Carrollton exit north on US 227 and drive to the park entrance, two miles southwest of the river city.

Open Year-Around

5. Museum of History and Science
727 West Main Street, Louisville, Kentucky 40202
Phone: (502) 589-4584

The collections include material concerning the cultural and natural history of the Ohio River, hands-on science exhibits, and the outdoor Yarmuth Garden. There are programs, demonstrations, guided tours, lectures, educational programs, museum membership, and a gift shop.

The museum is easily accessed from I-71, I-65 and I-64. Free daily parking is available at 7th and River Road. Access from River Road only.

Open Daily 9:30 am - 5:30 pm   Admission Fee
Closed Thanksgiving, Christmas   Free to Members
and New Year's Day

6. Urban Alternative Homestead

813 East Chestnut Street, Louisville, Kentucky 40204
Phone: (502) 587-3028

Visitors may see working examples of solar and wind energy, water conservation, raised Bio-Dynamic garden beds, solar greenhouse and aquaculture food tank at the self-sufficient, inner-city demonstration home. Workshops, group tours by appointment, and individual drop-in tours are available. Free publications available on request.

From I-64 exit west on Mellwood Avenue/US 42 and drive to the intersection with Baxter Street. Turn left/south and proceed 2 blocks to Jefferson Street (one-way). Turn right/west on Jefferson Street and continue to Shelby Street and turn south and continue to Flexner Way. Turn left/east on Flexner Way which becomes Chestnut Street (one-way).

Open Monday, Wednesday, Friday and Saturday   Donations
9 am - 12 noon   Accepted

7. Kentucky Botanical Gardens

814 1/2 Cherokee Road, Louisville, Kentucky 40204
Phone: (502) 452-1121

The botanic gardens specializes in rare and endangered tropical plants from around the world. Orchids, bromeliads, ferns, begonias, gesneriads and aroids flower throughout the year. There are group tours, special lectures and a membership program. Future plans will re-establish the gardens at larger facilities in the eastern Louisville suburbs.

To reach the Kentucky Botanical Gardens from I-64 east Louisville exit onto Grinstead Drive and proceed west past Cave Hill Cemetery to Cherokee Street, one street before the Bards-Town Road. Turn right/north on Cherokee to 814 1/2.

Open Monday, Wednesday, Thursday 11 am - 3 pm   Donations
Sunday and Saturday 12:30 pm - 4:30 pm
Closed major holidays

8. Cave Hill Cemetery and Arboretum

701 Baxter Avenue at East Broadway
Louisville, Kentucky 40204
Phone: (502) 584-8363

Beautiful statue, monuments, memorial fountains, spring fed lakes and 500 varieties of common and rare trees and shrubs may be viewed at the 300 acre Cave Hill Cemetery (est. 1848). Foot traffic is welcome along the 15 miles of paved roadways that interlace the rolling memorial gardens designed in the English pastoral tradition. A visitors guide and map are available at the Renaissance Tower entrance on Baxter Street and from the administration building at the center of the cemetery. From I-64 exit west on Grinstead Drive and proceed past the cemetery to Bardstown Road.

Turn right/north and drive a short ways to the intersection with Baxter Avenue. Drive 4 blocks north on Baxter Street to the entrance. Automobiles and pedestrians only.

Open Daily, 8 am - 4:45 pm, Weather Permitting

9. Rauch Memorial Planetarium
2301 South Third Street
University of Louisville Campus
Louisville, Kentucky
Phone: (502) 588-6664

The "Theatre of the Sky" is a circular 30 foot in diameter auditorium equipped with an automated sky or star projector and stereo sky projector. There are guided tours, lectures, films, classes, bookstore and gift shop. Group rates available.

From I-65 exit 133 south of downtown Louisville, go west on Eastern Parkway to Third Street and turn north/right. The campus will be to the immediate right. There is free parking. The planetarium is behind, north and east of the J.B. Speed Art Museum.

Public Shows year around except August   Nominal Admission Fee
Wednesday and Friday at 7 pm
Sunday at 2 pm and 4:30 pm
Starlight Rock Show Friday and Saturday
8 pm and 9:15 pm
Children's Show Saturday 12:30 pm and 2 pm
Closed major national holidays

10. Cherokee Park
Eastern Parkway and Cherokee Road
Louisville, Kentucky
Phone: (502) 459-0440

Beargrass Creek winds through the 409 acre rolling landscape providing an urban outdoor setting for a myriad of recreational opportunities. The park was one of several Louisville parks designed by Frederick Law Olmstead, the "Father of American landscape architecture". Nettelroth Bird Sanctuary and the Big Rock area in the park's east end is of special interest to naturalists.

Trails are located near the Hill One picnic area. Other facilities include picnic areas, fountains, statues, pavilion, ball fields, tennis and basketball courts, golf course, clubhouse, bridle trails, bikeway, and archery range.

From I-64 exit west onto Grinstead Drive. Continue 1/4 mile to Lexington Road and turn left/east and proceed to the park's entry drives.

Open Daily, Dawn to Dusk

11. Beargrass Creek Nature Preserve
1297 Trevilian Way
Louisville, Kentucky 40233
Phone: (502) 459-0440

Directly north of the Louisville Metro park administration offices at Joe Creason Park, 41 natural woodland acres have been set aside as a nature preserve bordering Beargrass Creek. Birding is considered good here. Future plans are to build a nature center to serve as a public environmental education outlet for the metropolitan area.

From I-264/60 Henry Watterson Expressway exit 14 and drive north on Poplar Level Road to Trevilian Way. Joe Creason Park is across the highway from the Louisville Zoological Park.

Open Daily, Dawn to Dusk

12. Louisville Zoological Park
1100 Trevilian Way
Louisville, Kentucky 40233
Phone: (502) 459-2181

African Panorama, "hands-on" Metazoo Education Center, and the Polar World and Siberian Tiger exhibits are some of the special attractions at the Louisville Zoo. 800 exotic and native birds, mammals, and reptiles are viewed in 60 natural settings at this 73 acre zoo. Concessions, gift shop, mini-train rides, picnicking and animal nursery are available.

From I-265/60 Henry Watterson Expressway exit 14 north on Poplar Level Road and drive north to the intersection with Trevilian Way. Turn right/east on Trevilian Way. Continue to the free zoo parking area across from Joe Creason Park and the Beargrass Creek Nature Preserve.

Open Daily, May-September 9 am - 6 pm   Admission Fee
September - April, Tuesday - Sunday 10 am - 4 pm
Closed Mondays, Christmas and New Years Day

13. Farmington Historic Home
3033 Bardstown Road
Louisville, Kentucky 40205
Phone: (502) 452-9920

Guided tours are given of Farmington, a restored Federal style home designed from a plan by Thomas Jefferson and built by John and Lucy Speed in 1810. Patrick Henry signed the deed and Abraham Lincoln visited here. The surrounding 14 acres are designed and planted as a early 19th century garden with identified trees, herbs and flowers. Additional facilities include a barn and blacksmith shop and gift shop. There is an active membership program.

From I-264 Henry Watterson Expressway exit 16 north on the Bardstown Road and drive one block and follow the directional signs to the historic home.

Open All Year except Thanksgiving,   Admission Fee
Christmas, New Years Day and Derby Day
Monday-Saturday 10 am - 4:30 pm
Sunday 1:30 pm - 4:30 pm
Last Tour at 3:45 pm

14. Locust Grove Historic Home
561 Blandenbaker Lane
Louisville, Kentucky 40203

Maintained by Historic Homes Foundation, Inc., Locust Grove was the final residence of George Rogers Clark, Revolutionary War General hero of the Northwest Territory. The 55 acre house and out-buildings, gardens and grounds are reconstructed as a 1790 Georgia plantation. There are guided one hour tours and a gift shop.

From I- 264 Henry Watterson Expressway exit 22 and go west onto KY 42/ Brownsboro Road and drive past Zachary Taylor National Cemetery to Blankenbaker Lane. Turn north/right and follow Blankenbaker Lane to Blankenbaker Road and Locust Grove home.

Open All Year   Admission Fee
Monday-Saturday 10 am - 4:30 pm
Sunday 1:30 pm - 4:30 pm
Last tour at 3:30 pm
Closed New Years Day, Easter, Derby Day,
Thanksgiving and Christmas Days

15. Iroquois Park
Taylor Boulevard and Southern Parkway Louisville, Kentucky
Louisville, Kentucky
Phone: (502) 459-0440

Rustic woodland, Iroquois Park is one of several 19th century metro parks designed by landscape architect Frederick Law Olmstead.

The 720 foot high Iroquois Hill has two lookout points offering vistas of the city and south suburban hills. Outdoor activities and facilities within the 739 acres include an open air amphitheater, golf course, bridle trails, stables, bicycling, swimming, tennis, frisbee course, picnicking, playgrounds, pavilion, archery range, and disc golf course.

From I-264 Henry Watterson Expressway exit 9 on Henry Avenue to Taylor Boulevard to the park entrance with Southern Parkway. Eastbound I-264 traffic must exit right/west at Stanley Avenue.

Open Daily, Dawn to Dusk   Rentals Available

16. Jefferson County Memorial Forest
Scott's Gap, Bearcamp, Jefferson Hill and Mitchell Hill
Roads access southwest of Fairdale, KY
Louisville, Kentucky
Phone: (502) 459-0440

Over 20 miles of hiking trails traverse the 4,000 acres of forested knobs, southwest of Louisville. The blazed 6.5 mile (one-way) Siltstone Trail begins at the ranger station on Scott's Gap Road and ends several knobs east at Tom Wallace lake ranger station on Mitchell Hill Road. The blazed 8 1/2 mile Mitch McConnell loop trail begins and ends at the Holsclaw Hill Road Parking lot. Besides hiking, the memorial forest offers picnicking, pavilions, playgrounds, fishing, and archery range. Additional trails exist at McNeely Park and Cheoweth or Charles Vettiner Park in south county. The memorial forest is administer by the metropolitan Parks Department at Joe Creason park in Louisville.

From the Jefferson Freeway/KY 841 exit south to Fairdale. Just south of Fairdale take the Mitchell Hill Road to Tom Wallace Park. West of Fairdale, Blevins Gap Road accesses Scott's Gap and Bearcamp Roads.

Open Year-Around
Summer Hours 6 am - 10 pm April - October
Winter Hours 6 am - 5:30 pm November - March

17. Bernheim Forest, Arboretum and Nature Center
Kentucky State Road 245
Clermont, Kentucky 40110
Phone: (502) 585-3575
        (502) 543-2451

51 miles of trails interconnect within the 10,000 acre wildlife sanctuary of forest, knobs and lakes. Special tree collections of crabapples, maples, nut trees, dogwoods, rhododendrons, viburnums and dwarf conifers decorate the arboretum. The nature center features a native garden. Fishing and picnicking may be enjoyed on the landscaped grounds.

Founded in 1928 by the Isaac W. Bernheim Foundation, there are pre-arranged guided tours, field trips, library and educational programs for members and the general public.

From I-65 at Shepherdsville exit 117 and go west through town to U.S. 61 and turn left/south. Drive south on US 61 about 4 miles to Kentucky 245 and turn left/east and follow the directional signs to the entrance. The arboretum is located about 22 miles south of Louisville, Kentucky.

Open Daily, March 15 - November 15
9 am - One hour before Sunset

18. Otter Creek Park and Wilderness Area
Box 165, Route 1
Vine Grove, Kentucky 40175
Phone: (502) 583-3577
(502) 942-3641

This 3,600 acre, city of Louisville administered Ohio River park, offers nearly 20 miles of self guided hiking trails along wooded Ohio River overlooks and Otter Creek. Visit the nature center to obtain trail maps and see the wildlife exhibits. Other offerings include picnicking, fishing, boating, bridle trails, ball courts, playfields, swimming pool, frisbee and mini-golf course, lodge, spelunking, rappelling, cabin rental and camping.

Otter Creek Park is located 30 miles southwest of Louisville via US 31 west and KY 1638. From the Ohio River crossing at Indiana SR 135 Brandenburg bridge, go east on KY 1638 to the park entrance 2 miles east of Fort Knox. Historically the site of the destroyed town of Rock Haven by the 1937 Flood.

Open Year-Around, Closed major holidays

19. Owensboro Area Museum and Planetarium
2829 South Griffith Avenue
Owensboro, Kentucky 42301
Phone: (502) 683-0296

This regional city and county funded natural science and history museum features collections of astronomy, botany, geology, zoology, insects, shells, Kentucky freshwater fish, Indian artifacts and live reptiles. Sky Shows are presented every Sunday afternoon. The cultural facility also offers guided tours, lectures, special exhibits and services, classes, a library, museum membership and gift shop.

From the Ohio River Bridge/US 231 drive south to 5th Street and turn west/right to the intersection of US 431 and turn south/left. Proceed on US 431 south to Griffith Avenue and turn west/right and continue to the museum at 2829 South Griffith and College Avenue.

The world's largest sassafras tree grows in Owensboro along 2100 Frederica Street. The 300 year old tree is registered with the American Forestry Association.

Open Weekdays, 8 am - 4 pm   Donations Accepted
Weekends 1 pm - 4 pm

20. Ben Hawes State Park
Box 761, Route 7, Roost Road
Owensboro, Kentucky 42301

A one mile loop trail weaves through a mature beech-maple forest in the northeast section of the 297 acre state recreational park, 4 miles west of Owensboro, Kentucky.

Other seasonal and year around facilities include archery range, concessions, 18 hole golf course, pro shop, picnic shelters, two tennis courts, ballfields, playfields and playgrounds. No camping available.

In Owensboro take US 60 west 4 miles to the park entrance on the north side of the highway.

Open Year-Around

21. John James Audubon State Park
Box 547, US 41
Henderson, Kentucky 42420
Phone: (502) 826-2247

Several miles of self-guiding interpretive trails traverse the forested hilly terrain of the Wolf Hills where naturalist-artist John James Audubon studied, painted and ran a general store for ten years (1810-20). The first Kentucky state nature preserve was established here and includes nearly half of the 692 acre park.

The French provincial styled Audubon Memorial Museum features an Auduboniana collection and natural history of the region. Additional facilities and activities include picnic shelter, playgrounds, golf course, tennis courts, boating, boat rental, fishing, beach swimming, nature interpretive center, gift shop, seasonal naturalist, seasonal cottage rental and Class A camping.

The park entrance is located in north Henderson, Kentucky along US 41, 2 miles south of Evansville, Indiana.

Open Year-Around   Admission Fee
Museum in Winter, Weekends Only   at museum

Sunset, Ohio River

ILLINOIS PRAIRIE, OZARKS AND WABASH RIVER

1. Lincoln Trail State Recreation Area
Rural Route 1, Box 117, SR 1
Marshall, Illinois 62441
Phone: (217) 826-2222

The 2 mile Sand Ford Trail passes through a variety of east central Illinois habitats. Nature walkers will enjoy the 1/2 mile Beech Tree Trail that skirts an Illinois climax beech-maple forest nature preserve.

The 1,000 acre state park also offers picnicking, shelterhouses, a summer naturalist, playground, winter sports, lake fishing, boating, concessions and Class A and D camping.

Lincoln Trail SRA is located 2 miles south of Marshall, Illinois and I-70 and US 40 on SR 1, about 25 miles southwest of Terre Haute, Indiana

Open Year-Around   Seasonal Admission Fee

2. Red Hills State Park
Rural Route 4, US 50
Sumner, Illinois 62466
Phone: (618) 936-2469

Several hiking trails exist in these wooded hills 25 miles west of Vincennes, Indiana. The 40 acre lake south of US 50 has 2.5 miles of walkable shoreline. Nearly 6 miles of loop trails are established on the north property across US 50 from the lake and campground. Picnicking, shelterhouses, playgrounds, summer naturalist, boating, fishing, hunting, archery range, winter sports, bridle trails, airstrip, concessions, and Class A camping and tenting are available.

Red Hills State Park is located one mile northeast of Sumner in Lawrence county between Olney and Lawrenceville on US 50, about 20 miles west of Vincennes.

Open Year-Around

3. Chauncey Marsh Nature Preserve
Chauncey-Birds Road
Chauncey, Illinois
Phone: (618) 936-2469

There are no established trails at this Embarras River bottomland state nature preserve however the property is open to visitation. Fine examples of sloughs, bottomland woods, open fields, dry and wet prairies and riparian communities are found here. Hiking and hunting are permitted on the adjacent north 300 acres. Further information may be obtained from the Red Hills State Park office.

The nature preserve is located 4 miles west of Chauncy and 4 miles east of Bird at the Embarras River. Go west on US 50 from Vincennes, Indiana to Lawrenceville, Illinois and turn north on SR 1. Drive about 6 miles north on SR 1 and turn west on the Chauncey-Bird Road and continue to the preserve.

Open Year-Around

4. Beall Woods Nature Preserve and State Park
Rural Route 2, Mount Carmel, Illinois 62863
Phone: (618) 298-2442

Of all the original deciduous forests remaining in the eastern United States, Beall Woods is the largest existing single tract. The 635 virgin acre "Forest of the Wabash River" contains 64 species of upland and bottomland hardwood trees including the largest Shumard oak in the nation. The nearly 6 miles of well marked, tree named, forest trails begin and end at the Red Barn Nature Center, picnicking and playground area. No camping is available.

Beall Woods is located 6 miles south of Mount Carmel near Keensburg east of SR 1 at the Wabash River. Follow the directional signs.

Open Daily except Christmas and New Year's Day

5. Shawnee National Forest
Route 45 South
Harrisburg, Illinois 62946
Phone: (613) 253-7114

Southern Illinois is rich in natural areas and historic sites that are open to public visitation. The national forest service has developed miles of hiking trails on their 1/4 million acre properties. Best areas to hike include Garden of the Gods, Pounds Hollow, Rimrock National Recreation Trail, Bell Springs, and the 80 mile River-to-River Trail. In addition several miles of trail exist at the nearby state parks of Cave-in-the-Rock, Dixon springs, Fern Clyffe, and Giant City.

Interstates 24 and 57, US Highways 34 and 51 and Illinois state routes 1, 13, 127, and 151 pass through the "Illinois Ozarks" region. Contact the national forest offices at Harrisburg and Murphysboro or the ranger stations at Elizabethtown, Vienna, or Jonesboro.

Open Year-Around

Garden of the Gods, Shawnee National Forest

American Medical Association. Handbook of First Aid and Emergency Care. New York: Random House, 1980.

Angel, Heather, and Wolseley, Pat. The Water Naturalist. New York: Facts On File, 1982.

Baker, Ronald L., and Carmony, Marvin. Indiana Place Names. Bloomington, IN: Indiana University Press, 1975.

Borror, D.J., and White, R. E. A Field Guide to the Insects of America North of Mexico. Boston, MA: Houghton Mifflin, Peterson Field Guide Series, 1970.

Brown, Vinson. Knowing the Outdoors in the Dark. New York: Macmillan Publishing, 1972.

Brown, Vinson. Reading the Woods. New York: Macmillan Publishing, 1969.

Brown, Vinson. The Amateur Naturalist's Handbook. New York: Prentice-Hall, 1980.

Brown, Tom Tom Brown's Field Guide to Nature Observation and Tracking. Berkley Books, 1977.

Buchholtz, K. P., Grisgby, B. H., Lee, O.C., and others. Weeds of the North Central States. Champaign, IL: Agri. Exp. Station, 1954.

Bull, John, and Farrand, John. The Audubon Society Field Guide to North American Birds: Eastern Region. New York: Alfred Knopf, 1977.

Bull, Alvin T., and Runkel, Sylvan T. Wildflowers of Indiana Woodlands. Des Moines, IA: Wallace Homestead Book Company.

Carra, Andrew J. ed. The Complete Guide to Hiking and Backpacking. New York: Winchester Press, 1977.

Conant, Roger. Peterson Field Guide to Reptiles and Amphibians of the United States and Canada. Boston, MA: Houghton Mifflin Company.

Danielsen, John. A. Winter Hiking and Camping. Glen Falls, New York: Adirondack Mountain Club, 1977.

Deam, Charles C. Flora of Indiana. Indianapolis, IN: Indiana Dept. of Conservation, Division of Forestry, 1940.

Deam, Charles C. Grasses of Indiana. Indianapolis, IN: W. B. Burford, 1929.

Deam, Charles C. Shrubs of Indiana. Indianapolis, IN: Indiana Dept. of Conservation, 1932.

Durand, Herbert. Field Book of Common Ferns New York: G.P. Putnam and Sons, 1928.

Fletcher, Colin. The Complete Walker III. New York: Knopf, 1984.

Frey, Robert W., and Lane, Michael A. eds. A Survey of Indiana Geology. Bloomington, IN: Indiana University Dept. of Geology, 1966.

Gerking, Shelby D., and Nelson, Joseph S. Annotated Key to the Fishes of Indiana. Bloomington, IN: Indiana University Dept. of Zoology, 1968.

Golden Guide Series. Racine, WI: Golden Press.

Hedge, Christine. Indiana: A Guide to State Forests, Parks and Reservoirs. Indianapolis, IN: Dept. of Natural Resources, 1987.

Henbest, Nigel. A Spotter's Guide to the Night Sky. Mayflower Books, 1979.

Indiana Dept. of Natural Resources. Directory of Indiana's Dedicated
Nature Preserves. Indianapolis, IN: 612 State Office Bldg., DNR, 1988.
In Addition:
Indiana Dept. of Natural Resources. Publications include maps,
canoeing, hiking & nature preserve guides, dept. magazine Outdoor
Indiana, and statewide flora & fauna information.
Kals, W.S. The Stargazer's Bible. New York: Doubleday, 1980.
Kellar, Charles E., Shirly A., and Timothy C. Indiana Birds and their
Haunts. Bloomington, IN: Indiana University Press, 1979.
Kellar, James H. An Introduction to the Prehistory of Indiana.
Indianapolis, IN: Indiana Historical Society, 1983.
Lawrence, Gale. A Field Guide to the Familiar. New York:
Prentice-Hall, 1984.
Lindsey, Alton A., ed. Natural Features of Indiana. Indianapolis, IN:
Indiana Academy of Science, Indiana State Library, 1966.
Lindsey, Alton A., ed. Natural Features of Indiana. Indianapolis, IN:
Indiana Academy of Science, Indiana State Library, 1966.
Lindsey, A.A.; Schmelz, D.V.; and Nichols, S.A. Natural Areas in
Indiana and their Preservation. Lafayette, IN: Indiana Natural Areas
Survey, Dept. of Biological Science, Purdue University, 1969.
MacFarlan, Alan. Exploring the Outdoors With Indian Secrets.
Harrisburg, PA: Stackpole Books, 1982.
Madison, James. History of Indiana. Bloomington, IN: Indiana
University Press, 1986.
Martin, Laura C. Wildflower Folklore. Charlotte, NC: East Woods Press,
1984.
McClane, A.J. Field Guide to Freshwater Fishes of North America.
New York: Holt, Rinehart and Winston, 1978.
McPherson, Alan and Sue. Wild Food Plants of Indiana.
Bloomington, IN: Indiana University Press, 1977.
Milne, L. and Milne, M. Audubon Society Field Guide to North
American Insects and Spiders. New York: Knopf, 1980.
Mitchell, Christie and Frank. Practical Weather Forecasting. New York:
Barron's, 1978.
Mumford, Russell E., and Keller, Charles E. The Birds of Indiana.
Bloomington, IN: Indiana University Press, 1984.
Mumford, Russell E., and Whitaker, John O. Mammals of Indiana.
Bloomington, IN: Indiana University Press, 1982.
Perry, T. G. Fossils: Prehistoric Animals in Hoosier Rocks.
Bloomington, IN: Indiana Geological Survey, Circular no. 7, 1959.
Peterson Field Guide Series. New York: Houghton Mifflin Company.
Petrides, George A. Field Guide to Trees and Shrubs. New York:
Houghton Mifflin, 1972.
Pough, Frederick. A Field Guide to Rocks and Minerals. Boston, MA:
Houghton Mifflin Company, 1976.
Powell, Richard L. Caves of Indiana. Indianapolis, IN: Indiana Dept. of
Conservation, Circular no. 8.
Scifres, Bill. Indiana Outdoors: A Guide to Wild Crops, Fishing, and
Hunting. Bloomington, IN: Indiana University Press, 1976.
Shaver, Robert H. Adventures With Fossils. Bloomington, IN: Indiana
Geological Survey, Circular no. 6, 1959.

Shull, Ernest M. The Butterflies of Indiana. Indianapolis, IN: Indiana
Academy of Sciences, 1987.

Simons, Richard S. The Rivers of Indiana. Bloominton, IN: Indiana
University Press, 1985.

Starling, Bud. Enjoying Indiana Birds. Bloomington, IN: Indiana
University Press, 1978.

Stephens, H. A. Poisonous Plants of Central United States.
Lawrence, KS: University Press of Kansas, 1984.

Stokes, Donald W. A Guide to Observing Insect Lives. Boston, MA:
Little, Brown and Company, 1983.

The Nature Conservancy. A Guide to Indiana Preserves and Projects.
Indianapolis, IN: Updated annually.

Thomas, Bill. Talking With The Animals. New York: William Morrow &
Company, 1985.

Thomas, Lowell J., and Sanderson, Jay L. First Aid for Backpackers and
Campers. New York: Holt, Rinehart, and Winston, 1978.

Ursin, Michael J. Life in and Around Freshwater Wetlands. New
York: Crowell, 1975.

Watts, May Theilgaard. The Winter Tree Finder. Nature Study
Guild, 1963.

Wampler, Mary Rose. Wildflowers of Indiana. Bloomington, IN: Indiana
University Press, 1988.

Welch, Winona H. Mosses of Indiana. Indianapolis, IN: Bookwater
Company, 1957.

End of the Trail, Morgan Monroe State Forest

ABBREVIATION USAGE

Am.	American
approx.	approximately
arb.	arboretum
arbor.	arboretum
ave.	avenue
BSA	Boy Scouts of Am.
CCC	Civilian Conser. Corps
conser.	conservation
Co.	county
DAR	Daughters of the American Revolution
Div.	division
elev.	elevation
est.	established
ft.	foot
FWA	Fish and Wildlife Area
Hist.	historic
Hq.	headquarters
HT	horse trail
I	Interstate
IN,IND	Indiana
IL	Illinois
KY	Kentucky
Lk.	lake
Land.	landing
Mem.	memorial
Mus.	museum
N	north
Nat.	native, nature
NF	National Forest
NM	National Memorial
NP	Nature Preserve
NWR	National Wildlife Refuge
OH	Ohio
Pl.	place
Pt.	point
PFA	Public Fishing Area
Planetar.	planetarium
Pub.	public
Recr.	recreation
res.	reservoir
SF	State Forest
SFA	State Fishing Area
SFWA	State Fish & Wildlife Area
SP	State Park
sp.	species
SR	state road
SRA	State Recreation Area
SW	southwest
Tr.	trail
USGS	United States Geological Survey
wilder.	wilderness
WR	wildlife refuge

ENVIRONMENTAL ORGANIZATIONS WITH OUTINGS

Regional and State

GREAT LAKES CHAPTER/SIERRA CLUB
506 S. Wabash, Suite 525, Chicago, IL 60605, (312) 431-0158

HOOSIER CHAPTER/SIERRA CLUB
6140 North College Ave., Indianapolis, IN 46220
(317) 253-2687

IZAAK WALTON LEAGUE, UPPER MISSISSIPPI RIVER REGION
6601 Auto Club Rd., Minneapolis, MN 55438, (612) 941-6654

THE NATURE CONSERVANCY
1330 West 38th Street, Indianapolis, IN 46208, (317) 923-7547

SIERRA CLUB/MIDWEST OFFICE, (IA, IL, IN, KY, OH, MI, MN, MO, WI)
214 N. Henry St., Suite 203, Madison, WI 53703, (608) 257-4994

THE SASSAFRAS AUDUBON SOCIETY
P.O. Box 85, Bloomington, IN 47402,

National Organizations

AMERICAN HIKING SOCIETY
P.O. Box 86-W, North Scituate, MA, 02060

AMERICAN RIVERS
801 Pennsylvania Ave., S.E. Suite 303, Washington, D.C. 20003
(202) 547-6900

FRIENDS OF THE EARTH
530 7th St., S.E. Washington, D.C. 20003, (202) 543-4312

NATIONAL AUDUBON SOCIETY
801 Pennsylvania Ave., S.E., Washington, D.C. 20003, (202) 547-9009

NATIONAL PARKS & CONSERVATION ASSOCIATION
1015 31st St., N.W., Washington, D.C. 20007, (202) 944-8530

NATIONAL WILDLIFE FEDERATION
1412 - 16th St., N.W., Washington, D.C. 20036, (202) 797-6800

SIERRA CLUB (NATIONAL HEADQUARTERS)
730 Polk St., San Francisco, CA 94109, (415) 776-2211

SIERRA CLUB (WASHINGTON, D.C. OFFICE)
408 C St., N.E., Washington, D.C. 20002, (202) 547-1141

THE WILDERNESS SOCIETY
1400 I St., N.W., 10th Floor, Washington, D.C. 20036, (202) 842-3400

It's Easy to See the Beauty of Sierra Club Membership

Since 1892, the Sierra Club has been working to preserve our magnificent wild places and protect our natural environment. The Sierra Club has played a major role in the formation of America's National Park and Wilderness Preservation Systems, safeguarding over 132 million acres of irreplacable public land.

With your help, we can continue working to preserve additional wilderness areas, especially forests and deserts that remain at risk from encroaching development.

As a Sierra Club member you will have the satisfaction of knowing that you are helping to preserve and protect our natural heritage. **Join today!**

MEMBERSHIP FORM

☐ **Yes,** I want to join! I want to help safeguard our nation's precious natural heritage. My check is enclosed.

New Member Name _____

Address _____

City/State _____ Zip _____

MEMBERSHIP CATEGORIES
(for 1993)

	INDIVIDUAL	JOINT
REGULAR	☐ **$35**	☐ **$43**
SUPPORTING	☐ $50	☐ $58
CONTRIBUTING	☐ $100	☐ $108
LIFE	☐ $750	☐ $1000
SENIOR	☐ $15	☐ $23
STUDENT	☐ $15	☐ $23
LIMITED INCOME	☐ $15	☐ $23

Annual dues include subscription to *Sierra* ($7.50) and chapter publications ($1). Dues are not tax-deductible.

Enclose check and mail to:

Sierra Club

Dept. H-111 • P.O. Box 7959
San Francisco, CA
94120-7959

W652

FRIP No.

Sierra Club Midwest Region

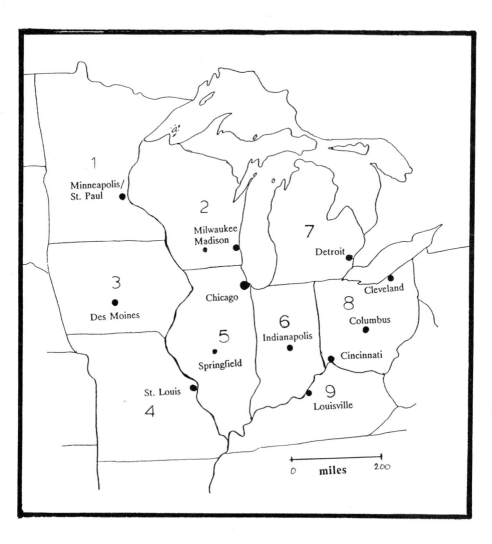

Midwest Local Chapters

1. North Star
2. John Muir
3. Iowa
4. Ozark
5. Great Lakes
6. Hoosier
7. Mackinac
8. Ohio
9. Cumberland